For the W[...]
Library' count[...]
Michael Orban, auth[...]
of Souled Out: Memoir
of War and Inner Peace,
and my friend.
Nancy K.

Written in ink
fueled by passion
refined by fire...

For my wonderful supportive family
and their enduring love –

my parents, Elspeth and Walt,
my children, Julian and Vanessa,
my cousin, Jeff McCormack,
and my husband, Kenny

Although based on a true story, this is a work of fiction. All characters depicted, names used, and incidents portrayed in this novel are fictitious. No identification with actual persons is intended nor should be inferred. Any resemblance of the characters portrayed to actual persons, living or dead, is purely coincidental.

Published by NK Marketing

ISBN 978-0-615-14123-7

BELIZE SURVIVOR:

DARKER SIDE OF PARADISE

a novel by

Nancy R. Koerner

Nancy R. Koern

April 2009

BASED ON A TRUE STORY

DEDICATION

In Memoriam

For

JACK WOOD

1916 – 2006

My mentor, literary confidante, best friend,
role model, and personal superhero,

whose infinite love, faith,
guidance, humor, and inspiration
made this book a reality.

I will always love you.

"Adventure is nothing

but discomfort and annoyance,

recollected in the safety

of reminiscence."

Gary Jennings

* * * *

"We shall not cease from exploration,

And the end of all our exploring

Will be to arrive where we started,

And know the place for the first time."

T. S. Elliot

preface

The country of Belize exists, and although this story is a work of fiction, it was inspired by actual places, characters, and events which shaped the experience of the author in real life. Can that which is rooted in fact be more bizarre than fiction? Yes, indeed. For the hand of destiny, with its proclivity for unseemly twists and playful ironies, writes that which no mortal can imagine or foretell.

Many years ago I saw a cartoon in a newspaper in which two people stood together in a deep valley. Each slope posted a different sign – one pointed the way to "A Meaningful Life" and the other to "An Indifferent Existence." The caption below read, "Funny, isn't it? No matter which way you go, it's still uphill."

This story is about a woman who equates a meaningful life with an adventurous one. Few people search for adventure in the classic sense of jungles and waterfalls, since most are content to remain in comfortable surroundings familiar since childhood, preferring to seek their rewards through traditional vocations such as the trades or the corporate world. But it must be remembered that, either way, the path still leads uphill. Neither alternative can guarantee a rich and satisfying life. Nor will either preclude the prospect of utter boredom.

In the springtime of youth when the path beckons and the passion for life runs hot, who can then foresee which choices will assure our mortal happiness and spiritual fulfillment?

 **ALEXIS**

chapter 1

Refusing to surrender, the rain god, *Chaac*, continued to veil the land in rainy shrouds. It was February of 1987, and for almost five months Alexis had watched the thunderstorms drench the jungles of Belize. Now another front of bruised clouds emerged from the east. A brisk wind rushed through the trees, and ozone filled the tropical forest with fragrance. Burning fiercely in the far western sky, *Kinich Ahau*, the sun god, fought to defend his meager patch of blue; there his bright face still opposed the forces of the storm.

From the wide balcony of the six-sided house, Alexis looked out over the lush yard. In the late afternoon sun, the rain sparkled on the giant *llora sangre* tree that shaded and protected the clear blue artesian spring beneath it. As the sun crept higher, a brilliant rainbow appeared. Although she'd seen many rainbows during her twelve years in Belize, they were all far away and illusory. This time it was a double rainbow, perfect and complete, so close she could almost touch it, the luminescent colors radiating just beyond her fingertips like a vivid banner against the steel-gray palette. The unique phenomenon brought a flood of emotions, washing over her like the colors in the sky. She breathed in the pure mountain air and forced herself to be calm. It was paradise, but the price had been great. Moments later the double rainbow was gone and black clouds obscured the sun. In a matter of seconds, darkness changed the mood of the land once more as another blast of driving rain rose over the mountains.

In spite of the rainstorm, the herd of horses grazed contentedly. They raised their heads only long enough to search for the next clump of grass. It was a rare event to have a day off from the horseback tour business; during weekends and holidays the riding roster was always full. Only once in a great while did Alexis have the opportunity to enjoy a quiet day with no guests on the books.

It was just as well. At this time of year, many of the trails were nearly impassable. The horses disliked the sloppy muck almost as much as she did, and facing another day of inclement weather, week after week, had become increasingly difficult. Only the guests didn't mind. The ride was only one day of their vacation; the mud was a bonus, more adventure for their money. In another three weeks the coming dry season would change everything. Trade winds would become steady and predictable; the rains would taper off until the sun burned down with such power that the clouds would evaporate, leaving a blazing ball of sun against the cobalt sky. All through March, the heat would intensify. Mud on the trails would shrink, flatten out, harden, and eventually turn to dust.

Tropical plants flourished in the forests of Belize, home to four-fifths of the world's botanical species. Strangler figs, mahogany, giant ceiba, palm, rattan, and immense clinging philodendrons grew in such close proximity that very little sunlight penetrated the high canopy. The effect was that of a false twilight, even at midday. The pungent scent of the bush was its most singular feature; Alexis loved its damp, spicy, moldering odor, fragrant with humus and rot – the smell of fresh new growth and ancient decay. But above ground was only half the magic. Below lay an infinite system of subterranean pipes and channels. Carved through the limestone bedrock by the acidic waters born of organic decomposition, countless caves of enormous proportion remained secreted within the rocky outcroppings. Hundreds contained relics of the ancient Maya civilization that had flourished a thousand years before.

Her mind drifted back to the previous day, the essence of this utopian lifestyle. An ideal day for riding, the sunshine had been brilliant, the breeze fresh and brisk. Seventy-five degrees of temperate perfection had lifted her spirits after the long months of rain. Nothing could compare with the sun and wind on her face as she cantered with her group of sightseers through the high pine ridges, slowing down only for steep ravines or a rushing watercourse. Around noon the riders had reached the waterfall and, after securing their mounts, made the one hundred-fifty-foot descent into the river valley. A horseshoe-shaped cascade made a sheer drop into the chasm of granite boulders below, while clusters of orchids dotted the canyon in bright splashes of pink and fuchsia. Guests and guides alike sought the special niches among the river rocks for an effervescent hydro-massage.

It was an incredible way to live all right. As a matter of priorities, Alexis had always chosen lifestyle over money. As a result she'd never had much money but had always enjoyed a lifestyle that most other people envied. However, none of her previous adventures in Key West or California compared with this: the ranch, the horses, the trails, and the high bush. It was the kind of fantasy lifestyle people described when asked what they would do if they won the lottery.

Alexis still lived with much uncertainty. Her situation with Max had taken years to create, and trying to undo the past would take even longer. Her heart ached for her two children, Jordan and Jessica, now eleven and six. Someday it would be over and she'd have them back again. Someday, but not yet.

The symbolism was inescapable. The raindrops, like the tears she had cried, were a part of the reality. The rainbow, ancient symbol of promise, was her hope for the future. *Chaac* still gripped the Land of the Mists. As if he would never relinquish his hold, he mocked *Kinich Ahau*, and dared him to show his golden face.

How had it all started, she thought to herself? How had it all begun?

* * * *

Alexis had been ten years old in 1962 when she'd first heard of the little country then known as British Honduras. At that tender age she never dreamed that she would ever visit Belize, let alone live there for the greater part of her adult life. The least known country in Central America, it had only about 130,000 people nationwide, 30,000 of them in the former capital of Belize City. The official language was English. And for some reason, the nation seemed to have a conspicuous deficiency of common tropical exports such as bananas, rice, corn, or beef. Years later, Alexis would learn that Belize also had the largest area of unspoiled rainforest in Central America, a wealth of wilderness, waterfalls, rare colorful birds, exotic butterflies, and the ruins of countless Mayan temples, as well as the largest and longest living coral reef in the western hemisphere.

During the summer before college, Alexis became influenced by the cultural revolution that would impact all the years that followed. Dressed in a T-shirt and old patched jeans, she rejected the traditional values of her parents, school, and church, abandoning her nice clothes as well as her bra, wearing her hair long with a flower tucked behind her ear.

Countless others embraced the idealism of the dissidents as the rebelliousness of the late sixties resulted in the formation of the radical movement. The message of Dr. Timothy Leary was to "tune in, turn on, and drop out." As fierce anti-capitalists, their purpose was to reject the very society that had spawned them. By demonstrating their supposedly unconventional attitudes and individuality by letting their hair grow and wearing secondhand clothes, the ironic result was that they all looked different in exactly the same way. In retrospect, their attempt to create a new order had developed a culture that was just as standardized within itself as the one from which they were trying to deviate.

Nevertheless, Alexis saw her former high school friends come home from the Vietnam War with broken bodies and twisted minds. She attended marches in which protestors wore arm bands: militants wore red, anarchists wore black, green was for amnesty. Everybody had explicit convictions. Political demonstrations were frequent as were marches, love-ins, and boycotts. The incident at Kent State shocked the world senseless when four college students were killed during a protest turned police action. Tricky Dick Nixon became the arch villain while Joan Baez, Country Joe, Bob Dylan, and Simon and Garfunkel became the conscience of the new crusade.

The classes Alexis was supposed to attend at college were the last thing on her mind. At Christmas she came home and announced to her parents that she was dropping out. A few days later at three o'clock in the morning, her self-appointed hour of departure, they all stood there in the driveway together. Her parents expressed their love and they made their goodbyes. It would be years before she understood their pain.

As the hours of driving passed, Alexis was filled with an exhilaration she had never known. She was seeking her fortune. For the first time she had taken control of her own life and could do whatever she wanted. There were no parents, no teachers, and no peer pressure; she was totally and utterly free.

The scenery was beautiful as she crossed the state line from Kentucky into Tennessee. The sides of the mountains had been cut back and the diagonal strata of exposed rock curved gracefully in tilted disarray. In one spot, a huge outcropping of rock protruded from a jagged mountainside. Looking like a waterfall cast in stone, it appeared to be a tumbling cascade, frozen in time. The rock formation was spectacular. In appreciation of the moment, Alexis pulled over, and considered her assets.

I have a few hundred dollars, she thought. That's enough to get me to southern Florida. I'll need a place to live, and some money to keep my car going. Why is it all about money? Why do we have to pay for insurance and taxes, or have an income and pay rent? Wouldn't it be great just to live somewhere, like on a beach, or in a cave? To enjoy the earth in its natural state and pull fruit from the trees; to live like the Native Americans did? We should be able to live in harmony with the Earth, not at odds with it.

Alexis had always believed she'd been born in the wrong century, preferring that she'd belonged to the era of discovery – of adventurers, explorers, and pirates. Perhaps the lifestyle she sought had disappeared long ago. But there had to be more to life than being locked into what everybody else expected you to do, and she intended to discover what it was. Getting back in her car, she took a last look at the stony cascade of rock and resumed the pleasant euphoria of her new found independence. Hours passed and the mountains of Tennessee gave way to the high plateaus and red clay of Georgia. It was still cold, but something in the air whispered a promise of warmth as she pressed south.

It was just after ten o'clock before Alexis pulled over at a rest area in northern Florida near Jacksonville. She'd been driving for almost nineteen hours straight through. Curling up in the back seat, she was dead to the world in a matter of minutes.

The next day Alexis headed east toward the coast to get a whiff of the ocean air at the earliest possible opportunity. Then she saw her first palm tree on the beach and delighted in the picturesque windy seascape. However, the majestic palms didn't sway gently in the breeze as the poets suggested. Instead, she saw that they defied the harsh winds that battered their leafy crowns and resisted riptides with tenacious roots that clung to the sandy shore. Watching them, Alexis couldn't have known at the time that it was more than an ambiguous analogy; it was to be an omen of her turbulent destiny.

 KEY WEST

chapteR 2

It was the Key West social event of the day, simply known as "sunset," when the island inhabitants gathered nightly at Mallory Pier to watch the drama of red and gold play out on the shimmering horizon. Young women wore homemade clothes, flowers, and beads, and were accompanied by their young men with Jesus-like hair and flowing beards. Most walked or rode bicycles to the wharf as befitted the tiny island community. Dancers, mimes, and acrobats entertained the crowds. Musicians came with their guitars, flutes, dulcimers, or banjos. Some played for free; others passed the hat in hopes of avoiding a real job a little longer. Colorful reptiles clung to the shirt of the lizard man, and conch salad was served in paper cups from a bicycle basket for a dollar each. The island, a long-time haven for pirates, wreckers, and ne'er-do-wells, now occupied by an array of artists, writers, homosexuals and wannabees, was as varied in charm and hue as the changing colors of the sunset sky.

As the people waited on the quay for the magical moment, the giant ball of fire touched the surface of the ocean and cast its reflection forward, creating the illusion of a giant keyhole on the horizon. When the last red sliver of sun was about to disappear, a hush fell over the crowd, and at the final moment, there was a round of applause.

"Hey, Alexis, come here," Eddie called. "There's someone I want you to meet."

Eddie was half Italian, half Syrian, pure artist, and all gay. He lived in Hialeah and specialized in nude and still-life works of art. After her excursion down the east coast, Alexis had picked him up hitchhiking near the University of Miami, and he had talked her into going to Key West. It had sounded like exactly what she was looking for.

"Alexis, meet Marcy. Marcy, this is Alexis," said Eddie. "Marcy's been posing for my paintings lately. I hope to enter one of them in an art show at the university next month."

Marcy was a stunning girl. Eighteen years old, five-foot nine, and deeply tanned with long shapely legs, she had a knockout figure that made even other women stare. Her hair was dark brown, long and straight, with wide brown eyes, full lips, and high cheekbones that revealed her three-quarter Cherokee blood. With a suggestive sway to her hips and a bizarre collection of revealing clothes, she drove most men to distraction. There was no spite or malevolence involved; she was a sexy good-time party girl who loved to laugh.

"So where are you staying, Marcy?" Alexis asked. "I've decided to look for a place and stick around for a while."

"There's a communal house over on Eaton Street, the big pink one, not far from the Naval Base. There are only about seven of us, so there's probably room for another person. Feel free to check it out. Just ask for Sergio."

Alexis visited the house the very next day. She fell in love from the first moment she saw the large airy room on the second story of the old wooden house, and rented it the same afternoon. The following morning, just after sunrise, the lemon-colored warmth filtered through giant palms outside and spilled across the breezeway. Inspired by the sunrise, she began to write:

> Wanderer, moving towards the next horizon.
> Wonderer, how long shall I journey?
> Listener, for the voice in song.
> Watcher, for what someday may be.
> Loner, until companionship comes.
> Patience, a virtue absent from me.

Over the weeks that followed, she lived simply, reading poetry, listening to music, and writing in her journal. Visiting the Cuban section of Old Town Key West, Alexis made line drawings of the shabby frame houses, watched the seafaring birds, and walked the beaches. At night she went stargazing or took long walks along the quiet streets. Lining the sidewalk was a profusion of tropical exotics – colorful hibiscus, hedges of curly aralias, pink and white oleander, and rubber banyan trees. In some areas, whole fences of moonflowers came alive in the moonlight, their white petals opening so quickly that the movement was barely perceptible to the human eye.

One night as she walked, Alexis was enveloped by a glorious fragrance. The rich scent was overwhelming. She sniffed the air, hunting for its source, until she discovered an ordinary looking shrub in front of a nearby house with clusters of pale tiny trumpet-shaped flowers. Bending over she breathed the heady perfume, a scent so sweet and delicious it was almost dizzying.

"It's night-blooming jasmine." A voice came from a shadow on the front porch, and a tall blond handsome young man came forward from the semi-darkness. "You won't smell it in the daytime. Potent stuff." Picking off a bunch of the blossoms, he gave them to her and smiled. "Here, have some."

"Thank you. They're lovely. Do you live here?"

"No. This is my sister's house. I have a sailboat at the marina. I visit when I'm in port. My name's Paul Halliday."

"Nice to meet you. I'm Alexis Dubois. Do you live on your boat full time?"

"No. I'd like to, but it's very hard to make a living unless you're a pirate, shrimper, fisherman, or a smuggler," he laughed and his eyes twinkled. "And although I have assumed all of those roles at some point in the past, I don't qualify for any of them right now. Most of the time I live in Fort Lauderdale; I have some property and investments there. But I decided to take a break for a while and spend as much time on the water as possible."

Paul and Alexis stood talking for a while and then walked together down the empty streets of Old Town. The architectural style was reminiscent of New England, aging frame houses with elaborate gingerbread detailing on the eaves and wide verandas.

"The ship's carpenters came mostly from Maine and Massachusetts," Paul explained. "See the small balcony on the roof with the railing around it? That's the 'widows walk.' The wives would go there to watch and wait for their sailors to come home." As he told of the magic of the sea and sky, she sensed a special warmth and magnetism. He was very attractive, and Alexis started to wonder if Paul was meant to be a part of the adventure she was seeking.

"I'm about ready to go back over to the marina, Alexis. Would you like to join me? Or do you have to be somewhere?"

"Oh, I'd love to see it. There is no place I have to be, and I have no promises to keep."

"Sounds great. Let's go back to my sister's house first so I can pick up my provisions. Hope you don't mind walking though. On land, my feet are my only wheels."

"Luke? Are you here?" Paul carried the box across the gangway, and then gave Alexis a hand as she crossed to the deck. As she admired the lines of the sailboat, a beautiful forty-two-foot trimaran, a mop of blond hair attached to a lithe wiry body bobbed out of the forward hatch.

"Yeah, I'm here," said a gruff voice. "Paul, listen, about those new lines on the spinnaker, I think we ought to – well, well, who do we have here?"

"Luke, this is Alexis. Alexis, meet my boat mate and partner in crime, Lukas Howe."

"Pleased to meet you, ma'am." He made a formal bow and kissed her hand. "Where did our Captain Paul find a good-looking little ladyfish like you?"

"We met over at my sister's house," Paul answered for her. "Serves you right for making me do the shopping all the time. You might meet somebody too if you weren't always here on deck playing with the rigging."

"I wouldn't mind playing with her rigging," laughed Luke.

"Control yourself, you horny sailor. Besides, I saw her first," Paul retorted. "Why don't you make yourself useful? Break out a bottle of wine and roll up one of your famous New York pin joints while I show Alexis the boat."

"Aye, aye, Sorr. Harrrrr," Luke growled good-naturedly as he went below.

Paul turned back to her. "Sorry about that. Luke's got a one-track mind when it comes to pleasures of the flesh. We've been out at sea for ten days, so he needs a woman real bad."

"Well, I've got good news for him. Tomorrow is going to be his lucky day," Alexis laughed, "I know a girl named Marcy that he'd just love to meet!"

As the hours passed, the moon sank slowly toward the horizon and they sipped the last of the wine. It was late, and the conversation had turned philosophical. Luke had long retired to his quarters, uninterested in anything that didn't directly relate to sex and women. Paul reclined next to Alexis on the deck. They were intensely aware of each other, feeling the effects of the wine and weed. The breeze was cool now.

"Would you rather go below where it's warmer?"

"No, it's so beautiful on here deck. Just look at that moon."

Paul got up and disappeared into the galley and brought back a blanket. As he reached across to cover her, his face brushed her cheek. Their eyes met and their lips touched; the kiss was unhurried, long and lingering. Then they lay back together under the cover and watched the moon go down, listening to the sound of the halyards flapping against the mast.

...The misty air was thick and sultry. The Dark One lurked in the shadows just beyond the gray curtains of sanity. Alexis screamed, yet no sound came out. She knew if she could just run fast enough, she could take off and fly, at least above the treetops, high enough to flee the menacing fiend. Looking down she saw its claws; the razor tips grazed her bare skin. Smelling the stench of decomposed flesh on its hot stinking breath, the sulfuric fumes enveloped her. She was running, running, but the demon creature was almost upon her...

Alexis awoke with a hoarse scream, her body cold and dripping with sweat. Shaking from the horror, it took time to fully escape from the nightmare. She was back in her second story room in the pink house on Eaton Street. Where did my subconscious come up with that? For many years, Alexis had prided herself on her ability to dream creatively. Lucid dreaming, it was called. She could often change the course of a dream for the better if it took a turn for the dark side. Even in her flying dreams, she was sometimes able to manifest a strong updraft that could boost her higher into flight. During those moments, Alexis became a bird. She could see over long distances with the eyes of an eagle. Soaring with arms outstretched, she saw a recurring vision of a faraway land. Could it be that the dreams were actually premonitions? For years Alexis dreamed about a particular river, a secret place with a green snake of water threading its way northward through a shaded tropical forest. At times she saw the river from a different perspective, wherein it seemed to flow from the east instead of the south, and was blue, rather than green.

Alexis shook off the fragments of the nightmare and started to think about the coming day. The foursome had been nearly inseparable for the last few weeks, and now Paul and Luke had asked Marcy and her to join them for a three-day sail to the Dry Tortugas. Together they would see in the New Year.

The sailboat anchored cozily on the lee side of the deserted island of mangroves and palm trees, a thin rind of white sand edging the beach. Large patches of purple sea grass patterned the ocean floor near the shore. Turquoise in the shallows changed to deep sapphire where the ocean dropped into the deep. A soft breeze textured the surface of the water, creating flickering reflections of light. Sky and sea met on a pure and perfect horizon, touched only by God's hand.

"Alexis? Are you awake?"

"Yeah, Paul. Just daydreaming and taking a good look at paradise. That sun feels so good on my skin. I just can't believe I'm really here, right now, doing this. How's my back look? Am I brown yet?"

"Your back is brown and your white ass is red. You'd better give it a break. What do you say we go over and take a look at the island?"

"That sounds great."

Getting up, her practical side took over as she started to gather a few items to take along in the dinghy: some fresh water, a couple of oranges, a towel or two.

What the heck are you doing?" Paul asked with a quizzical look. "This isn't an overnight camping trip. I thought we were just going over to the island."

"We are. I'm just trying to decide what to take."

Paul stood looking at her, shaking his head in amused tolerance. He was six-foot-four with a crown of below-the-shoulder golden hair, vivid blue eyes, and a thick gold ring in his left ear. His teeth were incredibly white in contrast to his browned body. He stood there like some golden sun god, glistening with vibrant youth, absolutely naked and carrying nothing. Alexis would never forget what he said next; it would forever be a standard as to what was really important.

"Well," he said, slapping his bare thighs and laughing, "I've got what I need." Without another word, he dived into the water from the starboard bow. Astonished by the simplicity of his actions, Alexis followed and swam with him to the shore.

They ran along the beach until they were breathless. Playing tag, they tickled each other and played like children in the sheer joy of being free. Then, sitting in the sand, they watched the sailboat rocking gently like a graceful white bird.

"How long have you had her, Paul?" Alexis asked.

"It's been about three years now since Luke and I first bought her, but she spent a lot of time in dry dock while we were getting her outfitted. She's only been out on the water for about two months now. Would you believe the owner was selling her for only fifteen grand? She's worth more than twice that price. And when she slices through the waves with a stiff breeze at her stern, you get a feeling of, well, that's how she got her name, the *Déjà Vu.*"

"She's the most beautiful boat I've ever seen. And speaking of Luke, do you think he and Marcy are still at it?"

"Probably," Paul laughed, "It's not often that Luke finds a chick with a sexual appetite to match his own."

"Are you insinuating that I am lacking in some way?" she joked.

"Oh no, baby," he said, reaching for her, "You're fine. Luke's taste just runs a little toward the bizarre."

"Yeah, well then Marcy fits the bill. I don't know anyone else with her style."

"You mean the quarter-inch mesh fishnet blouse with nothing underneath and her nipples poking through like pencil erasers?"

"Yeah, and don't forget the hip-hugger jeans with the zipper at half-mast and the Rolling Stones tongue logo sewn in the crotch," Alexis laughed. "Crazy chick."

It was simple. The sexual revolution was on, and if people liked each other, they made love. In those innocent days, when the worst consequence of intimacy was a dose of the clap, the counterculture had its own standards of conduct. If the mutual chemistry was there, and the signs of the Zodiac were compatible, that was enough.

"Well, he can have her," said Paul, appraising Alexis' tawny body, "I know what I like." She looked up at him and smiled. Her long hair, bleached to a honey color from the salt and tropical sun, blew carelessly in the breeze. "Why don't we hang out for a little while here?" he continued, "Give them some more time alone. I'm sure we can occupy ourselves." He kissed her face, neck, and shoulders softly. Then he eased her backwards, and in total solitude, they made slow and lazy love on the deserted beach.

The wind picked up considerably after they hoisted anchor and left the shelter of the island. In gusting winds, the salt spray flew across the bow as the speed of the sailboat increased. With Paul at the helm, Luke trimmed the sails and the wind pushed the *Déjà Vu* to a full twelve knots.

"How do you like this, Alexis?" Paul shouted above the roaring wind and waves.

"Unbelievable! Exhilarating! How fast can it go?"

"She's been clocked at twenty-two knots. That's one hell of a speed for a sailboat!"

Alexis clung to the rigging as she inched her way forward and dropped down, lying prone on the center bow. Watching the starboard pontoon slice through the water, a porpoise appeared right beside her. The intelligent creature looked up at her sideways and chattered happily; staying topside and maintaining the same speed as the sailboat, it was obviously enjoying itself. Greek mythology told of a dolphin who rescued a drowning sailor, and Paul had mentioned that swimmers were safe from sharks whenever a school of dolphins was nearby.

"Paul!" Alexis screamed with delight. "There's a dolphin here. Come quick!"

Luke took over the helm while Paul went forward and lay down on the bow beside her.

"Look, Paul, he's smiling at me! He's beautiful. Oh, I wish I could touch him!"

"Go ahead. He won't bite you. I'll hold on to you. Reach out and see if you can touch his head." Delightedly, she made the daring attempt, but the porpoise chattered again and smiled, then disappeared beneath the waves.

The water got rougher as the wind blew harder. Marcy and Alexis both made their way aft to the helm. Paul resumed control of the wheel while Luke attached a rope onto a cleat on the transom and made a loop around his body. Then he stripped off all his clothes and smiled.

"Now, what's he up to?" Alexis asked aloud.

"I don't know," said Marcy, grinning at Luke's nakedness, "but I like it so far."

Luke stepped up on the transom and prepared to jump overboard. "Watch this, girls," he said. "I'm maintaining my reputation as a wild man."

Giving a Tarzan yell, and making an ungainly splash into the water, Luke reappeared a few seconds later. Still hanging onto the rope forty feet from the sailboat, he corkscrewed around like a demented fishing jig. It was obvious then why he'd taken his clothes off; the water would have peeled away anything he was wearing.

"Why is he doing that, Paul?" asked Marcy.

"Isn't it dangerous?" said Alexis.

"You bet. I wouldn't do it. Dangling on the end of a line turning round and round like a silver fishing spoon? That's shark bait." It was a sobering thought.

Later in the afternoon the sea calmed and the skies cleared as the troupe made their approach toward the Dry Tortugas. As they tacked hard to port, the mainsail of the *Déjà Vu* came about with a loud popping sound, and Alexis saw the faint outline of Fort Jefferson. An hour later, they dropped anchor. While Paul made a fire in the hibachi, Marcy passed around a few beers, Luke cleaned some yellow-tail snapper they'd trolled for along the way, and Alexis cooked a pot of fragrant saffron rice alongside the flame-grilled fish. The mood was mellow on deck as they prepared and ate a leisurely meal.

It wasn't long before four insignificant humans on an infinitesimal speck of a sailboat watched in awe as the sun set and the full moon rose over the eastern horizon. It was the dawn of 1972 and it brought a confluence of celestial events: New Year's Eve, and a rare 'blue moon,' when two full moons occur within the same month. Far from civilization, it was hard for Alexis to imagine that there was still a world of time clocks and traffic jams, of police sirens and inner city crime. The sea was satin black, and when the moon slipped its veil, the departing clouds were edged in a lacework of purest silver. Paul leaned against the mast, putting his arms around her. Together they drank in the sights and sounds, and watched the interplay of the winds, waves, and sky.

"Have you ever heard of the *Nuestra Señora de Atocha*?" Paul asked. "She went down in these waters several hundred years ago, taking with her a large cargo of treasure: pieces of eight, gold doubloons, pearls, jewels, and riches beyond imagination. My uncle is second in command of the Mel Fisher expedition. They've got her narrowed down to one square mile of ocean and expect to find the *Atocha* within a year."

"A real treasure hunt," said Alexis. "Imagine what it would be like to be involved in something like that. Do you scuba-dive, Paul? Have you ever thought of joining up?"

"Yeah, but I'd need a lot more experience to get involved with an elite group of guys like that. They're professionals, underwater demolition experts and such."

"Mmmm," she mused, "I'm fascinated by history, explorers on the high seas of the New World, the Egyptians, the ancient Greeks, the Mayas, the Aztecs, and the Incas. When I was little, I wanted to be an archaeologist. Of course, I wanted to be a cowgirl too," she laughed. "Most of all, I have always wanted to seek out my own answers. I still do. Not just be left with a lot of regrets when I'm old. Maybe I'll even find the answer to the great question of WHY."

"Oh, I can tell you that," Paul laughed. "The answer is the great BECAUSE."

"Smart ass." She leaned over and kissed him.

The following day they sailed closer to the fort, anchoring about a quarter mile away. Then, instead of taking the dinghy, they decided to don their snorkeling gear and swim to the island. The submerged footings of the sea wall created a spectacular artificial reef, supporting a rich marine life of lobster and blue crab, sponges and conchs, yellowtail, and amberjack. There were green turtles and loggerheads, leopard rays, moray eels, and evil-looking barracuda. Formations of brain coral, stag horn coral, and sea fans were everywhere. As a penal colony, Fort Jefferson consisted of perimeter walls containing the individual prison cells and a large central yard area for exercising the inmates. Once they made landfall, Paul started searching for a particular cell.

"Fort Jefferson is famous for having imprisoned Dr. Samuel Mudd; he was convicted of complicity when he treated John Wilkes Booth after the assassination of President Lincoln," Paul said. "When I visited here last, I found a custodian who told me about Dr. Mudd's chamber."

They eventually found the cramped cell, no more than eight feet square, its cement walls sweaty with condensation. There was no evidence of prisoners having the privilege of a bed, sink, or toilet. One tiny hole in the wall, ten-by-five inches, served as a window. In contrast to the dazzling beauty of the open sky and sea just beyond the walls, the cell was abominably dank and depressing. Apparently Dr. Mudd had given outstanding service to the inmates in an outbreak of yellow fever; it was easy to imagine how disease could run rampant in such conditions.

"Check this out," Paul continued. "This cell has one very unique feature from all the others. See this shallow depression in the middle of the floor and the little trough leading into it? That was dug by Dr. Mudd to draw some of the water away from the walls, and give him a relatively dry place to sit."

"How did he make it? He had no tools?" Alexis asked.

"But he had a spoon, and many years to use it."

For the next five months Alexis lived in a virtual dream world. She and Paul were ecstatically happy together, and although she had little money, her lifestyle was one of enviable spiritual wealth. But in early June, Paul and Luke got the opportunity to go to Miami Beach and race hydroplanes for a successful stockbroker. It was an offer too good for them to pass up, and Marcy and Alexis had to resign themselves to the fact that the men needed to leave Key West for a while. Saying their goodbyes, Paul and Alexis lay together in the hammock on the wide veranda of the big pink house on Eaton Street. He kissed her on the forehead and gave her a squeeze. "We'll be back in about six weeks," he said. "Meanwhile, we'll keep in touch. Are you going to stay on here at the house?"

"As far as I know," she replied. "Marcy and I might go to that new RV Park on Ohio Key. They're hiring people to plant trees and shrubs. It sounds like we can make a little money. I'll miss you, Paul. Please be careful. I care for you. I really do."

"You're a very special woman, Alexis. We'll be back in a few weeks."

Alexis never saw him again. Two days later the radio announcer spoke of a freak explosion. Paul Halliday and Lukas Howe were both killed when their two-man hydroplane had flipped over backwards and spontaneously ignited. They had died instantly.

Throughout the year that followed, Alexis managed to make just enough money to get by. Initially, she and Marcy spent three weeks on Ohio Key, and later Alexis found a job back in Key West as a waitress. Her artistic talents inspired her to buy a few simple hand tools, and she used them to make souvenirs out of beach debris, driftwood, dried flowers, and shells which were sold to tourists whenever the opportunity presented itself.

Although Marcy was not similarly affected by Luke's death, Paul's had a profound effect on Alexis, having never lost anyone close to her before. She continued to write in her journal, finding small comfort in the written word.

> I've drawn your face
> On napkins in restaurants across the island
> Tracing your smile with my index finger,
> Making your hair just so
> Until now you're more of what I want you to be
> Than what you are.
> I can paint your eyes blue and say
> This is where I have lived
> For twenty minutes or more.
>
> I order grapefruit, and pay for the ruined napkins.
> And between morning and evening,
> I draw your face a little fainter every day.

* * * *

There were many bars in Old Town, all within a few blocks of Mallory Pier. Sloppy Joe's had been Ernest Hemingway's favorite haunt; Captain Tony's was the infamous gay bar, and Lou's had the best live music, but the Old Anchor Inn was still the place to be.

One evening just after sunset, Alexis passed by the Anchor Inn and saw an old East Indian man standing outside. With a long black beard and nut-brown skin, he noticed her, and broke into a toothy grin. Behind his bald pate, long frizzy hair extended half way down his back. He was tiny, lean and spry, weighing less than a hundred and twenty pounds. As she returned his smile, she saw Marcy walk up to him and kiss him on the cheek.

"Hi, Ron," Marcy said. "What's going on with you?"

"Just cooling off, darling," he said. Marcy noticed Alexis standing across the street and called to her. "Hey, girl, come over here and meet one of the finest people on the island. This is Indian Ron."

"Oh, so you're Indian Ron," said Alexis, walking over. "Ron from Ceylon. I've heard of you; I hear you're a wonderful storyteller."

"He's also got the best *ganja* on the island," added Marcy.

"Now that part is absolutely true," Ron admitted, "and I would be happy to confirm it if you lovely girls would care to join me for a smoke back at my place?"

The breeze was balmy as the three of them walked down Elizabeth Street to Ron's second floor apartment. As they ducked under the yellow tie-dyed curtain, they could smell the lingering scent of sandalwood and curry. The orange ball-shaped paper lantern suspended from the high ceiling gave off soft muted light. A legless sofa had a low table in front, and a lava lamp glowed in a far corner. Beautiful oriental drawings decorated the walls and large pillows indicated that all Ron's guests sat on the floor.

"Excuse me for one moment while I put on some music and change into something more comfortable. Then I'll prepare us something to drink." He parted the strands of beads in the doorway and stepped into his bedroom. A minute later Ron came back, having traded his jeans and T-shirt for a one-piece garment deftly tucked in about the waist. "I enjoy my American clothes but they are very restrictive. In the evenings I like to put on my *dhoti*," he said. "Shoes are even worse because I am cursed with these Pisces feet. I guess I'm still Sri Lankan at heart, even after all these years in the United States. I suppose I should honor my ancestors with some good Ceylon Black, but living in Key West has given me a passion for Cuban coffee. I hope you don't mind."

After serving the refreshments, he sat cross-legged, opposite from Alexis and Marcy, holding an elegantly carved box of ebony and brass. Taking out a small amount of marijuana, he crushed it reverently and packed it firmly into a straight clay pipe. Before lighting it, he lifted it to the sky.

"*Bom Shankar*," said Ron, as he passed the pipe. "It's a sort of blessing. The closest translation is probably 'God, here we come.'" As they passed the *chillum* again, Indian Ron began to tell a story:

There once was a journeyer seeking a vision, a great truth to live by .The traveler crossed hot deserts and trampled through forests and swamps. Throughout his wanderings he encountered the wicked and the good, found victory and suffered defeat. He won at love, only to lose it again. Through time and space, he learned and grew. At last, the seeker came to the top of a hill where he rested against the base of a large tree overlooking a beautiful valley.

As Indian Ron spoke, Alexis noticed his long and supple fingers, his sculpted hands communicating what words alone could not express. She and Marcy were transfixed by his imagery; his eyes were full of fire and magic.

The traveler saw a vision of rolling green fields before him, as if freshly washed by the summer rain. The sky, in a gentle overcast gray, intensified the grass green hue. Then people appeared, all dressed in shining white robes, standing there in the fields, as though also washed in the summer rain. There were thousands upon thousands of them, as if all the people who had ever lived and all those yet to be born were there before him. He saw faces of all colors, bodies of all stature, people of all ages and eras, from every part of the world. Each looked into the sky with the light of their inner spirit glowing in anticipation. They stood there waiting. Then, before his eyes, each person began to melt like a bright candle until, of each one, there remained only a small nugget of gold.

Ron paused as his guests sat breathlessly at his feet.

Now before the traveler lay the green valley, and upon it rested all the souls of those who had known Earth. Suddenly a divine wind started to blow, causing all those golden souls to rise together on the same plane. The journeyer realized his own golden essence was rising with them, that he was a part of it all. As they rose, a whirlwind began in the center, pulling them inward toward each other. They began to melt together forming into one great mass.

The traveler looked below for a last glimpse of Earth. The green fields were gone. Instead, he saw the horrifying ruins of what had once been the Earth: its surface now covered by twisted sheets of rusted iron and tortured steel. It was burning, smoking, and foul. With no sign of life, the remains of the Earth fell away into a mist, and were gone.

Then the gray sky turned brilliantly blue all around them. The golden souls of the people drew relentlessly toward the center, joining together. In a last enormous rush of the wind, they amassed as One. And, together, they formed God.

Indian Ron became a great friend to Alexis after that memorable evening. Although she didn't know it at the time, their lives would continue to intertwine for years to come. It was a non-physical love, spiritual in nature, rather than sexual. Alexis lived only a few blocks away and visited him several times a week. Together they made up fanciful tales and spoke of philosophy and poetry.

"Ron?" she asked one day. "I've wanted to ask you something for a long time. Do you ever get scared? Really scared?"

"Yes," Ron replied thoughtfully. "At times, I do. For one thing, I'm not getting any younger. Most of my life is over. I have experienced many things, traveled, raised a family. I worry about my health like anyone my age. I'm not so enlightened as to have no fear of death, but I try not to let it consume me. Why do you ask? Remember, the future is always unknown. It's out there waiting for us, regardless of whether we fear it or not."

"I'm not afraid of that," said Alexis. "To me the future is an exciting prospect. I want to get out there and live it. But sometimes this horrible fear comes over me out of nowhere, a fear with no name."

"Come here, Alexis," said Ron gently. "What has happened? More dreams of tropical green rivers?"

"No. A nightmare."

"Come let me hold you. Tell me about your terrible dream." He put his arms around her. She leaned her head on is chest.

"I'm walking along a deserted beach," she began. "I'm heading north on an eastern seacoast. A strong breeze is blowing. The sky is ugly and gray and so is the ocean. The seaweed and sand are cold and wet under my bare feet. I feel an aching grief, too heavy to bear. There's a hopeless desperation, one that nothing can resolve. It's as though I've lost something terribly important and I don't know what it is. The wind has an evil sound. It accuses me over and over saying the words `unworthy, unworthy.' I keep walking and walking. It's terrifying. What do you think it means?"

"Sometimes dreams are manifestations of what we want. Other times, they are just the ramblings of the subconscious mind," Ron said, in a soothing tone. "Some people say dreams are premonitions of things to come."

"This can't be a premonition," Alexis countered. "I'd have to have done something I'd really regret to feel what I'm experiencing in this dream. It couldn't be that. I decided a long time ago that I'm not going to regret anything I do in my lifetime. I'll make my decisions wisely and I'll live with them."

"Ah, darling, sometimes I forget just how young you really are. You'll not live life without regrets," said Ron. "You will make errors in judgment, just like everyone else. Some mistakes will be unimportant. Others will be serious. You can't expect to hang around this planet and not get some cuts and bruises. We live and we learn; our mistakes teach us to make better choices." He paused. "Would you allow me to write something in your journal?"

That night when she went home, Alexis lit a candle and read the lines he had written:

> *Because hate is legislated, written into the primer and testament, shot into our blood and brain like a vaccine or vitamin; because our day is of time, of hours, and the clock-hands turn; closes the circle upon us; and black timeless night sucks us in like quicksand, and leaves us totally without a parachute, a key to heaven, or a long last look. Because a slow negative death withers the world and only 'yes' can turn the tide, we need love more than ever. We need love more than hope, money, wisdom, or a drink, because love has your face and your body and God has made no other eyes like yours.*

As the shadows flickered across the room, she lay down on the bed and added her own words.

> A bittersweet day,
> A day of sunny mystics and rainy strangers,
> Of wispy free spirits, of fear and of laughter.
> A day in the curio house, and not so curious,
> A day, like any other Key West day.

* * * *

Another tourist season had come and gone, and with the departure of the snowbirds, the restaurant business slowed, and Alexis' boss told her to take a week off. On a whim, she decided to drive up the Keys to visit her old friend Eddie in Hialeah, and see his new display at the art gallery.

The Seven Mile Bridge was a marvel of engineering. With its long uninterrupted expanse of steel and concrete, the pilings were imbedded deeply in the ocean floor to withstand the brutal riptides. Often a traveler could see sandblasting crews hanging precariously over the edges of the bridge on scaffolding. Nets underneath protected them from the sweeping currents of the shark-infested waters.

Passing Pigeon Key, a picturesque island belonging to the Marine Biology Department of the University of Miami, and the town of Marathon, she headed for Grassy Key, an island beach where camping was possible without police harassment, if done discreetly. Following the subtle landmarks, Alexis wandered through the scraggly pine and mangrove swamps until she found a suitable site. That night, after her campfire had burned out, she lay in the sleeping bag and looked at the stars.

Funny, she thought. When I was little, I used to be able to see a zillion stars from my backyard. The Milky Way was so bright and obvious back then, now I can hardly see it. Fewer stars? No, that's not possible. Haze or pollution? More likely. Or maybe I just remember it wrong, she thought. In childhood, everything was so much more vivid. In the dim starlight, she could make out the white curling edges of the waves lapping the shore, molding and shaping the beach as they'd done from the dawn of time. Alexis drifted into sleep and dreamed about ancient sea creatures and the evolution that caused the first proto-amphibians to brave the dry land. One by one they had crawled from the warm womb of salt water and taken the first breath of air, which must have seared their new lungs like fire...

Alexis left Grassy Key early the following morning and arrived at Coconut Grove a few hours later. There were hundreds of beautiful sailboats in the marina at Dinner Key, and she heard the halyards slapping on their masts as they rocked gently at their moorings. It was a familiar sound, sad and nostalgic, reminiscent of Paul. She walked through Love Park, watching the sunlight streaming through the banyan trees for which the park was famous. The ancient trees grew aerial roots which, upon contact with the ground, became rooted. As the years passed, these also became trunks until the trees turned into a series of cathedral-like arches. Kids were on swings and people walked their dogs. Some were having picnics, or throwing Frisbees. Suddenly, the sound of a crash made Alexis turn around. A station wagon had just pulled into the spot where her car was parked. The rear of the VW beetle looked like an accordion. A middle-aged woman stepped out of the station wagon.

"I'm terribly sorry," she said. "Your car was so small and pulled so far into the space; I never even saw it until it was too late. Do you have insurance?"

"Yeah," Alexis sighed, grateful that her dad had talked her into a modest policy. She knew it would cost more than the hundred dollar deductible, and her car wasn't going anywhere for a while. She went through the motions of exchanging insurance information with the woman and making out the police report. Then the tow truck came and took her car away. The repairman at the garage said the car would be ready in about four days.

"OK, great," she mused aloud, as she plopped down on the curb. "Now where am I going to stay?"

"Hey, are you OK?" The voice came from a Hispanic boy she'd seen throwing the Frisbee in the park. "I saw what happened to your car. That was really a tough break." He was no more than sixteen, thin, with narrow shoulders. Other than a jagged scar on his right cheek, his face was lovely with dark eyes, long black lashes,

and a mouth that was full and sensuous. From his demeanor, she guessed he was a street person and, most likely, homeless.

"Yeah, I didn't need that hassle," Alexis replied. "It sure is bumming out my visit."

"Well, unlike me, at least you have a car. Or you will when they fix it." He grinned and stuck out his hand. "Hi, my name's Rico."

"Hi, Rico, I'm Alexis."

"Did you say that you don't have a place to stay for the night?"

"Actually, I did have a place. I was planning to visit a friend of mine in Hialeah. But now that my car's in the shop I don't know what I'm going to do."

"Well, about an hour ago I was talking with some people who told me about a guy in a van who offered them a place to stay. He must have plenty of room at his house, because he said if we knew anyone else who needed a place, they could stay there too. I'm going to hook up with them later. Are you interested?"

"Sounds too good to be true," said Alexis. "Was this guy cool?"

"I don't know; I guess so. They didn't say."

"So when are you going to meet up with them?"

An hour later, backpacks in hand, Alexis found that Rico's new acquaintances were not attractive people; they were dirty and in need of a good shower. Roger was tall and skinny with a straggly brown beard, and Barbara was short and heavy with greasy blond hair. These were the types that gave hippies a bad name. She could never understand how anyone could go without bathing. Even Rico, as homeless as he was, wore clean clothes and did not smell bad. There was always a way to get clean if you wanted to.

When the van showed up, Alexis was surprised to see that it was a work of art, with a custom paint job depicting unicorns and rainbows. The man's name was Alberto, a Cuban, who looked to be in his late fifties. With thick salt-and-pepper hair, his black eyes were beady under the heavy eyebrows, but he seemed jovial and easygoing. Alexis figured him to be one of those lonely older men who desperately wanted acceptance by the younger generation.

"You're all welcome to stay at my place," Alberto said. "I've got some wine and good music. Some excellent hashish too. I live in Hialeah. I've got a big house with a pool and everything." Perfect, Alexis thought. This is great. She'd stay there for a night and then look up Eddie the next morning.

It seemed to take a long time to reach Alberto's house. Rico sat in the passenger seat while Roger, Barbara, and Alexis sat in the back. Alberto hardly spoke, and when Roger asked him a question, he seemed preoccupied by other thoughts.

"Wow. Is this your place?" Rico asked, as they drove up the palm-lined driveway. The house was white with black wrought-iron grillwork on the windows and a Spanish tile roof. The manicured lawn and flowering plants added to the presumption of wealth.

As they got out of the van, Alexis whispered quietly, "Hey, Rico, this doesn't look like any hippie crash pad to me. People like us don't live in places like this. This guy has money, big money."

Rico whispered back. "So? He's friendly and he's rich. We lucked out. That's all."

"I'm not so sure," she replied. "Something's not right here. Besides, if he's so cool, then why are we whispering?"

"Come on, kids, bring your backpacks in and I'll show you the place," Alberto called out. They piled their stuff in the living room and Alberto gave them a tour. The living room was spacious, lavishly decorated with cream-colored walls and burnt-orange carpeting. Dramatic black drapes closed off the outside world, giving the house a cave-like feeling. The spotless kitchen looked like it had never been used to prepare a meal. The guest bedrooms were immaculate and color-coordinated – one in shades of pink and one in golden yellows. A large outdoor pool surrounded by a high wooden fence could be seen just behind the glass sliding doors of the blue bedroom in the back. Uncomfortable with the opulent surroundings, the four young people sat on the floor around a low coffee table, unsure of what would happen next.

Alberto was in a good mood. He pulled a large ornate hookah from the closet. It was solid brass with six flexible braided-cord mouthpieces. He warmed a small chunk of hashish with a match and crumbled it into the bowl of the pipe. "What do you say we enjoy a good buzz and get to know each other a little better?"

"Yeah, all right," Roger said eagerly. "That looks like some good stuff. What kind is it?"

"Lebanese blond," replied Alberto. "A friend of mine brings it into the country in the most ingenious way. He buys a fancy candelabrum made out of olive wood. Then he cuts a slab off the bottom and hollows out the base and packs it with hashish. When they x-ray the piece as carry-on luggage, it doesn't show because the olive wood is the same density as the hash."

"Way to go," said Barbara. She took a big hit off the pipe and pushed a greasy hank of hair behind her ear. "I heard of a pregnant woman who carried two kilos of cocaine underneath her belly. The customs officials started to search her because they thought the belly was fake. But when they saw her nipples were dark, they realized she really was pregnant and they stopped searching her."

Alberto's eyes flickered; he liked her story. "Hey, good idea. I've got some coke in the fridge. Shall I cut us a few lines?"

Everyone responded enthusiastically, except Alexis. She had snorted cocaine a few times and liked it. For that exact reason, it was a drug she never intentionally sought out. But it was still difficult to turn down if it was right in front of her.

Over the next two hours, they found themselves having a hell of a good time. The coke was excellent and there was lots of it. Their host poured the wine and the pipe was kept full. The music on the sound system was fantastic. Through the haze of indulgence, Alexis forgot her misgivings.

"God, I feel good," said Rico. His face flushed a deep rose, his pupils dilated. "I feel hot though. I'm sweating like a pig."

"What do you say we all go for a swim?" Alberto suggested.

"Ah, that would be perfect right about now," said Roger.

Barbara giggled. "I don't have a bathing suit."

"That's okay," said Alberto. "It's more fun to skinny dip anyway. Hey, it's my place. We can get as loose as we want."

Under the influence of the drug, Alexis peeled off her clothes and plunged into the water. After swimming its length twice, she reclined back against the side of the pool. It felt wonderfully sensuous on her bare skin. Roger and Barbara were walking into the pool by degrees. They were even less attractive unclad. Alexis saw Alberto watching her out of the corner of his eye until he was distracted by Rico

climbing out of the pool. A furtive smile crossed Alberto's lips when he saw Rico's slim naked hips and effeminate walk.

Just after midnight, the party began to break up. Everybody was coming down from the high and nothing seemed to be as much fun as before. Alexis started to wonder if all the guests were going to be sharing the same room. She found herself hoping they would.

"Roger, if you're ready to crash, you and Barbara can have the gold room," Alberto said. "Rico, you can have the pink. Alexis can have the blue."

"Where's your room?" asked Alexis.

"Oh, my room's off on the other side of the house. I didn't show you that one. Would you like to see it? It's very different from the others."

"No thanks," she replied, as an unexpected shiver ran through her body. "I'm really tired. I think I'll call it a night. Thanks for the great party. Goodnight, everybody."

Alexis grabbed her stuff and went into the blue bedroom, closed the door behind her and locked it. Then she lay on the bed, fully clothed, unable to sleep. Something was wrong in this place. Faint voices could be heard from down the hall. Despite muffled noises, she eventually began to doze. A short while later, an abrupt knock on the door shocked her into full consciousness.

"Alexis!" Rico's voice crackled and he sobbed. "Quick! Open the door. Let me in."

Her heart began to race. "What's the matter?"

"It's Alberto," he cried. "He came to my room. Please hurry. Let me in. For God's sake, Alexis, open the door! Now!" Cold fear prickled up the back of her neck. "Hurry, Alexis! He's coming down the hall." As she reached for the lock, something crashed against the other side of the door. Rico screamed.

"You little pussy faggot," Alberto growled. "You only perform for your *maricon* friends, is that right? What's the matter? I'm not pretty enough for you? C'mere you little cocksucker, so I can bend your skinny ass over and show you how we do it in the Big House."

"No!" Rico screamed. "*¡Parate!*" he cried. "*¡Madre de Dios!* No!"

From inside the blue room, Alexis heard the sounds of solid blows against flesh and Rico's muffled screams. In terror she stuffed a few things into her backpack. Outside the door, the brutality continued, culminating in a final slam and the sound of a body slumping to the floor. Lightheaded with horror, she saw the bright red blood seeping into the carpet from underneath the door.

"Now for you, you little bitch!" Alberto snarled. He beat on the door with both fists. "You goddamn hippies give away free love to everybody but me. Open this door right now and I'll give you a thrill you'll never forget. First I'm gonna fuck you blind, and then let my knife do the same. Just like your little gigolo boy here, except I'm gonna cut off your tit and use it for a tobacco pouch!!" His voice screeched higher with maniacal laughter. "Oh yeah, baby. There won't be nothin' left. When I'm finished with you, they'll have to scrape you off the floor and bury you in a fuckin' bucket!"

Beyond panic, Alexis grabbed her backpack, slid open the glass doors, and ran out on the deck. She tossed the backpack over the fence, and then somehow, through the power of adrenaline, she pulled herself up, and over the wall just as Alberto came running around the side of the house. His face was a contorted mask of insanity, his hands and shirt red with blood. She dropped down on the other side, and escaped into the darkness. She never looked back.

Alexis ran like she had never run in her life. Terror gave her wings. Thinking someone was behind her, she saw headlights and ducked behind some bushes. Keeping her head low, she waited for the vehicle to pass. But where was there to go? She was all alone in a strange city at two-o'clock in the morning.

Eddie! That's it, she thought. I've got to find a phone and call Eddie. What was it again? The Chelsea apartment complex? Where the hell is that from here? Oh God, Rico is dead. He must be dead. What happened to Roger and Barbara? I've got to find a phone. Still hiding behind the hedge, Alexis waited until she was sure she was not being pursued. Then she fumbled through her things and found her address book.

The street lights lit up the sidewalk in macabre shades of gray as she looked for familiar landmarks. As she walked the streets, an eerie feeling gripped her. The long night was not over yet. Turning the corner, she realized she had reached the bad part of town. A party was going on in a nearby house and she approached several people sitting on the front steps.

"Can I please come in and use your phone? I'm in trouble and I need some help."

One young man turned to her. Alexis could see the drug-induced disorientation in his eyes, even in the dark.

"Oh sure, sweet thing," he said, putting his finger to his lips. "But be careful. They're having a séance in there. Black spirits, you know." He pointed to the door behind him. "They have called the name of Lucifer. The table is just starting to rise off the floor." Her pupils dilated, and she staggered. Backing away slowly without a word, Alexis struggled to keep from blacking out. She turned a corner and saw a convenience store a few blocks away. There was a public phone outside, and she dialed the apartment in Chelsea.

"Hello, Eddie? This is Alexis from Key West. Yeah, I know it's the middle of the night. I'm here in Hialeah. I came to visit you and see your new gallery. I was just attacked by some insane guy." She fought to keep her voice calm. "No really, Eddie. There are dead people. You've got to help me. I'm in trouble here. Can you come pick me up?"

The next morning the newspaper headlines told of a triple murder in Hialeah by former convict and drug dealer, Alberto Alvarez. The horribly mutilated bodies of two men and a woman were found in his home. All three had been sexually assaulted and one had been partially dismembered. Identities of the victims were being withheld pending notification of next of kin. Alvarez was also wanted for questioning in regard to several other area slayings. Apparently, police had apprehended Alvarez around dawn when he was found walking the streets, bloody and incoherent.

It took time to get over the brutish ordeal. Shaken, Alexis returned to Key West and, over the summer, spent a great deal of time with Indian Ron. He hadn't been feeling well. Together they shared more stories and talked of dreams, but slowly she came to realize that her time in Key West was coming to a close. The island had been a good place to start, but now other adventures waited. It was time to move on.

"I'll miss you so much, Ron. You've been more than a friend to me," said Alexis.

"I know, darling. I'll miss you too, but friends like us are never really apart. You only have to think of me. Besides," he smiled, "Key West gets in your blood. You'll be back."

"Do you think so?"

"You'll be back," he repeated.

"You know, I've kept my journal ever since I've been here. Now I have only one page left. Maybe it's symbolic. Maybe it's just coincidental, but somehow I think it's a sign that it's time to go."

"Signs, meanings, symbols," he laughed. "Don't forget, Alexis, some things don't mean anything." She laughed with him as she wiped a tear from her eye. "Just think of me." He laid his hand gently just above her left breast. "I'll be right here." He hugged her then. "God bless you, darling. We'll meet again."

That night as she stared at the four walls of her apartment in the flickering candlelight, Alexis took out her book and turned to the last page.

> As I lie here writing on page number last,
> I think of the future and remember the past.
> I think of my calling, today is the day,
> Nothing will stop me, I'll no longer stay.
> The sunshine, the joys, the loves, and the tears
> Have called through long months
> Which have felt like long years.
>
> And now I will answer, the time is now nigh
> To leave mother ocean under great father sky.
> To again seek my fortune and follow my heart.
> The story is written, now the sequel must start.

The following morning, Alexis called her parents. The phone rang, and her mother picked it up. She told her she'd be coming home.

"Only for a visit? Only for a short while?" Liz's voice betrayed great disappointment.

"Yeah Mom, I still haven't found what I'm looking for. I'm only going to stay for a few weeks, and then I'm going to California."

 CALIFORNIA

chapter 3

In the intense heat, the VW Beetle had coughed and sputtered all across the Mojave Desert, running on three cylinders instead of four. With cartoon visions of bleached longhorn skulls in her head, Alexis was afraid to stop and reset the timing for fear the car would never start again. After a short stint in an auto repair shop in the smog-laden city of Los Angeles, she continued north, threading her way around the famous hairpin curves of El Camino Real. Sometimes the road hugged the lower beaches; in other places it wound along vast coastal cliffs perched hundreds of feet above the water line. From the kelp beds near the rocky shore to the far reaches of the distant horizon, the deep indigo of the Pacific Ocean seemed to stretch into infinity. Being a romantic at heart, Alexis visited places she'd read about or heard in song, stopping briefly in Monterey and pausing again among the windblown Joshua trees near Carmel. Once in San Francisco, she couldn't resist the impulse to go to the intersection of Haight and Ashbury, if for nothing more than to see the famous signpost. She was in California all right, but as a stranger in a strange land, she didn't have a clue as to where to go. A friendly waitress in a little soup kitchen on Castro Street provided the answer.

"Oh, the Haight scene, huh? That's long gone," said the girl, as she placed the steaming green split pea soup in front of Alexis. "Berkeley's got a lot happening if you like the city, but most of the old late-sixties freaks have gone up to the mountains. They're organizing communes up there. There's a place called Nevada City. It's just beyond Grass Valley, about 30 miles north of Auburn."

Nevada City, California, nestled in the heart of the mother lode country on the western slopes of the Sierra Nevada Mountains, still had the remnants of authentic Old West charm. The Gold Rush of 1849 had created a boom in the tiny town which still boasted an assay office for weighing gold. After the short three-hour drive from the Bay, Alexis found herself exploring the quaint mountain village with its leather shops, arts and crafts, second-hand stores, and modest museum.

The front room of the Herb Shop was bursting with spicy fragrances emanating from the bundles of drying aromatic plants suspended from the ceiling. Dozens of large glass jars on broad wooden shelves were labeled with the name of the herb and its purported benefit. There were silvery leaves, dusky barks, mottled seeds and pale petals, bunches of dried yellow flowers, and bins of twisted brownish roots, all claiming effectiveness against ailments ranging from cancer to female complaints. Reading the labels, Alexis was smiling in quiet amusement when a middle-aged man with a long red beard, wire rim glasses, and patched jeans appeared in the rear doorway that led to the herb garden. He wiped his feet on the mat, and as he stooped to set down his trowel and gloves on the step, his waist- length red pony-tail fell forward over his shoulder.

"Hello," he said pleasantly, looking up. "Come in. My name is David Cooper. Would you like the ten-cent tour, and perhaps some tea? I just made some chamomile." Alexis accepted graciously and followed David as he explained the benefits of the various herbs and blends. He was very informative; his views on natural healing were fascinating and insightful. Until now, all of her friends and acquaintances had pursued altered levels of consciousness through marijuana or hallucinogens. This was her first contact with the true naturalists of the counterculture. They embraced an advanced new-age lifestyle, followed strict organic vegetarian diets, drank cleansing herbal teas, and ingested no artificial stimulants.

David and Alexis sat across from each other at the simple unpainted wooden table in the front room and sipped their tea.

"So you've taken a great trek across the country to get this far," David began. "What are you going to do next?"

"I guess I'm looking for a place to live for a few months. Since it doesn't rain in California in the summer, I'd like to live outdoors, someplace natural, and hang out with some like-minded people. Do you think you could help me with that?"

"Well," he answered, "there are some great places on the Yuba River, or you can join a communal farm like the one in Camptonville. In fact, I was going to hike in to visit some friends on the South Fork for the weekend. It's my partner's turn to take care of the shop. Would you like to go?"

"Great, perfect."

"You're welcome to stay the night," David added, kindly. "My old lady and I live in the little house next door. There's an extra bed in our back room. That way we can get a fresh start in the morning."

"Thank you. You're very kind," said Alexis. "I'm grateful."

The next day she and David drove through the winding mountains, heading for the South Fork. The morning colors were spectacular as the sun rose, shining crisply on the dark verdant greens contrasted against the black shadows of the deep northern forest. The bridge came into view, and Alexis saw the Yuba River for the first time. Far below, the river crashed against the granite boulders, violently dividing and rejoining in swirling eddies of white water. The rocky flood plain above the waterline was bordered with live oak and manzanita that led upward into the steep ravines of towering ponderosa pine. After parking on an old logging road, Alexis and David hiked the twenty-minute trail above the river bed, drinking in the sweet scents of pine, wildflowers, yarrow, and scotch broom. At that point she could see a cliff far ahead, jutting out over the river, and a tiny rough cabin perched high above. Below, a dozen or more people were sunbathing naked and swimming among the river rocks.

"There they are," exclaimed David, pointing. The vigorous exercise had made his face almost as red as his hair. "How're you holding up?"

"Whew! These packs are getting heavy," said Alexis. "But I'm doing OK. What are we carrying anyway?"

"Candles, brown rice, matches, kerosene, oats, wheat bran, dried fruit, carob powder, and honey," he said, a little breathless. "You'll like these folks. Some of them belong to the commune in Camptonville, but they still spend most of the summer here. Others are transients like you."

For six weeks, Alexis lived on the rocky banks of the Yuba and listened to the song of the river, enjoying an idyllic moment in time for self-reflection and communion with nature. Sitting on the rocky banks, discussions with the river people were usually metaphysical in nature and laced with double meanings. Where you were at, or where you were going, was more than a physical destiny, it was a frame of mind.

"For me, the ultimate would be a little farm," said one of the young men. "I just want a place where I can grow my own food, live off the land, have a couple of kids and raise them in a clean, pollution-free environment."

"I'd like that," said another. "But it should be two farms: one in the north for summer and one in the south for winter. Like Florida."

"Or Oaxaca in Mexico," said one of the girls. "Or Costa Rica. I was there last year."

"I don't want to have to go outside the United States to find the right place," Alexis responded. "There must be a perfect place here in the U.S."

"Well, let us know if you find it. We'll join you and together we'll establish the ultimate flawless society," the first young man laughed.

Most of them worked at some type of handicraft: sewing, macramé, carving soapstone, baking, or weaving, to provide enough money to get by. About once a week, two or three made the trip to town for food and supplies. But finally, summer had turned into a lingering Indian summer, and by the time the roadside blackberries were ripe, her finances were exhausted. The real world beckoned. But this time Alexis knew where she wanted to go – Berkeley.

* * * *

Although San Francisco still symbolized the very heart of the hippie counterculture, the focus had shifted east to the University of Berkeley. Running south from Sather Gate was the famous Telegraph Avenue, where all the contrasting charisma of the times seemed to line its sidewalks. On the shady side of the street were the pessimists, the cynics, and existentialists. These were children of the night, the jilted, and the lovelorn. Many wore the ravaged faces of hard drug abuse. On the sunny side were the optimists, the spirituals, the hopefuls, those who made direct eye contact, believed in love and peace, and trusted their fellow man. They were the writers, the poets, the dreamers, and philosophers; the sweet scent of marijuana lingered in their clothes.

Street vendors lined the sunny sidewalk while musicians, corner poets and orators, bubble-blowers, and Frisbee throwers created an air of festivity. Handcrafted wares were strewn across brightly colored blankets and sold to passers-by. Hari Krishnas paraded in the street, wrapped in orange mantles, shaking their tambourines, and chanting the praises of Rama. Everybody, it seemed, was an extremist of some type: vegetarian, fruitarian, macrobiotic. There were those who ate only sprouted wheat grass or engaged in prolonged fasting until they barely looked human and resembled walking skeletons. Some had taken a vow of silence and had not uttered a single word for years; others mumbled incoherently, oblivious to everything around them. New-born babies were named Rainbow, Cloud, Tree, or Star. It was the post-Haight-Ashbury era in California – the dawning of the Age of Aquarius.

Mark Donovan became Alexis' first real friend in the city. A student at the university, they had met while playing Frisbee on the campus grounds and struck up a conversation. A few days later when he invited her back to his uniquely decorated crystal-laden apartment, Alexis found out that Mark was an accomplished guitarist. He was also fascinated with pyramids and prismatic power.

"I've been doing research for a term paper," he said, sitting down at his desk. The low evening sunlight shone through the dozens of hanging crystals in the window, creating a room full of rainbows. He pointed behind him. "See that book *In Search of Ancient Mysteries*? It claims that a razor blade will stay sharp inside a pyramid no matter how often it's used."

Alexis examined an Indian print hanging on the wall above the bookshelf. Below it was a brass incense burner and a handmade clay pot with an arrangement of dried flowers and eagle feathers.

"Who's this Hindu god? And why is his skin blue?"

"That's Shiva. See the cobra around his neck? The blue skin symbolizes that he survived the effects of the venom; it also represents the universality of oceans and water."

"You're really into this stuff. You don't worship them, do you?"

"No," Mark laughed. "But I have respect for all religions and their teachers: Gandhi, Jesus, Buddha, and Confucius. They all had good things to offer. In fact, it seems that most religions say much the same thing: you should love other people, respect yourself, and try to be the best person you can be."

"That's what I believe too." Alexis relaxed into a yellow bean-bag chair in the corner and stretched out comfortably. The rainbows still played their colors on the wall, but the sun was getting lower.

"On a more mundane level, have you found a way to make money yet?" Mark asked.

"Actually, I think I'm on to an excellent prospect. The other day, I hooked up with a couple of craftsmen who make ceramic flutes. They're looking for someone to be their street vendor on Telegraph."

"What do the flutes look like? Just conversation pieces, or real instruments?"

"Oh, they're real instruments. Accurate too," Alexis told him. "I checked out their factory in Crockett and saw the whole operation. These guys have spent two years developing the mold. They're made out of California white clay; the holes are cut with brass tubing. It's all done with great precision: the size and shape of the holes, the individual bevels, and the distance apart. All the measurements are absolutely critical because the flute shrinks in the kiln. Then they glaze them with different color schemes. They really look and sound exceptional."

"Do you play?"

"I used to play a little in high school and probably would have majored in music if I hadn't dropped out of college. But I have a good ear and can pick up just about any instrument, so I figure I'll give selling a shot. I'm supposed to pick up my first crate tomorrow and I'll see how it goes."

"How about a place to live?" Mark inquired. "Did you find one?"

"Sure did. I found a place in Oakland with those two gay guys I told you about, Hank and Danny. All I need is about seventy-five bucks and I can move in."

"That's great. It sounds like things are coming together."

"I hope so. Listen, Mark, I'm going to go up to Tilden Park to watch the sunset. Kind of a Key West habit I picked up. Wanna go?"

"I can't. Thanks anyway," he said, giving her a hug. "But let me know how the flute thing goes. I'll be off to Santa Cruz for the weekend; I'm going to visit my buddies in the redwoods." Mark sighed, then yawned and stretched. "Yep. Bonny Doon. No place like it on Earth. You should go there sometime. Good people there, so peaceful and beautiful."

"Sounds great. I'll keep it in mind. See ya later."

Leaving his apartment, Alexis started the drive up the winding road to the hills above Berkeley. Reaching the summit, she parked the car and wandered among the new fallen leaves. Autumn had that pungent scent, enhanced by the aroma of the eucalyptus trees. Picking up a handful of the aromatic cone-shaped seeds, she sniffed them like fine perfume and put them in her pocket. She rolled a thin joint, lit it, and sat back against a tree to savor the sights.

With the sun poised over the Golden Gate Bridge, the panoramic view spread out before her while the hand of God began painting bold splashes on the backdrop of the muted sky. Below lay the San Francisco Bay in its entirety – Berkeley beneath, Oakland to the left, and looking far across the water she could see as far south as Palo Alto, and as far north as San Rafael. As Alexis watched day change into night, the steady stream of east-west traffic became a great moving snake of headlights slithering across the Bay Bridge to the twinkling City of San Francisco. Alcatraz sulked in lonely solitude in the encroaching darkness while Angel Island and Mount Tamalpais rose like specters from the mists. Lost in thought, Alexis stayed on the hillside of Tilden Park until the afterglow had faded completely from the sky. There was peace in her heart. Life was unfolding, and it was very good.

"Alexis?" Danny whispered. "Are you awake?" He was leaning over the bed shaking her shoulder gently.

"What time is it?" she asked, groggily.

"It's three-fifteen. Do you still want to go to the Flower Market with me this morning? If you do, I'm leaving in about ten minutes."

Danny Sutherland had lived with Hank Berman for four years in an old wooden house on the fringes of the ghetto. Together they owned a floral business in the downtown area of Oakland. Unlike other flower shops with sterile ambivalent racks or rows of plants laid out in supermarket fashion, when a visitor stepped through the door of Hank and Danny's flower shop, they stepped into a virtual rain forest, a sweet-smelling jungle, complete with small waterfalls in each corner. Plants of all shapes and sizes nestled together from floor to ceiling; there was no telling where one began and the other left off. Three times a week Danny got up early and drove to the enormous Flower Market in San Francisco where he did his wholesale buying. On several occasions he had invited Alexis to go along, and for the first time, she had decided to accept the offer. It was still pitch-black as they headed west across the Bay Bridge toward the lights of San Francisco.

"Hank and I will be taking another trip to Mexico soon," said Danny. "We're going to close the shop, but wondered if you would mind taking care of the plants for a few days?"

"Of course not; I'd be glad to. What are you going to do in Mexico?"

"Walk through the jungles and look at the plants, of course." He smiled.

"Jungles? I thought Mexico was all deserts. You know – cactus, striped blankets, and sombreros."

"That's true of the northern areas. But in the mountains to the west and south there are tropical rainforests with wall-to-wall plants. That's where they used to make all the old Tarzan movies."

"I loved Tarzan movies!" she exclaimed. "But I thought they were filmed in Africa."

"Nah, that's what they wanted you to think," David replied. "Besides, most of Africa doesn't even have jungle. The big cats they used in those movies weren't even leopards; they were jaguars. And again, jaguars are from Mexico, not Africa. But the plants..." he said dreamy-eyed. "Just imagine, philodendrons with leaves big enough for a full-grown person to hide behind, dangling from sixty foot vines. *Ficus lyrata*, eighteen feet tall with trunks that are four inches thick. And orchids. In the high canopy of the rainforest, the vines crisscross to make natural baskets that fill with leaves and animal droppings, the perfect growing medium for millions of beautiful orchids. To me, Mexico is paradise on earth."

By then Alexis had lost her point of reference in the maze of streets, but somewhere near the Embarcadero, Danny made two left turns and parked. Together they walked into the largest warehouse she had ever seen. Filled with every type of flower and houseplant imaginable, it was there that her love of tropical flora was born.

A few days later, Alexis obtained a solicitor's permit and began to sell the ceramic flutes on Telegraph Avenue amidst the purveyors of colorful tied-dyed T-shirts, ceramic wind chimes, leather belts, cherry-wood pipes, and African trade beads. Fellow vendors turned into friends, and the sidewalks near Sather Gate became Alexis' second home.

In December, the weather turned unseasonably cold. The Bay, which rarely saw temperatures below fifty, felt the bitter chill of near-freezing temperatures. But business was as brisk as the weather, and Alexis found herself making trip after trip to the factory in Crockett. She played and sold the ceramic flutes all day long, becoming more proficient as the weeks passed.

"Tell you what," customers would dare her, "I've never been able to get a single note out of any flute. If you can help me do that, I'll buy one."

"It's all in the embouchure, the way you position your lips and blow across the hole," she told them, loving the challenge. "The air splits, half goes down the hole, half goes over the top. If you can blow across a bottle, you can get a note out of a flute." Selling came easily to Alexis. With Christmas coming, she did well, and in spite of her professed anti-capitalism, she managed to clear almost two thousand dollars in a little less than two months.

However, everything changed after the first of the New Year. Hank and Danny decided to move to a nicer house in the hills, and they told Alexis she'd have to find another place. Wishing them luck, she promised to stay in touch. Within a few days she found a little garage in Berkeley to rent for cheap, fixed it up as a studio apartment, and called Mark to tell him the news.

"Hey Mark, how are you doing? How was your holiday?"

"Great," he replied. "I spent Christmas with my people in the redwoods. I just got back a few days ago. Regular sessions don't start until Wednesday, so that gives me a couple days to get organized. I'm off to a lecture right now. Stephen Gaskin's Monday Night Class. Ever hear of him?"

"Yeah, I think so. Isn't he the guy that preaches communal living?"

"Right. He's got a big following now. Stephen's really into a new philosophy. Eventually he wants to take a caravan of busses across the country to spread the word."

"What else are you studying this semester?"

"I've decided to take a course at Ali Akbar School of Music studying Indian flute. Maybe you're rubbing off on me." He grinned.

"So how was Santa Cruz?" she asked.

"Incredible. Every morning I watched the sunrise over the redwoods, worked in the garden, took steam baths in the geodesic dome, and tended the goats. When are you going to take my advice and go there?"

"To tell you the truth, I was considering just that. Telegraph Avenue is pretty dead. No buyers, no vendors. Do you really think it would be okay to just show up?"

"Sure, they're good folks. Just help out around the place and chip in on groceries and chores. They'd love to have you, I'm sure."

* * * *

Seven miles north of Santa Cruz on the upper end of Monterey Bay, the mountains ran close to the ocean, separated only by a narrow plateau. On the western side of Highway One were broad fields of Brussels sprouts, hardy plants that thrived in the harsh sun and wind above the cliffs where the salt spray wafted up from the sea. On the eastern side, the hills rose from the flats, and redwoods stood in grandeur as they had for thousands of years.

Alexis made a sharp left at the sign and followed the long dirt driveway edging the redwood forest. Pulling up to the gate, she saw the white two-story farmhouse, the barn, and a large acreage all surrounded by a white picket fence, just as Mark had described it.

"Hi," she called. "Is anybody here?"

"C'mon in," came the reply from the house. A young woman came to the door and beckoned, her hands dusty with flour.

"Hi, I'm Annie," she said. "Forgive me for not coming out; I was trying to get this bread kneaded and set to rise before the men get back."

"My name's Alexis. I'm Mark's friend from Berkeley."

"He told us about you. Welcome to Bonny Doon. Come in and have a seat."

Alexis mounted the creaky steps and took the proffered chair in the kitchen as Annie kneaded the dough. The faded orange curtains fluttered gaily in the window. The house felt comfortable; the vibes warm and friendly.

"It's beautiful here," she said. "Mark says this is actually a working commune, right?

"Well, most of the time anyway," Annie replied. "Some folks are permanent; some are short term. As long as people are helpful and contributing, it works out for everybody. If they're lazy and just taking advantage of a good thing, they are asked to leave."

"How many people are here right now?"

"Only four. But some are still visiting relatives because of the holidays. There's me and my old man, Martin. There's Greg, and a guy from Canada named Max. There are two other couples who live here permanently, plus a single guy and a lesbian couple; eleven all together. Even though the holidays are over, they probably won't be back for a month."

When the kneading was done, Annie greased a bowl, and flipped the dough twice. As she covered the smooth rounded loaf with a clean cloth and put it on the back of the stove to rise, they heard the sound of a truck pulling in through the gate.

"Is that the men coming back?' she asked. "Perfect. I got that bread done just in time. Want to give us a hand? The guys are bringing back a load of firewood." Alexis followed her outside as the truck pulled in.

"Martin, Greg, Max, this is Alexis, one of Mark's friends from Berkeley. Alexis, meet the guys."

Martin was skinny and tall with a scraggly beard and thin brown hair. Greg had a ruddy complexion, strawberry blond hair, and wore a red bandanna around his neck. He was attractive and had a mischievous twinkle in his eye. Max had dark straight hair that fell to his shoulders and hazel eyes deeply set in a heart-shaped face. His nose was straight and angular, shaded by heavy brows. The chin was too short but his lips were bowed, full, and sensuous. It was an arresting face, not exactly handsome, but certainly distinctive.

That evening, dinner was a simple meal, served on a trestle table on the screened-in side porch that acted as a sitting room and a spare bedroom as well. There was a sort of meatless meatloaf made of soybeans, steamed sweet potatoes, homegrown zucchini, fresh green alfalfa sprouts, and Annie's homemade bread. The conversation was lively all through dinner. Then Martin picked up his guitar and strummed a few notes as a soft winter rain began to fall outside.

"Anybody in the mood to take a little ride? Who wants to go over to Gino and Gracie's and play some music?" he asked.

"Sounds good to me," said Max. "They're the ones with the drums, right?"

"Yep," Martin answered. "They've got a couple of guitars, some conga drums, and a banjo." He turned to Alexis. "I understand we have a flute player in our midst, right?"

"I'm not very good," Alexis admitted, "but I'd love to jam a little."

A few minutes later they piled into Greg's van and headed down the road in the general direction of Santa Cruz. Martin and Annie sat up front, with Greg and Max in the back with Alexis. As they drove toward town, she realized that she felt a strong physical attraction to both men.

Although Alexis considered herself to be a very passionate person, she wasn't "easy" – at least not within the counter-culture context. She wasn't like Marcy, who would have sex with just about any man, or woman for that matter; enjoying one-night-stands and sexual encounters with no significant rapport. For Alexis, there needed to be a connection of spirit, if not long-term commitment. Few had actually entered her heart-of-hearts and won a place there for life. Long ago, it seemed, there had been Paul. Indian Ron too, but in a different way.

"So how long have you played flute, Alexis?" asked Greg.

"Not long. I've only been playing seriously for about three months now, selling these ceramic flutes on Telegraph Avenue. How about you, do you play anything?"

"No. I'm the storyteller and comic in the crowd," said Greg. "Former class clown. You know the type. But I do like to—"

"I play hand drums," Max interrupted, not realizing his momentary rudeness.

"Hand drums?" asked Alexis.

"I don't play a full drum kit with sticks. I play congas, *djembes*, or *doumbeks*."

"Where are you from, Max? I can't place your accent. Annie said Canada, but you don't sound Canadian."

"I spent time recently in Canada, but I'm originally from South Africa. I learned to play congas in the Zulu *kraals* on my father's sugar farm back in Natal."

"I'd like to hear about it sometime," said Alexis, diplomatically. "Sorry, Greg. What were you saying?"

"It's okay, nothing important," Greg said politely, but his smile had faded.

The evening turned out to be great fun. As the rain drizzled softly outside, the pot-bellied stove kept the cabin in the redwoods cozy and warm. Gracie danced, while Gino and Martin played guitars. Max kept a steady but creative rhythm on the congas while Alexis took the lead on flute. Between songs, Greg kept everyone in stitches with jokes and funny stories.

"Let me try to play that drum, Max," said Alexis. She took the conga from him and beat out a few notes on the rim. "Ow, that hurts my fingers. How can you play these things?"

"You have to have hands like a monkey's *arse* to play congas," he said earnestly.

She laughed as she mimicked his British accent. "Now how would I know what a monkey's *arse* is like?"

"Well, you see, monkeys sit on rocks most of the day, picking nits off each other and eating them—"

"Eewww, gross," shouted Gracie from across the room. "Just tell the story."

"Anyway, they get these two round hard corns on their butts. When you've got hard horny calluses on your hands, like a monkey's *arse*, then you can play hand drums with the best of them. By that, I mean the Zulus."

"What's this about 'horny' over there?" Greg teased, as he stoked the fire. "Let's keep it clean."

That night Alexis was pensive as she bedded down alone on the side porch. She could have chosen to sleep in closer proximity to Greg or Max, but she didn't feel like it. At least, not yet. Funny, how it was always the woman's ultimate choice. Men did the chasing and women did the choosing. Greg was sweet, funny, and American; Max was different, foreign, and mysterious.

"Somebody needs to take a run into the health food store in Santa Cruz," said Martin. "Do I have any takers?" It was just after breakfast and Greg, Annie, Max, and Alexis were all helping to clear the table.

I'll go," Max volunteered, raising his hand. "Alexis, would you like to go with me?"

"Sure," she replied.

The rains from the previous night had scattered and the day was again warm, breezy, and sunny. Grabbing a hand-woven shopping bag, they got the list from Annie, and walked together down the gray weathered steps of the farmhouse to where the vehicles were parked. The sky was brilliant blue; the temperature, perfect.

"My car or yours?" Max asked. "Do you have a preference?"

"Since you asked, let's use mine. Your car smells like a goat," she said, truthfully.

Max smiled good-naturedly and shook his head. He got in on the passenger's side of the VW and rolled down the window to let in the fresh air. "Hey, it's true. What can I say? I milk the goats around here." Max was quite aware that his car was a little over-whelming in natural scent. Out of necessity, he'd transported a few of the Bonny Doon goats in the back-seat on more than one occasion.

"Just teasing," Alexis said, as she started the car and headed toward the highway. "It's part of your charm. So tell me a little bit more about you."

"Like what?"

"Let's start with what's your last name?"

"Lord." He paused, "OK, I might as well tell you the rest; my full name is Maximilian Augustus Lord."

"You've got to be kidding!" Alexis started to laugh, and then caught herself. He was actually serious. "I'm sorry. It's just that I've met so many California people who name their kids Dewdrop and Moonbeam and stuff. Is that your real name?"

"I got the Augustus from an uncle." He smiled, amused. "The rest, I have no excuse for."

"I thought your real name was probably Bob or something, but somehow I think Maximilian suits you. I knew a Chicano named Jesus."

"Just imagine if he was my brother," Max laughed. "He would have been Jesus Lord."

The comment set the tone for fun, and by the time they reached the health food store the two of them were giggling like children. From the tofu burgers to the organic Chinese *bok choy*, everything seemed funny.

"*Bok, bok*," Alexis mimicked a chicken. "What the *bok* is a buckwheat groat?" she clucked. "*Bok, bok. Bok CHOY!*"

Max was laughing so hard, he could hardly stand upright. Then suddenly he grabbed Alexis impulsively and kissed her hard, right there in the store. It was only a fleeting moment, but it was filled with passion and in the pit of her stomach, she felt the unmistakable ache of desire.

Later that day, Max and Alexis left Bonny Doon for a second excursion, opting to take a walk in the Brussels sprout fields, skirting the edges of the rocky outcroppings where the cliffs plummeted hundreds of feet to the crashing waves below. The sky seemed enormous, still brilliantly blue, although now, giant puffy cumulus clouds billowed across the sun, casting immense undulating shadows across the flats. This time Max kissed her deeply. In return, she held him tightly, loving the feel and the touch of his caress. She stroked his beautiful thick dark hair and felt the hard muscles in his back and shoulders. From that moment on, neither of them could wait for the coming night and the promise of passion it held.

Max came to Alexis' bedside on the screen-in side porch about an hour after sunset. In the darkness, they kissed and held each other gently, knowing that the night was long and their lovemaking could be unhurried. Slowly he undressed her; his excitement grew as he stroked the firm smooth curves of her body. She ran her hands over his hairless muscled chest and felt her own fire start to burn. A moan escaped her lips as he penetrated her for the first time.

They made love for hours that night. Around two o'clock am, utterly exhausted, they took a brief respite, but awoke an hour later with renewed strength and passion. By first light, destiny had brought their lives together.

The next few weeks passed like a dream. Everyone on the farm knew that something had happened between Max and Alexis. Martin and Annie were happy for their sakes, although Greg had become uncharacteristically sullen, and no one was surprised that he left suddenly for an impromptu visit to San Francisco. Early on, Annie had kindly suggested that Max and Alexis use one of the still-unoccupied furnished bedrooms of the sprawling farmhouse, and she quietly hoped they would both stay on as communal members.

In early February, Alexis lay with Max, watching the early morning shadows on the wall. Cradled in his arms, her head on his chest, she could hear his heart beating. She thrilled to the very sound of it.

"Max?" Alexis said quietly. "Are you awake?"

He brushed her hair aside, and stroked her cheek. "Yeah, what is it?"

"Sorry if this sounds like a pick-up line – but what sign are you?"

"Leo, the lion," he replied. "From the jungle."

"What was it like there in Africa? You started to tell me before. I've always had a fascination for it."

"My father had a sugar plantation near Zululand," Max replied. "When I was little, he grew wattle trees as a cash crop and later, sugar cane. Being born and raised on a farm, I guess I've always loved the land and the soil. I even built my own thatched house on the edge of an enormous gorge on the farm. Someday I'd love to find another place like that – my own little corner of the world."

"So you're a lion from the jungles of Africa, and your name is Augustus, the name of a king. It all fits." Alexis sat up playfully. "I'm a Gemini, sign of the twins." Symbolically, she gave him a brilliant smile, and then an intentional scowl, followed by another smile to drive the point home. "But fair warning. With me, you get more than the twins – you get a whole harem."

"Sounds great," Max said, as he reached for her. "I'll never be bored."

Settling back into his arms, she paused before speaking again. "I'm going back to Berkeley today."

"Why do you want to do that?" he cried out. "Don't you want to stay here with me for a while longer? Don't you feel the same way I do?"

"What I feel for you …I can't put a name on it." Alexis looked at him, and then looked away. She could see the hurt on his face. "I don't know exactly. Right now my life is still there in Berkeley, not here. Even though I don't really have a job there at the moment, my ties are there. My little place and the people I've met here in California. Bonny Doon was only meant to be a vacation, not a permanent move."

"I think I love you." Max hadn't meant to say it so soon. His hazel-green eyes shone liquid and warm.

Alexis looked up at him through her long thick lashes. "Tell me that in Zulu."

"*Ngi atanda wena.*"

"That's a beautiful language. But how can you know? How can I know? We've only spent a few weeks together."

"My sign is Leo, Alexis. Lions mate for life and I think I may have found you." Max sighed, and hesitated before he spoke again. "Also, I happen to believe that anybody can live with anybody and make it work, so long as the other person feels the same way; so long as they both strive for that common goal."

"It's strange that you should say that. I've often thought the same thing."

"Well, if you feel it and I feel it, doesn't that tell you we should be together?"

"Maybe. But if we're meant to be together, we'll best find out by being apart."

* * * *

Living Love was painted on the side of the bus, along with a yin-yang, an OM sign, and other spiritual symbols, all on the backdrop of a tastefully multicolored sunrise. It was parked across the street from Alexis' garage apartment. Returning from her Santa Cruz adventure, she eyed it casually as she opened the door to go inside. After a leisurely shower, she thought about Bonny Doon again, and wondered for the hundredth time what Max might be doing.

Two hours later, the bus was still there. At last Alexis' curiosity got the best of her and she knocked on the door. A young long-hair in a tie-dyed T-shirt answered.

"Come in, come in," said a disembodied voice, not from the young man, but from the back of the bus. "Welcome to my home." The old bearded gentleman came rolling forward in a powered wheelchair and smiled at her.

"Hi," she introduced herself. "My name's Alexis DuBois. I live across the street in that little garage." She gestured. "I couldn't help noticing your vehicle."

"Hello, Alexis. I'm Ken Keyes, and this is the Living Love bus, my traveling ashram," he welcomed her graciously. "My followers and I are looking to find a home here in Berkeley, to establish a permanent base."

"Your...followers?" She noticed that there were three others in the bus with Ken besides the young man who let her in. "Are you a guru?"

"Perhaps in India," he laughed kindly, "but here in America, I simply call myself a spiritual teacher. We follow the positive precepts of many great religions of the world: Hinduism, Christianity, and Buddhism – and, although we have no direct affiliation with any of them, Living Love is officially a church and is registered as such."

"Where do you come from?"

"Originally, from Miami. Come in, sit down or let me give you a tour. Would you like some fresh juice or some herb tea? I was the owner and founder of Keyes Real Estate, a large company in southeastern Florida." Alexis studied the man; she'd heard of Keyes Real Estate. He was perhaps sixty years old with thin mousy-brown hair and wire-rim glasses. Ken was a quadriplegic, his body atrophied from decades of physical inactivity. He had only enough muscular control to hold up his head unaided and use one of his claw-like hands to move the simple toggle switch on the electric wheelchair.

The inside of the converted Greyhound combined spiritual inspiration with high-tech efficiency, allowing Ken maximum freedom and mobility. Besides the front room, there was a small but complete kitchen, extensive shelving for the stereo, amplifier, speakers, reference materials, tapes, and a substantial library of books. Toward the back was a complete bathroom with a toilet, sink, and a small sit-down shower. The well-rounded rear of the bus was Ken's bedroom which he referred to as the "OM Dome." Ornate with Indian prints and a heated waterbed, it afforded his gaunt body as much comfort as possible.

Alexis stayed for several hours. Ken was a fascinating man with an agile mind. Stricken with polio at age twenty-seven, the disease had changed his physical life forever. Yet, mentally, he refused to be victimized. Not only had he survived the debilitating psychological effects of the disease, but had become a highly successful businessman in spite of them. Eventually, Ken had escaped corporate life and had chosen to pursue spiritual enlightenment. His family thought he was losing his mind when he announced the purchase of an old bus and travel plans to set up his own religious order in California. Intelligent and forthright, unlike many of the other spiritual leaders of the day, he was not an extremist. His message was simple: live to the fullest, live in the here-and-now moment, and love others unconditionally.

Three days later, Max phoned Alexis. She had just come back from having coffee with Mark at the Café Mediterraneum in Berkeley, where she'd told him about Max. She'd been giving the whole situation some serious thought; three days had felt like three months.

"Max! What a wonderful surprise. I'm so happy to hear from you."

"I've been missing you so much." Eighty miles away, Max stood in the kitchen of the Bonny Boon farmhouse. "I can't stop thinking about you."

"Me too," she admitted, heaving a sigh and sitting down quickly. "Do you still want to be with me?"

"Yes, with all my heart," he said, softly.

"Then come to Berkeley. Come as soon as possible."

"I'll pack my stuff and be there tomorrow. What about a place to stay?"

"For now, there's my little garage apartment. But I met a spiritual teacher who just arrived in California. They have plenty of space in their big converted Greyhound, and he and his followers sure could use some help finding a location for his new ashram. How about you meet me at Sather Gate in front of the University at noon?"

Staying on the bus, Alexis and Max needed to adapt to the routine quickly. It didn't take long for them to realize that they probably should have kept the garage apartment to retain their privacy and get more sleep on a regular basis. Every night, Ken kept his followers up until midnight, talking, listening to tapes, or reading from various spiritual books like Ram Das' *Be Here Now* and *The Only Dance There Is*. Being limited to a wheelchair, Ken found it virtually impossible to exercise, and as a result, he slept very little. Waking at three-thirty or four in the morning, he would call for Max, or one of the other men, to carry him to the toilet, wipe him, wash him, and brush his hair and teeth. Devotees were expected to perform their own daily ablutions at the same early hour. Then, well before dawn, the morning began with *pranayama* yoga, singing, and meditation. After breakfast, there were various errands to be run: shopping, banking, and following up on potential ashram locations. Still a competent business man, Ken ran an extensive operation from his wheelchair. It was amazing how he lovingly compelled them to get things done for him – and how they reciprocated with open hearts.

Every evening after dinner, Ken Keyes formally addressed his followers as mentor and leader, speaking at length on the Living Love philosophy. His message was poignant; Max and Alexis were drawn to his truths.

"When you are involved with any menial task," Ken said, "think of the pleasant aspects of the job. Learn to appreciate the very fact that you have the mental and physical ability to do it in the first place. If you are doing the dishes, don't focus on how much you dislike the task. Concentrate on the warmth of the water and the slipperiness of the soap. Take delight in the foaming bubbles and the contrasting hardness of the dishes. Be in that space and praise God for it. Many people would give anything to be able to perform this activity.

"When you feel that things are going wrong with your life, take the time to appreciate the fact that you can breathe, walk, and talk. Be glad you have food and a place to sleep, that your basic needs are covered. Live inside this moment. Remember that whatever is troubling you now is forgotten in a year.

"And when it comes to others, just love," Ken continued. "Love, not because of what someone can do for you, but simply love for the sake of loving. So many songs reflect the selfish love, the sentiment of 'what you can do for me,' or 'how you make me feel.' True love is like the song 'Bridge Over Troubled Waters.' It expresses what you will do for someone else. 'I will lay me down,' the song says – for you. That is love.

"Real love is loving someone, no matter what; it's not ambivalently dependent on the other person keeping up certain standards of behavior. In real life, people let other people down. They go astray at times. Unconditional love survives all adversity. Live the love that does not die. Love your fellow man without conditions," Ken concluded. "Love, because it is so very good to love."

Later that night, as Max slept, Alexis thought about the lesson. Was such a thing possible? Could a man and woman love each other to such a profound extent as to be considered 'unconditional'? Could a husband and wife love so much? Did she love anyone so much, so unconditionally? Did parents love their children to such a degree that they would never turn against them, no matter what?

By March, Max and Alexis succeeded in helping Ken locate a beautiful old fraternity building just off the campus of the university. Once he had made the decision to buy Toad Hall and establish the Living Love Center, they told him they'd decided to go a different direction. Ken was sorry to see them go; he'd hoped they might join the ashram. Nevertheless, he expressed his deepest gratitude for their help during the transition.

Meanwhile, during the short time that Alexis had known him, Max had become increasingly preoccupied with the desire to secure a piece of land. Someone else's property would do for a start, but ultimately he wanted to find a place to put down roots, as well as seeds. Ideally, he foresaw it as being semi-tropical, with good farmland, and a long growing season, most likely outside the U.S. In Max's mind, the United States was a convenient first-world stopover, a source of making money before hitting the road to some uncivilized backwater where he could carve his own little kingdom. Now, as the famous Cafe Mediterraneum on Telegraph Avenue in Berkeley buzzed with the conversations of the regular coffee crowd, the two of them sat in a quiet corner talking about the possibilities of homesteading.

"Hawaii's too expensive," said Max, "and Florida doesn't have enough diversity. Maybe Jamaica, or Costa Rica."

"I'd really prefer a place somewhere inside the U.S."

"That's only because you've never been outside its borders, Alexis. There's a whole world of countries out there." They'd been drinking coffee and talking for about ten minutes when a tall man with a rugged face and jar-head haircut walked past their table, then paused and turned back.

"Excuse me," he said, "but I couldn't help overhearing what you were saying about a back-to-the-land retreat. That seems to be a popular subject these days. But if you two are looking for a place in the tropics, I could tell you about a little country that might interest you."

"I'd like to hear about it," Max said. "Won't you join us for a few minutes?"

"Well, I wouldn't want to impose–" said the man.

"No, believe me," said Alexis, "you'd be doing us a favor. Have a seat, please. What's your name?"

"Patrick McConnell. Formerly, Lieutenant McConnell, U.S. Army."

"I'm Alexis, and this is Max." They all exchanged handshakes.

"Glad to meet you," Patrick said, pulling up a chair. "Have you ever heard of Belize?"

"Belize? Where's that?"

"It's in Central America, a little country on the Caribbean, southeast of Mexico," Patrick said. "I spent about three months there. It used to be called British Honduras."

"I remember that from grade school," Alexis said. "So what's it like?"

"Well, most people would say that Belize hasn't got much going for it. The country is poor, but the natural beauty is impressive. There's no mineral wealth, no oil, no real employment for the masses. Not that there's much of a population either. But it's tropical, agricultural, and land is cheap. Off the coast are some beautiful islands and a spectacular reef."

"What were you doing there?" asked Max. The waiter came by, and brought their order of mochas.

"I was sent there as part of a temporary peace-keeping force when the British thought Guatemala was going to invade."

"The British?" said Max. "What do they have to do with it?"

"Belize is a British protectorate," Patrick continued. "It used to be a colony. Her Majesty still has troops stationed there."

"They speak English?" Alexis asked.

"A pidgin dialect called Creole, but it's still English. A lot of people speak Spanish too."

"So why were the Guatemalans going to invade?"

"Guatemala has argued a claim on Belize for years. A long time ago there was supposed to be a roadway built from Guatemala to the Caribbean so the Guats could have an eastern port, but it never happened and they blame the Brits. So every few years the Guats rattle their sabers. It's really only for show; a war will never happen. The Guatemalans are capitalists just like the British; they may be fascist, but they're still capitalists. Permanent British troops are stationed in Belize. It's the only country in the world never to have been invaded."

"I wonder why that is," said Max. He sipped his coffee.

"Basically because there's nothing worth taking," Patrick laughed. "Maybe because the people there are lazy – after all, they've never invaded anyone else either! But if you're looking for a place where you can carve out your own homestead, you should check it out."

Alexis realized later that a seed had been planted inside Max that day. He had been enchanted with McConnell's story and had taken it to heart.

The following week Mark Donovan invited Max and Alexis for dinner at his apartment near the university. New plans were unfolding, and they wanted to thank him and say goodbye.

"So I guess you're glad you went to the commune at Bonny Doon," said Mark, settling into the bean-bag chair.

"You were the one who brought us together." Alexis squeezed Max's hand. She told Mark that they were planning to go back to Nevada City; that they would not be staying with Living Love.

"I can't take the city for too long," replied Max. "I'm still a farmer at heart. I have to get my hands back into the soil."

"Max isn't happy unless he has dirt under his fingernails and smells like a goat," said Alexis. "So we're going to go back to the mountains. David, from the Herb Shop, found a piece of land we can rent near Lake Vera. The owners said we can grow a garden, and there's a little trailer to live in until we decide our next move."

"And in a few months, if we can get the money together, we may consider a more permanent back-to-the-land move. Like Belize."

"Belize? I've heard of other folks going there. Or maybe it was Costa Rica. Anyway, a lot of people seem to be turning pioneer," said Mark. "Except I always thought boats and water were more your style, Alexis. Didn't you always say that you gravitate toward the sea?"

"Most of the time that's true," she replied, smiling at Max. "But right now I'm under the influence of terrestrial forces. Max and I are going to plant some seeds and make some good things grow."

As April began, the winter rains of the Sierra Nevada Mountains continued nonstop. Still too cold to begin the gardening project, claustrophobia set in as the young couple tried to make the best of their home inside the tiny trailer on the edge of Lake Vera.

"You know, I can't stop thinking about that soldier's story. It makes me really want to give Belize a try. It makes me homesick for South Africa – or at least for the good parts."

"Why did you ever leave Africa if you loved it so much?" she asked.

"It's a long story."

"Well, it's raining outside and we don't have anything else to do, that's for sure. You started to tell me once. Tell me now. Tell me how you ended up here."

Max took a deep breath and began.

 **MAX**

chapter 4

Born in England, Max's father, Guy Lord had come to South Africa looking for wide open spaces and the opportunity to work the land. Over the years he had scrimped and saved, foregoing the indulgence of marriage and children until, in 1947, at the age of forty, he'd purchased a farm which he named Good Faith. At first, the cash crop had been wattle trees, the bark of which produced an extract used for tanning leather. When modern chemicals replaced wattle on the market, Guy had turned to sugar production.

On a trip to Capetown he'd met Max's mother, Ellie, a down-to-earth woman with a strong back and a will to match. The fact that she'd had two children from a previous marriage didn't intimidate Guy. He wanted a family anyway and figured, from a farmer's point of view, that the man who'd planted the seeds wasn't important; it was the man who tended them and made them flourish.

After courting for several months over the distance, at last they were married. When the time came for her to set up housekeeping on the farm, Ellie arrived from Capetown at the train station in Durban with little Timmy and Eunice. She had expected her new husband, yet it was a full two days before he showed up. When Guy finally arrived, he explained that the weather had been perfect for planting beans; he'd had to get them in the ground before it got too late in the season. If Ellie had any previous doubts about Guy, she knew then that he was a true farmer.

The other three children had come in quick succession. First Ellie had given birth to Clarice, then Max, and then little Sophie. With the brood of five, her husband, a crew of domestic girls and Zulu farm workers to look after, it was a wonder that Ellie could get anything accomplished, but she managed. Her household ran with almost military precision. She shouted orders and expected performance. The Zulus called Ellie *misxhla mamba*, eyes-of-the-snake, meaning that nothing ever got by her. She kept track of the stores of provisions for the Zulus in the compound and maintained a running list of chores to be done. She knew who was an enemy of whom, and from which quadrant the next problem would arise. Although Guy was the master of the plantation, Ellie was the disciplinarian; the farm was run with an iron hand.

Being the only white woman in the area, Ellie was expected to be an encyclopedia of medical information. Castor oil was a great cure-all, especially because the *Bantu* believed that the worse something tasted, the more potent it was. She delivered babies from breech position and cured all manners of illness, from stomach aches to evil spirits. An old Zulu once lingered outside the door of her kitchen holding his hand over his chest. When she greeted him, he calmly explained that a bull had gored him, and she suddenly realized that the red meaty object protruding from the hole in the man's chest was his heart.

Actually, many of the medical emergencies came as a result of fighting. In spite of the Christian ethic of the early missionaries, the Zulus did not believe in forgiveness. If two men fought, whether it was over a bottle of cane spirits or a cow or a woman, the fight was always to the death. To simply wound the opponent was pointless; to forgive someone was altogether stupid. If one of the men was merely injured, he would enter the other man's hut and kill him as he lay sleeping. Most fights broke out at weddings, which often lasted a week or more. The Zulus would eat enormous quantities of meat and drink *twala*, a native beer made from millet, until they were so gorged and drunk they passed out. When they regained consciousness, be it day or night, the cycle would start over. Ellie had seen many vicious wounds from the razor sharp *pangas*, and had called the coroner more than once when a Zulu skull had been crushed by a *knobkerrie*.

"Mummy! The boys are being mean again," Sophie cried petulantly. "Max just has to have his own way and won't give anyone else a chance. He and Ian were chasing Clarice and me. They pulled my pigtails, too."

Ellie shook her head as she dried her hands on the dish towel. Already her hair was shot with silver and the face beneath it, lined from the hard physical labor, made her look far older than her years. Life on the farm was rewarding but difficult, and the constant chaos of raising five children didn't make it any easier. Ellie spoke to the kitchen girl in pidgin Zulu, telling her to keep on stirring the pot. Then she sighed and went out into the yard where the two boys stood.

"Ian Fairbanks," said Ellie. "Off with you this very instant. Get on your bicycle and ride home before I phone your mother and tell her what a troublemaker you are."

The smaller nine-year old blond boy didn't wait to be told twice. He hopped on his bike and waved. "See you tomorrow, Max," he shouted, and then gave his friend a secret hand signal that signified 'you're-in-trouble-again-so-good-luck.'

"And you, Maximilian Augustus Lord," she shouted, "I am sick and tired of telling you to cooperate with your sisters. Come here this instant!" The dark-haired ten-year old walked toward her with hunched shoulders. He knew the reprimand would be harsh. "You're too bossy, Max. I've told you over and over that you must let the other children have a chance, and treat your sisters with kindness and respect."

"But, Mum, I..."

"Don't interrupt when I'm talking to you. Why do you always have to be in charge? Can't you let someone else be the leader for once? Everyday it's the same thing. I thought they would have taught you more discipline at school."

"But, Mum..."

"Not another word out of you, young man. Now go over there and sit under that tree until I tell you differently."

Old witch, Max thought as he sat down dejectedly. She may be my mother, but she's a royal pain in the *nxhoza*. Why can't she be more like Dad? He never shouts or punishes me like Mum does. Dad's great. One day I'll be grown up and no woman will ever be able to do that to me again. I'll be a man, and I won't have to take it. The resentment on his face was obvious as he sat under the tree and scowled at her.

"Bloody chancer," Ellie muttered under her breath as she walked back into the house.

Max sat under the tree sulking until he saw his father walking up the flagstones to the house.

"Dad!" he said joyously, as he ran to his father.

"Hello, son," said Guy. "What are you doing out here all by yourself?"

"Mum told me I had to sit here until I learn how to behave. I was just playing with Clarice and Sophie. I wasn't doing anything bad. Really, I wasn't. Mummy's always on my *arse* about one thing or another."

Guy put his hand across the boy's shoulder. Max was his only blood son, and his favorite child.

"I'm sorry to hear that, Max. But I'm sure your mother has reasons for doing the things she does. You know she loves you very much. She just has her ways. Tell you what," he continued, "how about we eat an early supper and head up to Field Nine and cut a few toppies for the cattle? We'll get Mishame. He and the boys can give us a hand."

"Really? Can I drive the tractor?" Max asked eagerly.

"Guy?" Ellie said, as she stepped down from the veranda of the big stone house. "I didn't expect you home so soon."

"Hello, my dear," he replied. "I finished early. The boys are still going to check the animals, but I've called it a day."

"Max, what are you doing running around?" she said, turning her attention to her son. "I told you to stay put."

"Oh Ellie, don't be so hard on the boy," said Guy. "He's just a little high-spirited, that's all. Why don't you put our supper on the table? Max and I have a special project for this evening." Max looked at his father gratefully. His heart went out to the big man with the work-roughened hands and dust on his shoes.

Guy stood at Max's shoulder as the boy drove the tractor on the narrow dirt roadway between the fields. Max had been driving for over a year now, ever since his feet were finally able to reach the pedals. Christmas vacation was almost over and, in this land of reversed seasons, the South African summer would soon be at its peak. The sugar cane was growing thick and tall. Soon it would be time to burn the field which would eliminate the green leaves and make the cane easier to cut. Then the Zulu *induna*, or foreman, would bring in his crew to harvest the crop with their sharp *pangas* and work their way through the blackened stalks. Burning had other advantages: it raised the sugar content by stressing the plants, and it served to chase away many of the poisonous snakes that made their home there. Squinting into the sun, Guy lifted his hat, wiped the sweat off his brow, and whistled for the workers as he surveyed the backdrop of the beautiful hills and deep forested gorges of Natal. This land had been good to him.

Hearing his call, the Zulu laborers came running and vaulted enthusiastically onto the flatbed trailer. As they got underway, Mishame began to sing a work song in clear bold tones while his brothers chanted back haunting responses that echoed in the distant hills. When they reached Field Nine they leaped over the fence, hacked off the fresh green tops of the sugar cane, and tossed them onto the trailer. Once the pile was large enough, Max and Guy drove back to the cattle *kraal*. Together, Mishame and the others threw the sugary leaves over the fence where the waiting animals seized them eagerly.

"*Bayete!*" Mishame shouted to the huge black bull who presided over his harem of cows. "*Bayete, Nkulu!* I salute you, Great One." With renewed vigor he began a new chant as his brothers joined in. "*Bay-e-te. N-ku-lu. Bay-e-te. N-ku-lu.*"

Above all else, the Zulus loved their cattle. Guarding them zealously, they knew every animal by name and loved them as their children. In the homelands, the village huts formed a circle around a large enclosure made of deadwood thorn trees. As prized possessions, the cattle stayed inside the fence at night to protect them from prowling lions and thieves, and grazed during the day only under the watchful eyes of the little boys, called *umfaans*.

The first job of all *umfaans* was to watch over the grazing cattle on the grassy *veld*. Even at the tender age of five or six, they carried the responsibility of keeping the cattle from wandering too far, or running for help if a leopard or a snake came near. Barefoot, wearing only a string around their waist with a small flap in front, the little boys carried two sticks as their only defense. Their accountability was a serious matter; a sick or injured cow must be treated without delay, and a lost cow would result in a severe beating. Cattle were wealth, and the ultimate status symbol. To buy a wife, the prospective groom had to pay the bride price of eleven head to his future father-in-law. For that reason, the Zulus valued their female offspring. A tribesman with many daughters would one day be a rich man.

In the days before the coming of the white man, life had been simplistic for the Zulus. The men did the fighting, the hunting, and the drinking. The women had the babies, milked the cows, grew the household crops of maize, squash, and beans, and built the round grass houses that the Afrikaaners, descendants of Dutch immigrants, would later call *rondavels*. Zulu huts looked like little beehives made of thatched grass over wattle-and-daub frames. A single low hole served as a doorway, and the thick choking smoke from a dung fire burning in the center of the floor helped to keep the biting and stinging flies to a minimum. It was customary for the men to gather in the company of men only. Each man had his own bachelor's hut, off limits to all women, whether he was married or not. Women were regarded as inferiors and mingled only with each other socially. Each wife had her own hut for herself and her children and it was the man's prerogative as to when he would spend a night with one of his wives.

* * * *

Through the long years, boarding school had been pure anathema for Max, but somehow he had tolerated it and survived. Now, after graduation, at age 17, there was a brief homecoming before starting the next phase of his life. It was late afternoon on his first full day back on the farm. He jumped in the four-wheel drive and motored down to the Zulu compound looking for one specific black and friendly face.

"*Nkosana!*" said Mishame. The two boyhood friends regarded each other as young men.

"*Sabuona,* Mishame. *Ngi ya bonge,*" Max replied in perfect Zulu. "It is good to look at you again, my friend. You've grown tall; you are a man, and the chattering birds have told me that you now have a wife who will soon give you your first child. My father says you are one of his best workers and will soon wear the head-ring of the *induna.*"

With the same toothy smile from childhood, Mishame grinned and said proudly, "That's true, *Nkosana*. And I see you are also a man now. We have spent much time apart. I hope the time has not been wasted, and that they have they taught you many useful things in the white man's school."

"Numbers and words are good to know, Mishame, but there are times when the lessons mean little to me. Often my ears long for the sound of the wind through the wattle trees, and my dreams are of the red sunsets over the African grasslands."

"Ah *Nkosana*, you have the heart of a Zulu – different from other white men I have known. You alone understand how the soul stirs when the conga drums beat in the glowing light of the village fire."

"Yes, my friend, sometimes I feel that, under this white skin, my soul is *Bantu*."

Distressed by the political turmoil within the country, Max was indeed different from most of the white South Africans. He enjoyed the company of the Zulus and sometimes visited the late night jazz clubs where blacks and whites socialized together, contemptuous of the mandate on *apartheid*.

"You also make allowances for the errors of my people," Mishame said. "Do you remember the time I drove the tractor into the great tree and all of its yellow-green blood ran out the metal grid of its mouth?"

Max laughed loudly. "Yes, I remember. My father took the *sjambok* to your backside."

"But you understood," said Mishame gravely. "I was young, and there were many things I didn't know. Most white men think we are stupid, but we are only uneducated. We do not have the opportunity to go to the good schools so our people may learn. The radios that you have, the tractors and machines, they are still so new that most of my people regard them as witchcraft."

It was true, thought Max. They were a simple but proud people. The sun was round, their cooking pots were round, and their women were round. In their culture, there was no such thing as a right angle, let alone an internal combustion engine. The Zulus who worked the plantation were friendly to Max as an individual, but many carried a deep-seated resentment of other white men, with good reason. Black men could not vote, could not own guns, were not able to hold title on land, and must always carry a pass unless they were on the tribal reserve. They were not allowed to gather in large groups, publicly or privately, and demonstrations were strictly forbidden. It was the country containing the world's greatest wealth of gold, diamonds, and plutonium, yet four million whites held the authority in a land of twenty-two million blacks. As such, a great deal was at stake, and fear played a large role in the imbalance of power.

"*Nkosana*, my heart is glad to be with you again. Let us walk together. We can share the good *ntsanghu* my cousin gave to me. It's from Malawi, very black, very strong. *Pema mange.* Let us smoke now. *Woza.* Come."

"*Yebho*, Mishame, but not here. *Asambe.* Let's go to the bush where we won't be disturbed."

Together the young men walked toward the crest of the last hill and began the long descent into the dark forests of Ngotche Gorge. About halfway down the steep incline they stopped and sat on a flat rock. Mishame took a *chillum* from his pocket, as well as a small quartz crystal, which he placed inside the pipe in lieu of a screen. He took out the tubular roll of brown paper and broke off a piece of the marijuana, crushing it in the palm of his hand. The weed fluffed as the seeds and stems popped to the ground. Then he offered the pipe to Max in ritual honor, who accepted a light from Mishame. After the first ceremonial draw, he tamped the burning weed lightly and passed it back.

"*Nkosana*?" The black man's eyes were dark and sincere.

"*Yebho*, Mishame," Max answered in perfect Zulu. "What is it?"

"You have gone to the white man's school from the age of eight summers. When will you come back to live on the farm again? Your father is old already. Will you not take his place soon?"

"No, not yet. Although I am finished in the white man's school, the South African government now wants me for military service. It will be several years before I can come back to Good Faith to stay."

"And your *ntombi*? When will you make her your wife?"

"You've seen her?" Max smiled at the mention of Jane. They had been sweethearts since the age of fourteen.

"*Yebho*," said Mishame. "She is very pale, like the moon over the night skies of Zululand, and thin like a young wattle tree. Her hair is like the yellow silk of the corn when it is yet tender and green. For a white woman, I suppose she is beautiful, but I like my women black, sleek, and fat," his face split in to a wide grin, "with the haunches of a brood mare, so they can bear fine sons and comely daughters."

Max laughed. He started to reply when they heard a strange howl echoing through the forest. "What was that sound?"

"I do not know," said Mishame. Their laughter had halted abruptly. They were silent for a few moments and then heard it again. "Perhaps evil spirits have been disturbed by our presence."

"No, not spirits," Max began. "Although I have never—"

Again the cry rang through the great valley. Neither of the young men moved, Mishame out of fear, and Max out of curiosity.

"*Nkosana*, I don't like this noise. In the days of my grandfather, a howling demon, half-man and half-beast, was known to have walked this valley, carrying his severed head in his hands," Mishame said. "I am frightened."

"Don't be afraid," Max said. "It is only an animal of some kind."

"Let's go back to the compound. The darkness is coming and my blood runs cold at the thought of meeting a phantom of the night."

"Be at peace, my brother. *Ntsanghu* makes your fear greater. But we will go. It's getting dark and my belly rumbles for food."

"Yes, *Nkosana*. The bush is beautiful when the sun shines down into the valley and lights the shadows, but at night it is well known that the forest has more eyes than leaves."

Ellie had prepared a picnic for Max and Jane, and now the young lovers held hands as they walked across the grassy savannah toward the edge of the deep forested gorge. Their time was short.

"I can't bear the thought of being away from you," Max said, as he held Jane tenderly. "It's been bad enough being at boarding school for all these years, but now I have to go to military training. Oh God, I don't know how I can stand it. Boot camp will be nine weeks with no leave." He looked into her eyes tenderly and squeezed her again. Then he turned and began to spread the cloth under a shade tree while Jane knelt down beside him to unpack the picnic basket.

"You're always with me in spirit," said Jane. "Maybe it won't be so bad. After all, it's officer's training school. Better to pick the rank of officer than to be picked for the infantry."

"Yes, but that means I'll be in for twice as long. I can't stand the thought of being told what to do by a bunch of Boers – those stupid hairy-back rock-spiders! I suppose I could hitchhike down for a weekend once boot camp is over, but then again, it's over six hundred kilometers from Pretoria. How much time would we have left to be together?"

"I don't know, but somehow we'll survive it," said Jane, lightly stroking Max's face. "Nigel promised to fend off any prospective suitors – with a *knobkerrie* if necessary."

"Nigel's a good guy, my best friend." Max sighed. "What else can we do, except be patient?"

"Here's something for you to take with you," Jane said, handing him a small box. "Might as well. No one else is going to see them." Max unwrapped the package slowly and pulled out a pair of her white lace panties.

"Oh my darling, I'm going to miss you so much," he said, kissing her with renewed fervor.

Impassioned hours passed and, too soon, the daylight turned to twilight. Max walked Jane back the stone house at Good Faith and then drove her home in the truck. Along the way, there was little conversation; it had all been said. At her doorstep, they used the traditional Zulu words of parting.

"*Hamba gashle*," Jane said softly. "Go in peace."

"*Shala gashle*," Max replied. "Stay in peace."

* * * *

"Atten-tion!" barked the sergeant as he entered the room. "Heinman, suck in that gut. You look like a bloody swine! Van DerVeer, get that silly-*arse* grin off your face. Brent! Stand up straight! You're creeping around like an *aape*," Sergeant DeGroot growled in guttural *Afrikaans*. Actually, this was uncommonly polite, as his more colorful remarks often implied deviant sexual behavior on the part of one's mother or sister. But having drunk too much liquor the night before, he wasn't in the mood to do any real bellowing so early. It was five o'clock in the morning, yet the men had been up for an hour already, cleaning their quarters, scrubbing the showers, and tucking in their bed covers. Now they stood at attention as DeGroot inspected them one by one. Max hated boot camp worse than anything else he'd ever experienced. As the only Brit in the otherwise all-Boer troop, his Afrikaaner superiors gave him a hard time, but this particular drill sergeant delighted in his own brand of humiliation.

"And you, Little Miss Maxine. You still have an attitude problem, do you not?"

"No, sir," replied Max, also in *Afrikaans*. He detested the sound of the language as much as he detested the people who spoke it. But the South African government was run by Afrikaaners; everyone was required to be bilingual.

"I can't hear you, soldier!"

"No, sir!" He shouted.

The sergeant put his face next to Max's, so close that their noses were almost touching. Max looked straight ahead, avoiding the man's eyes, but he couldn't escape the stink of stale brandy on his breath, and DeGroot was enjoying the revulsion on the young man's face.

"I'm checking your personal quarters today." With the men still standing at attention, the sergeant took out a white glove. Running his hand along the top of the locker, he was visibly upset when the glove came up clean, and Max smiled inwardly, glad that he had anticipated such a move. The big florid sergeant checked the corners of Max's bed and, still unable to find fault, took out a coin. He was disappointed when it bounced on the tightly-made bed.

"You think you're pretty smart don't you, Private Lord?"

"No, sir," shouted Max.

"Shut your face, *arse*hole. I'm not bloody deaf, you know." Then Sergeant DeGroot gave him a wicked smile. "About face!"

Max turned around obediently.

"Now open your locker. Let's see what you have in here."

"Yes, sir!"

Max shuddered as DeGroot saw the photograph on the locker door. It was something he had overlooked. There was Jane on the tree swing, looking so like a girl, and yet so much a woman. Her face shone in the morning sun, her flaxen hair streaming behind her in the breeze. They had strolled through a meadow that day in the early summer two years ago, and had made love for the first time among the wild flowers.

"Hmmm, who is this little vixen?" he said as he ripped the picture rudely off the locker door. "Nice tits."

"Sir, she's my girlfriend, sir."

"Ah, she's your girlfriend. Isn't that sweet?" Tossing the photo on the bed, he continued rummaging around in the bottom of the locker. "And what do we have here?" he said, as he pulled out Jane's panties. "Will you look at this? It's a darling little pair of lace knickers," he said, holding them up so all the other men could see. "Tell me," he yelled loudly. "What do you do with these? Wear them?" Max's ears started to turn red as the anger welled up inside him. "Or do you lie here at night thinking of her, pounding your pecker and jacking off?"

Still Max remained silent.

"Come on, you little *soutpiel*. Tell us all. Is she good?" he said lasciviously. "Does she lick you and suck you until your toes curl, hmmm?" DeGroot came up close to his face again and sneered. "It must drive you crazy to think about all the other guys fucking her while you're stuck here with me scrubbing toilets with a toothbrush."

Seething with rage, Max clinched his fist, fantasizing the crunch of cartilage and the blood spurting from the man's nose. He despised DeGroot with his every fiber and detested his impotence to do anything about it.

"Oh so you do have balls, do you? Good. That's what we want in a soldier. Now hit the deck and give me fifty."

Max began the pushups; the hatred and loathing were overpowering. At that moment he swore an oath from the depths of his heart: once he got out of the army, he would never let another human being degrade him, or tell him what to do, again. Not ever.

Winter was desperately cold that July as Max stood hitchhiking on the edge of the highway. Even with the warm outerwear, he was still chilled to the bone. Now that boot camp was finally over, his thoughts were only of Jane; he had to be with her. His friends at the base had covered for him Friday afternoon, enabling him to get a good start south toward Zululand, but the trip was long and vehicles were few. Now, after almost ten hours, he was in the middle of nowhere and still only halfway home. Through the darkness, he saw the lights of a cane truck coming toward him. As the driver slowed, Max made a pleading gesture with his hands. The kindly old Boer farmer took pity on the young man and pulled over, happy to have someone to talk to through what would otherwise be a long lonely night. But the ride turned out to be a mixed blessing, for although the truck was warm, it would not go more than sixty kilometers per hour. It would be late morning before Max reached his destination.

"Hello, Mum," he said calmly as he stood in the doorway.

"Max, my dear, I didn't expect you home!" said Ellie, hugging him firmly and pinching his cheek just a little too hard. "How good to see you. What a surprise. How did you get here?" He walked in the door and headed immediately for the fireplace, where he stood rubbing and warming his hands.

"I hitched a ride – several rides actually. Technically, I'm on leave this weekend, but most of it is going to be spent on the road. I have to get back by Monday morning role call or I'll be declared AWOL."

"I wish you had told us in advance. No one is here this weekend except me. Your brother and sisters went with your father to Durban for an agricultural fair. But I'll cook your favorite dish and we'll have a nice chat, you and I."

"Mum, I really came to see Jane."

"I see," she said, slowly. "Have you told her you were coming?"

"No, I didn't know myself until yesterday morning. I wanted to surprise her."

"Did she write you about the pageant?"

"No. What pageant?"

"Jane won the title of Miss Sugar Queen of Zululand. Quite a big honor. She's been running all over the country lately, even down to Capetown, endorsing products and making public appearances. Didn't she tell you?"

From the moment he heard the news, Max had a bad feeling about the whole affair, and after spending the least amount of obligatory time with his mother, he used his father's truck to drive over to the Hartley estate where he found it teeming with activity. There were vehicles from local news agencies, and television stations. A large archway and trellis decorated with winter garlands had been added to the front of the house. Max swallowed hard, a feeling of dread rising as he knocked on the door.

"Max," said Mrs. Hartley, as she stood in the doorway. "What a surprise! Jane didn't tell me you were coming. You certainly picked a crazy weekend for a visit. Would you like some tea?"

"She didn't know I was coming," Max said. "I hope I'm not intruding. What's going on?"

"Oh, another photo shoot. There have been so many lately, ever since she won the title."

Max stood there awkwardly; Mrs. Hartley had made no further move to admit entrance. "May I come in?"

"Of course, how thoughtless of me. Come in and join us for tea. Jane's changing outfits again. Bennington Clothiers are doing all her apparel for the telly spot, and they want to make a bid for an exclusive if she runs for Miss South Africa."

Max's jaw dropped as he heard the news. "She's going to compete for Miss South Africa?"

"Yes, didn't she tell you?" But before Max could answer, Nigel Upjohn walked into the room wearing a tuxedo. Max looked at him for a long moment, then continued. "No, Mrs. Hartley, she didn't. In fact, it seems like there are a lot of things Jane hasn't been telling me."

"Well, excuse me, gentlemen," the older woman said, warily eyeing the two young men and backing away. "I'll get the tea. Have a seat on the divan and make yourselves at home."

"Maximilian, old boy," said Nigel, walking over, trying to conceal his uneasiness as he shook Max's hand. "I didn't expect to see you. You're home from the wars, what?"

"What are you doing here?" Max growled.

"Take it easy, old chum. Jane simply needed an escort for the different functions she's been attending over the last month or so. She asked me if I'd help out. Remember, you did ask me to watch out for her."

"Hasn't exactly been tough duty, has it?"

"Look, pal, I..."

"Hello, Max," Jane said, as she entered the room. Max took a deep breath. The young woman looked like a goddess. For a moment he doubted that she was even the same girl. Her face, captivating without makeup, had been artfully transformed to lustrous perfection. Jane's flaxen hair had been lightened to the shade of moonlight. A peach satin evening gown, accented with a stole of white fox fur, enhanced the luscious curves of her body.

"Jane, darling. My God, you're beautiful." He reached for her with open arms, hungering to crush his mouth against hers.

"No, Max, don't. You'll muss me."

He stopped in mid-stride. His mind flashed back to DeGroot, and a hundred lonely nights without her. "Darling, aren't you happy to see me?"

"Of course I am," she said quietly. "It's just that I didn't expect you."

"Can we talk in private for a minute? Nigel, do you mind?"

"Of course not, old boy," he said, turning to leave. "See you in a few, Jane."

They sat on the divan between the tall marble statuary, and Max picked up her hand and held it between his. He barely had time to begin. "You just have no idea what the last two and a half months have been like for me—"

"Miss Hartley," interrupted the cameraman, poking his head into the room. "They're ready for you now."

Without hesitation, she replied, "Thank you, Mr. Simms. I'll be right there. I'm sorry, Max. You want to wait a few hours so we can talk? I'll be free around five o'clock. Nigel invited me to dinner but I'm sure he won't mind if I cancel this once."

"What do you mean, 'this once'?" Have you been seeing him?"

"Well, of course I've been seeing him," replied Jane frankly. "He's been my official escort. Naturally we spend a lot of time together. You understand."

"No, I don't understand. What the hell is all of this doing to you and me?" Max grasped her hand tightly.

The man popped his head in again. "Miss Hartley? Sorry to bother you, but everyone's waiting."

"Really, Max, I must go." She tried to pull away. "Why don't you watch the shoot?"

"Look – I've traveled six hundred kilometers to see you. I've gone without sleep for thirty-some hours. Soon I'll need to start back to the base."

"Max," she insisted, "You're hurting my hand. I must go. I'm sorry." He released his grip and closed his eyes as she left the room. Hot tears squeezed from between his eyelids as he lay down quietly on the divan. In spite of the flurry of activity around him, total exhaustion claimed him and he fell asleep.

Hours later, Mrs. Hartley found him. "Max, wake up," she said, shaking him. "I thought you'd gone back to Good Faith."

Groggily, he mumbled, "Jane said she'd see me after the photo session. Is it five o'clock yet?"

"Yes, a quarter past. Why don't you go freshen up and I'll tell her you're still here."

Max went into the bathroom and splashed cold water on his face, but it still looked haggard and dark. As he used the towel to dry off, he heard Nigel and Jane's voices coming down the hall outside. In a few seconds they would pass right by the door. Instinct told him to pull away, but instead he pressed his ear against the wood.

"I told you. I didn't know Max was coming," said Jane. "Actually I thought he'd left during the photo shoot. I should have known better than to think he'd simply walk away after traveling so far."

"Well," said Nigel. "He's making things damn difficult. I think you should just tell him the truth. You should have written him a letter, weeks ago. Then we wouldn't be having this problem."

"I suppose you're right. I just didn't want to hurt his feelings, that's all. Now it's going to be even harder. Also I told him I'd have dinner with him and that you'd understand."

"Well, that's going too far. I love you and you love me," said Nigel, petulantly. "Max is just going to have to deal with it."

"But you're his best friend."

"Well, I was – until the day I started making love with his woman."

Behind the bathroom door Max staggered and fell back against the wall. The blood drained from his face, but the hot sweat soon changed to cold chills as he walked into the living room where Nigel stood with Jane. Without a word, he walked up to Nigel and gave him a hard uppercut to the chin that knocked him flat.

"Max, please listen," Jane began.

Without even turning around he said, "Save your breath, slut."

Max didn't go back to Good Faith that night. Another chat with his mother was the last thing he needed. Instead, he drove to a bar in town and made passionate love to a small, but lethal, flask of cane spirits. Somewhere in the back of his mind a voice told him that he should get started back to the army base, but the pain was too great. By one o'clock in the morning he was quite drunk and ready for the Blue Note, a late-night jazz club where *apartheid* was largely overlooked and people of all colors gathered for music and liquor. The smoky semi-darkness comforted him like a womb, as he switched to scotch and stared numbly at the faces.

A little chocolate-colored girl, no older than fourteen, sat down across the table. She didn't speak, but studied his face as he sipped his drink. He paid no attention, continuing to think about Jane, his feelings alternating between love, anger, and hurt. He thought of Nigel caressing her and suddenly felt himself hard with lust. It was then that he realized the little chocolate girl was rubbing his crotch with her toes. She stuck out her pointed pink tongue and licked her lips, exposing small, even, and perfectly white teeth. With a movement barely discernible, she gestured toward the back of the club.

The room spun dizzily as Max came back to consciousness the following day. His head, splitting in agony, reminded him of the night before, and he was suddenly filled with remorse. He raised his body to a sitting position, holding his head, cringing at the mildewed walls and filthy bare mattress. The black girl was gone, as was his wallet and watch. But he had the good sense to give thanks she hadn't stolen his shoes and pants as well. The room was rank with the smell of stale liquor, and Max's only thought was to get out as quickly as possible. In the street, the glaring light of midday blinded him. His heart skipped a beat when he found out from a passerby that it was already one-fifteen in the afternoon. He called Good Faith.

"What do you mean you're heading back to base? I thought you were going to spend time with Jane and then come home," said Ellie. "Where were you last night? Where did you sleep? Max, are you in some kind of trouble?" Her raucous voice punished his eardrums like a squawking chicken with a British accent.

"No, Mum, I'm fine," he lied. "I spent the night with a friend. I've been here too long already. I've simply got to head back to the base, or I'll end up in real trouble."

"Well, I'm thoroughly disappointed in your behavior and I'm sure your father will be as well. I would have expected that you could have spent at least a little time with your old mother."

"Mum, please. I'll make it up to you next time, I promise. I'm going to go now. You can have Timmy pick up the truck here in town at the petrol station. I'm sorry. Bye, Mum."

"Max! Don't you hang up on me," she said. "Max?"

Worse than the cold on the way down, now a freezing rain blew across northern Natal as Max hitched his way back to the base. He felt sick and disgusted, disenchanted with life in general and women in particular. By the time he reached the camp it was eleven-fifteen Monday morning, and Sgt. DeGroot had already had the supreme satisfaction of declaring him AWOL.

Max was committed to solitary confinement for three days. The tiny cement structure was only six feet by six. The menu consisted of thin soup, bread, and water. Served twice a day, it was garnished with a few greasy hairs, courtesy of the fat Afrikaaner cook who brought his meals. The three days of incarceration made for an experience beyond Max's worst nightmare. He'd seen men come out of the dog box drooling and babbling nonsense. In the cold and damp, among the scuttling roaches, Max reaffirmed his embittered vow to never again be a victim of the system.

* * * *

As the pale blue VW bus passed by the quaint cottages of Brighton nestled among the immaculate gardens of the southern English countryside, Max Lord and his childhood friend, Ian Fairbanks, congratulated each other on the success of their trip. So far, it had been flawless.

"It doesn't get any better than this, does it, old boy?" said Max, slapping Ian's shoulder good-naturedly. "I thought I'd never finish my time in that stinking Boers' army. Really, chum, it was a brilliant idea. And what a concert that was! The Isle of Wight is sure to go down in history." He squinted slightly and pointed ahead. "Looks like a couple of good-looking birds hitchhiking. Want to give them a go?"

"OK," said Ian, with an impish smile, "but only if I get the dark-haired one."

"Deal," Max replied. "But you'll be sorry when you get a good look at the redhead. She's a knockout." The van slowed down and pulled over; Max had the door open even before they came to a complete halt.

"Hi! Thanks for stopping," said the dark-haired girl, as they both climbed in. "My name's Janine and this is Gabrielle." The girls arranged their backpacks on the floor on the van and settled themselves comfortably in the backseat. "Where are you guys from?"

"South Africa, Natal Province," Ian answered for both of them, as he put the vehicle in gear and brought it back up to speed. "This is Max Lord and I'm Ian Fairbanks."

"Gabby is from California, and I'm from Chicago," Janine added. "I'll bet you were at the Isle of Wight concert, huh?"

"I'll say! In fact, I feel like I'm still there. The music's still playing over and over in my head; I've barely started to come down from the buzz," said Max.

"I'm sorry we missed it, but unfortunately, we just got to England yesterday," said Gabby. She and Janine had met at Heathrow and decided to knock around Europe together for a while. They were going to France and Spain first. "How 'bout you guys?"

"Europe first, of course," Max answered. "Then on to India. It's almost eight thousand kilometers overland. We're not really sure. But we've got nothing but time, so it doesn't really matter. Why don't you girls hang out with us on the Continent for a while? You need the ride and we'd sure enjoy the company."

Ian jumped at it. "Yes, I second the motion. How 'bout it, ladies?"

Over the next several weeks, the foursome enjoyed the little cabarets of Spain and France, partying, dancing, and plying themselves with wine and French pastries. They finally parted company in Milan when the American girls decided to go south to see Florence and Rome. Per the original plan, Max and Ian intended to continue their trek east through the Balkans to Turkey and on into the great deserts of the Middle East.

All across Eastern Europe, they'd heard frightening rumors about the safety of the Turkish border crossing, so naturally, they were apprehensive when they found no one at Immigration to check their papers. After waiting nervously for someone to see them through, when the border guard finally arrived, he was smiling and friendly. And in spite of the language barrier, he sold them some prime-quality hashish, stamped their papers, and sent them on their way with a crooked yellow smile. Pleased with such an auspicious entrance, Ian and Max changed their image by purchasing Arab-style clothing. Clad in native headdresses and flowing robes, they further endeared themselves to the local population by making a sign for the front of the van that read *Inshallah* – if Allah wills.

In the months that passed, the van trundled bravely across the Middle Eastern deserts in spite of incredibly harsh conditions. The desert was blistering by day and freezing by night. In many seemingly unending stretches, there were no roads, no signs, only the faint tread marks of previous vehicles in the shifting sands. On occasion, a truck would approach from the other direction, putting on its high beams within a hundred meters of the vehicle. Both Max and Ian had screamed curses at this impudent behavior until a helpful English tourist explained it as a local courtesy to prevent collision with stray camels. Through the weeks and months that followed, the elevation increased sharply, and not long afterwards, the jagged mountain peaks of the great Kush of Afghanistan pierced the distant sky.

Once into India itself, Ian and Max visited the Vale of Kashmir, reputed to be one of the most beautiful places on Earth. In Benares, the great holy city of India, they visited the Theosophical Society, where Max spent many hours in the immense library, enriching his mind with the teachings of the great philosophers and holy men. Slowly, he began to soften and forgive the wounds of the past, giving up much of his anger and hurt, especially when his eyes were opened to the suffering and poverty of India's masses. He read of Mohandas Gandhi, the struggle for freedom under Lord Mountbatten, the last viceroy of India, and the destruction that followed in the tortuous separation of Hindu India and the Islamic Pakistani states. At last, in Bombay, Max and Ian sold the van and boarded a ship bound for the Seychelles and the ports of eastern Africa.

Of all the places he'd been, the Seychelles most embodied Max's ultimate fantasies. He sat on the beach under the *coco de mere* palms found nowhere else in the world. The women were the most beautiful he'd ever seen, the French ancestral blood mixing with the dark-eyed Ceylonese and the smooth features of the East Asians. The weather of the islands was always perfect, as it varied little from the median temperature of seventy-five degrees Fahrenheit. As he stared into the cobalt blue of the ocean's depths, Max realized he'd found the tranquility he'd sought and was ready to return home. Ian postponed his departure. Finding a dark-eyed beauty of his own to distract him, he opted to stay in the Seychelles for a few weeks longer, but they arranged to meet in Durban in one month's time.

Max advised his family regarding his return, and asked if they could come to Durban to meet him. Then he boarded the boat heading due west from Victoria for the final leg of the journey down the African east coast. Visiting the ports of call one by one – Mombassa, Dar es Salaam, and Lorenzo Marques, he realized he had come a long way, and not just in the geographical sense. He felt different, looked different, and carried peace in his soul for the first time. With new eyes he saw a new Africa; his experience had taken him outside the provincial world in which he'd grown up. Now he was ready to return to his father's plantation in Zululand; where he wanted to put his newfound knowledge and compassion to use, to assume his position on the farm, and begin a new life.

Having been gone for just over a year, it was at once strange and familiar to be returning home. As Max walked off the gangplank in Durban, he tried to get the attention of his father, who was still searching the deck for him.

"Here, Dad!" he yelled above the clamor of the crowd. The dock carried the sharp acrid odors of curry, stale sweat, and urine. Departing passengers shouted to their relatives, carrying live chickens or leading goats as they shoved through the crowd, their children scurrying behind.

"Over here," he shouted again. "Dad, Mum, Clarice! Here I am."

"Max!" shouted Sophie, spotting him and pointing. "Mummy! Look at Max!"

As the family got closer, they stopped short, staring at a person they no longer knew.

"Max," said Ellie, "What the devil happened to your clothes? Look at your hair."

"It's good to see you, son," said Guy, breaking the ice. "But where are your shoes? What's happened to you?"

Max suddenly realized how drastically his appearance had changed. His hair had grown more than six inches since his departure and was now down to his shoulders. He sported a full beard, cutoff blue-jean shorts, an Afghani sheepskin vest with no shirt underneath, and leather sandals. Under one arm was a set of bongo drums, and a small backpack was slung over the other shoulder. Looking back at them, ignoring their looks of shock and disbelief, he smiled and said serenely, "I was gone and now I'm back."

Industrious and productive, Max moved with a purpose, loving the dawn of each new day. After a few weeks, he had things so well in hand he convinced his parents to take an extended trip to England to visit Guy's relatives. While they were gone, he set out to accomplish a project that had daunted his father for years: the plowing and cultivation of Field Six. He was convinced that the way to plant the steep hillside was not in lateral rows, but rather straight up and down. First, he took apart the tractor and spent a fortnight rebuilding the worn sprockets, one by one, so the halftracks would not slip. Then he designed and built a special braking system for the plow so it could go straight downhill without running up over the tractor. Through weeks of diligent work, Max finally plowed the precipitous incline. With the help of his old friend, Mishame, he planted the small nodes of cane, sure to produce a fine crop.

The call had come in early that morning. Ian was back from the Seychelles and headed out to Good Faith. Max saw his vehicle approaching and raced down the drive to meet him.

"Ian, you old dog! Good to see you again," said Max, embracing him fondly. "When did you get in?"

"Day before yesterday. I was going to see you first but I decided to stop by Simon Frye's digs in Durban first. Are you staying out of trouble?"

"Pretty much so," Max replied. "Haven't had you around to be a bad influence."

"Well, I can change that." Ian's characteristically impish smile was back. "I've got something to show you. Look at this." Together they walked over to the car, and Ian pulled out a record album from behind the front seat.

"Yeah? So?" Max was confused. "Led Zeppelin. It's a great album. So what?"

"Check what's inside." From between the cardboard record cover and the inside sleeve Ian pulled out a sheet of translucent white paper with faint demarcations in half-inch squares. Holding it to the light, Max could see that each square contained a drop of dried liquid.

"Holy shit!" said Max. "LSD?"

"The best acid you'll find anywhere," replied Ian. "Manufactured right in Simon's basement, guaranteed to be fresh, top quality. Same stuff we had at the Isle of Wight."

"Holy shit," Max repeated. "What are you going to do with it?"

"Well, old buddy, I'm going to give half to you and take the other half down to East London and Port Elizabeth. I'm sure it will sell for at least forty *rand* per hit. Surely you know a few people who might be interested."

"Ian, this is Natal, not the U.K.," said Max. "People here don't know about this stuff."

"Enough people have gone abroad to have had a taste of the real world. They've all grown their hair and they've smoked *ntsanghu* for years. That friend of yours, what's-his-name down at the Blue Note, knows a ton of people. I'll bet we could create a regular market with very little effort. Make a little money."

"I don't know. It's a lot different from weed. The Boers would lock us up forever for this."

"Who's going to know?" said Ian. "Simon's going to have another batch ready in about two weeks. Just keep an open mind, and let's just see what we can do. If it doesn't fly, I'll just tell him we're not interested."

When Guy and Ellie returned from England four months later, they were thrilled at the progress on the farm. The first thing Guy noticed was a haze of green shoots covering the steep hillsides of Field Six, and this was only one of many improvements. Max had made repairs to numerous outbuildings, including the grain room and storage sheds. He'd had the workers dig ditches around all the farm buildings to prevent water damage from heavy rains. With Mishame's help, he'd coordinated an effort to improve sanitation in the compound by supervising the digging of new latrine pits and reeducating the Zulus on personal cleanliness. He'd repaired every piece of machinery on the entire farm, and serviced every device with moving parts, from the tractors right down to Ellie's sewing machine. Long hair aside, Max had become a model son, and their hearts were filled with pride.

But his parents had no inkling of some other things that had gone on during their leave of absence. Max had enjoyed free rein as lord and master of Good Faith. On many nights the stereo had pumped out rock-and-roll music while Max and his friends had enjoyed wild parties, smoking Durban Poison, a particularly potent strain of marijuana, and tripping on Ian's LSD. Surrounded by black lights and fluorescent posters, the young people indulged in whatever bizarre behavior came to mind. Max had found a market for Simon's basement product at the Blue Note and now had a steady following of key people. It became a bit trickier to keep up the distribution when his parents had returned from England, so Max built himself a huge thatched house overlooking the rim of Ngotche gorge. There he could be his own man in the privacy of his own home.

A young Zulu girl was scrubbing the floor under Ellie's supervision, and she was taking a long time to do it badly. The harsh knock on the door of the main house startled her, and when she opened it, a large heavy-set army lieutenant stood menacingly in the doorway. Behind him was an army transport vehicle. Ellie stared at him in surprise.

"May I help you, *Menheer*?" she asked politely.

"I would like to speak to Maximilian Augustus Lord, please."

"I'm sorry. He's not here right now."

"Very well" he said, in a thick Boer accent. "Then it is my duty to inform you that your son is required to attend two weeks of Reserve Army training at the base in Pietermaritzburg. We expect him to report in one month's time. This is his official notice. Please sign here." He handed her the clipboard and pen. Dutifully, Ellie signed the slip and was given the carbon copy. "Make sure he receives this notification. It is a punishable offense if he does not appear."

That evening when Max came in from the fields, his mother presented him with the letter. She had made him a special dinner, but his appetite evaporated instantly when he opened it. Memories of Sergeant DeGroot and his army days came back to him; it felt like a physical blow. I can't do this, he thought. I can't. There's got to be a way. I've got to get out of here, somehow. I can't go back to that. They'll shave off my hair and, with it, my dignity. No, never again. He excused himself from the table, hurried to the telephone in the back room, out of earshot from this mother, and made a phone call.

"Yeah, that stinks, Max," Ian agreed, after hearing the news. "It really does. Is there anything I can do?"

"I honestly don't know, but I'll tell you one thing, I'm starting to think about getting out of here."

"Getting out? Where would you go?"

"I don't know, but I'm damn glad I got a proper British passport. Good thing Dad was actually born in England. I can go a lot more places on that than a South African one."

"That's helpful, at least. You really think you'll leave?"

"I don't know. The sad thing is that I've really been enjoying South Africa ever since we came back. Come over and let's drink a few beers, OK? We need to talk."

"Sure, old chap. Anything to help."

After he'd been served notice, Max remained in his thatched house on the edge of Ngotche Gorge. He felt trapped. Everything was falling apart. His parents couldn't understand his angst. It was only two weeks of reserve training, after all, and what would be so bad about having to cut his hair? It all came to a head one rainy afternoon when the police, rather than the army, arrived at the door of his private domain. Too late to duck and run, he stood there in disbelief.

"Maximilian Lord, you will come with us, please. You are wanted by the authorities for questioning in regard to possible involvement in illegal drug trafficking."

Handcuffed and taken into custody, the next few hours were sheer torture. The counter-culture of the U.S and England had yet to trickle down to the South African police, and the fact that his hair was now well below his shoulders didn't help his image. By evening, Max found himself in jail under the official charge of "suspicion of treason against the state" – a catch-all phrase long-used against the Zulus to detain them for months on end for unspecified reasons.

The next day Ian came to bail him out.

"You mean my parents won't put up the money?" Max asked incredulously.

"Probably they will, but I thought it would be better if we did it first," said Ian. "All of your buddies, including myself, put this money together so you could get the hell out of here. If your parents did it, then you might feel guilty about jumping bail."

Max's eyes grew wide in amazement. "What?" he whispered softly.

"Why, of course, old boy. Can you imagine what would happen with the army and the drug thing combined? No. You need to go – with our blessings."

There was no longer anything to think about, the decision was made. Max was too far ahead of his time to stay in a country of rural *rooineks* and rock-spiders. In seeking a more modern environment, it wasn't hard to figure out where to go. He wanted to be where the length of his hair was the standard, where sandaled feet were acceptable, where the women gave free love, where beads and flowers were worn by everyone, and marijuana was a part of the culture.

*   *   *   *

The cold rain still fell outside the tiny trailer as Max finished telling his story.

"See, *Ntombi?*" said Max, warmly. "There was only one possible destination for me – California."

 **NORTHLANDS**

chapteR 5_____

As the weeks passed, and the winter rains of northern California continued to fall steadily, close quarters eventually bred short tempers.

"Maybe we should go on another fast," said Max, irritably. "Fasting is so good for you. It's nature's operating table"

"Oh please, not that again," Alexis protested. "Why does everyone in California have to be an extremist when it comes to food?"

"I just think that natural cures are best. That's why God gave us herbs and grasses. You don't need to be a scientist to be healthy. When I was a kid I had bad tonsillitis regularly. My grandfather, back in England, was a naturopath; he didn't believe in modern medicine, and always said that God doesn't hand out unnecessary body parts, so I never got my tonsils out."

"Still, there's a lot to be said for modern medicine. I'm sure you still took antibiotics every time you had a flare-up, and they're products of the twentieth century."

"Penicillin is made from bread mold," he argued. "That's natural."

"Okay, never mind," Alexis said, now also irritated. "Sorry I brought it up." She held his gaze for a moment. "I didn't mean to snap at you. The claustrophobia must be getting to me."

"I know what you mean," said Max, his tone softening. "At least we'll have a piece of land to work on as soon as the rains let up. This land and trailer were a lucky break for us. It might not be much, but it's cheap."

When spring finally arrived in mid-April, they broke ground and began planting snow peas, lettuce, radishes, carrots, broccoli, and cabbage. Max put up an eight-foot fence to keep out the numerous deer, and they made plans to drill for water with the coming of the dry California summer.

"Did you ever read a book called *The Magic of Findhorn*?" Max called from three rows over, as he shouldered the spade and walked over towards where Alexis was working.

She opened the seed packet carefully and dropped a single kernel into the hole, covering and tamping it gently "No. What's it about?"

"It's a commune in northern Scotland where they grow huge organic fruits and vegetables. Supposedly, they call on the *divas*, plant spirits, or sing to them, to bring forth the bounty of the land."

"Sounds like a fairy tale," Alexis laughed. "Is it supposed to be for real?"

"That's what they say." Max turned over several other shovelfuls of soil to prepare the rest of the row for her. "Why don't you try singing to the seeds while you plant them? Maybe they'll grow better."

"Oh, come on. Give me a break. I'd feel stupid."

"Okay, then sing for me instead. The Zulus always sang while they worked in the fields. I wrote to my parents and told them I'd met an American girl who could sing like an *nyoni*, like a songbird."

Alexis gave him a winning smile and began to sing softly. A few minutes later he walked over to her, brushed the long hair away from the back of her neck, and kissed her.

"Alexis?"

"Hmmm?" she said absent-mindedly.

"What would you say to us getting married?"

"What?" she exclaimed, truly surprised. "Why married? We could just live together."

"That's true. But you know I'm only visiting here right now. The U.S. Government thinks I'm a Canadian. If we married, then I could stay."

"Wait a minute. I thought you were a British South African traveling under a British passport."

"I am. But I also have a South African driver's license, a South African passport, Canadian Social Insurance card, and a Canadian driver's license."

"Isn't that slightly illegal? How did you get the Canadian ID?"

As it turned out, Max had taken advantage of a little glitch in the system. He'd found out that Newfoundland didn't have any birth records before 1949, so when he got to Canada, he told the authorities that he was born in St. Johns in 1948, and they'd given him both ID's without question.

"Now you're confusing me. Which passport do you travel on?"

"Always on the British one. A South African passport is very limited as far as which countries you can visit. You see, I was born in 1948 before the Union of South Africa became the Republic of South Africa. And because my father was born in England, I was allowed a choice as to what citizenship I wanted. So I was able to get a British passport issued in England. I also had a South African army reserve card, but I burned it before I left. As soon as I have some good United States identification, I plan to burn my South African passport too."

"I take back the 'slightly' part," she said, "that sounds extremely illegal."

"Of course, it could get tricky if I were ever searched. But if we were married, I could stay here in the United States – that is, if neither Belize nor Costa Rica works out. But beyond all that, I just always want to have you by my side. I want you to be *ntombi eyami*, my woman," he said affectionately. "Will you marry me?"

Within a few months the preparations for the wedding were complete – food, flowers, what to wear, invitations. Friends from all over California had already promised to share in their happiness, and Alexis' parents were flying in from Pennsylvania. Everything was in line for the big day.

On the day before the ceremony, Max and Alexis decided to head to the North Fork for a swim at a spectacular nude swimming hole called Oregon Falls. As the couple relaxed on a rock, Alexis saw a tall young man she vaguely recognized from the previous summer on the South Fork. She called out to him, and the young man squinted in the bright sunlight, smiled, and walked over to greet her with a platonic kiss on the cheek.

"Alexis, right? Sure, I remember you. Long time, no see."

"Doug, I'd like you to meet Max, my fiancé. We're getting married tomorrow."

Doug congratulated them both. Max stared at him and accepted the handshake, but said nothing.

"Have a seat," said Alexis. "Join us."

"No, really I can't," he said. "I've got some friends over there. We were just leaving."

"Well, maybe you'd like to come to the wedding tomorrow. Twelve-thirty. We'd love to have you." She told him the location, and he said he would try to attend. After exchanging a few pleasantries, Doug rejoined his friends. After a few minutes passed, Alexis realized that Max still sat in silence.

"What's wrong, Max? You're not saying anything."

"I don't like the way you were looking at that guy. Who is he really? Some dude you were screwing back on the river last year?"

"Take it easy. He was just a friend from the cabin on the South Fork. What are you so pissed off about anyway?"

"You, that's what. You couldn't take your eyes off that big dick of his, could you?"

"He's only a friend, and I rarely, if ever, saw him with clothes on. What are you so upset about? He's not a former lover, but even if he was, so what? What difference does it make? You're the only one for me now."

Max continued to stare into the water in anger. "I just can't stand the thought of another man touching you."

"Well, I still have men friends. That's not going to change."

"Maybe it is, maybe it isn't."

Now Alexis reacted to the irksome statement. "What's that supposed to mean?"

"Tomorrow you're going to marry me, not somebody else," he said, his voice getting louder. "I don't expect to ever see you look at another man like that again – especially one like Mr. Long Dong back there."

"Looking at him like what? My feelings for a man are not in proportion to the length of his penis. You're just going to have to get more confidence in me, or maybe yourself. I don't mind you having opinions, or even dictating certain aspects of our relationship, as long as they're reasonable. I've probably always been a little too headstrong anyway. But you can't tell me how to live or who to be friends with. Otherwise we'd better call off this wedding and just have a big party for our friends instead."

"Yeah, well, maybe we should."

"You're overreacting! I can't believe this. We have a life planned together. We're going off to find a better place, remember? Make a home for ourselves in the tropics somewhere. You sold our cars and bought the van so we could. What about the unconditional love that Ken taught us? Don't you believe that we're supposed to be together? What happened to the theory anybody can live with anybody if they work at it hard enough? Don't we love each other? Have a little faith." She stroked his arm lovingly. "Max?"

He sat there in stony silence for several minutes before he answered. At long last he said, "Yeah, I guess so."

Alexis didn't notice it at the time, but Max never actually admitted to being sorry. In fact, during the six months they'd been together, she realized then that she'd had never known him to apologize for anything.

Two days later Alexis lay awake in the quaint hotel room whose picture window overlooked the forested banks of the Russian River. It was late morning. She could hear Max moving around in the bathroom. Quietly she lay on the bed, letting her mind drift back to the wedding.

It had been a splendid day in a fairy-tale setting of flowers and good friends under the cool shade of the ponderosa pines. Ken Keyes had brought the huge lumbering bus from Berkeley to officiate the ceremony. Martin and Annie had come from Santa Cruz; Mark Donovan had made the trip from Berkeley. Hank and Danny had arrived from Oakland, and David and the Yuba River people had also joined in the festivities.

Frank and Liz, Alexis' parents had also attended; Liz enjoying the unique and unusual setting of a California hippie wedding, and Frank barely tolerating the bizarre array of long-haired attendees. And although he wouldn't hurt Alexis by saying so, he fervently wished the groom had been someone else – anyone else.

Alexis had worn a simple white dress, and Max, an embroidered cotton tunic and pants of pale green. Danny and Hank had designed beautiful wreathes of flowers for their hair, and the couple had stood before the assembly of friends making unrehearsed declarations of love, rather than traditional vows. After the wedding, there was a celebration of music, presents, dancing, champagne, and a feast of organic dishes. The party lasted until after dusk. Eventually the crowd thinned and a large campfire was lit. For several hours, the last few happy people sat around playing guitars, staring into the flames, talking of destinies and the road ahead.

Now Alexis and Max were married. This was their honeymoon and everything should have been perfect. Yet somehow she felt a terrible void. Their recent lovemaking left her feeling detached, and a feeling of emptiness had invaded her being. Not like something was wrong, more like something was missing. A still small voice seemed to question her – is this all there is?

Max and Alexis checked the tiny local library in Nevada City and, finding nothing, made the thirty mile trip to Auburn just to get more information. As they sat together at the table in the Public Library scouring book after book, they tried to come up with any random information that would be helpful to their quest. Belize. Now it was all Max talked about. Obsessed with the hunt for information, they were finding that the country was virtually unknown. The only maps of Belize were in the encyclopedias, so Alexis was obliged to copy them dutifully and highlight the districts and towns. As Max's interest waxed, his patience for living in the United States waned, and he became increasingly moody and negative as he harped about the failings of the country.

"You just don't understand, *Ntombi*. Here in the States I feel like Big Brother is watching," Max complained. "I considered straightening out my ID problems, but there's too much red tape and bullshit. This country is good for only one thing – making money and getting the hell out." He went on to explain how much money they'd need, and what could be done to get it. Meanwhile the vegetable garden was producing, but selling organic broccoli and lettuce would never make them rich.

But on the way back from Auburn, the van made the decision for them when its engine suddenly blew up. As quickly as their plans had been made, they collapsed.

"You mean, because of this expense, Central America is out of the question right now?" asked Alexis.

"Yep, for the time being. We're going to have to rebuild the engine, and it's going to cost us plenty. We can't just pick up and go to a foreign country on a shoestring. With vehicle expenses, we simply don't have enough money."

"So what are we going to do instead?" she continued tenuously.

"I guess we're going to have to devise a moneymaking scheme and work for a couple of years first," he replied. "I hate the thought of staying in the United States, but maybe we can find a nice farm somewhere temporarily. Realistically, we should have at least five or ten thousand dollars to make our new start."

Although excited by the thought of a unique culture, overall, Alexis was relieved. She didn't want to admit it, but she wanted to stay in the States, and somehow the thought of going alone with Max to another country was no longer her idea of paradise. He was too intense; sometimes he scared her.

*   *   *   *

After rethinking their plans several times, Alexis finally talked Max into going back east to live somewhere near her parents' home in Pennsylvania as a temporary move. Over the phone, Liz and Frank immediately offered them a place to stay until they could locate one of their own. After tying up loose ends in California and saying their goodbyes, they packed their belongings, made the long trek across the U.S. – over the Rockies, across the Great Plains, through the cornfields of Iowa, Illinois, and Ohio until they arrived, at last, in Alexis' hometown in northwestern Pennsylvania.

Max was less than thrilled with the prospect of living with his in-laws, and the resentment was mutual. Alexis' father, Frank, had an aversion to his son-in-law from the moment they'd met at the wedding, and his dislike was further piqued when Max approached him for a loan to finance carrying their daughter off to another country. The long hair was one thing, Frank said, but there was something else he just didn't trust. Although Liz shared this opinion, she took a more philosophical approach. Since there was nothing they could do about it, the best bet was to give the marriage as much emotional support as possible, and be there for Alexis if she needed them.

The first incident occurred just a few days after Max and Alexis moved in. Frank was at work, and Liz had gone grocery shopping. Staying in the guest room downstairs, they were alone in the house when the argument erupted. "My parents are not cheap," Alexis insisted, "I'm sure they had their reasons for not wanting to lend us money."

"Well, of course you're going to defend them; they're your parents," Max said. "But I still think they're cheap. What's wrong with them anyway? Talk about 'conditional love.' My folks would have helped us in a heartbeat if they weren't twelve thousand miles away; they would have lent us money on a handshake. Your father wanted collateral, and terms, and a deadline – like I wasn't family or something."

"Give them a chance, Max," she said, as she folded the laundry on the bed. "We made the decision to come east, and all of a sudden we're living in their house.

They hardly know you. Hell, the way you've been acting lately, I feel like I hardly know you."

"What's that wisecrack supposed to mean?"

"I don't know," she said, her eyes downcast, taking a chance and telling the truth. "You're different, ever since the wedding, maybe even before. I don't know. All the rapport we had – it doesn't feel like it used to. It's almost as though now that you've got me, you don't have to be nice to me any more."

"Just what the hell are you saying?" demanded Max.

"Maybe I don't even know who you really are." She stood up to face him. "I don't know much about you, except what you've told me. I married you without even meeting your parents. Maybe it's Africa that I've been in love with all along. Tell me the truth, Max. Did you just marry me so you could stay in the United States?"

"You little bitch," he hissed vehemently. His hand shot out and he smacked her across the cheek. The unexpected blow caught her off balance and she fell. "You better have more respect than to ever talk to me that way again. If you're going to act like a black *kaffir*, then you can expect to be treated like one."

Alexis sobbed as she heard her mother come in the front door. Max left for the kitchen abruptly and she could hear him talking to Liz as she put the groceries away. "I just don't know what got into Alexis," Max said. "She became hysterical for no reason at all. I had to slap her to bring her out of it. She's probably just pre-menstrual."

A few minutes later, Liz saw the black and blue imprint on her daughter's face when she came up the stairs. A terrible feeling of foreboding came over her.

Within two weeks, Max and Alexis were offered a job on a ranch in an adjacent county, about twenty miles away. The three-hundred-acre ranch was owned by Owen Marshall, a wealthy shipbuilder, and he was looking for someone to manage his beef operation and oversee his breeding program. The big house on the southern end of the property was for the shipbuilder's family on their infrequent visits. The two-bedroom overseer's quarters suited Max and Alexis perfectly, and with Max's background in farming and ranch management, Owen considered himself lucky to have found them. The three Quarter horses available to Alexis turned out to be an extra bonus.

"Sure, you can ride her whenever you want," Owen explained. "Dana, my foreman, and the other boys usually just whistle up the cattle, but it helps to have one of the horses saddled and ready to round up any stragglers. There are two other riding horses, but the others are still wild. Have you ridden a lot?"

"Since I was twelve," said Alexis. "I took lessons from an instructor, English style. Then I rode western on the neighbors' horses every summer until I went to college. So for me, this will be a real treat."

Through the months that followed Max and Alexis learned the routines of the ranch, as well as the care and feeding of the animals. Workmen were involved in the construction of a new barn, as well as assorted repairs on the bulldozer, tractor, and other vehicles. The breeding bulls had to be kept separate from the cows and calves, and young steers were on a special feed-lot so they could be fattened for sale just before winter. When the calves were old enough to be separated from their mothers, they would be appraised as breeding stock, or sold with the steers on the meat market.

It was almost sunset and the bare branches of the trees made intricate patterns against the cloudless October sky. Alexis stood next to the corral and watched the horses. Their coats shone from the vigorous brushing. "So how about it?" Dana said, as he walked up behind her. "Are you gonna ride one of these here critters, or just treat them like pampered children?"

"I'd love to ride Storm."

"Yeah, she's a great little horse. Real peppy. My favorite filly. You wanna to get on her and help us round 'em up?"

"Right now?" Alexis asked in delight. "I'd love to. Which tack should I use?"

"Well, you'll have to 'rein' her since she's always been a cattle horse. But it don't matter much which saddle you're using." He smiled. "Unless you reckon on ropin' some cows, in which case you'd be shit outta luck without a horn." He laughed and smacked the top rail with his gloved hand. "I'll tell you what. You bring her on over to this here hitching post outside the corral. I'll fetch the tack from the barn."

With delight, Alexis haltered the young horse and brought her out through the gate. She stood stroking her velvety muzzle while Dana brought the tack, and within a few minutes, the filly was saddled and ready to go. He gave her a boost and Alexis walked the horse into the pasture.

First, she trotted the filly and found that riding had lost none of its magic. The field smelled like fresh rain, tangy manure, and autumn leaves. On the far side of a low ridge, the horse saw two straggling cows and their calves. Alexis had never rounded up cattle before, but Storm took the initiative and she decided to let the filly do what she did best. The horse cut behind the stragglers and got them headed toward the barn. As one cow turned back a second time, the horse angled sharply again and brought her back into position. With virtually no effort on Alexis' part, the cows and calves were soon in the barn with the rest of the herd.

Too soon to stop, Alexis turned the horse around and sped back to ride some more. The evening light began to dim as she rode Storm to the farthest end of the pasture and nudged her into a canter, gradually going faster into a full-on gallop. Thrilling to the sound of pounding hooves, she laughed aloud, but the wind carried the sound away. Her thighs hugged the saddle, and rider and horse ran as one.

"Where the hell have you been?" asked Max angrily, drumming his fingers on the table as she came in the door of the overseer's house. "I've been waiting here for almost ten minutes. Dinner isn't even cooked, let alone sitting on the table."

Alexis took off her denim jacket and hung it over the back of the chair. She washed her hands at the sink, and grabbed her apron. "I'm sorry, Max. Dana asked me if I wanted to round up the cattle so I took a spin on Storm to help out."

"Yeah, well the cattle have been in the barn for over a half an hour. What were you doing after that?"

"I...I rode around in the pasture afterward. It was so great to ride again. Then I had to put away the gear and give the horse a quick once-over with the brush. Really, I'm sorry about the dinner. Let me get it for you right away."

"Well, you sure have some screwed-up priorities. You take better care of those horses than you do of me. I work my guts out on this ranch all day long and then I don't even have a decent meal. Not that you know how to cook anyway."

"I thought you liked my cooking."

"Oh yeah. You're great with salad and mashed potatoes and boiled squash," he said sarcastically. "What are we having tonight?"

"I made brown rice with vegetables and some corn bread. You like that, don't you?"

"Okay," he said, winding down a little. "But next time, be sure and have my meals ready on time."

"I will," she said softly, shaking her head as she turned on the stove.

Some days it was still good between the two of them, times when laughter could be heard inside the little farmhouse in the evening hours after the day's work was done. They would touch in the old way, lie in front of the fireplace, and make love on the floor. During those times he was the old Max: the seeker, the spiritual traveler, the man she'd fallen in love with, the man she'd married. They would talk about the future and raising a family and suddenly all of Alexis' fears disappeared. She snuggled in his arms, breathing a sigh of contentment, wondering why she'd been concerned in the first place. Other days he hardly spoke to her at all, totally preoccupied with the objectives of the day. When he did speak he was critical and demanding, seemingly unsatisfied with whatever she did do, and whatever she didn't do.

A dismal November arrived with cold rain and driving winds. As the days shortened and temperatures dropped, so did Alexis' spirit. Nothing was green anymore. The once-bright autumn leaves now lay in soggy heaps and a cowardly sun stayed hidden behind a dull gray veil. After the years of sunshine in Key West and California, it seemed that life was devoid of color, both inside and out. Even as a child Alexis had hated winter. Now her depression grew daily as she felt the world closing in.

Each day started in the cold darkness before dawn. The alarm clock rang rudely, and Alexis shivered as she padded barefoot across the floor to put on warm clothes. The fluorescent light in the kitchen was brutally white, like that of a prison. The clock on the kitchen wall ticked defiantly as she put on the kettle. When the tea was on the table, Max came in and sat down. He drank it in silence, his mind focused only on the day ahead. Then the chores began.

First Max fed and checked the cattle, turning out the ones that would pasture for the day. He talked to the ranch hands and laid out the daily work schedule. Then he inspected the progress on the new barn. It was anybody's guess as to whether the new one would be completed before the old one fell down. Max fretted over the rotted flooring and termite-eaten beams groaning under the weight of the tons of alfalfa hay. He topped-up the oil on the tractor, checked the tires, and welded a weak spot on the dozer. Wood repairs were needed on the horse corral and the watering trough had a bad leak, making it necessary to refill the tank every day. The three-year old horses had to be shod and he made a mental note to call the ferrier. Also, a veterinary check would be necessary for the several cats that were supposed to be controlling the rats in the barns. Max cursed softly as he noted the chewed ropes and gnawed leather in the tack room.

Meanwhile, Alexis was busy with her share. Max insisted that everything be done a certain way. After washing the dishes and cleaning the house, she glanced over at the cranky old washing machine and opted to ignore the pile of dirty clothes temporarily. Instead, she decided to go into town and stock up on groceries. Max was so fussy about what foods he ate and how they were prepared.

On the way to town she remembered the lecture that Max had given her the day before about the proper way to make tea.

"What have you done to this tea, Alexis?" he had said.

"What do you mean? Is there something wrong with it?"

"Yeah. It doesn't have the right flavor, like you left out one of the steps."

"I made it like I always do. I boiled the water, used loose tea instead of bags, steeped it in the teapot, and put one-and-a half spoons of sugar and a little cream."

"Hmmm. Tastes like you boiled the water too long. Either that or you didn't let it steep long enough."

"Shit, Max."

"What do you mean – shit? Is it too damn much to have you make me a decent cup of tea? Didn't your mother teach you how to do that either?"

"Look if you want it different, just tell me. Leave my mother out of it."

"Okay, little Miss Shit-for-brains. Since this is one more thing you never learned, let's start at the beginning. First, you let the cold water run for at least fifteen seconds. And don't forget to rinse out the kettle first. Then you fill it with fresh cold water. Put in just enough for the number of cups you're making, plus one extra cup; if you put in too much water, then I have to wait unnecessarily. You must stand there and watch it come to a boil. As soon as the steam shoots from the spout, lift it off the burner at that precise moment. Not before, and certainly not after. Over boiling affects the flavor and makes it bitter. Then you warm the pot."

"What do you mean warm the pot? Warm it how? Heat it up in the oven?"

"Damn, you are a lost cause, aren't you? No wonder it never tastes right. 'Warming the pot' means that you pour a little of the boiling water into the teapot, swirl it around, and dump it out. Then you put one rounded teaspoon of loose tea for each cup you're making and one for the pot, and pour the boiling water on top of the leaves. Give it a quick stir, put the lid on the pot and let it steep for exactly five minutes. You should really put a cozy on it too, but we don't have one."

"A what?"

"A cozy. It's a little cloth cover that fits over the teapot to keep the heat in. I'll show you what it looks like. It won't take you long to make one on the sewing machine. Now, where was I? Oh yeah. After five minutes, you open the teapot and give it one more quick stir. The tea will be floating and if it's been steeped properly it will sink to the bottom after you stir it. Pour it into the cup through the tea strainer, and make sure to put in the sugar first, and then the cream. That way the sugar melts completely and mixes with the tea before the cream cools it off too much. Actually, the English way would be to put in the cream and sugar first and then pour the tea onto it, but I like it better this way."

Alexis winced as she remembered how she'd had stood there, dumbfounded. Surely the man couldn't be serious. Yet he was staring at her like he'd just awarded her with critical scientific information. It was tea, not rocket science. She didn't know how to respond.

"Okay, Max," she said. "I'll do my best in the future."

"Don't do your best, *Ntombi*. Just do it right."

Two hours later, Alexis returned from grocery shopping. Max came in from the barn and flew into a temper over the unwashed clothes.

"But it was a matter of priorities. I did the shopping, baked some bread, and cleaned the house. Besides, you still had two sets of work clothes before you really needed those overalls. So I didn't do the laundry yet. I just didn't have time."

"Priorities again. Just what we discussed the other day. You know I like to wear those brown insulated overalls when it's this cold outside. They're the only ones that are big enough to fit over my long underwear and my shirt and jeans. Just because that washing machine isn't brand new, you go out of your way to do everything else first – just to avoid a little water slopping on the floor."

Alexis rolled her eyes, exasperated. "It's not just a little water," she protested, as she put away the groceries. "The washing machine is faulty; you know the automatic water shut-off is broken. It keeps filling up until it overflows. Do you really think it's a good use of my time to literally stand there and watch it the whole way through both cycles? It means that I can't really do anything else; it's wasting my time."

"Stop arguing with me. My mother raised five kids and still ran a smooth household. The house was always clean, the meals on time, and the clothes washed. You can't even seem to do that with no kids."

This time Alexis couldn't stifle her reply. "Well, it sounds like you already had the perfect woman then, didn't you? Why did you ever leave Africa if you had your mother?"

He roared and backhanded her. "You fucking bitch. Get the hell out of my house."

This time Alexis ran out the door and up the hill to the barn. Max got in the truck and spun out the driveway. Good, she thought. I hope he stays away. Then the tears came as the enormity hit her all at once. Alexis felt trapped. It was the second time he'd struck her this month. What am I going to do? This whole marriage thing isn't what it's supposed to be. I don't know how I can go on like this. It seems that the longer I stay, the more I have to lose. I've already invested a year. Do I want to make it work? Confused and hurt, she went over to Storm's stall. The horse whickered softly as she heard Alexis' voice.

"Hey there, baby. How're you doing? How 'bout a little snack?" She wiped away her tears and got some grain from the barrel. But as she tried to go into the horse's stall to put the grain in her feeding trough, the filly was so anxious she wouldn't let Alexis pass. Still frustrated by Max's behavior, she slapped the horse sharply on the flank.

"C'mon Storm, let me through," she snapped, angrily. "Get over, you cow."

Quickly, the horse whipped around and fired a double kick at Alexis. One shod hoof landed squarely on the thick quad muscle of her right leg. Her world exploded as she reeled from the blow and scrambled out of the stall door, collapsing on the cement floor. The walls spun, but even in her disoriented state, Alexis sensed that Storm had already forgotten the incident and was munching the spilled grain. Alexis tried to scream but no sound came out. Surely her leg was broken. She could feel it swelling inside her pants. Fighting to remain conscious, she knew she needed help. But who? Max was gone and the workmen – that's it, she thought. She forced her voice to shout, "Help! Somebody please help me! I've been kicked!"

The men came running when they heard her cry but by the time they reach her, she was unconscious. The next thing Alexis remembered was being on the couch in the living room. Dana stood over her with a pair of scissors. A look of deep concern was in his eyes. The other men were gone.

"What are you going to do to me?" Alexis said. In her pain and confusion, the scissors didn't make sense. She felt threatened and helpless, her mind muddled between fear and trust.

"Honey, I'm gonna have to cut those jeans off of you. That leg's fixin' to bust the seams. I got to look at your leg." Delayed shock had set in and powerful chills racked her body. Dana wrapped some heavy blankets around her, then began cutting.

"Be careful," she whimpered softly.

By the time he reached her knee there wasn't enough room for the blade to slip between her skin and the fabric of her pants. The sweat beaded up on his forehead like a surgeon in an operating room as he tore the jeans the rest of the way. The leg was a mass of bloated purple flesh; it looked more like a war wound than a horse kick. The muscle was crushed and pulpy, the skin lacerated from the sharp edges of the iron shoe.

The doctor came out of the emergency room and walked toward Max. "Well, believe it or not, it's not as bad as it looks," he said. "Your wife was lucky. That's the strongest part of her leg and she was fortunate that's where the hoof landed. If it had been anywhere else on the front of her body: stomach, chest, knee, or head, the result could have been grave, or even deadly. As it is, the muscle has been badly traumatized, but the femur fracture is only a greenstick. I've immobilized the leg. Your wife will wear a cast, but not for too long. She'll be on crutches for a month and walk with a cane for several more after that. But she's young and strong. She ought to mend well, given the time."

Max and Alexis rode in silence on the way home. She stole a sideways glance, but saw he was looking straight ahead showing no expression at all. The pain was dulled only slightly from medication, and every little bounce and sway still caused her to cringe. The doctor told her to expect a fever caused by the intramuscular toxins released into the bloodstream. Already Alexis could feel her temperature rising, and it was accompanied by a sense of unreality.

"Well, I guess you'll have to take it easy for a while," said Max, in measured tones. "It's going to be tougher on me if you can't do anything around the house."

"I probably won't have much choice," Alexis replied cautiously. "Look, I'm sorry it happened. It was an accident."

"Owen wants to shoot the horse."

"No!" she practically shouted. "No, absolutely not! He can't do that."

"He can do anything he wants. It's his horse."

"I'll convince him not to. Storm's just high-spirited," Alexis said emphatically. "Besides, it wasn't really her fault."

"Are you saying it was yours?" Now his tone had a perceptible edge.

"No, not exactly. I...was...I was still mad at you. I slapped her to move over, that's all."

"Oh, so you brought this on yourself, and me, because you lost your temper?"

"You're turning it all around. You're the one who hit me, remember?"

"Oh, so it's all my fault then?"

"Yes...no...I don't know. Look, can we please just not do this. I feel horrible as it is. I'm sorry for my part. Could you please just be nice to me? Please? I'm feeling so bad."

"Apology accepted," he said, triumphantly. Max thought quietly for a minute and then added, "Maybe you could make that tea cozy I mentioned to you the other day. After all, we've got to find some way for you to be useful."

Alexis discovered the meaning of being handicapped over the next few weeks. In the beginning she could do practically nothing. The pain was intense as she lay in the grip of a high fever. She felt thirsty and didn't have the strength to get up for a glass of water. When she used her crutches to reach the sink, the water had to be drunk standing right there because she couldn't carry the glass back to the couch and use the crutches at the same time. Alexis didn't get much help from Max, but, under the circumstances, it was difficult to blame him. He was having a hard enough time just handling the outside work on the farm and making his own meals. She knew he considered her a burden, a liability, useless.

Finally, Alexis called her mother, and Liz came and spent a few days helping out. Max put on a great performance for his mother-in-law, letting none of his anger and resentment show. Being an intuitive person, Liz still felt the undercurrent of animosity, but it was simply not her place to interfere.

* * * *

The rolling mountains of North Carolina were covered in pine forests as the old VW van struggled up one incline after another through the steep passes. The top-heavy vehicle swayed badly on abrupt curves, chugging and sputtering. Something was wrong with the timing, no doubt. Damn stupid air-cooled engines, Alexis thought. Damn! Listen to me. I sound like Max, she thought, criticizing herself even more. She shifted her leg to the right of the accelerator and used the cane to hold down the pedal. Her leg ached from the hours of continuous driving, but it didn't matter. At last she'd escaped from what had become an intolerable situation. She had left Max and was going back to Key West.

Poor Mom and Dad, she thought. They deserved more than that spaced-out note I left them. But what could I say? How much worse would they feel if they knew what had been going on from the start? What if they advised me to go back to Max?

Angry, yet saddened, she was hopelessly torn. In good faith, she had married Max and had hoped to stay with him, raise children, and grow old together. Yet they had also said that if it didn't work out, they could always get divorced and part friends. But somehow it wasn't like that. Marriage did something to people that was hard to untangle. They came together as two human beings, and ended up as one-and-a-half. In merging their lives, something changed, and honorable intentions became lost in obsession and avarice. Now Alexis felt grief but no remorse. The decision was made. The only way was straight ahead and south. Back to mother ocean and the call of the sea, back to the days before Max and cold northern winters.

By the time she reached South Carolina, she finally got up enough nerve to call her parents from a gas station.

"Hello, Dad?"

"Honey! It's you! Thank God you called. Are you all right? We've been so worried about you. Wait a minute so I can get your mother on the other line..."

Before Alexis could say anything more, she heard Frank calling out, and her mother replying with relief. "Hi, honey," Liz said, when she got on the phone. "Are you all right?"

"I'm okay. I'm sorry I scared you. I didn't know what to do, or what to say."

"We figured you'd call eventually," Liz continued. "I'm just glad you didn't wait any longer. Where are you? We won't tell Max unless you want us to."

"No. Don't tell him, at least not yet. I'm in South Carolina."

"How are you managing to drive with your bad leg?" Liz interjected. "You only just got the cast off a few weeks ago."

"It hasn't been easy. It still hurts a lot, but I'm managing."

"So what are you going to do? Are you leaving Max, or was this just something that will pass?" Frank asked.

"No," said Alexis, controlling the slight quiver in her voice. "I wouldn't have left over something trivial. Maybe I just made a mistake when I married him – a big mistake. You were right all along, Dad. Max is different from when I first met him. Or maybe it's just his cultural background."

"Do you still love him?" asked Liz, taking over the conversation.

"I don't know, I'm all confused. I don't want to call it quits; I just want him to be the way he used to be. How did he react when I left?"

"He's been a mess, like a lost child," Liz said emphatically. "At first he spent a lot of time over here at our house; he was drinking heavily. It wasn't easy for us. Things are falling apart on the ranch. Owen has been very upset."

"Mom, please. I feel like a fool as it is, but Max was being totally impossible. I just couldn't take it any more."

"He's remorseful now."

"You mean he's actually sorry?"

"Well, he says he is. He says he's been stupid and only wants you back so he can prove how much he loves you. He says he'll treat you like a queen if you'll only give him a second chance. We talked to him last night on the phone. He called us from somewhere. Sounded like a party going on in the background."

"How depressed can he be if he's out partying?"

"I don't know, dear," said Liz, tenderly. "We're not passing judgment one way or the other at this point. All I can say is he sounded very sincere and very unhappy."

"Do you think I ought to take him back? Is it worth what I've already put into the relationship? I mean, if it's not meant to be, it would be better to end it now, rather than later."

"Only you can be the true judge of that, honey. You'll have to do what's right in your own heart. If you still love him, then maybe it's worth another try. If not, then you still need to say what needs to be said, face to face."

"I'm going to Key West," she said petulantly. "I've got to get away from the cold; the winter is so gloomy and depressing. Once I get to the sunshine again maybe I'll be able to think. Nothing is clear right now. I need space and time."

"What about the farm meanwhile?" said Frank. "The job with Owen?"

"I'm sorry. There's no way I can go back to that house. Not with Max."

No one said anything for a minute.

"Honey?" her father said finally. "Promise us that you'll stay in touch. Just don't cut us out of your life. We're here to help you, even though we're far away. Promise us you won't do anything rash."

"Don't worry. I'll stay in touch. I love you both. I'm sorry I left the way I did."

"It's all right, dear," Liz added. "You just get yourself sorted out. We love you too. Call us again soon."

When Alexis arrived in Key West, the sun indeed helped to warm her, both heart and soul. She rented a tiny cottage on Grinnell Street, and soon found herself walking familiar beaches, visiting old haunts, and seeking the nostalgic scent of night-blooming jasmine. Having returned to the island, just as Indian Ron had said she would, Alexis passed by the marina, and the sound of slapping halyards brought back a heartache named Paul. She wondered what had ever happened to the sailboat. Like its name, *Déjà Vu* was a wound that had never completely healed.

Everywhere she went she asked about Indian Ron, but no one seemed to know where he was. Someone said he'd bought a house on Petronia Lane, just southwest of the old cemetery, but hadn't been seen on the island for months. More than anyone, she wanted to see Ron. She needed his insight and hoped to find comfort in his presence and his wisdom.

Her other wound was perhaps one of those that time should not heal. But nevertheless, over the weeks, the bad memories associated with Max began to fade. Alexis began to see more clearly, or so she thought. Was it truly clarity, or was it loneliness? She didn't know, but Max was still her husband after all. Maybe the relationship deserved another chance. Eventually, the pain subsided, and the remembrance of the good times overpowered the bitterness.

"*Ntombi eyami!*" Max cried when he picked up the phone. "Oh Alexis, I've missed you so much! I've been such an idiot. Can you ever forgive me?"

"Hi," she said quietly. "I will ask you only one question. Do you still want to be with me?"

"You asked me that once before in California. I'll say now what I said then," he replied. "With all my heart."

"Then come to Florida. I'm willing to try again."

They set up housekeeping together in the little Grinnell Street cottage which was really one of four identical dwellings situated within a picturesque courtyard among the rubber banyan trees in the heart of Old Town. And it was like old times, indeed. Max was not only conciliatory, he was wonderful. He treated her like a queen, and Alexis was sure she had made the right decision. One day, late in the afternoon, as they sat together on the front porch swing, Alexis decided to tell Max about some ideas she'd had. "Wouldn't it be great if we could get a band together down here so we could play music? Like at Bonny Doon? I mean – one way or the other we've got to make some money soon. Why not something we really enjoy?"

"You're right about that," Max said agreeably. "Those guys, two doors down, are musicians. I think one plays bass and the other plays lead. Getting a group together is a great idea."

"I was also thinking how I used to make different kinds of handicrafts when I lived here before. We could buy some twine or jute. I could make some plant hangers, or macramé chokers, or maybe even weave a hammock. We could look into a vendor's permit like I had in Berkeley, or even rent a little shop."

"I like it." He nodded approvingly. "Ok, let's keep an eye out for some possibilities."

Sunset at Mallory Pier was still a ritual, as it had been and would continue to be for decades to come. The young couple attended the celebration of sun and sea almost every night. Alexis still used her cane occasionally and walked with a slight limp, but the warm weather was helping her heal at a faster pace. Max had bought bicycles for both of them, the perfect transportation for the island, and as they rode home that night after sunset, the sky became a lustrous backdrop of purple, slashed with brilliant fuchsia. A soft balmy breeze began to blow, and the velvety palpable darkness started its descent over the island. Pulling up to the little gate at the white picket fence, Max was quick to jump off first and open it for her. As she dismounted and wheeled her bike past him, she paused. He was looking down at the ground pensively, but then purposefully raised his eyes to meet hers, her face filling his vision. His sincerity was unquestionable. With a marked tenderness, he said, "I love you, Alexis."

Keeping an eye out for an available shop space became a priority. If they were going to make the investment, Alexis was determined to find an extraordinarily worthwhile location, right in the heart of things. As a result, she made sure to check the ultra-touristy section of Old Town on a regular basis – Front Street near the Conch Train Depot and the two northernmost blocks of Duval Street between Green and Caroline. There was also a fruit vendor tucked away on Tift's Aly. He made the best coconut-banana smoothies ever, so she usually stopped there when making her rounds. She saw the vaguely familiar form, the black crinkly hair and nut-brown skin.

"Ron!" she called out, as she ran to him. "Ron, is that really you? Where have you been?"

"Alexis," he said in that dear familiar voice, as he opened his arms wide to her. She embraced him tightly, refusing to let go. "It's so good to see your beautiful face again. I have traveled much of the time we've been apart; I returned to Sri Lanka. Many of my relatives are very old now and I knew I'd never see them again. And you, my dear? Where have your adventures taken you in these last years?"

"I spent time in California, and I got married to a British South African. His name is Max. We've been back in Key West now for about two months or so. We're looking to open a little gift shop somewhere in Old Town."

"He doesn't happen to play conga drums, does he?" Ron asked. She told him yes, and asked how he knew. "I met a conga player from South Africa two nights ago at Mallory," he continued. "He told me he was looking to rent a shop with his wife, but of course I didn't have any idea he was your old man."

"Yeah, that's him," Alexis said brightly. "I didn't go the other night. I injured my leg a while back and sometimes it still gives me grief."

"I'm sorry to hear that. Unusual person, your husband."

Her smile faded. "In what way?"

"Nothing certain. His eyes perhaps, or his aura, as if he were troubled by the past." Ron seemed a bit subdued. "Are you happy with him?" Alexis took his hand, and together they stepped in to the shade.

"Some severe ups and downs. We spent some time apart recently, and only just got back together. It figures you'd sense it."

"Sometimes you're quite sure, and other times you're still in great doubt?"

"Yes. I see you've lost none of your ability to read me. What do you foresee?"

"I pick up vibrations from people," Ron said, kindly. "Sometimes I see things, but I have never been a fortune-teller. I can only give my blessings for whatever your future may hold." Alexis was silent. She didn't know what to say.

Changing the subject, Ron said, "Believe it or not, I saw a mutual friend of ours last week in Miami on my way down. It was Marcy."

"Really?" said Alexis, her interest piqued. "Oh, I've thought of her so often. How is she? I lost track of her a long time ago. Is she all right?"

"More or less, I suppose, but she's quite different from the person you knew. She lives in the fast lane now, fancy clothes, and when I saw her she was wearing red snakeskin boots with four-inch heels. Her boyfriend is a jockey at Hialeah Race Track, and is a whole head shorter than she is. That puts him right about at the level of her breasts" he laughed, "which I imagine is just about where he likes to be."

"Can't say that surprises me. Is she all right? I was worried about her when we lived in the pink house. Looked like she was headed for trouble – sex and drugs."

"Pretty accurate. She's heavily into drugs and hangs out with a rough crowd at the track. I must admit I fear for her. But as you know, each person must choose his own *dharma*. We can influence at best, but no one else can decide the fate of another. Beginnings are scary, middles are exciting, and endings are sad. It's the way of the world. Throughout our lifetimes, we gain family, friends, and possessions, and then we lose them one by one."

"It's so true, but sometimes it's hard to let go."

"Attachment is the cause of all sorrow. The older I get, the easier it is to let go of some things and the harder it is to let go of others. For example, my dear, it will be hard to let go of you, right now. I'm leaving Key West again in just a few minutes. It was only mere coincidence that I ran into you at all. I'm going to New York for an extended visit.

"Oh no," Tears welled in her eyes. "I just found you again. Don't tell me that."

"I haven't been well these last few years," he confided. "I'm going to have some tests done in the hospital. While I'm there, I'll visit my children. Of course, they're all grown now, with families of their own. Although they don't much approve of me, it still pleases me to see how the little ones have grown."

"I can't believe it," Alexis said. "You mean, this is it? After so long apart, we see each other for a few minutes? That's all?"

Ron lifted her face and kissed her softly on the lips, this time a lover's kiss. With closed eyes, she accepted the caress as though it were a benediction. "I am only grateful that we were able to meet at all. Serendipity. Perhaps our paths will cross again soon. We will look forward to that day, but then again, for people like us, it matters little. Time and space are relative to you and me; they always have been. We share a common spirit. Our souls understand and love each other. We are never far apart. Give me a hug." The small spry Indian man held her tightly for a long moment, then released her slowly. "Bless you. Go with God."

Smiling through a veil of tears, she wondered if she would ever see him again.

On the west side of Simonton, just north of Dey Street, a new local tavern had been constructed. Unique to the area, the main bar was under one thatched roof, an entertainment hut with a raised stage under another one. A series of additional thatched-roof huts arranged in a circle were all connected by slatted wooden walkways that skirted huge living trees that had been left in place, rather than cut down. Brightly multicolored paper lanterns contrasted with the night sky and a band from Miami played calypso music. Patrons danced on the circular central dance floor under the stars and enjoyed drinks made with exotic fruits like papaya, *anona*, *guanabana*, and sapodilla. The bar was crowded that night, with nearly every table at capacity. Max and Alexis sat at the table closest to the band and, as the last song finished, a young couple looking for a place to sit asked if they could join them at their table. They made the usual introductions. Richard and Rita lived in Miami but were originally from Santa Cruz.

"No kidding!" Alexis said enthusiastically. "That's where Max and I met."

"Another one of those 'small world' things, I guess." Rita smiled. "What do you both do?"

"Since we got here about two months ago, we've just been having a good time, but we're working on opening a little gift shop," Max answered. "Got to make a living, you know."

"Isn't it a drag when money keeps getting in the way of your life?" quipped Richard. "I'm an artist; Rita's a yoga instructor. We own a gallery in Coconut Grove."

Rita signaled the waiter and ordered a round of drinks for everybody. A few minutes later when the server arrived, Max raised his glass and toasted his hosts.

"That was some good music in the last set," Alexis said wistfully. "I wish I could have been up there."

"Why? Do you play?" asked Rita.

"We both do," Max interjected. "I'm a conga drummer. Alexis sings and plays flute."

"If you're musicians, you guys are in for a treat," said Richard. "That's why we came tonight. Wait til you hear this next group. They're originally from Kansas City but I met them in a recording studio in Monterrey. The lead singer's outrageous. Wait a minute. They're coming on now. Watch this."

The stage lights went up. The bass player, drummer, keyboardist, and rhythm guitarist struck the first clean chord, then launched into a heavy, yet funky, solid rock-and-roll beat. As they got into the theme, a striking blond with a Les Paul guitar leapt out on stage and attacked her instrument. She was an absolutely stunning woman with long shapely legs, tapered hips, and perfectly rounded breasts. Masses of strawberry-honey hair fell over her bare shoulders as she swung the neck of the guitar seductively to accent the beat of the song. But when she belted out the lyrics, full-throated, alternately wailing and crooning sweetly, Max's jaw dropped. He did more than look at her, or listen to her, during the course of that song; he devoured her. In those few seconds, for the first time since they'd been together, Alexis clearly saw an obvious raging desire for another woman.

"She sounds like Bonnie Raitt, don't you think?" said Richard. "Her name's Katrina. Is she hot or what?"

"Wow. She plays her own lead," murmured Max. "You weren't kidding. She's great."

"Would you like to meet her after the set?"

"Ahh…yeah," Max could hardly talk. "Definitely."

Although he would try to deny it later, there was intense chemistry between Max and Katrina from the start, and it wasn't just one-sided. This became particularly apparent during the first break when Alexis returned from the ladies room to find them dancing cheek-to-cheek. Later, finally, she dragged Max home. He was more than a little drunk. Luckily, Katrina's tour bus was scheduled to leave town the next day.

* * * *

The shop was perfect. Located right on Duval Street next to Howie's Bar, half a block from Front Street, they'd found it two days earlier, and Max was so pleased that he'd put down a deposit immediately. They decided to call it *Rondavel*, after the Afrikaaner word meaning "round house," and together they had made plans to create an inventory of Alexis' new macramé line, as well as other consignments of pottery, belt buckles, paintings, and jewelry.

"I really think it's a good idea for you to go to Miami and check out this wholesale house," Max said, as they walked around the shop. "It sounds like they have an incredible selection of beads and cordage. Obviously we can't just buy supplies retail and then expect to resell the finished products for a decent price. We've got to get the stuff cheap enough so we can wholesale the chokers and plant hangers too. That means purchasing in quantity. And with Richard and Rita offering you a ride and place to stay for the weekend, it's not like it will cost us a lot of money."

"Are you sure you don't want to go?" Alexis said. "We always do everything together."

"No, I should stay here and fix up the shop. It needs carpentry work, floor matting, and I've got to make the place secure from theft before we put any stock in here. You go. Have a good time. Everything else will be fine."

 **JORDAN**

chapter 6

From the McArthur Causeway to Miami Beach, white skyscrapers reflected majestically on the rippled surface of the intercostal waterway. As huge ocean-going vessels made their way to Dodge Island and the Port of Miami, tall-masted sailboats glided gracefully over the face of the water, while an assortment of sleek low-slung speed boats cut through the light chop, leaving a V-shaped wake like a flock of geese heading south for the winter.

The House of Crafts was to beads and cordage what the Flower Market in San Francisco was to plants. Within its one-hundred fifty thousand square feet of warehouse, Alexis, Rita, and Richard saw semiprecious beads of every imaginable size and description: jade, carnelian, lapis, bloodstone, rose quartz, sodalite, turquoise, malachite, tourmaline, garnets, and tiger eye. Within the variety contained in bins, tubs, and baskets were round beads, barrel beads, flat beads, square beads, and nuggets. There were hundreds of colors and cuts of glass beads, as well as trade beads of Venetian glass and African amber – both antique and contemporary versions. In another partitioned area, enormous spools hung from strong steel supports in the ceiling with all manner of fibers: waxed linen, unwaxed linen, nylon, cotton, wool fiber, rope, string, and jute – all for sale by length or by weight. Now faced with the individual decisions that might spell success or failure, Alexis took her time, spending the entire afternoon making her purchases. She had to decide what styles, colors, and designs would be saleable in the Key West tourist market. After all, it would take a realistic combination of Max's good business sense and Alexis' artistic flair to make or break the enterprise.

The mood was mellow that night. Richard and Rita's house was extraordinarily old-fashioned, yet artistically deliberate, tucked there at the edge of affluent Coral Gables. Throughout the house were beautiful wall hangings, exotic plants, and Richard's distinctive artwork: framed line drawings, palette knife acrylics, watercolors, and oil paintings. With a warm and colorful atmosphere, her hosts had been helpful in every way. And now that Alexis' traveling bag was comfortably ensconced in the loft along with her bead purchases, she was feeling that the trip had been most worthwhile.

"Alexis?" Rita called from the kitchen. "Richard should be back any minute. He just ran to the market to pick up the wine. Are you ready for some dinner?"

"Sure," she called back from the loft. "Can I help? Want me to make a salad?"

"That'd be great."

Alexis descended the steep stairway and went in to join Rita. As she chopped the vegetables on the built-in cutting board on the island in the middle of the room, Rita finished wiping down the rest of the kitchen counter tops, and then went into the living room. She knelt on a large dark red pillow beside the coffee table, and opened an ornate hand-tooled leather box.

"Are you up for a toke?" she called out.

"Heck yeah, anytime," Alexis said, as she finished drying her hands on a towel. She came into the living room and began to peruse the artwork as Rita busied herself rolling a joint. "Does Richard do all these paintings himself? There are so many different styles."

"Yes. Amazing, isn't it? He started out doing impressionism, later changed to surrealism, and then surprised everyone by doing primitives. His newest thing is charcoal nudes."

"My girlfriend, Marcy, in Key West used to do some posing for a guy in Hialeah. He had a showing at some gallery there, years back."

"How about you? Did you ever pose?"

"In the nude?" Alexis smiled. She looked at Rita, and then realized she was serious. "Yeah, actually," she admitted. "In college once or twice."

"Richard told me he was going to ask you."

Alexis shivered involuntarily. Wouldn't it make Rita feel strange? Besides, Max would freak out.

"Oh, don't worry. I don't care," Rita added light-heartedly. "Our relationship is very relaxed. You'd be doing him, and me, a real service. I recognize that it's hard for him to find appropriate models."

"Well, I don't know if I'm...I'm comfortable with that," Alexis stammered. She thought about all their help and hospitality. How could she diplomatically refuse?

"Please?" Rita pleaded. "As a personal favor to me?"

An hour and a half later, Alexis found herself sitting on a bar stool, wrapped in nothing but Rita's white terry cloth robe. She shifted nervously as Richard first arranged various low-level spotlights and reflective umbrellas around her to create the optimal lighting effect, and then used a knife to pare down the point of his favorite charcoal pencil. Opening his oversize portfolio case, he took out a large sketch pad, and positioned it on the easel. Just then Rita called from the front foyer. "Richard? I'm all set; I'm leaving now."

"Okay, have fun," he responded casually.

"Rita? You're going out?" asked Alexis, taken aback. "Where're you going?"

"I have to go teach my yoga class in Coconut Grove. I'll be back in a few hours. You guys have a good session. See you later." The door thumped shut with finality.

Alexis sat there, dumbstruck. "I didn't know she wouldn't be here tonight."

"Yep, she teaches classes three nights a week," Richard mumbled absent-mindedly, as he looked down and made an adjustment to the easel. "Okay, you can disrobe now. Just drop it around you, I'll tell you how to position yourself, and then after that, don't move. It's easy." Then he looked up at her. "Relax. It's okay." Reluctantly, Alexis followed his instructions. "Good. Now to the left, just a touch. Perfect. Hold it."

Every few minutes, Richard coached her into a slight variation of the original position. But after seven or eight poses, he came over and physically rotated the stool so her back faced him. Then he angled her upper torso sideways so the profile of her breast, and its perpetually hard nipple, stood proud. He lifted her chin, bringing her face around to look back over her shoulder, moved her arm, and arranged her long blond hair to fall forward seductively.

"That's great, Alexis. Now just turn your head a little more toward me; bring down your chin. Drop your shoulder a touch more. Good. Okay, hold it right there. This is some good stuff I'm getting. You have marvelous high cheekbones, and great curves. The lighting is perfect, and your eyes just sparkle all the time. You really are lovely, you know."

Like all women, Alexis needed compliments from time to time, and it was nice to feel appreciated. As he drew, she studied Richard and suddenly realized how attractive he really was. His features were fine, yet paradoxically, rugged. His hair was short blond and curly, yet appealing. Of medium build, he was lithe, yet muscular, with strong features that contradicted the usual stereotype of the effeminate artist.

"Now this time I want you to face me, full front. Extend your left leg, front and center. Let's keep the modesty with your right foot on the rung of the stool and your knee raised a little. Good. Now give me that preoccupied look – like you've got a lot on your mind."

I do have a lot on my mind, she thought. I can't stop looking at you.

An hour later, it was time to take a break. Alexis was surprised that posing was actually hard work; it wasn't easy to hold still for that long.

"All right, let's take fifteen," said Richard. "Get dressed, and we'll continue shortly. Would you like a some wine?"

"Sounds great. Thanks." He poured two glasses, gave one to her, and they walked out on the screened lanai together. It was a lovely room, full of lush ferns, philodendrons, hanging Swedish ivy, and tall ornamental bamboo.

"You know, Alexis, you're a very appealing woman. You're passionate; your energy and vibrancy are obvious. I think you're just beautiful, inside and out." He paused meaningfully and looked into her eyes. She took another sip of wine to cover her uneasiness. He reached out and caressed the side of her face. "I've been an artist all my life. I've drawn women, been with women, and have certainly seen lots of unclad bodies. It's art; it's what I do. But I have to admit that I don't think I've ever felt so turned on before while doing my sketching. With you, I can hardly concentrate. To tell the truth, I've been tempted by you from the moment we met in Key West." Alexis dropped her eyes self-consciously. She felt like Max was watching, and almost bolted from the room. "I want you – bad," he continued. Simple and direct; he had come right out and said it. "I really want to make love with you. Here. Tonight. Right now."

"I can't do that, Richard. I'm married. Not that I don't find you attractive, because I do. But what about you? What about Rita?"

"We have an open marriage and are involved sexually with other people from time to time. It doesn't harm our relationship. We've been together for five years. For us, it works."

"I don't believe it. It never works," Alexis stated adamantly. "People are possessive and jealous by nature; it's that ownership thing. It would never work for Max and me. Neither of us could handle it. Are you telling me Rita wouldn't freak out?"

"No, she wouldn't. She thinks you're beautiful too."

"You mean...?"

"That she's bisexual? No, not exactly." He paused. "Let's just say she has an eye for beauty. With Rita, art is art. It could be a man, a woman, a sunset, a painting, architecture, or a flower arrangement – just as it is for me. That's why our relationship works."

For a breathless moment, Alexis closed her eyes and gave in to the fantasy of reckless sexual diversion with Richard. Wouldn't it be fun, and wild?

"No, I can't." She'd made her decision. "Free love used to be part of my life. Now I take my marriage seriously. I could never face Max again. I like you very much, and I'm flattered, but I can't."

"I won't pressure you," he said, smiling softly. "Forget I even said it. Would you like some more wine?"

"No thanks. You know what? I'm really exhausted. It's been a long day, and if you wouldn't mind, I'd just as soon adjourn with the posing and turn in." She hugged him and climbed the stairs to the loft. "Thanks for being so understanding."

"Goodnight," said Richard, warmly. There was no animosity in his tone. "Sleep well."

The next day Alexis thanked her hosts and boarded the bus. She'd made good time with her purchasing and would be arriving back a day earlier than expected. Once arriving in Key West, she decided to walk the few blocks from the bus station. Her leg was improving, and the load was not that heavy. As she rounded the corner of Grinnell Street heading home, she saw Max embracing a tall shapely woman with strawberry-honey hair. Hidden in the shadows of the tropical exotics that bordered the street, Alexis watched them kiss. His hand slid from her trim waist to her tapered buttocks. Her touring bus was parked around the corner; it had never left. She waited for Max to part company with Katrina and enter the cottage before she walked in and made known her arrival. A few minutes later, all hell broke loose.

"What do you mean it was nothing?" Alexis screamed, righteously. "Did you sleep her or not?"

"Okay, okay. Yes, I did. I admit it. The band was supposed to leave but they ended up staying over for another three shows. It didn't mean anything, I swear. I just really dug her singing. She was foxy; I was high. After it was over, it just made me want you more anyway."

"What a crock! So what does that mean? You were comparing us? What were you doing, thinking of me while you were screwing her? Does that mean you'll be thinking of her while you're screwing me?"

"Calm down. You're hysterical."

"You're damn right. This time I am hysterical. Tell you what – this weekend in Miami, I had my chance too. But did I take it? No. A gorgeous man with brains, talent, and class – he begged me to go to bed with him. But I refused him because I take our relationship seriously. What an ass I am. There I was saying no, while you were getting it on with Katrina. How was it afterward? Do you love her now?"

"Of course not. I love you. After it was over, it was over. It was only sex."

"That's the most shallow, callous attitude I've ever heard. There I was, buying all these supplies for our new business venture and...I don't know, Max. Maybe getting back together was a huge mistake. I thought we were making a new start. Maybe we should just call it quits."

"I really do care...," he began. Then he paused and sighed. "But maybe you're right."

The relationship maintained a stiff awkwardness for the next two months. Neither of them spoke much, although Max was again as good as gold. Alexis went ahead and began work on the handicrafts; it was too late to stop what they'd already put into motion. But then something unexpected happened one day as the result of a routine office visit at the doctor's.

"A baby," Max said, incredulous at the thought. "That's wonderful! That's really great!"

He and Alexis were sitting in the open doorway of *Rondavel*, when she told him the news. He'd been busy organizing her supplies and wares, making a work desk for her, and hanging the finished artwork and jewelry displays.

"Is it wonderful?" she asked him. "Is it great?"

"Oh yes, honey," Max said sincerely. There were actually tears in his eyes, the first time she'd ever seen them. "To me this is a sign that we have to stay together. I was starting to think that it wasn't meant to be, that maybe we should end it like you said. But we can work out anything. I swear, what happened with Katrina will never happen again. I do love you, Alexis. I swear to God I do. We'll make it work. I'll take care of you; we'll have a family. Wow, my own son."

"Child," she corrected mildly. "Maybe it will be a girl."

"You can have a girl next time," he jibed, testing the waters for a little light-hearted banter. "First, I want a son. You know, a man and his son – carry on the family name, and all that."

"Oh no! You're not planning on calling him Augustus, Jr., are you?" The tension broken, they both laughed.

"Heck no, I wouldn't stick that on the poor little guy."

"Or on a girl. No little Augustina, either."

"Okay, I promise. Actually, come to think of it, maybe you should have a girl instead. Girls would be more profitable," Max teased. "I get eleven head of cattle for a daughter."

"You're nuts," Alexis said. He was plucking at her heartstrings again.

"Yeah, nuts about you," he said. "You're going to be a beautiful pregnant woman, and I'm going to stand by your side, and provide for my family."

Over the next few months, Max and Alexis became happier as a couple than they'd ever been before. They checked the pregnancy book at least once a week to monitor the baby's development. Alexis acquired the rosy flush of pregnancy, eating only pure foods to give the growing baby the very best nutrition. Of course, there were times when Max became overbearing about what she ate, how much, and when. But they were both committed to the same goal: to deliver a healthy child. Alexis went to the obstetrician every month and everything appeared to be progressing normally.

As planned, they had opened the little shop in Old Town Key West. Sales were good, and Alexis continually replenished the large artistic inventory, taking in consigned works from their friends as well.

"Check out this book I found in the bookstore," said Max, one evening. They were sitting outside on the little veranda of the cottage under the shade of the rubber banyans. "It was written by that Stephen Gaskin guy who did the bus tour across the country and wrote *Caravan*."

"Oh, I remember him. Stephen Gaskin. Remember Mark Donovan from Berkeley used to go to his Monday Night Class?"

"Yep, same guy. Apparently, when they were done touring, they decided not to return to California. Instead, they purchased a back-to-the-land retreat and established a commune in Tennessee. They call it 'The Farm.' It's all right here."

"Let me see," said Alexis, leafing through the book. "They grow their own organic food, build their own houses, and use different types of New Age energy. Looks like they're big on soybeans and brewer's yeast. It says that they contributed to the relief effort in Nicaragua after the earthquake by shipping sweet potatoes and beans."

"Read on a bit. It also says their chosen sacrament is marijuana, and they also offer a free midwifery service for people looking for natural alternatives to hospitals. Is that great or what? I don't like the thought of our baby being born into a sterile environment of bright lights and bullshit," he said. "The first thing they'll do in a hospital is put silver nitrate in his eyes, and whack off his foreskin."

"What?" Alexis exclaimed, with some alarm. "Not have the baby in a hospital? Dr. Monahan says plenty of things can go wrong during a birth, especially a first one. I'd be scared to have the baby at home. There's placenta *previa*, breech birth..."

"Come on. Don't be a wimp. Women have been having babies since the beginning of time. Back in Africa when the Zulu women are ready to deliver, they put down their hoes, go behind a rock, pop out the baby, strap it on their backs and go back to work."

"I'm not a Zulu," she protested, uncomfortable with his tone. "Besides, that's a little exaggerated, don't you think?"

"Well, maybe. But the point is still that the process of birth is a perfectly natural occurrence. I don't see why it has to be seen as something unnatural and cost a fortune to boot."

Alexis flinched. She was remembering an earlier time, flashbacks to California when Max had gone into a tirade about fasting and the evils of antibiotics.

"You mean you never intended for me to have this baby at a hospital?"

"Of course not. Why? Did you? I just always assumed we would have it at home. You know, natural." Suddenly, he eased off, remembering his promise. "Tell you what. Let's just look into The Farm as an option."

"I guess it would be a happy medium between a hospital and a home birth," she conceded. "Besides, I do like the idea of natural lighting, and submerging the baby in warm water like the French method."

Business seemed to grow as fast as Alexis' belly. Besides macramé, stained glass work, leather, and other consignments, Max and Alexis discovered a new faddish jewelry called *heishi*. Manufactured in the Philippines, small pieces of flat shell with a hole in the middle were threaded on heavy string, then ground on a wheel to a uniform cylindrical shape, sanded, and polished to a lustrous finish. A new style was created when the shells were restrung and interspersed with silver beads or with centerpieces of jade, agate, or other semiprecious stones. More elegant than macramé, this whole new market began to turn over a good profit at the little shop on Duval Street. As the season went by, they expanded their selling at craft shows and street fairs in Miami, Key West, and Fort Lauderdale, combining selling trips with buying trips. By the time Alexis was seven months pregnant, the shop was providing an adequate income.

"'Every baby brings its own bread,'" said Alexis. "Isn't that how the proverb goes?"

"I guess so, *Ntombi*. We've cleared a few thousand bucks, and things are definitely looking good. But we're going to have to plan ahead now. *Heishi* is about played out in this area. We caught the fad just at the right time for the Florida market, but now everybody's getting into it. Once the retail department stores start to carry it, it's time to get out and find something new. Either that, or take the *heishi* to a more provincial area where it hasn't been seen before. I've been thinking of a new plan."

"You usually are. Okay, let's hear it."

"Well, first I think we should go to Stephen's farm in Tennessee and have the baby there. Then we could go up north and find a farmhouse to rent within a hundred or so miles of a big metropolitan area, like Washington D.C. We do a major wholesale purchase by ordering a bunch of *heishi* directly from the Philippines. No middleman. We would be the importers, the wholesalers, the artisans, and the retailers, making all the profit. While you're home with the baby making jewelry, I can be wholesaling it to shops in the city. When we have a big quantity of stock, we could do a grand finale: find a retail target market right before Christmas and sell the hell out of the stuff. After that we sell the business and move to Belize, just like we planned."

"Wow, Max. Are you thinking big enough? That's not a scheme, it's a scam. You're amazing. Do you really think we could pull off something like that?"

"I'm serious. We need to make money. We need to create the lifestyle that we want for ourselves and our child. I'm a Leo. My motto is 'I will.'"

Alexis' belly became mountainous. The pregnancy created the most dramatic physical changes she'd ever experienced. Somehow, seeing other women pregnant just hadn't seemed real. But this baby was real, and there was only one way out of her body: to be born. The child turned inside her, occasionally pushing out an elbow or a knee to create an odd point on the otherwise round contour of her abdomen, or to aim a well-placed kick to the bladder. At times, a suffocating fear would come over Alexis; there was no turning back the hands of time. She studied people on the street and tried to imagine that, for every person she saw, a mother somewhere had gone through pregnancy and birth. Women had been giving birth since the dawn of time. How bad could it be?

* * * *

At the end of March in 1975 they closed the shop, packed up their belongings, and Alexis said goodbye to Key West for the second time. It was still cold as the young couple drove through northern Florida and into the heartland of Georgia. By the calendar, spring was just around the corner, yet the landscape stayed locked under gray skies and icy drizzle. Following the map to Tennessee, Alexis and Max were excited about their arrival at The Farm. Friends in Key West had recommended it as a great place to have their baby, and at last Alexis had overcome her fears. From everything they had read, it sounded like a haven where their child would be born in a true ambience of peace and love. The sign on the gate said,

Welcome to The Farm.

"Hello. Can I help you?" said the gatekeeper.

"Yes, I'm Max Lord and this is my wife, Alexis. We read Stephen's book and came here to take advantage of your midwifery service. We called ahead about a month ago. Our baby is due in two weeks."

The young man seemed confused. He asked them to wait there at the gatehouse while he made a phone call. Alexis looked at Max and he shrugged. Through the glass, they could see the man shaking his head and gesturing emphatically as he spoke on the phone. Finally, he hung up and poked his head out again.

"Okay, you're all set," he said, finally. "See that log cabin up there that says Welcome House? Just go on ahead and park there. You can wait inside and someone will be with you shortly."

"Great. Thanks. By the way, buddy, everyone here will enjoy our visit. We brought an ounce of primo Columbian to share. I understand that *ganja* is your sacrament so we thought we'd make a contribution," said Max, as he stepped on the accelerator. "See you later." The young man's eyes dilated at the comment, but by then they were already through the gate and on their way to log cabin. "Did you see the look on that guy's face?" asked Alexis. "He looked like he was going to drop over. Honestly, the guy looked visibly upset."

Once inside the Welcome House, they waited for what seemed like an eternity for someone who could explain what would happen next. "Hi, are you the couple who came here to have your baby?"

"Yeah, I'm Max and this is Alexis."

"I'm Christopher," he said gruffly, extending his hand. "Come into my office and have a seat." Then the questioning began. Christopher grilled them, cross-examining them about where they were from, what they did, who they knew, how they had found out about The Farm, and what their intentions were. After ten minutes, Max finally put his foot down. He wanted to maintain a feeling of serenity, but things weren't making sense.

"Look, man, I don't know what's going on, but it's really very simple. We read Stephen's book and came here to have our baby. Why are we getting the third degree? You seem like a nice enough guy. Why don't you just level with us and tell us what's going on?"

Christopher looked them straight in the eye, leaned across his desk, and took a deep breath.

"Okay, here's the deal. Apparently, you guys mentioned when you came to the gate that you'd brought some weed with you. That's a real touchy subject on The Farm these days, ever since Stephen was arrested on marijuana charges. He just got out of jail, so there's a lot of paranoia. Everybody's afraid of narcotics agents being planted here by the Feds. If we get caught again, they could close down The Farm, and we could all lose everything."

"Oh, that's terrible," Max said. "We had no idea. Listen, man, I swear we are who we say we are. We don't want to cause any problems. We're just grateful for the midwifery service, and thought we could contribute in a way that would be meaningful. Are you saying that nobody smokes around here anymore?"

"Let's put it this way," Christopher said. "We don't talk about it. Now let's see who you're going to stay with."

"Oh, we don't need to bother anybody. Alexis and I bought a big tent before we left Florida and have a stove and propane heater, everything we need. We're self-contained, self sufficient. If you'll just show us where we can park, get water, and have access to a toilet, we'll be all set."

"Oh no, that's not how it's done here," he said emphatically. "We like our guests to stay with permanent residents so we can all interact. It's part of the rules." Seeing their expression, Christopher forced a sheepish grin. "Oh yeah, we have plenty of rules. Give me a couple minutes and I'll call the Big House. They take care of all the arrangements."

"The Big House?" Alexis repeated.

"Yep," said Christopher. "Where Stephen lives with his wives."

As he went over to the phone, Alexis looked at Max and mouthed the words silently. "His wives?"

Converted army tents and ramshackle shelters of wood and tin dotted the rounded hills of Stephen Gaskin's property in Tennessee. Approximately seventy-five feet from each individual dwelling stood a metal water tank. Each tank was mounted on a two-foot tall platform and positioned on the edge of a dirt utility road which ultimately connected the widespread residential areas to the communal center, church, motor pool, clinic, and store. An assortment of cranky-looking rusty vehicles were scattered haphazardly; none of them looked serviceable. It appeared to be a strange combination of indigent hippie and poor white trash. The Big House stood alone on a hill.

For the first day, Max and Alexis stayed in an eight-person framed army tent. There were two couples: William and Helen, Daniel and Elaine and their two kids, a young single pregnant woman named Leah, and an older man named Thomas. Alexis and Max learned immediately that only full names were acceptable; no one was permitted the use of nicknames. Apparently, it was considered disrespectful. They also learned that many things at The Farm were not as they appeared. On the exterior, people were smiling and cheerful. Yet, inside the family domain, hostilities quickly surfaced.

Alexis settled their things into the corner of a partitioned area in the rear of the tent, and then walked around, incredulous, staring at the green canvas walls of the bleak dwelling. Max covered his edginess by helping Helen put some more wood into the Franklin stove. The others sat around on old threadbare furniture or rude wooden crates covered with thin green army blankets.

"Yeah," Daniel growled. "The hierarchy sits up there in their fancy house on the hill with their running water and hot showers while we live in these cold drafty army tents. Like everyone else, when I first came here, I took the obligatory vow of poverty and gave all my worldly possessions to the collective. Their part of the deal was to take care of me and mine. Everybody was to be treated equally, but you learn real fast that some are 'more equal' than others."

"It's true," said Elaine. "You might have read about how we sent all those sweet potatoes to Nicaragua when the earthquake hit in 1972. A great humanitarian gesture, except that it left only the third-grade sweet potatoes for us – more appropriate for animal feed. They're so rotten and full of bad spots that sometimes we have to cut up twenty-five or thirty of them just to get enough for one meal. But at the Big House, they eat first grade sweet potatoes."

"The water situation is the worst part," said Thomas. "All the family units have their own tanks, but we have to depend on the water truck to deliver before we run out. It seems like no matter how much we conserve our supply, we wake up one morning and the tank is dry. And do you know why? Because our neighbors run out of water first and they steal ours in the middle of the night. Sometimes I stay up all night outside just protecting our water tank. These aren't bad people. They're our friends. But when you need water, there's no choice."

That night, lying on clean sheets with nice blankets and pillows atop the inflatable mattress they'd purchased in Key West, Max and Alexis almost felt guilty for enjoying more comfort than the permanent residents.

"Why did they want us to interact with the permanent people if we'll hear all these negative remarks?" Max whispered to Alexis,

"Maybe the Big House is unaware of what goes on," she whispered back. "But I'll tell you one thing, I'm already sick to death of everyone calling you 'Maximilian.'"

"This place is all wrong," he said. "It's not what a commune is supposed to be."

The next day, after a few bargaining sessions with the hierarchy, the young couple was finally allowed to set up their solo tent in a secluded area on a wooded ridge, and Alexis felt better immediately in their own space. Unable to sit still, she followed her nesting instinct and kept arranging and rearranging the comforts of their little temporary home. Physically, Alexis was so huge and uncomfortable that, at times, even breathing felt impossible. Otherwise, her outlook on the prospect of motherhood was positive. Later that day, she attended a pre-natal checkup, met the midwives who would assist in the delivery, and was given a clean bill of health. On the way back, she planned to pick up some food supplies at the communal store. In the book Max had originally showed Alexis, The Farm had emphasized the importance of organic foods and healthful living. So, naturally, her grocery list included soybeans, yogurt, honey, fruits, vegetables, and herbal tea. But in the store, the shelves were absolutely barren of anything that could be considered wholesome. There was a bin of white sugar, another of white flour, three tins of baking powder, a bag of salt and a few fuzzy gray sweet potatoes. A disinterested young man sat in the corner on a stool trying to hide the fact that he was munching a Snickers bar and two empty Dr. Pepper bottles lay in the corner. She backed out of the store, and gave it a wide berth.

"You know," Alexis said to Max when she returned to the tent, "I really think they've got some junk-food junkies on the sly. They praise the almighty soybean, but they bring back chocolate bars and Pepsis from Summertown. I mean, if people choose to eat junk food, they should at least be allowed to do it openly. They shouldn't be forced into being hypocrites."

"Yeah," Max agreed. "It's only been two days, and the longer we're here, the stranger I think this place is." He and Alexis had both looked for evidence of alternative energy sources like solar and wind during their stay. But instead they'd seen a motor pool of fossil-fuel-burning machinery. Heavy tractors had seemingly trampled the vitality out of the soil, and it appeared that they'd given up organic farming after the very first crop.

"I get a feeling the hierarchy doesn't trust us either," Max continued. "This place appeals to the backpacker types, the true homeless hippies. Hey, if you've got nothing going for you, The Farm's a good deal. But if you've got your act together, it seems to threaten the system. We're probably just too independent for them."

"Yeah," said Alexis. "I never really thought about us being 'capitalists.' It's always been a dirty word to me. But now 'commune' is starting to sound a lot worse. I feel sorry for them. This isn't just a commune; it's communism."

"To me, *Ntombi*, the perfect path is one that combines free enterprise with spirituality. Most people don't think that's possible; they think you either have to be a cutthroat businessman or a dreamer. But I believe there's middle ground."

The first twinges of labor hit at four o'clock on Saturday morning, six days after their arrival. From the beginning, Alexis knew it was the real thing, and from that moment on, sleep was impossible. Realizing it would be a long process, she and Max decided to take a leisurely walk and then go into Summertown to have lunch at a new organic food restaurant. By three-thirty in the afternoon, the pains had increased to the point where Alexis was ready to go back to The Farm and lie down. Soon it was dark and the long night began. One of the midwives came at nine o'clock and determined that Alexis was only dilated two centimeters. With the contractions being twenty-five minutes apart, it was unlikely that the birth would happen during the course of the night.

"I'm scared, Max," she said. "I can't believe how much it hurts and it's only just beginning. I can't believe how tired I am."

"That's why they told you to try to sleep between contractions. You should try to do that."

"Yeah, right. I'm going to push out a watermelon, and I'm supposed to catch forty winks in between." But she did manage to drop off from time to time, and at last dawn arrived. Again the midwife came, but there had been very little progress. Alexis was only four centimeters dilated and the contractions were still fifteen minutes apart. Throughout the entire course of the day, she continued to do the level one Lamaze breathing, but by dusk she was desperate and exhausted.

That second night, racked by agony, she lay on the bed staring at the twin eyes of the kerosene lamps winking at the far side of the tent. Trying to relax and concentrate, Alexis went through every meditation and breathing technique she could think of. She felt like her back was breaking, and she turned and positioned tennis balls on her sciatic nerves for counter-pressure. Max was awake much of the time; she had to give him credit for that. But after forty-eight hours, his breathing slowed in sleep. She was alone.

By dawn of the second morning Alexis felt she had reached the end. Some women died in childbirth and now she understood why. She wished for a drug to kill the pain almost as much as she wished for sleep. Yet every time her body drifted off, the next contraction brought her back. At eight o'clock, Ida May, the head midwife walked into the tent with two other attendants.

"Still in there, huh?" she said, directing her comment toward Alexis' bulging belly. "Well, it's high time that baby comes out into the world."

"What are you going to do to me?"

"Honey, if we don't get that baby out of you, you're going to have to go to the hospital to get a zipper." She flexed her fingers. "Okay, girls. Showtime."

By eleven o'clock, Alexis no longer even knew who or where she was. Her water had broken. The midwives massaged her belly and breasts to stimulate the birthing process and wiped her sweating naked body with a damp cloth. The sun shone through the red canvas roof of the tent and played colorful tricks on the walls. Sometimes she could see three Maxes and other times none. The world spun away as if she was being sucked into a funnel. In her more lucid moments, she was sure her vertebrae were shattering. Nothing could relieve the pressure, except pushing that baby out. Mohammed didn't know anything about moving mountains, she thought. Women did.

"I can see the head," said Ida May. "Okay, Alexis, bear down. Push. Push hard.

Okay, girls, it's crowning. Get ready. Come on, Alexis. PUSH!" she commanded. Every fiber of Alexis' mind and soul directed itself into that one moment as the baby's head emerged from her body. "The head is out. Now, one more push for the shoulder. Come on, Alexis."

"I–can't–do–this," she gasped, as she bore down one final time. With a gush of blood and fluids, the baby was born and gave a vigorous cry.

"It's a boy!" cried Max.

Just then Stephen walked in and smiled.

"Do we have a new human being here?" As he spoke, the baby's tiny penis stood up, and in the relative coolness of his new environment, he peed. Stephen laughed and spoke for the infant. "Ahhh, I've been waiting to do that for months."

Alexis stared down at the multicolored baby lying between her legs. Looking surreal, the colors swirled before her eyes. The infant appeared to be red, blue, pink, and white – all at the same time. The umbilical cord was thick and curly; it pulsated with new life. The midwives cleansed the baby and laid it on Alexis' bare body. As she touched the infant for the first time, another powerful contraction caused the placenta to be born. Holding the mass of tissue high, they waited until all the life-giving blood drained into the child's body before cutting the cord. Putting the tiny mouth to her breast, Alexis felt a delicious pang as the infant began suckling. She looked into Max's eyes and knew it was the greatest moment either of them had ever experienced. Outside their tent, the world had burst into a riot of color. Spring, too, had been born; the dogwood bloomed, shy violets peeped from the woodlands, and the sun shone brightly in the skies over Tennessee.

Ida May shook her head, as she held the baby.

"He's looking a little yellow," she said. "I want to take him outside for a moment and check him in the sunlight. This color in the tent here makes it hard for me to tell."

It had been the most incredible three days of their lives. Of course, Max had nearly reneged on his promise by wanting to call the baby Maximilian Augustus II. "Because he looks so much like me," he had said. But they'd finally agreed to call the baby Jordan, and still spent hours simply staring at the newborn, sharing the amazement of new life. The baby had already taken in plenty of rich colostrum, and now Alexis felt the fluid change to milk. Nursing was uniquely pleasurable for her. She felt none of the soreness or distress other mothers had described. It was as natural as breathing, and holding the baby to her breast felt beautifully maternal and safe.

"Yep, I'm afraid he looks like he's got a high bilirubin count," Ida May announced as she came back inside the tent. "I think we should take him to the hospital and get him checked out."

"What does that mean?" said Max. "Is it dangerous?"

"It can be, if the count is very high," she replied evenly. "About one-third of all new babies get a slight jaundice after a few days because their liver isn't functioning properly yet. If the count is higher than twenty, it's possible for the baby to suffer brain damage." Frightened, Alexis had been prepared for the physical part of having a baby, but nothing she had ever read in a book could have prepared her for the intense love she felt. She understood now why mothers could give up their lives for their children. "I'm going to take him into Summertown Hospital and get him tested for a bilirubin count."

"Max, you go with them." Alexis wanted no argument.

"Look, Maximilian, that's unnecessary," said Ida May. "You stay here and support your old lady. She's the one that needs you."

"No, I'm fine. Really," Alexis said anxiously. "I'd feel much better if Max went along with Jordan."

"You know, you two are so intense!" the midwife criticized loudly. "We handle things like this all the time. Just let us take care of it."

Max and Alexis exchanged looks. The very reason they'd chosen The Farm was to avoid hospitals, drugs, and doctors. Now, they were expected to send their baby into that very environment? A place where he'd be out of their control? Fighting for composure, Alexis finally said, "Okay, but only to test him. Not to admit him."

"Right," Max chimed in, swallowing hard. "I don't want you to allow the hospital to do anything else to him. And for heaven's sake, don't formally admit him without my permission, whatever you do. You just advise us as soon as you know something."

Alexis felt sick, both physically and mentally, from the moment the midwife took her baby away. Her milk was coming in; she took to her bed as she became feverish. Midmorning changed to afternoon, and the hours dragged on into the evening with still no word. At nine o'clock they found out the midwife had been back for several hours and was taking a shower.

"Taking a shower?" she heard Max yell into the telephone. "Where's our baby?"

A few minutes later Ida May came to visit and explained that Jordan's bilirubin count was seventeen and a half, and she had felt it necessary to admit him for infrared lamp treatments and antibiotic injections.

"You what?" Max screamed.

Alexis' world plunged into despair. After three days with their precious baby, now he was in the hands of strangers, and only God knew what they were doing to him. She couldn't stand the thought of someone feeding her baby a chemical formula while she lay sick with milk fever. Her enormous breasts were hard as rocks and throbbed in pain, with no baby to relieve the pressure.

"Max, is there any way I can have a bath?" Alexis asked the next morning. She was miserable, in total despair. "I need to soak in a tub so bad."

There were communal shower houses at The Farm, but the water was almost always cold. On the rare occasions when the truck brought propane, people lined up outside by the hundreds. Then, instead of politely rationing themselves so everyone could enjoy a little precious hot water, the first ones took twenty-minute showers, selfishly drowning themselves in bliss. Soon the heat was gone or the water was gone, one or the other. Desperate to provide, Max took the matter into his own hands. He found an abandoned fifty-five-gallon drum and scrubbed it clean, inside and out. Taking a chisel and hammer, he laboriously cut the drum in half and bent the sides down in sections so as not to leave a sharp edge. Then he found some old cinder blocks and set them under the drum, allowing enough room to build a fire underneath. Working like a draft animal, he labored to carry polyethylene buckets of water from a distant stream, load after load, until he'd filled the drum three-quarters full. Finally he started a fire and brought the water to just the right temperature. Then, with uncharacteristic charm, Max insisted on leading Alexis to it, blindfolded, and surprising her.

"It's a 'cannibal bath' and I made it just for you. Do you like it?"

She slipped off her clothes and stepped in gingerly. Then she settled back in the luxurious warmth of the water. "Oh Max, this is heaven. I think this may be the nicest thing you've ever done for me."

"I sure hope it makes you feel better. Take as much time as you want, but when you're done, I'm next. And tomorrow we're going to see our baby."

The next day their worst fears were realized when they saw little Jordan through the glass of the newborn ward at Summertown Hospital. He had a bandage over his eyes to protect him from the purple-white rays above, and the nurse on duty was giving him an injection in the thigh. Alexis' letdown reflex reacted at the sound of his cry and immediately her shirt was drenched with milk. When Max tried to comfort her, she could not be soothed, and when the careless nurse picked up the baby and allowed his head to fall backward, Alexis snapped.

"Stop!" she screamed, banging on the door. "You're hurting my baby! Give me my baby. Stop it!" At the sound of her voice, doctors and nurses started pouring out of the doors and into the hallways like a firedrill.

"What on earth is going on here?" demanded the head nurse.

"That nurse in there is hurting my baby," Alexis yelled. "We didn't want him admitted in the first place. The Farm did it. I can't stand this anymore. I want him. Give me my baby back." Like a mother bear, Alexis was in a complete frenzy. Her claws were unsheathed, and she was ready to tear apart anyone who made further attempts on her cub.

"I'm sorry, ma'am," Max said to the nurse, trying to maintain courtesy. "We are visitors at Stephen Gaskin's Farm. The midwives admitted our baby into this hospital against our specific instructions; they had no right to do that. Yes, my wife is hysterical, but I'm supporting her on it one hundred percent. The truth is that she needs to hold that baby and nurse him."

"It would be against policy and against all medical advice to release him at this time. He's still in need of treatment for the high bilirubin count. With all due respect, Mr. Lord, I hope you know what you're doing."

Max went to the lobby and started making phone calls. Within twenty minutes he'd found a naturopath in Nashville who agreed to treat the baby. They made the decision to take Jordan out. Signing a waiver, he was delivered into Alexis' arms.

Returning to The Farm, Max began packing up their tent and other belongings immediately, while Alexis waited in the van nursing Jordan. As he finished loading the last of the gear, Ida May showed up and began to reprimand them for a second time.

"It's just as well that you people are leaving. Ever since you got here you've been troublemakers. You just think you're better than everybody else, don't you? Well, around here, what's good enough for one is good enough for the other. Just like the fifty-five gallon drum. You just couldn't wait and take a shower like everybody else. You just had to set up your own system, didn't you? This is a commune, not an entrepreneurial enterprise. People like you don't know how to go with the flow. You just have to make things happen yourself."

"Oh yeah?" Max retorted. "And you don't? Is that why you were in your own private hot shower at the Big House on the night you deserted our son in the hospital? You people have some very screwed up priorities around here."

"Why you ungrateful son-of-a-bitch," she said, angrily.

"No," interrupted Alexis. "Enough please. We're leaving now, so we'll be gone. We're grateful for your help in delivering our baby. I just think Max and I have discovered that we like to be in charge of our own, to think and work and fend for ourselves. We have different ideologies; we are entrepreneurs, not communists. Thank you for all you've done." Alexis extended her hand. "Goodbye."

The old doctor in Nashville diagnosed that Jordan was out of danger, prescribing gentle morning and evening sunlight, ironically, a natural cure to break down the rest of the bilirubin. He was very kind and refused payment on the grounds that he hadn't really treated the baby. The grateful couple thanked him heartily, then continued north, free at last to pursue their journey.

* * * *

A rare bit of good luck at the House of Musical Traditions in Berkeley Springs led them to find a farmhouse for rent just outside the rural artistic town. The West Virginia property was a hundred or so miles outside of Washington DC, just as Max had planned, and with the baby being born, everything was starting to fall into place. Although surrounded by beautiful hills, woodlands, and apple orchards, the house itself was in a dreadful state of disrepair. An old farmer and his wife had lived there for most of their sixty years of marriage until a sudden stroke rendered the woman comatose. While visiting his wife in the hospital, the husband had died of a sudden massive heart attack at her bedside, and she followed suit within forty-eight hours. Everything had been left in its place, assuming and awaiting their return, but they had simply never come back.

Under the kitchen sink, Alexis found a pink Depression glass bowl with open handles, circa 1930's, an ancient quilt in excellent condition, with soft gold and teal tassels, lovingly crafted by little old ladies in a circle, no doubt. With the peculiar and slightly creepy feeling of unexpected and untimely abandonment, there were still dishes in the sink in the old farmhouse, medicines in the bathroom cabinet, and the old woman's support hose on the towel rack behind the bathroom door. The water pipes under the house had burst in the previous winter's cold. The flue in the fireplace was blocked with debris. Thick layers of dirt and filth were everywhere among boxes of clothes that had never been removed by relatives. Huge pieces of sheetrock stood stacked against the living room wall for a remodeling job that had never come to pass. Cleaning the place was a Herculean task. For everything that needed to be done, four other things had to be done first. Max worked hard, and Alexis carried little Jordan in a front carrier so she could work using both hands. After a week's effort, quite unexpectedly, everything was finished. They walked out on the front porch as the sun was setting, sat down on the wooden swing, and looked at the long stretch of driveway leading to the bridge over the creek. All was still, except for the chirping of the crickets.

"Tomorrow I'll call the Philippines and order our wholesale *heishi*," said Max. "It's time to follow through."

Three months later the plans were in full swing. The Filipino shipment had been sizeable, and Alexis produced as many as twenty *heishi* chokers a day. Max found markets in the Georgetown area and was making runs to Washington, D.C. twice a week. Jordan was healthy and growing; already he weighed seventeen pounds. Max and Alexis made friends with other couples in the area, most of whom had tired of life in the city. Through the course of the summer, a half dozen couples developed a ritual of weekend get-togethers for potluck and volleyball.

But all was not peace and love at home. Once again their relationship seemed to be deteriorating. Throughout the summer and into the fall, Max began to bark at Alexis incessantly, complaining about the way she managed her household and the baby. If Jordan cried, Max expected his wife to continue taking action of some kind until the crying stopped, no matter what was required, even if it meant leaving the house so Max could get his sleep. As a new mother, Alexis had a mental list of things to try when the baby cried and wouldn't stop. Is he wet? Too hot? Too cold? Tired? Hungry? Teething? Restless? If he was still crying when she reached the bottom of the list, she'd start at the top again.

More than anything, Max was driven to provide, yet his whole focus seemed to be that of providing for his son's future, rather than for his family as a whole. He no longer treated Alexis as an integral part of the big picture; he acted as though she were nothing more than an assistant in the raising of his son. It got worse as he badgered her, and ran her ragged with physical and emotional demands.

Max was fanatical when it came to the subject of diapers. Alexis knew from other mothers that most babies went through perhaps twelve to fourteen diapers in twenty four hours. Yet because of Max, she used almost two dozen within the same time period. Other women used disposable; Max insisted on cotton. He insisted that they were not only cheaper, but also that his child must be surrounded by natural fabrics only. Not really cheaper, thought Alexis, I'm still the one who has to wash, dry, and fold them. Refusing to buy, or even accept as a gift, any article of clothing that contained any percentage of polyester, Max even argued with her over the use of waterproof plastic baby pants to cover the cotton diaper, until she convinced him there was absolutely no substitute.

Max had opinions about domestic issues that most people considered to be completely outside, or even beneath, a man's domain or interest. Even her father, Frank, had remarked on it. Household matters, such as how Alexis arranged the kitchen utensils in a drawer, what she cooked for dinner, and how she folded the towels – nothing was immune from his criticism, and apologies only seemed to pique his irritation. Worst of all, Alexis knew now that she was bound to him forever because they had a child together. Over a period of time, she was forced into further subservience, and Max began to truly enjoy the sensation of power. Alexis was a woman, not his mother, and he realized he could treat her any way he pleased.

As the huge stockpile of finished product accumulated, Max became obsessed with finding the ultimate retail market in time for Christmas. In late October, he found a mall in nearby Harrisburg that was renting space to artisans for the Christmas season, so he paid for a prime corner-spot and made arrangements to set up shop at the beginning of December. Then Max sold their VW van, bought a '59 Ford step-van, parked it in the barn, and began remodeling the inside. Alexis was not enthused, and it showed in the timbre of her voice as they sat at the dinner table in the old farmhouse. It was mid-November, and winter was upon them. She could smell the cold, and the snows were not far behind.

"You mean we're actually going to live in that old step-van while we're doing the stint at the mall?" She barely picked at her food, and was concentrating on watching Jordan with the toys in his play-pen in the other room.

"Yeah. Have you got a problem with that?" Max barked.

"Where is it going to be parked? In the mall parking lot? The security people would never let us do that. What about water, and electric, and sewerage?"

"I'll fix it so we can be completely self-contained. Then we'll just have to talk the security guy in to letting us do it. Bribe him, if necessary."

"This isn't Africa; you're not dealing with *Bantu*. What if he won't go for it?" she argued.

"He'll go for it. It's not a problem," Max spat back.

"Sounds like a serious loophole to me." Alexis couldn't help it; her ire was up. "I don't want to work in a shopping mall and then sleep in a parking lot in a truck with a baby for three weeks. That's not a life!"

"God damn it, Alexis!" Max exploded in anger. "You're always rowing in the opposite direction, so all we ever do is go around in circles. Why don't you pull your finger out and get with the program?"

"I'm just trying to be realistic," she protested, refusing to back off. "If they won't let us park there, it'll blow the entire scheme. Then what will we do? Spend all the profit on hotel rooms?"

"Oh, bullshit. You're just being contrary as usual." Max's face was dark and red, and he was seething. "I ought to knock you. All you ever do is contradict me. You're getting to be a total pain in the ass!" A loud cry interrupted their argument. "Now look what you've done," he reprimanded. "You've upset Jordan. Go take care of him. Better yet, I'll do it." Max walked over and picked up the baby. He shoved his hand down into his diaper. "He's wet again," he said with finality. "Take him up and change him."

Alexis took Jordan from his father's arms and carried him upstairs to the bedroom. As she started to remove the diaper, she realized it was completely dry. Shaking her head, she brought the baby back downstairs.

"Are you disobeying me again, woman? I told you to change that baby. You've only been gone for thirty seconds." His rage had begun to build, and Alexis could feel a cold chill as she saw his fist at his side.

"He was bone dry, Max."

"Bullshit," he snarled. "I'm going to take that kid upstairs, and check for myself. If there's any wetness in his diaper, you can prepare yourself for a little lesson in discipline."

Thirty seconds before the baby had been dry. But what if he peed again before Max could check him? This is ridiculous, she thought nervously, as her husband disappeared up the stairs. Max returned a minute later and stared at Alexis with steely eyes.

"He was dry. You're lucky."

 **BELIZE**

chapter 7

Heat waves shimmered on the asphalt surface ahead, creating a distant mirage of water as the old step-van rumbled through the arid desert of northern Mexico. Although the U.S. border lay only a few miles behind, the landscape was already abysmally bleak. A solitary piece of tumbleweed blew across the road, providing a brief distraction from the desolate landscape of sagebrush, cactus, and sand. Max drove, keeping his hands firmly on the wheel, his eyes forward as Alexis sat in the passenger seat holding little Jordan, now nine months old. Uncomfortable in the intense heat and dust, he fussed and fidgeted as he nursed. Without air conditioning, the open windows provided nothing more than fresh blasts of hot gritty dust.

Alexis wiped the sweat from his face and neck and thought about the mound of cotton diapers accumulating in the sealed plastic bucket in the back of the truck, wondering when and where she'd able to wash them now that they were out of the land of coin-operated laundries. Glutted with milk at last, Jordan's head dropped sleepily to the side. She carried him to the crib secured in the rear of the step-van and put him on his stomach inside the protective padded bars.

"Well, Alexis," said Max cheerfully. "We've made it. No more U.S.A. No more taxes, traffic, or industrial pollution. We're free. Free to go where we want, find our special corner of the world and carve out our little empire, just like we said. Damn, I feel good."

The adventure had begun, all right. Did it feel good? Alexis wasn't sure. After all, wasn't she bound to find the unspoiled natural paradise that had always seemed just outside her grasp? She remembered the conversation on the Yuba River about the ideal place to live, Danny's comments about Mexico, and what they'd heard about Belize and Costa Rica. Now it was happening. The anticipation was great, the prospect exciting; yet many things frightened her. Max frightened her, and the despair expressed by her father and mother still echoed in her head.

The ambitious Christmas sales project at the mall in Harrisburg had been a huge success. She and Max had cleared over just over six thousand dollars. It wasn't much of a nest egg, but enough for a couple of young people with a dream. After the holiday they'd visited Alexis' parents in Pennsylvania. Only years later would she really understand what her parents must have gone through in those final days before their great trek south. Dropping out of college and going to Florida was one thing, but now they were headed to another country.

"What about money?" Frank asked anxiously. First Max had taken his daughter and now he was taking his new grandson; they were going far away to a land and a lifestyle that were incomprehensible to him.

"I told you, Dad," Max said, making Frank cringe at the familiar term. "We'll buy a small piece of land and set up a homestead, growing what we need and selling the overflow for cash. I've got a good agricultural background."

"What about medical care?"

"I've done research," Max said. "The British Army has troops posted in Belize. If the local medical care isn't up to snuff, we can rely on the army. Of course, we may end up in Costa Rica instead. From what I've read it's even more civilized than Belize."

There was no point in rhetoric. No amount of challenging by Frank would make Max change and no explanation could ease her father's mind.

"What about earthquakes?" asked Liz.

"Come on, Mum," he said. "You could trip in the street and drown in a mud puddle, or get hit by a train, or struck by lightning. People die in automobile accidents every day. If we were flying to Central America instead of driving there, you'd be worried about a plane crash. Relax. There aren't going to be any earthquakes."

In the end there was nothing Frank and Liz could do, other than to give the young family their blessings. But part of their world died when the van pulled out of their driveway in January of 1976.

Through the dust and flickering heat, they both spied a small rickety building in the distance.

"What's that up ahead?" asked Max. "Do you think that's the checkpoint they told us about?" As the van came closer, a faded Mexican flag out front gave mute testimony to its purpose. "Have you got that Spanish dictionary handy?"

"Yes," Alexis replied. "But I wish it had verb conjugations instead of just nouns. Now I'm sorry I took French for the last three years of high school instead of sticking with Spanish. The only phrase I can remember from seventh grade is *No me gusta las albóndigas,* which means 'I don't like meatballs.' And I don't think that particular vocabulary will be of much help at an Immigration checkpoint."

The burly sweaty Mexican in a uniform motioned them to step off the van as it pulled to a stop. *"Ven,"* he said. *"Ven aquí, Ustedes. Tienen armas? Que tienen por allá? Armas? Televisiónes? Que tienen al dentro?"*

"What's he saying?" asked Max.

"Damned if I know, but it looks like he wants us to get out. Something about televisions. I'm not leaving the baby. You go."

"Televisions? What's that got to do with anything? Can't you say something in Spanish?"

"I'll try. Ahhh, *Señor, no puedo* come over there. *Niño.* I have a *niño* sleeping back here." She made a motion with her two hands to indicate rocking a baby, and then closed her eyes put her hands under one cheek to indicate sleep, and motioned to the back of the step-van.

"Esta bien, pero su esposo necesite venir para la inspección de sus papeles."

"He wants to see your papers, Max. Go ahead while I check in the dictionary."

Armas...armas, she thought as she flipped through the pages. Here it is.

"Guns!" she shouted out the window after Max as he entered the building with the fat Mexican. "He wants to know if we have guns or televisions with us." Max nodded. She held her breath until he came out of the building a few minutes later.

"All set," Max said, in a great mood, as he got back in the driver's seat. "All I had to do was give them a few pesos. The third world's the same wherever you go. Even if you don't speak the language, money talks. If we did have guns, all I'd still have to do is give them a little more money, and they would have let us go." He laughed, and shook his head. "This lifestyle is going to be a piece of cake." As they drove away, he reached into his crotch and pulled out a small baggie. "Here, roll us a doobie and let's celebrate."

"You brought weed into Mexico? I thought you were going to get rid of it before the border?"

"Throw away perfectly good pot? No way," he laughed again. "It's one of the best reasons to go to Central America in the first place. Roll it up."

For the rest of the day and most of the next, the scenery didn't change. As Alexis stared at the never-ending dreariness of Tamaulipas, she wondered if she'd ever see a tree again, let alone a jungle.

"I'm hungry, said Alexis, finally. "The ice in the cooler is melted, so now the bread is all soggy, and the cheese and fruit are gone. So are the nuts. There's one yogurt left, but it's got a hole in the top and the water leaked in. Can't we stop somewhere and get a real meal?"

"I swear, you eat like a goddam horse," Max muttered.

"I'm nursing," she countered. "It takes a lot of calories to produce milk, so I probably need even more food than you do right now. I know there aren't a lot of places to stop out here, but I've seen a couple of signs saying *abarrotes*. I have no idea what that means, but whatever it is, I'll eat it."

"Okay," he said grudgingly. "We'll stop the next time we see a place."

About forty kilometers later they saw an old wooden building with the same sign. It was barely a building – really just a large shack with no walls, a few upright beams, and a rusty tin roof. A pleasant old Mexican woman came out to serve them. With a hollow ache in her stomach, Alexis said hopefully, *"¿Abarrotes?"*

The woman smiled and gestured to a large old-fashioned top-loading cooler behind her. *"Si, señora. Por allá."* At her invitation Alexis went over and lifted the lid. Soft drinks. Nothing but soft drinks. In desperation she paged through her dictionary. *"¿Comida?"*

"No. Lo siento, señora," the woman replied apologetically. *"Pura bebidas."*

"Oh Max, all they have are soft drinks! No food."

"Well, so much for your eating *abarrotes*."

"Señora, por favor," Alexis pleaded. *"Mi niño – leche,"* she gestured to her breasts. *"Comida, por favor."* Her mind struggled back to the seventh grade for the right words, *"Hambre, señora.* I'm very hungry. *Tengo mucho hambre."*

The woman understood. She looked beyond the rear of the wooden building to her own dwelling and pointed. *"Solamente huevos y frijoles. Esta bien?"*

"Max!" Alexis shouted with glee. "That means eggs and beans. I remember those words. *"Si señora, huevos y frijoles. Muy bien."*

The old lady nodded and disappeared into her small thatched house. Twenty minutes later she brought out two small plates with a tiny amount of beans and eggs on each. She set them on the red checkered tablecloth with a large stack of steaming corn tortillas wrapped in a clean cloth, and a bowl of green salsa. Alexis grinned as she thanked the woman sincerely. Although the place obviously wasn't a restaurant, the old matron understood motherhood, and she had provided for them out of her own meager stores. The portions were nominal, but Alexis figured that the stack of tortillas could go a long way if she put just a dab of beans and eggs on each. Max commented on the diabolical-looking green sauce.

"Think it's safe?"

"It looks pretty deadly. I don't much care for hot stuff either but I'm so hungry I feel a little reckless. I'm going to have some."

Their hostess was pleased with the acceptability of the meal, and she held out her hands toward Jordan. *"Dame su niño mientras."*

"I think she wants to hold Jordan, *Ntombi*. Africa's like that too. All the old ladies love to fuss over yellow-haired babies. Let her hold him so you can eat."

Simple fare, but it was a meal Alexis would never forget. Piqued by rampant hunger, the tasty tortillas with their flavoring of eggs and beans and the tangy hot sauce were nourishing and satisfying. Breaking their own rules of healthy eating, Max and Alexis washed it down with a couple of cold Cokes. As they left, they thanked the woman heartily and paid twice what she asked. With a fond *adiós* the young family climbed into the truck and continued south, feeling like they'd arrived in the real Mexico.

After the river-ferry crossing at Tampico, the look of the landscape became more inviting. Gradually, the dry flat lands gave way to curving hills and abundant greenery. As the road wound through the areas near Poza Rica and Papantla, Alexis finally saw lush jungle for the first time. Instead of the blazing heat, the rickety van and its occupants found refuge in the cool of the tree-shaded roads. Pulling over at a roadside stand to buy some fresh juice, they noticed that the men wore long white shirts and white cotton trousers. They were a physically beautiful people, immaculately clean. One of them saw the Americans and approached the vehicle.

"¿Piña pie, señor?" he said. *¿Señora? Solo catorce pesos,* one dollar. *¿Quiere pie de piña? Barrato. ¿Lo quieren?"*

"That means pineapple, Max. Ooh look, a pineapple pie. Mmm, it looks good."

"Señora, señora," interrupted another man, as he too crowded at the door of the van. *"¿Quiere vainilla? Tengo vainilla para vender."* He quickly opened his palm to reveal a scorpion! Alexis nearly jumped out of her skin until she realized it was some kind of seed pod. When he gestured that Alexis should smell it, she realized it was a vanilla bean, the pod from a special tropical orchid used to make vanilla extract.

"¿Otra forma? Tengo otra forma tambien. Solo tres pesos cada uno," said the little man. He pulled out another vanilla bean work-of-art, this one in the design of a crucifix.

It was an interesting choice of styles – a scorpion and a crucifix, obviously two important influences in their everyday lives. Alexis took one of each and the pie too, and hung the crucifix from the rear view mirror. When in Rome…she thought.

She sat back and smiled to herself. Feeling much better, she was looking forward to spending the night in the little coastal village of Tecolutla, where Max had promised they would treat themselves to an actual restaurant meal and a clean hotel room for the night.

The old step-van persevered southeast, passing alongside the coastal city of Veracruz and going through small villages with exotic names like Alvarado, Lerdo de Tejada, and San Andreas Tuxtla. Alexis studied the map, knowing that soon they'd have to make the big decision.

"It shows here that there's a fork in the road at Acayucan. At that point we can go south to Guatemala City and on to Costa Rica, or continue east through the Yucatan and on to Belize."

"How far is it to Acayucan from here?" Max asked.

"Mmm. Looks like about seventy-five kilometers, less than forty miles. That doesn't give us much time. And once we head east to Belize, it's pretty much cut off from the rest of Central America. It looks like there is only the one decent road that comes in from the north. Amazing. And there's only one single skinny red line that leads from the west of Belize into Guatemala. And nothing to the south either; no roads down there at all," she emphasized. "Probably just heavy jungle. It'll be a tough decision to reverse once we make it."

"That's true, but if we go to Costa Rica, then for sure we won't go to Belize. If we go to Belize first and don't like it, we can always go on to Costa Rica."

"Belize is a lot closer to the States," Alexis reminded him. "It would be much more expensive to travel back from Costa Rica."

"So who wants to go back?"

"Don't be like that, Max, my parents are there. Even if we set up permanently in Belize or Costa Rica, I'll want to be able to come back to see them."

"We haven't even gotten there yet, and already you're talking about coming back."

"No, I'm not," she protested. "I just want to consider all the factors."

"Yeah, right," Max said, sarcastically. "You're real good at soft adventure inside the U.S. Once you're the foreigner, you're a wimp."

"Come on, please. Let's not fight."

There was silence for a good five minutes before he spoke again.

"Well, I still think we should go to Belize first. Then we can see if we like it." There was no point in arguing.

Of all the spectacular country they'd seen in Mexico, there was an incomparable magnificence in the rugged beauty just before Acayucan. As the narrow road curved treacherously along the hairpin turns, precipitous cliffs dropped off into the gorges on either side, and the heady perfume of orange blossoms from the nearby groves sweetened the early morning mist. Reaching the fork in the road, they bore left without hesitation and continued due east, bypassing the route that would have taken them south across the Isthmus of Tehuantepec and on to Guatemala. Descending rapidly from the highlands, the old step-van trundled towards a black smudge that lay thickly on the horizon. The closer they came to the coastal city of Coatzacoalcos, the more the air reeked of the petroleum emissions belching from the smokestacks of hundreds of oil refineries. As they reached the city itself, the thick smoke engulfed their vehicle. There was no longer a sky above them, only the choking purple-orange haze from which there was no escape.

Desperation seized Alexis as Jordan fussed and struggled. All three of them were wheezed and fought for breath, and tears streamed down their cheeks as the caustic fumes burned their eyes, lungs, and skin. The only answer was to counter the movements of frantic taxis and pedestrians in the narrow streets and get out of that city as quickly as possible. It was a good eighty kilometers east of Coatzacoalcos before the burning feeling began to subside.

"My God, what a stink-hole!" exclaimed Alexis. "My throat is raw and my eyes are still watering. My poor baby," she said, rocking Jordan back and forth on her lap. "He's still coughing." She stroked his head gently. "How can those people live there?"

"I don't know," said Max, "but those refineries, or whatever they are, made it bloody impossible to breathe. So far it's only been an inconvenience not having air-conditioning in this old wreck, but in Coatzacoalcos you could damn well die without it. What's the next major town?"

"Villahermosa," Alexis answered. "It means `beautiful city' in Spanish."

"Well, it didn't take a genius to name that one." Max gave a smirk. "Any city would be beautiful compared to the last one."

As it turned out, Villahermosa, located on the banks of the Rio Grijalva, wouldn't have won any awards for urban splendor either, but with its shining white buildings and colorful gardens, it had been, at least, a temporary reprieve. But again the scenery degenerated as Alexis and Max continued eastward to the little village of Francisco de Escarsega.

"This is ghastly country." Alexis grimaced. "Everything has been such a letdown since Acayucan. Villahermosa wasn't too bad. But look at this place. Escarsega – it's the ends of the earth. There's nothing here. A bar, a church, a restaurant where you'd surely die of salmonella poisoning, and one gas station that sells nothing higher than an eighty-two octane. A few broken-down buildings surrounded by a barren flat. No trees, no nothing. God, it's ugly. I hope we've got better things to look forward to in Belize."

Max immediately took the remark as an attack. "So you're saying it's my fault we didn't go south to Guatemala?"

"I didn't say that," Alexis protested. "We made the decision together. I just hope the countryside improves, that's all." But through the dry wasteland of Campeche, the landscape only deteriorated. With their spirits at the lowest ebb, Max and Alexis arrived at a god-forsaken spot on the map that made Escarsega look like a thriving metropolis.

Once a center of the Mayan empire, the village of Xpujíl was now a wretched outpost of desolation. There was one grimy gas station with a sagging roof and a few dilapidated huts. Filthy snot-nosed children played on the edge of the road beside the wreckage of a burned-out automobile. A couple of mangy dogs chased after a hairless scabby bitch and tried to wrestle a suspicious-looking piece of meat from her mouth. Alexis' head pounded from the blinding sun, the pain made worse by Jordan's incessant crying. A terrible heat rash tortured his little body, and his mother's constant ministrations seemed to do no good. Max was silent and morose as he pumped the gas into the old step-van. His skin was covered with a sticky plaster of sweat and dust. His tongue felt thick and swollen. Although he would not admit it, at that point even he had misgivings.

Max was still busy, so Alexis stepped down from the truck holding Jordan and walked around the back to take advantage of its shade. Immediately she smelled the vile odor of rotting flesh. There, ten yards away, lay the bloated corpse of a pig festering in the hot sun. The iridescent green and pink meat was blanketed with flies; the open thoracic cavity squirmed with white maggots. One of the male dogs had finally claimed the gruesome prize from the bitch; it was the snout of the pig with a tattered ear still attached by a piece of grisly hide. Having lived all her life in the United States, Alexis had always seen dogs as pampered pets, cherished and cared for. She'd never seen anything like this.

But it was far worse to see the condition of the children.

"Señora, señora," the little children called as they ran to the van. *"¿Dinero, por favor? ¿Pesos? ¿Pesos?"* Alexis could have cried as she saw their physical condition. One little girl looked up at her with one good eye, the other blinded by a blue-white mass of hardened scar tissue. Her crippled brother tried to reach out and touch Jordan, and Alexis recoiled as she could see the lice crawling on the boy's head.

"Let's get out of here," she cried out, running back into the van. This place is hell on earth. Can't we do something? Can't we give them some money?"

"There's nothing you can do, *Ntombi.* See that drunken bum leaning against the wall over there? That's their father. Besides begging me for money, he's been watching you with those kids. I can guarantee that if you give them anything, he'll take it away in two seconds flat and spend it on more rum. Even if the kids could keep it, they'd spend it on sweets, not food. You can't save the world – not the first world, and certainly not the third world." She paused reflectively as his words sank deep. Alexis would remember them forever.

By the time they came to the lower end of Bajia Bacalar and took the final turn south, the night sky was jet black. Not one star or street light illuminated the lonely stretch of road leading south from Chetumal. Even the parking area of the tumbledown shack at the border crossing was veiled in darkness except for a feeble beam of light shining through the rickety wallboards. They parked and got out of the car, approaching what they assumed to be Immigration. The source turned out to be a single naked light bulb dangling from an electrical wire on the ceiling.

"I've got the passports," said Max, taking Jordan from her. "Let's go."

Inside, the building was so dim it was almost impossible to make out the contents of the room. Not that there was much to see. The two men behind the counter were as black as the night sky outside. They mumbled to each other in some incomprehensible language as they fiddled with a cheap scratched-up radio.

"I thought they spoke English here," Max whispered.

"Supposedly they do," Alexis whispered back. "But I sure as hell don't know what they're saying."

"Look hyah mon. Dis ting no work correc at all," said the shorter man as he twisted the knobs.

"Mon," replied the taller one, *"Da yu, no de radio. Yu no know noting bout how de ting funkshun propah. Yu use de laudge button first, den de small one fu fine-tune di ting. Den yu get de stayshun clare, clare."*

Max cleared his throat. "Excuse me?" The taller man glared at Max, severely inconvenienced. "Hi. Is this Immigration and Customs?"

With an air of importance the shorter man stood up and walked over to the young couple.

"I de Immigrashun mon. He de Customs mon. Mek Ah see yu paypahs."

If it had been difficult to go through Mexico without being able to speak Spanish, the language barrier of Belize was proving to be an even greater problem. Asking the border officials to repeat themselves was useless and frustrating, as an unintelligible word, spoken more slowly, is often just as unintelligible. Not only were the men officious, self-righteous, and belligerent, but the Immigration officer was highly suspicious of their motives for entering the country in the first place. How long they were going to stay? Where would they stay? Who did they know?

How much money did they have to spend? The Customs man wanted to know what they were bringing into the country. TVs? Guns? Watches, metal detectors? Tools, alcohol, or illegal drugs? In exasperation, Max finally slipped each of them five U.S. dollars, and again, it worked.

At one-thirty a.m. on January 20, 1976, the Lord family gained legal entry into Belize, the land of promise. They drove several more miles into the consummate blackness before stopping for the night. A peculiar anxiety troubled Alexis as she tried to fall asleep in the airless van beside her husband and baby. Outside, there was no evidence of people. There was no breeze. The jungle loomed on both sides of the narrow road. The darkness was so complete, the stillness so absolute, and the sultry air so oppressively humid, that Alexis felt she'd entered the uninhabited interior of Dr. Livingston's darkest Africa.

At the dawning of the following day, a new world came into focus. The menacing gloom gave way to a bright landscape, revealing fields of sugarcane bordered by fruit trees and palms. In the distance they could see the sun sparkling on the ocean just beyond the town of Corozal. The little town was named after the *coroso*, the American Oil Palm, which grew in abundance. Unlike the modest fronds of coconut palms, the leaves of the *coroso* grew up to sixty feet, and instead of coconuts, the trees bore clusters of egg-shaped *cohune* nuts that hung on thick stalks from the base of the fronds.

From the scant information they'd found on Belize, Max and Alexis had decided to skip the flatlands of the north. Their plan was to pass through Belize City on the coast and head toward the western district, which claimed to have the best climate and the greatest number of American inhabitants. Deciding was one thing, getting there would be another. The route south from Corozal to Orange Walk Town was a decent stretch of highway. With sugarcane as its main export, the Public Works Department of the northern districts maintained a good road for the cane trucks to deliver to the sugar factory at Libertad. But once south of Orange Walk, the road became a dangerous winding track surrounded by scrub and bug-infested undergrowth. It dwindled abruptly to a single lane of broken asphalt with potholes deep enough to break a spring even at twenty miles per hour. The lane of blacktop was so narrow that when a vehicle approached from the other direction, Max had to pull completely off the crumbled tarmac, and the drop to the dusty white shoulder was a full five inches lower than the road's surface. Although the bush was not thick enough to qualify as true jungle, the nearby mangrove swamps housed millions of hungry mosquitoes, which swarmed through the open windows of the van seeking fresh blood.

"Can't you drive any faster?" Alexis said, as she swatted another one.

"God damn it! You think I enjoy getting eaten alive? If I drive any faster the bottom of this crate will fall out and we won't go anywhere. Keep those bugs off Jordan, would you? Put some more of that citronella oil on him." Max slapped his neck twice in a row. "Man, this is bullshit."

It took almost two and half hours to complete the tortuous stretch from Orange Walk to Belize City, and when they arrived, the squalor that Alexis and Max found there defied comprehension – at least by North American standards. The narrow city streets were filthy with discarded boxes, rotten fruit, broken glass, and other refuse. Unpainted frame houses huddled one next to the other in various stages of disrepair, some leaning as much as fifteen degrees. Other buildings, such as schools and churches were made of sturdier cinderblock, but they grew a disgusting black mold on the lower walls, especially where drunks and dogs urinated on them. Run-down bicycles, people on foot, ancient pickup trucks, and aged taxis all competed for space in the grimy streets, while battered trucks growled noisily and belched noxious fumes that mingled with rank odors from the nearby fish market. Since all the streets were one-lane, and therefore one-way, there was a limited pattern of circulation that allowed a vehicle to get from one place to another. Unfortunately, there were no signs marked accordingly.

A navigable waterway sixty feet wide divided the city, and only a single bridge in the center of town provided for the traffic from east to west. Once on the west side, Max and Alexis saw the most loathsome characteristic of Belize City: the network of disgusting canals that acted as open sewers. With no indoor plumbing available, people simply collected their wastes in "night buckets" and emptied them into the fetid canals in the early hours of the morning. With no substantial circulation to move it along, the slimy green-brown scum wafted sluggishly to the main waterway in the center of town and finally drifted out to sea.

"Do you think we made a drastic mistake by coming here?" Alexis asked as she looked around. She felt nauseous and was sure she was going to throw up.

"I don't know," said Max. "Maybe. But I can't believe the rest of the country is this bad. Apparently, there are quite a few Americans here, and they sure as hell don't live in places like this."

Continuing west, with the city now forty miles behind them, the country still remained devoid of beauty – a tedious wasteland of eroded flatlands and small stands of scrub palmetto and saw-tooth palm. The soil was reddish-yellow with a coarse grainy texture – a highly acidic content in which nothing else would grow. An occasional smattering of gaunt southern pine accented the otherwise barren landscape, but there were no real trees and, again, no shade. However this no-man's-land did have one thing that made it memorable: a small black biting insect known as the "bottle-ass" fly. Landing silently, it delivered a voracious bite that left a distinctly flat raised welt with a little blood spot in the middle, which itched and burned for hours. Alexis looked up from her map and suddenly pointed.

"Max, look over there, to the south. Mountains, I think, unless it's just clouds on the horizon. No. look, there are mountains coming up from the south, angling toward the west. See them?"

"All right!" said Max, enthusiastically. "I want to see some elevation again, and some decent vegetation." And sure enough, within ten minutes the scene changed dramatically as an area of thick forest and giant cohune palms came into sight. After crossing a good-sized bridge, they found themselves at the first T-junction they'd seen in fifty miles, followed by a small village. The ramshackle houses were mostly unpainted; others sported uncomfortably gaudy color combinations.

"Do you realize we haven't seen a single road sign since we crossed the border? And whoever heard of a border guard that can't provide a map of his own country? Let's see if we can find a store. We could get something to drink and find out where the heck we are."

"Maybe this is Belmopan," said Max. "But it doesn't look like a capital. There should be government buildings. This just looks like a village."

The little cinderblock store was dingy on the outside, and even more dismal inside. A tall black-skinned man behind the counter watched them without much interest.

"Excuse me, sir, is this Belmopan?

"No, Miss, Belmopan is back south at de crossroads. Dis da Roarin' Creek Village."

"What do you think, Max?" said Alexis, shifting Jordan to her other hip. "Want to go there and check it out?"

"No. Let's head west first. We can always come back this way if we want."

"What kinds of juices do you have for sale please?" Alexis said, turning back to the owner.

"I no got juice. Only sof drink."

"With all these oranges around, you don't sell orange juice?"

"No Miss, but we got de o-ringe fruit if yu wan eat it right-so." Alexis noted that he accented orange on the second syllable, instead of the first. No wonder it was hard to understand their pidgin.

"Okay, we'll take three oranges," she said gratefully. "We'd like to buy some cheese and crackers too. Also what kind of nuts do you have?"

"Well, we no got no cheese or noting like dat. Sometimes we got peanuts, but right now we no got. Only Coke, Red Fanta, and powda bun."

"Give us two Cokes, please," said Max.

"We're going to die of food carcinogens at this rate. Look at the shelves up there," Alexis whispered, pointing behind the man. "That's the selection? Nothing but canned goods and six different kinds of rum? What do these people eat? And what the heck is a *powda bun* anyway?"

"I don't know. But they sure don't have any snack foods available, at least not the kind we're used to. It's like Africa. People were healthy until the white man introduced them to Coca-Cola and white bread. Then they started getting diabetes, cancer, and rotten teeth. Obviously, the sooner we can cook for ourselves, the sooner we're going to eat properly again."

Max paid for the drinks with a red five-dollar bill, noting its oval portrait of Queen Elizabeth. There must still be a strong English influence, Alexis thought, as she saw the cracked and faded picture of the Royal Family, circa 1963, hanging crookedly on the far wall.

"Dere yu go," the storekeeper said, giving them their change. *"Tree dollahs an eighty cents. Tank yu ver much."*

"What's up this way if we keep going west?" asked Max.

"Yu got small villages. Den yu get to Cayo. Dat bout twenty miles more up."

"Cayo? Is that near San Ignacio?"

"Dat ah de same ting. San Ignacio is de town; Cayo is de distric. But dey still call de town Cayo anyway."

"Thank you," Alexis said. "You've been very helpful."

"No problem, Miss," said the man politely.

* * * *

Three days had passed since Max, Alexis, and Jordan had crossed the Hawkesworth Bridge to Cayo and parked their truck on the western savannah of the

Macal River. The sight of the impressive river had been the first time they'd been able to breathe a sigh of relief, that maybe Belize might have the features they were looking for after all. It was Saturday, and Alexis was at the water's edge washing Jordan's diapers when she saw a dugout canoe coming from upriver. A skinny old white woman carrying an empty plastic handbag stepped lithely onto the bank. At the stern, a slim black man wearing a cowboy hat manned the small outboard motor. It was impossible to tell his age. His eyes seemed old, yet his skin was smooth and unlined, his body lean, but muscled.

The woman saw Alexis watching her and smiled.

"Hello," she said, speaking with a slight European accent. "Did you just arrive here in Cayo?"

"A few days ago. I can't believe how beautiful this river is."

"I never tire of it and I've lived here for fourteen years now. My name is Mrs. Whitmore."

"Nice to meet you. I'm Alexis Lord." She stood up and extended her hand.

"Are you here with your family? Your parents?"

"Oh no, my husband and baby. We own that truck over there."

"So you're visiting Belize. Will you be staying long?"

"Permanently, if we can find what we're looking for. We want to find a piece of land to start our own farm."

"Ah, homesteaders. A lot of young Americans have been coming to Belize with that on their minds. I've seen many new faces in recent months." Mrs. Whitmore lived several miles upstream. Her husband had died the year before, and she lived with one of her sons and her two young teenage daughters. "I'll be glad to tell you about the area, but you'll have to come with me to market. I want to get my fresh eggs from the Mennonite before they're all gone."

"I'd love to go. Let me get my baby first. My husband's looking after him."

After introducing Max to Mrs. Whitmore, Alexis put Jordan into his backpack, slipped on the shoulder straps, and spent the rest of the morning making the rounds. She couldn't believe the variety of skin colors. Many people were shiny coal black; others varied from dark brown to *café con leche*. She saw three Chinese, some Lebanese, a few white Americans, some Mennonites in their horse-drawn wagons, and six or eight British soldiers in uniform. As they walked, Mrs. Whitmore kept up a steady commentary about what to buy and where to buy it. Together they purchased fruits, vegetables, and eggs, all at different stalls. She advised Alexis which store had the freshest flour, sugar, and rice. The old lady was eccentric, but sweet and informative. She explained that the local dialect was called Creole and that everybody learned to speak it eventually. She talked and talked, about her farm, her children, her late husband, and the excessive rain in recent months. Then Mrs. Whitmore waved to a young boy selling some kind of leaf-wrapped food from a plastic bucket.

"Try one of these," she said, as she peeled back the corn husk for Alexis. "They're called *tamalitos*. You take fresh green corn, cut the kernels off the cob, and grind them in a *molino*. Then mix in a little oil, some salt and chopped hot peppers, and wrap the mixture in the same husks the corn came from. Then you steam them for about twenty minutes."

"Wow. They're delicious," Alexis said, taking a bite. "What do you mean 'green corn'?"

"In Belize we don't have sweet corn. It's too soft and rots in the high humidity. Green corn is actually field corn, or what you'd call 'dent corn.' But when it's young, it's perfectly tender and juicy. *Tamalitos* are my favorite of all the local street foods, but it's very seasonal. Corn matures quickly as the dry season begins."

Later, they stood on the edge of the savannah waiting for the dugout that would take the old woman back up the river. Still enjoying the spotlight, Mrs. Whitmore told Alexis more about the river. Above the bridge, although broad and majestic, the river was navigable only by dugout. It had two distinct personalities – dry season and rainy season. In the dry season, although it retained its width, the level of the river dropped so low that the mahogany dugouts, called dories, often scraped their bottoms on the shallow rapids and were never steered straight up the middle. Instead, specific channels had to be followed. The river changed constantly, not only year by year, but even within the course of the season. Only a dory man who stayed familiar with every alteration was safe from its hidden dangers. During the floods of the rainy season, the river became a brown deluge. Mrs. Whitmore told Alexis that when the river flooded, it could rise at a rate of four feet an hour, sometimes spreading to more than a quarter mile wide. Sometimes flash floods would occur, and a wall of water would sweep the banks, engulfing anything or anyone in its path. Mrs. Whitmore told her that once she had seen a squealing pig and two chickens marooned on a pile of sodden debris, swirling helplessly in the torrent. Under the surface of the river lay the evidence of countless floods, submerged boulders of immense proportion, and the remains of giant trees. Once the Macal River flowed north past San Ignacio and the Hawkesworth bridge, it flattened into treacherous shallows just before its merger with the Mopan River from the west. Together, the two branches formed the River Belize, which wound its way slowly to the sea.

Previous to the building of the Western Highway, the Belize River had been the only practical means of transportation between the mountains and the coast. Flat-bottomed steamers known as Cayo Boats traveled the waterway in the dry season, carrying supplies upstream for the *chicléros* and loggers. During their three week journey to the western uplands, the boatmen stopped at villages with curious names like Baking Pot, Double-head Cabbage, Young Gal, Teakettle, Burrell Boom, More Tomorrow, Guinea Grass, and Never Delay. In the course of this passage, the Cayo boats had to contend with one hundred thirty-three "runs" or rapids where they often ground out on the shallows. By using long ropes attached to trees on the banks, the crew painstakingly winched the unwieldy crafts yard by yard against the current until they reached deep water again. Once they had arrived in Cayo and loaded the cargo of *chicle*, the return trip east was a virtually effortless float downstream to Belize City, taking a mere two days.

As they stood waiting for the dugout to come back, Mrs. Whitmore turned suddenly. "Alexis, I'd like to make you and your husband an offer. I told you that I have another son, an older one named Michael; he recently left for the States and will be gone for quite some time. His property is adjacent to mine. There's a house on the hill above the river. Would you and your husband like to consider renting it?"

Alexis' eyes lit up with delight. "Oh, Mrs. Whitmore! On the river? That's just too good to be true. Wait 'til I tell Max. When could we see it?"

"We'd have to ask Matthew if he has room in the dory for all of us. If he does, I suppose we could go right now, by river, to take a look. With the amount of rain we've had lately, you couldn't possibly get there any other way. The road is too bad right now."

"I can't tell you how much we appreciate an opportunity like this. Do you want to hold Jordan while I run up and get Max? I'm sure he could be ready to go in a couple of minutes."

Max was just as astonished when he heard of the offer.

"That's great. Heck, yeah. Let me lock up here and grab a few things. What did Mrs. Whitmore say the boatman's name is?"

"Matthew Richardson. Why?"

"It just seems funny that someone as black as he is would have a name that's so English. I would have imagined something more African."

"Mrs. Whitmore says the British have been a long-time influence. They have interbred with the local population for two hundred years or more, and left their names behind. I understand that Jones, Smith, Waight, and Brown are all common names here. Others have Scottish names like McDonald and McKay, and a lot of them are as dark as Matthew."

Upon arrival of the dory, Mr. Richardson agreed to take the newcomers. He would wait while they looked at the property and then bring them back to town.

"Whoa!" exclaimed Alexis as she stepped into the tipsy craft. "I guess there's a right way and a wrong way to do this."

Matthew stood to help her. *"Yu mus step inna de middle of de bottom, so de dory don rock."*

"Sit low and try not to move your upper body," added Mrs. Whitmore. "Most of all you have to relax."

First Matthew arranged the people and cargo for ideal balance and weight distribution. Then he started the outboard motor, shoved off from the bank with a short stick, and pointed the bow upstream. Once past the bridge, Alexis could hear Max talking to Matthew. Since she sat in the bow with Mrs. Whitmore in the middle, she could only catch snatches of the conversation at the stern.

"...and these big trees on the banks...are they the ones that are used to make the dories?" Max asked.

"No, replied Matthew. *"Dat is de one de Maya call 'ceiba.' It is very sof. We call it cottonwood. De correc tree for dories don grow close to de river. Wat yu wan is de mahog'ny or de cedar trees wat grows inna de high bush. De wood is very hard. Dem trees have to be at least bout six feet right tru de center for have de big heartwood. Inna de old days they used mules fu drag de tree. Now-days yu get a friend wit a tractor to drag it close by de river. Den yu cut away all de sof sapwood from round de outside wit de chainsaw if yu got one, so only de hard heartwood lef. Den yu dig out de center wit de tool called de 'adze'. You know de tool?"*

"Yes," said Max. "I know what an adze looks like."

"It take one long time fu mek it, an yu mus be careful when yu dig it out. It have to be jus right on the bottom curve an de point correc, or de dory drag sideways inna de water."

With acute awareness, Alexis looked around her and observed a fantasy world of tropical grandeur. Around the first big bend, she saw a concave wall of rock. Two boulders, each as big as a three-story house, rose proudly above the surface. The upper portions of the rocks had been smoothed by a thousand floods, and the algae-covered bases were shrouded in deep water. Beyond the rocks on either side of the river, peculiar-looking trees rose out of the underbrush. Enormous gray-green iguanas, up to four feet in length with long black and orange tails, sunned themselves lazily on branches overhanging the river, plopping into the water as the dory came too close. From time to time, stretches of bush bamboo gave way to open pasture. Thatched houses shaded by tall cohune palms came into view. Brahma cattle grazed on the slopes, standing contentedly as white egrets feasted on the fat purple ticks embedded in the humpbacked beasts. The river was a haven for all types of birds. Crested blue kingfishers seemed to skim no more than an inch above the water's surface. There were flycatchers, warblers, tanagers, doves, orioles, and curious-looking woodrails with their gaudy orange feet.

It was obvious that Matthew was a skilled dory man who stayed in tune with the shifting channels and obstacles left by the floods. At times he hugged the far left side, staying within an arm's reach of the bank, forcing his passengers to duck the brambles of thorny bamboo. Then, abruptly, he crossed diagonally to the extreme right, squeezing through a narrow channel between sharp rocks. Other times he guided the boat right up the middle of broad open pools, skirting the boulders in the swirling eddies. Farther upstream, Alexis saw a large log above their heads in the fork of a tall tree. Puzzled, she turned and shouted back to the driver, "Matthew, how did that big log get up there?"

"Well, Miss Alexis, de flood lef it."

"Up there? That's fifty feet above the river!"

"Yes, ma'am, I seen dis river go up bout sixty five feet inna de hurricane. Why yu tink de houses built so high up away from de water?"

Alexis tried to imagine herself fifty feet under the floodwaters. What on earth did this river look like when it filled the valley? It was an awesome thought. "Mrs. Whitmore? That pointed hill up there on the ridge, is that natural?" she asked.

"You have a good eye. It's a Mayan ruin," the old woman replied. "This area has hundreds of them. Some are just house-mounds like that one. But if you know what to look for, you'll notice larger ones from time to time. At first you might think it's just another hill. Then suddenly you'll realize it's the covered remains of an ancient temple. Of course, all the mounds near the rivers were robbed by diggers long ago. But no one knows how many temples are still hidden deep in the high bush."

"What kinds of things did the Mayans leave behind? Gold and silver?"

"Maya is the name of the people; Mayan is the language and culture," Mrs. Whitmore corrected mildly. "But to answer your question, no, the Maya didn't have metals, or the wheel, or beasts of burden. But they did have beautiful works of jade and pottery. Sometimes you find small potshards just lying around the house mounds."

"How do you know they're real, and not fake?"

"Where would anyone get imitation artifacts around here?" she laughed. "This is the jungle."

"Is there a museum anywhere in the country? Stuff like that has always fascinated me. I'd sure like to see some artifacts one day."

"Not in Belize, but there's a wonderful museum over the border in Guatemala at the ruins of Tikal. All we have here is a vault in the Archaeology Department in Belmopan. But if you go there on a Monday, they let people go in and look, accompanied by one of the supervisors, of course." Mrs. Whitmore nodded, then turned and pointed to the left.

"There's the house," she said. "That's the property ahead."

"Yu wan dat I pull in here first, Mrs. Whitmore?"

"Yes, please, Matthew. We'll stop here and show them Michael's first, then we'll go on to my place. Look, the Brahma stud's here. Victor must have finally dropped him off so he could breed the cows."

As Max and Alexis stepped onto the narrow sandy bank, they shared one common emotion from the first moment they saw the place – they not only wanted to rent it, they wanted to buy it. The plain unpainted rectangular wooden house stood about seventy-five feet up the hill from the river, and like many of the more substantial wooden and tin-roofed dwellings in Cayo, it was solidly rooted into the bedrock by means of enormous twelve-by-twelve hardwood posts. Upon closer inspection they found that, except for a front veranda and railing, the rear of the house was identical to the front with a central staircase and door, the western one facing the river, and the eastern one butting up against the adjacent hillside behind. The house had eight windows with heavy wooden shutters, two on each side. Surprisingly, there were no screens. Mrs. Whitmore assured them that, unlike the coastal areas, all the land near the river had good drainage and therefore very few bugs. The house was unfurnished except for a small butane stove and fridge in the kitchen; the living room was empty as was the only bedroom. And yet, crude and unsophisticated, the entire house was built of solid mahogany. However, the lower level beneath the house had one major difference; it had been reinforced with cement blocks between the stilts, creating solid walls, and therefore, an enclosed workshop and storage area.

"…and this is a spice tree. You know it as 'allspice'," said Mrs. Whitmore as she continued her tour of the grounds. "The local people use the seeds in a delightful dish called *escabeche*. It's a chicken soup made with white onions, a little vinegar, and allspice seed. Sometimes they collect the spice seeds for export, although it's not a big market. And here is an *achiote* bush." She popped open the Brazil nut-shaped casing with her forefinger and thumb to expose the red-orange berries inside. "The people crush these and mix them with salt, pepper, and other spices to make *recado*, a flavoring and coloring agent for stewed meat. The Mayas also used it for dye and painting their faces. This is a tamarind tree. Its fruit is sweet and tart at the same time and it makes a cooling drink. My girls love it. See these pods? They're still green, but they'll be coming into season soon, during the dry."

"When exactly is the dry season?" said Alexis.

"Well, it's almost the end of January now. The heaviest rains are over, although we'll still get some in February. The dry will begin in early March, but it won't really get hot until April. May is the hottest month. June and July are wet and humid, but the rains are more like gentle summer showers than real downpours. In August, there is a little mini-dry that the locals call the *mauga*, or meager season. The real rains start in September, going right through until February."

"Something tells me we're not in Kansas anymore, Toto," said Alexis, under her breath.

"So, you haven't told me what you think of the house and property?" Mrs. Whitmore said.

"Well," Max said. "What would you charge for monthly rent?"

"How about seventy BH?"

"BH?"

"Belize dollars used to be called 'BH' for British Honduras. We've had our new name for eight years now, but I still can't break the habit. Seventy Belize dollars per month. That's thirty-five U.S."

"We'll take it," said Max.

Alexis was dreaming. She was out on the ocean in a sailboat. A gale force wind came out of nowhere and the boat began to rock. In a split second she was shocked back to reality, awake and trying to focus on what was happening. Where am I? Oh yeah, I'm in the house on the river, in Belize with Max and Jordan. Why is the house shaking? The cows, she thought. That big Brahma stud bull must have gotten into the yard and he's rubbing on the stilts. But then she remembered the cement blocks between the posts. It would take an elephant to shake the whole house like that.

"Earthquake!" cried Alexis. "Max, it's an earthquake!" The whole house trembled as Max was shocked from sound-asleep to wide-awake.

"Earthquake?" he said. "Geez, it's an earthquake!"

"It can't be an earthquake," Alexis shouted, illogically. "We've only been in Central America for two weeks!"

Two jars in the kitchen fell off the shelves and crashed to the floor. Alexis screamed, jumping out of bed and grabbing Jordan. The noise became deafening. Outside they could hear the land reverberating and groaning as shock waves rolled across the river valley. The wooden planks in the house creaked as though the whole structure were trying to tear free of the heavy beams that rooted it in place. With only one flashlight and no electricity, the experience was even more frightening. Sensing his parents' fear, little nine-month-old Jordan screamed and cried.

"What do we do?" Alexis shouted above the din. "Should we get out of the house?"

"I don't know," Max shouted back. "Both staircases are really steep, and they're wet; it's been raining. We could slip and break our necks, or the stairs could tear apart while we're on them. But if we stay in here and these main timbers give..."

The quaking built to a crescendo as the geologic plates shifted and settled. Panic stricken, Max and Alexis dodged back and forth from one side of the house to the other with the baby, not knowing whether it was safer inside or outside – whether to wait or abandon the house. After more than three minutes of mind-numbing fear, the quaking subsided

"Good morning, Belize. This is Radio Belize, the voice of the Caribbean, *la voce de la amistad,* the voice of friendship," said the gregarious DJ. "And how are all of you this morning in this beautiful little jewel of ours?" Max turned up the volume of the radio in anticipation. "So all of you in the western Cayo District had quite a jolt last night, *no true*? Well, we in Belize City felt only a jiggle. But it has been reported that there has been some minor damage in San Ignacio Town and Benque Viejo del Carmen on the western border. The real news this morning is in neighboring Guatemala. The epicenter of the earthquake was located just east of the Guatemala City and measured at 7.6 on the Richter scale. The quake occurred at 3:44 a.m. and lasted just over three minutes. Reports of major damage are starting to come in from Guatemala City. First estimates are that perhaps twenty thousand people are dead, and it is suspected that thousands more still lie buried alive in the rubble. Many churches and other buildings of historical importance were destroyed or severely damaged. We'll have more news on this breaking story as it becomes available. In other news this morning..."

Alexis put Jordan into the hammock crosswise, the way Mrs. Whitmore had shown her, and put the cut-off piece of broomstick in place, wrapping both ends in the material to hold it in the open position. Jordan loved it, falling asleep much faster than a cradle or rocking chair. Then she picked up the whisk broom and began to sweep where the jars had fallen, just in case there were still minute broken shards. Max sat on the windowsill drinking his morning tea. He looked out over the pasture and noticed that, miraculously, only a few trees had fallen. Like the house, timber seemed to have tremendous resilience.

Just at that moment another hard tremor began. Alexis' eyes opened wide. In one glance she and Max exchanged a thousand words. The aftershock lasted perhaps ten seconds.

"Is it over?" asked Alexis cautiously. He didn't reply. "Max?" she said hesitantly.

"Yeah?"

"If we'd gone south at Acayucan instead of east to Belize, we would have been in Guatemala City right now. Right at the heart of the quake."

 **SEASONS**

chapteR 8

Other than a few framed prints on the wall of the living room, the red and blue woven Guatemalan hammock was still the only spark of color in the otherwise austere surroundings. In the bedroom, the double mattress from the van lay frameless on the hardwood floor and sturdy cardboard boxes disguised with bright orange and yellow tie-died scarves served as makeshift night stands on either side. Jordan's baby hammock occupied one corner, its ropes securing it to the rafters. Space in the vehicle had been extremely limited. Max had brought hand tools, electric tools, farm tools, hardware, an old guitar, his congas, a generator, and a small welder. Alexis had brought personal items, cooking utensils, small handicraft tools, silver wire and bead supplies, her flute, sewing stuff, baby things, linens, and clothing. Furniture had been a foregone luxury.

Standing on the front veranda, Alexis looked at the spectacular river below. The water was not only clean and refreshing; this portion of the Macal was also free from dangerous reptiles that *gringos* so often worried about – and not without good reason. She and Max went swimming at least twice a day and little Jordan delighted in playing along the edge. But, more than recreational, the river was also a prerequisite to Belizean life in the dry season. The rains had stopped and the weather was getting hotter. Max had bought and mounted a water tank on the side of the house which managed to catch the last few rains off the roof, but soon the meager supply would be gone. Once that happened, any water needed at the house would have to be carried by hand. There was only one answer: Max needed to go find, and purchase, a water pump. And there were none to be had in Belize. No one sold them, anywhere.

"I should only need to be in Guatemala for two, maybe three days," said Max. "Just long enough to find the right mechanism for this type of application. A submersible jet pump would be great if we didn't have to worry about the floods taking it away. But I think a centrifugal pump would be the best choice for this application; the head is less than eighty feet. 'Head' is the appropriate term for the amount of lift you're trying to achieve."

"Ah geez, I was going to make a joke…" Alexis teased, but his stern expression took away her mood. "Sorry. I was just trying to be funny. You're so serious all the time; you never laugh any more."

"This is serious," Max emphasized. "We need to get the pump so we can fill the tank from the river. The dry season's here. Do you want to keep washing diapers and doing laundry all the way down there? Water weighs eight pounds per gallon. Do you want to be carrying forty pound buckets uphill?"

"No. I don't. You're right," Alexis admitted. It was a sobering thought. She couldn't leave Jordan at the house alone, and if she took him to the river with her, he would get tired and cranky before she could finish the washing. Besides, then she'd have to carry both the baby and the wet laundry up the hill. "Are you sure you have to go to Guatemala?"

"Mrs. Whitmore said the only place to get one is over the border." Max raised his hands in agitation. "It's obvious that Belize doesn't have much in the way of technology."

"How do you know if you can get through to Flores? Do we know for sure if the road's been cleared from the earthquake?"

"The real damage was in the mountains west of Flores, closer to Guatemala City. Besides, and that was three weeks ago. We can't afford to wait any longer. You're not worried about staying here alone are you?"

"No,"Alexis lied. An hour later, Max was packed and on his way.

Now that the mud was beginning to dry up, Max had found that getting the truck in and out of Michael's property was achievable, but it was still far from easy. When first viewing the property, he and Alexis had both discovered that what was accessible by river was not, necessarily, accessible by road. The single dirt track heading south from the Whitmore properties through *Cristo Rey* village to the twin towns of Santa Elena and San Ignacio was a twisted snaking path, and what was six miles by river was ten miles by road – if it could be called a road at all. Barb wire fences separated the diminutive thatched huts and modest banana plantations from the jungle road whose long stretches of red clay, steeply pitched inclines of sticky white marl, bare limestone, abrupt curves, hairpin turns, and bold bony cobbles, threatened the oil pan of any vehicle, high clearance notwithstanding.

The next day was Saturday, and with Max gone, Alexis prepared to go to market in Cayo if she could catch Matthew's dory. As soon as she heard the sound of the outboard motor upstream, she put Jordan into his baby backpack and dashed down to the riverbank as fast as she could. There were no phones, no two-way radios. If Alexis was not present at the riverside, she would miss the boat.

That morning in San Ignacio, Alexis met Betty, a young American woman who lived with her husband and two kids up the Mountain Pine Ridge Road, just south of the National Forest Reserve. Apparently, her family had been among the first in the new wave of *gringos* to arrive. Alexis had ducked into the shade at a vegetable stand where an overabundance of tomatoes was selling for twenty-five cents per pound, and the two women had struck up a conversation – if you could call it that. It was really more of a rant, Alexis thought. Apparently Betty was so happy to meet another white woman that she couldn't wait to talk about every interesting thing she'd ever seen or learned about in Belize.

"...and we're surrounded by high bush, so naturally we hear the howler monkeys at night. We farm our land and grow most of what we need since Len and I are strict vegetarians..."

She might be a vegetarian, Alexis thought, but she's a walking controversy. Betty couldn't have weighed more than a hundred pounds, soaking wet. She drank Coca Cola constantly, chain-smoked cigarettes, abstained from meat, ate candy bars, and drank herb tea. It reminded her of the soybeans and Snicker bars on Gaskin's Farm. Or maybe she's just a natural speed freak, Alexis thought.

"...because, you see, our house is on the edge of a valley made fertile by a year-round creek, and it's critical that you have a dependable water source. Has anybody told you how bad the dry season was last year? A normal dry lasts for only about three months, whereas this one lasted almost eight. The cattle were dying. All the artesian springs, what the locals call 'eyes of water' or *ojos de agua*, had dried up; even the most reliable creeks virtually disappeared. Cattle skirted the fencing where it met the rivers and trampled other people's properties in search of a single blade of grass. It was the worst dry in anyone's memory. Terrible." Betty paused to take a large swig from her Coke to light another cigarette, taking two long drags before she continued. "Sure, it's still hot in the dry season, but where we are in the mountains at least you get lots of shade and a good breeze. All the mud dries up, the kids can enjoy playing outside, and laundry on the line dries in about ten minutes. It's also easier to visit friends, or go to one of the rivers up the Pine Ridge for an afternoon. Good swimming holes and waterfalls.

"Of course, here in town it gets miserable in the dry season. All the white limestone on the roads turns to a choking dust. It sifts through the screens and leaves a white film all over everything: floors, walls, furniture. Clean it off and it's back in ten minutes. There are swarms of houseflies. The temperature goes into the mid-nineties, and in May it gets smoky too. That's because the *milpaléros* start to burn."

"The what?" Alexis asked. Her mind couldn't keep up with the torrent of information.

"*Milpaléros*," said Betty. "The people who work their *mílpas* – little plantations. You see, the local people are so poor that their only tools are a machete, a file, and a pack of matches. Early in the dry season they go out and clear-cut a big piece of high bush. Over the next three months the fallen bush dries out in the heat, even the huge tree trunks, and when the dry season is at its hottest towards the end of May, they wait for a stiff breeze and then set a match to the whole piece. With a good burn, the whole *mílpa* goes up at once, nice and clean, leaving a big open space of ash-covered ground. When the ashes cool, they plant the corn, and hopefully, the rain falls immediately afterwards. The ideal situation is for them to set fire when the first rain clouds are visible on the horizon. That way their crop gets a head start on the weeds. If all goes well, the corn is harvested by the end of the *mauga* season in August."

"So then the next year they already have a piece of cleared land, right?" said Alexis.

"Wrong. That's the problem," Betty said, pleased to have an audience and the opportunity to elicit a little drama. "You see, the big trees aren't going to grow back. The only thing that happens is a secondary growth of weeds they call *wamill*. They can't deal with it just using a machete; weeds are too soft to chop. What the locals need is a tractor, which they don't have. Or herbicides, which they can't afford."

Horrified, she began to get the big picture. "So, you mean they..."

"Yep. They cut down a whole new piece of virgin high bush every year. When you figure that every single *milpaléro* does this every year, you have a country whose forest is rapidly disappearing."

"That's terrible!" Alexis exclaimed. "Can't it be stopped?"

"The Mayas have been doing it for thousands of years. And the politicians want them to do it; they consider it progress. The practice of 'slash and burn' is not going to stop in a couple of decades just because a few *gringos* tell them it's a bad idea."

"But in a couple of decades the forest will be gone!" Alexis protested.

"You know that and I know that, but the locals can't see the big picture. One of the best things we can do as Americans is to educate them before they screw up their own country. At least the population here in the west is still pretty low, but if the refugees from Guatemala keep entering the country illegally, the problem will get a whole lot worse." She paused for a moment. "But that's the dry. You want to know about the wet season?"

Alexis was shaken. "I don't know," she said nervously. "Do I?"

"If you're going to be here, it's better to know what to expect," said Betty, now fully enjoying the effect of her diatribe. "When the rains first begin, the ground is so dry it sucks up everything. But when it reaches the saturation point, there's simply no place for the water to go. The roads turn into rivers of mud and the creeks flood so badly that sometimes people aren't able to get to town for weeks."

"Is that why so many houses are up on stilts?" asked Alexis. "Because of the mud?"

"Well, that and other things. Being high up keeps your house cool in the dry season because you catch more breeze. In the wet season it keeps you out of the mud, but it also prevents most of the critters from crawling through your house."

"Critters?" said Alexis, not sure if she could take anymore. "Like what?"

"Mostly snakes and tarantulas. But pretty much anything can get in your house if it's on the ground. Of course, having your house on stilts won't prevent cockroaches and scorpions. And for sure it won't stop the army ants, although it might take them longer to get there. Do you know what army ants are?""

"No, but I have the feeling you're going to tell me."

"Ahh, they're not so bad. They're actually good because they clean all the other bugs out of your house. Army ants come by the millions when they're on the move. They cover the ground like a living black carpet. Whether your house is on the ground, or on stilts, they march right through, eating all the cockroaches and scorpions."

It was not a pleasant visual. "They only eat the bugs?"

"Yep. Natural exterminators. They don't even bite unless you step on them and get them pissed off. The best thing to do is just leave your house for a couple of hours and let them do their thing. They're harmless."

"Harmless. Uh-huh."

"The rainy season has other drawbacks too," Betty continued. "When you hang your wash on the line, it might keep raining for days, and then there's no way to get your clothes dry. There's so much humidity inside the house that your sheets and towels start to grow mildew sitting right there, folded on the shelf."

"It's a wonder you don't start growing a fungus on your skin," Alexis joked.

"Oh, you do," said Betty, triumphantly. "I have some right here on my stomach. Here, want to see?" she said, pulling up her shirt.

"No! Geez, that's gross."

"You'll get used to it. But there's an upside to the rainy season too. The new growth comes out and the look of the bush changes. Instead of being dry and brittle, it gets full and lush again. In June, the trees and plants bloom in the most gorgeous colors. There are beautiful rainbows, and wild animals, and huge psychedelic-blue butterflies with eight-inch wingspans..."

* * * *

Within the first ten days of March, the heat intensified in quantum leaps. The sun burned down fiercely; the air felt like a blast furnace. In spite of adverse growing conditions, Max and Alexis planted tomato and green pepper seeds in peat pots in the shade on the front porch and watered them three times daily. Their hope was to nurse the seedlings through the dry season and get them into the ground in June when the rains broke. With luck on their side, they would have tomatoes when no one else did, securing them a premium price at the market. The new water pump Max had purchased was making all the difference, and they were relieved to know that their water supply from the river would now be dependable, no matter how long the dry might last.

In the weeks that followed, Alexis and Max met more newly-arrived Americans at the Saturday morning market. Three couples, Tim and Maggie, Eric and Sheila, and Joel and Kirsten, had combined their financial resources to purchase a fertile tract of land tucked away in Baron's Creek Valley, about four miles south of Len and Betty. For the time being, they were all living in a single communal dwelling while their houses were being built out on the flat, just east of the little river that flowed alongside the sheer rock wall on the western side.

According to Maggie Davis, the southern end of the valley narrowed abruptly, marking the end of all human habitation, becoming a steep gorge of virtually impenetrable forest where even the bravest of *chicléros*, or *chiclé* gatherers, did not go. Rising into the undisturbed highlands where jaguars reigned supreme, the jungle abounded with deer and wild pig and other exotic-sounding tropical fauna such as: *peccary, tapir, kinkajou, agouti, coatimundi*, and *paca*. Boa constrictors, black-tails, coral snakes, and deadly fer-de-lance all slithered through the fragrant leaf mold of the forest floor, while great white falcons, king vultures, owls, toucans, and scarlet macaws flew in the upper reaches of the high canopy. Max and Alexis were intrigued, so when Maggie invited them to visit the valley, they accepted happily.

That night the four couples, and baby Jordan, sat together in the little communal house made of wood and thatch while the crickets and howler monkeys sang their evening song. The floor was raised about three feet off the ground and the thatch extended into an extra-long overhang to compensate for the fact that there were no walls. And other than a few hammocks and the single rough-hewn table of heavy mahogany around which they gathered, there were no chairs or couches, but comfort was not an issue. Laughing with their new-found friends, and passing a joint and a bottle of rum, Max and Alexis had at last found what they sought: like-minded people, other young expatriated Americans who had been prompted by the very same forces to seek the alternate lifestyle of a Belizean homestead.

"Tomorrow I'll take you to the water cave near my house site," Eric said, as he readjusted the bandanna lower on his forehead. "The cave's enormous, and Baron's Creek itself, which is really a substantial river, flows right out of the face of the mountain creating a huge blue-green pool called *Nohoch Sayab*. It means Big Spring in Mayan."

"Wow," said Max, impressed. "Can you swim up inside the cave?"

"Oh yeah, you bet," said Eric "The pool is cold though, and once you get around a couple of big rocks at the mouth and up into the cave itself, the water gets even colder. It's really dark too, until your eyes adjust. Then you can start to make out the details of this enormous chamber. The ceiling is vaulted like a cathedral; it must be a hundred and twenty feet high in there, at least. And there are huge stalactites everywhere, twenty or thirty feet long, and big rounded stalagmites underneath. The colors are beautiful too; all the formations are stained orange and green and brown with mineral deposits and molds."

"Sounds pretty intimidating," said Alexis.

"It is. But so spectacular," Kirsten said. "You can feel that the place doesn't quite belong to mankind. You can see river otter tracks on the bank and there's a heavy animal-smell, a musky, wild odor – like it belongs to them, and we're the intruders."

Joel agreed. "I swear you can feel the presence of the ancient Maya. It's...," he hesitated, "a feeling of holiness."

"I've got a cave story for you," Maggie said, "You'll like this one."

Alexis picked up Jordan and moved to the hammock where she stretched out and got comfortable. Baring her breast so he could nurse, she settled back to listen.

"Tim and I arrived here in the valley before Eric and Sheila, and Joel and Kirsten. It was dry season then, and the water was low. We thought it would be fun to build a house on twenty-foot stilts on the west bank, up against the cliffs, rather than out on the flat – almost like a tree house. But six weeks after completion, the rains broke unexpectedly, and then one night in early June it rained like hell for hours, big fat raindrops – like bullets. The noise of the roaring river woke us. It was directly beneath us."

"It was nerve-racking," emphasized Tim, "and terrifying, especially when I looked out with a flashlight and saw the white turbulent water halfway up the stilts. The force of it was pushing at the whole structure."

"We knew there wasn't much time," Maggie continued. "Twenty minutes later the river was only about thirty-six inches below the floorboards. We knew the whole house was going to collapse; we could feel it swaying," said Maggie. "It was time to bail out."

"Bail out where? How on earth did you get to safety?" Max demanded.

"We pried a long board off the veranda and crossed the gap between the house and the cliff. Then we literally `walked the plank' on our hands and knees and escaped up the side of the mountain. Five minutes later, the whole house was swept away. We spent the night in a cave. Hey – it came down to survival," Maggie laughed. "Anyway, when the water receded there was nothing left. Luckily, all these guys," she gestured, "had arrived by then, and that's how we all ended up living together, or at least until we have our own places finished. But you've probably been here long enough to have heard some 'dumb *gringo*' stories, right? Because if you haven't, you've just heard your first!"

During their visit, Eric had mentioned to Max that on the following Saturday there would be an auction over at the Mennonite settlement of Spanish Lookout, which was a few miles east of San Ignacio and north on the other side of the River Belize. Now, as he rested in the hammock back at Michael's house, Max proposed that he and Alexis they should go.

"Besides some household items, they're going to have Nubian goats for sale," said Max. "It would be great to have milk, especially for Jordan. That is, if you ever decide to actually wean him."

Alexis brought him a cup of tea, and stood beside the hammock with a neutral expression. It was hard to tell if he was making an attempt at humor, or simply needling her again.

"We could breed the nannies to Mrs. Whitmore's ram, keep the female kids, and sell the little billies for meat. I understand the Jamaicans in Cayo love curried goat."

"That would be your call. I don't know anything about goats, except the way your clothes smelled when we first met in Santa Cruz," she replied, trying to encourage the humor.

"You can learn," Max said crossly. "I end up teaching you everything anyway,"

"What do you mean by that?" Yep, she thought, he was being malicious again.

"Well, I had to teach you how to cook, and how to make a proper cup of tea. I'm teaching you how to care for tomato and pepper seedlings, so I guess you can learn how to milk goats too." Incredulously, Alexis walked away without a word. What had she done this time?

There were three separate sects of Mennonites living in Belize, and each group was easily distinguishable by their style of dress and transportation. The colony downstream from the Americans in lower Baron's Creek Valley was the most conservative; they wore simple homemade clothing; the men used buttons rather than zippers, and the women wore full bonnets that hid their faces, and long gray dresses covering them from wrists to ankles. Trips to town were arduous, using the traditional horses and wagon, or buggies, with iron wheels. Another sect wore modified clothing, the bonnets exposed more of the women's faces, dresses were mid-calf, and the wagons had pneumatic rubber tires. The colony at Spanish Lookout was the most advanced; even certain technologies were acceptable. The men drove tractors and trucks, dressed in jeans and plaid shirts, and wore baseball caps or cowboy hats. The women wore short-sleeved print cotton dresses hemmed just below the knee, and little white scarves tied behind their heads and tucked behind their ears. Of course, they still wore no makeup or jewelry.

As it turned out, getting to Spanish Lookout that day was an adventure in itself, as it necessitated the use of an ancient hand-cranked craft to take them over the river. Capable of carrying only two vehicles at a time, the ferry was tethered to a heavy braided steel cable stretching from one bank to the other with a single loop wrapped around a large drum, securely mounted to the ferry. Attached to the axle going through the drum was a welded rotating handle, and they stood watching in disbelief as an old man turned the manual crank to carry the ferry across the water. It was hard to believe that anything so old could even exist in the modern day world, let alone be functional.

"It's a museum piece," said Max, "and it looks like that guy's only job in life is to crank it back and forth across the river all day. I wonder why it's manned; it wouldn't take anything at all to put an electric motor on it."

Once on the other side, it was easy to see by the shops and farms that the Mennonites at Spanish Lookout were naturally industrious. The clapboard houses were neat and clean with well-kept yards and flower gardens. Irrigated fields of corn and sorghum thrived in long straight furrows. There was a dairy, a hatchery, and a chicken processing plant, as well as a gas station, an auto parts store, a welding shop, and a general store.

"It looks like Pennsylvania with palm trees," said Alexis.

By noon, Max and Alexis had purchased a large washtub, a corrugated glass washboard, some half-gallon Mason jars with glass lids and wire clamps, some Tupperware, four cans of thirty-weight oil, and two female Nubian goats whose previous owners had named them to match their personalities. Fine-goat was sweet and well-mannered with a quiet disposition. From all indications, Space-goat seemed to be the stereotypical irascible goat with an attitude problem. Both had the long droopy ears and huge udders for which Nubians are known. Fine-goat was said to be a particularly good producer, yielding over a gallon a day when she freshened. Both nannies were already pregnant, and since goats usually give birth to twins, Max figured the purchase guaranteed an instant herd.

Getting the goats back to Michael's property had been no easy task, and a month later Alexis was still not doing well at the not-so-gentle-art of goat-milking. Both nannies had given birth since the purchase and were newly freshened. Space-goat bleated and stomped the ground and turned with a baleful look in her eye.

"Hold still, you bitch," Alexis yelled. Grabbing her udder again, the nanny lashed out and knocked over the bucket of milk, turning her head a second time and glaring triumphantly. "Now look what you've done! Of all God's creatures, I have never known a more cantankerous animal."

"What's going on down there?" Max yelled from upstairs. The goats mostly lived outside within the fenced-in property, but Max had created a straw-lined quadrant under the house especially for milking.

"Space-goat kicked over the milk again," she yelled back.

"Damn it, Alexis. Can't you do anything right? That's the third time this week. For heaven's sake, control the animal."

"This goat is making it personal. I never have trouble with Fine-goat, except that her bag is harder to squeeze. She's got the upper hand. She knows she intimidates me. No wonder they say goats are evil," Alexis muttered. "With those horns and that beard, they have the silhouette of the devil."

The goats had been nothing but trouble since day one. Originally, Max had been concerned with keeping the goats from wandering off. The problem turned out to be just the opposite; they insisted on wandering IN, wanting to be part of the family. Being fond of animals was one thing, but finding a goat in the living room was something else. With their love of climbing and natural affinity for high places, the goats had simply mounted the steep front stairway, knocked over the precious tomato and pepper seedlings on the verandah, scattering the dirt everywhere, and then walked right into the house. In that particular instance, they found Space-goat on her hind legs amidst the ruin of pots, pans, and broken dishes, with her hoofed forefeet on the kitchen counter.

Stories and jokes about goats eating anything were also well-supported by Space-goat's capricious habits. Over time, she ingested one of Jordan's baby rattles, a small Tupperware lid, several crayons, and had actually chewed on tins cans and the clothes on the line in the yard – just like in the cartoons. But a few days previous to giving birth, the situation had turned serious when Max discovered Space-goat had eaten a tube of epoxy resin. She had been due to deliver at any time. As much as Alexis disliked the goat, she didn't want her to die.

"I don't know; she doesn't look sick, but I definitely saw her grab the tube from the workbench. See?" Max said, opening the goat's mouth and pointing. "She still has paint flecks from the tube label on her tongue. Maybe we should make her throw up."

"Good idea," said Alexis. "I'll go check natural medicine book." Ten minutes later she came back with a vile-looking concoction. "It's an emetic. Warm water, salt, and mustard. I thought this old glass coke bottle might give us the best chance of getting it down her throat."

Max nodded. "Good. Okay, I'll hold her head back and you shove it in." Together they forced the foul mixture down the throat of the struggling goat. After a half hour, still nothing had happened.

"I hate to do this, but I guess I'm going to have to go see the vet at the agricultural station at Central Farm. It's time to take action. Epoxy is highly toxic. We can't afford to lose her or the kids." Fervently, they hoped that Space-goat didn't have boys. Uncharacteristically, Fine-goat had delivered triplets, except they'd all been males. Yikes! Three billy-goats-gruff.

"It's still weird that she doesn't look sick." Alexis commented.

"Yeah, but we can't take a chance. You stay with her; I'm going for the vet."

It took Max a full two hours to drive to the agricultural station and back. And yet, when he returned, he was alone. "So where's the vet?" she asked as Max got out of the truck.

"He said it was pointless to come. The goat will either live or she'll die. The emetic was a waste. Goats are ruminants; they can't throw up."

At that, Alexis broke into laughter and then Max did too. "So she's got all that stuff inside her? The kids, plus the warm water, salt, mustard, and epoxy resin? Did the vet have any advice at all?"

Now Max could hardly get the words out, "Well, he did suggest that we feed her the other tube, the epoxy catalyst, so it could just mix together and she could hopefully poop out the whole thing."

Strangely enough, Space-goat had suffered no ill effects from the epoxy glue or the intended cure, thus confirming that goats really do have cast-iron stomachs. A few days later she gave birth to a single healthy kid. Unbelievably, it had been another male. In keeping with tradition, they had named the little billy, "Scapegoat."

* * * *

On the sixth day of June, the rainy season began. What started as a gentle breeze soon became a stiff wind that blew up the river valley, flipping the leaves upside down to expose their silvery undersides, and bringing the sweet smell of ozone that signaled the coming storm. Soon the torrential rains began their assault on the hard-baked earth, and within two days everything changed. The brittle forest of dead crunchy leaves became soft and receptive. The branches of the trees relaxed, gratefully opening their arms to the sky as they drank in the life-giving moisture. The ground transformed into a sea of mud.

Green and more green. Alexis never knew there could be so many shades of green – surely God's favorite color. There were the deep blue-greens of the distant pines scattered over the peaks, and the true forest-green of the high bush. Nestled in the river valley were innumerable varieties of bushes and plants in greens of every imaginable shade: spring green, jade green, dusty olive, brilliant chartreuse, kelly green, bright lime, dark bottle green, and shining emerald.

High in the mountains, the loose soil and debris of the dry season washed from the hillsides in the onslaught of tropical rains, sliding into hundreds of small springs that divided the valleys. Springs became streams, streams merged to become the Rio On, the primary branch of the upper Macal River. Restricted by the narrow canyon, the turbulent water churned, cutting between jagged rocks and boulders. Through miles of untamed jungle, the volume of water continued to race its course. At last, the flood reached the part of river valley where the Lord family lived.

From the house, Alexis watched the level of the Macal rise steadily as the water raged. Within the course of the morning, she had seen it rise twenty-five vertical feet, spill its banks, and spread across the lower pasture to twice its usual width. She knew it was dangerous to go closer, but felt the magnetism of its power. Walking down the hill to the edge of the surging floodwaters, she listened to its roar and felt vibrations deep in the earth.

A great crashing brought her out of her reverie, and Alexis stared dumbfounded as a giant tree came floating down the river. Over a hundred and twenty feet long, its enormous root mass came downstream first, bobbing up and down in slow motion like a sea serpent, its tremendous trunk and canopy of sodden branches trailing behind in majestic counterbalance. Suddenly as the forward mass of roots bobbed downward, they caught on some unseen obstacle under the surface. Unable to be restrained in the awesome force of the flood, the tree up-ended into the air and struck an arc of one hundred and eighty degrees across the sky, literally tumbling its leviathan canopied crown over its submerged foot. Breathless, Alexis watched as the monster tree continued its journey downstream.

Due to distances, transportation, weather, and lack of communications, homesteading *gringos* rarely saw each other unless they went to town. Going to San Ignacio on Market day was usually the only sure-fire way of touching base with most of the friends they'd made. But through unique circumstances, they'd met Rick and Suzy on the river one day. He was a tall fair-haired handsome Brit who had spent much of his life in Kenya. Rick impressed Alexis as one of those endearing hard-working mad-dog-Englishmen types, who earned and enjoyed his daily gin and tonic sundowners with good humor. His wife, Suzy, was a smart spunky curly redhead, a pretty girl with a good head for business and a full-steam-ahead attitude. As it turned out, they had been lucky enough to purchase a spectacular piece of land on the other side of the river from Mrs. Whitmore. Their friend, Anita, was from Chicago. With long gypsy hair and dark warm intuitive eyes, she was an earth-mother type who had spent many years living in the wilds of one of the most remote areas of Mexico. As an herbalist and naturalist, Anita had bought an adjacent smaller parcel next to Rick and Suzy. Her plan was to study ethnobotany and natural healing with an old Maya shaman she'd heard about in the Maya Mountains. At almost eighty years old, she was anxious to absorb as much of his knowledge as she could. Otherwise, when he died, it would be like losing an irreplaceable library of information.

One Saturday in mid-August when their crop was ripe, Alexis and Max took hundreds of pounds of tomatoes to San Ignacio, where they found them in high demand. Max had been right. Tomatoes were completely out of season, and people were paying a dollar-fifty BZ per pound at that time of year. Taking a red five-dollar bill for her purchase, and making change for one of the local women, Alexis looked up to see Rick, Suzy, Anita, and Eric walking in their direction.

"Hey, you guys!" called Alexis, as the girls all took turns hugging and the men shook hands. "How's it going? Long time, no see. What are you up to today?"

"Just making the rounds, buying provisions" said Suzy. "And Anita's been on a house call with Eric."

"Why? What's up?" asked Max, looking over at him. "Are you sick?"

"Not exactly, but I do have a real problem." Eric pulled off the red bandanna and exposed a huge raw red hole in the middle of his forehead. It was an eighth of an inch deep, and nearly the size of a quarter.

"Wow, are you working on your third eye?" said Max, covering his horror with an attempt at humor. "Or did you get hit with a pickaxe?"

"Neither of the above," Eric replied. "It's some type of weird infection that I can't seem to cure. Actually, I had it the first time you came to the valley. It was just covered up." Alexis thought back to the visit with Maggie and the others. Come to think of it, she had never seen Eric without a bandanna, and remembered seeing him adjust it frequently. "The British Army doctor says it's not bacteria, or a virus, but some type of protozoa," he continued. "I remember one day when I was chopping bush and I got bit by a sand-fly. It just started out as a little dot, but the damn thing has gotten bigger and bigger. I've used every antibiotic cream and cortisone junk you've ever heard of. Nothing seems to help. Now the doctor has scheduled me for regular heavy metal injections, shooting right into the rim of the sore itself."

"And I'm trying to help him avoid it," said Anita. "I've been searching my pharmacopoeia for natural cures, but haven't found anything yet. So I'm going up to San Antonio village sometime over the next few days to see if I can find this old shaman, the venerable Don Elijio. Maybe he will have some suggestions."

"I hope you can find something," said Eric, earnestly, "because I sure as hell am not looking forward to the British Army alternative." Just then, Sheila pulled up in the jeep to pick up Eric. "Well, that's my ride; I got to go."

"Take it easy," said Alexis. "Say hi to the rest of the gang for us."

As Eric got into the vehicle, Max said to Rick, "Did you see the size of that thing? There's one good reason why I wouldn't choose Baron's Creek to buy property: protozoa infection-bearing sand-flies. I know there used to be yellow fever in Belize, and I hear there are still cases of malaria from time to time. I'd just as soon live by the Macal River. Good drainage and reliable water. I sure hope Michael wants to sell."

"My feelings exactly, Max," Rick replied. "But don't hold your breath. We tried to buy that piece before old Jake Gardener sold us this one. Renting it is one thing, but I guarantee Michael won't budge and neither will Mrs. Whitmore. How about a beer, old boy?"

"You go ahead with Rick," offered Alexis. "I'll stay here and sell the veggies."

"Okay, thanks, *Ntombi*," said Max. "I'll take Jordan, so you can use both hands. See you in a few."

When he returned with the baby forty-five minutes later, Max saw Alexis speaking with a big strapping Spanish boy who was picking out tomatoes. As the handsome young man left with his purchase, she could see her husband's anger written all over his face.

"Who is that guy you were talking to?" he demanded.

"I don't know," she said. "I think he's one of Rick's workers. I don't even know his name."

"Well, stay away from him. You don't need to be hanging out with these Spanish guys."

Max was in a mood; she could feel it coming on, so for the rest of the day, Alexis remained quiet but tense. As much as possible, she gave Max a wide berth, and answered his questions without offering anything extra, trying to avoid any remarks that might be deemed controversial. But still, a feeling of foreboding came over her as they rode home together in the truck. Max was somber and she could feel profound fear creeping into her consciousness. As they pulled in the rear of Michael's property, and got out of the truck, Max started again with his verbal invective. As she carried Jordan up the back steps, she made the mistake of defending herself.

"I just think I should be able to carry on a conversation with whomever I want. It's not like I see other people very often. It gets lonely up in the bush. What's wrong with a little social time in Cayo on a Saturday? You had a beer with Rick."

"And who were you spending time with when I was in Guatemala buying the water pump? Some other little Spanish boy? Or perhaps that same one? If he works for Rick and Suzy, it's only a short ride across the river and downstream."

"You're being absurd. We didn't even know Rick and Suzy yet."

"Stop arguing with me, okay?" Max shouted. "You listen to me. I call the shots in this relationship and I don't want you associating with guys like that. End of discussion. Now just shut the fuck up."

Alexis shook her head, close to tears. She put the sleeping baby in his shortened hammock and set the stick to hold it open. Then she went back into the kitchen to put away the provisions they'd bought.

"Oh no," she said aloud. Things had just gotten worse.

"What's the matter now?"

"I forgot the box of provisions in town. I had the girl in the store box them up for me, and I forgot to pick them up on the way home."

"You dumb-ass!" Max said angrily. "I can't believe this. I have the responsibilities of running our whole show and you can't even remember to bring home the groceries. Now we're going to have to go all the way back into town tomorrow. That's half a day's work, plus gas and wear and tear on the truck. None of the dories run on Sundays. Hell, you'll be lucky to get the proprietor to open his store so we can get the stuff."

"I'm sorry, Max. It was a simple mistake."

"Right. 'Simple' being the operative word here. How the hell you gave birth, I'll never know. You're not mature enough to be anybody's mother. You still need a mother yourself, someone to wipe your nose for you."

Alexis burned at the insults. "I said I'm sorry."

"Words are cheap. Now fix me some dinner."

Without the groceries, there wasn't much of a selection. One thing that had been especially difficult for Alexis was to learn to prepare local foods, a situation made more difficult because many were best prepared by frying. Max preferred steamed or baked food; Alexis had a stove but no oven. She missed foods like cheese and apples, and yearned for crackers, yogurt, and whole wheat bread. Face it, she thought. All she could fix tonight would be a little leftover beans, some steamed plantain, and maybe fried eggplant. She hoped it would be adequate because that was all they had. Nightfall came quickly in the tropics, and Alexis constantly fought with the kerosene lamps. They were dim and temperamental. She was already emotional, and could barely see what she was cooking. At last the meal was ready.

"Here's your dinner," Alexis called as she put the food out. "I'm putting it on the table. Please eat it while it's still hot."

Max walked over and sat down. "Aren't you having any?"

"No. I'm not hungry. I'm just tired. I think I'll go to bed."

She had been in the bedroom less than one minute when she heard the crash of the plate and Max's cursing. He stormed in and tore her out of bed, hauling her into the living room by the arm. "What do you mean by putting that crap in front of me?"

"Shhh, not so loud," she said, terrified. "You'll wake the baby."

"I don't care if I wake the whole goddamn river valley," he screamed. "What's the big idea of putting that pig slop on my plate? Do you really expect me to eat that? You sure as hell aren't having any."

"I don't like eggplant. I thought you did. I'm sorry."

"Sorry!" he screamed in rage. "I've heard sorry out of you a few too many times lately. This time you're going to learn sorry."

Instantaneously, he cracked Alexis on the side of the face. She screamed and backed away from him as he grabbed her by the shoulders and shoved her against the wall. He crushed her nose sideways with his finger and cursed her again.

"You've had this coming for a long time, you uppity little bitch."

Then he drove her head against the corner of the exposed beam and she collapsed, feeling the warm blood trickle down the back of her neck.

"Stop! Please don't hurt me," she cried.

"You fuckin' bitch! What about your smart mouth? All the times you've hurt me? How about all the times you humiliated me in public? Associating with people you have no business hanging out with? How about when you flirted with that jerk with the big dick on the day before our wedding? Huh? Go on. Answer me. You always have an answer for everything. Well, this time you can scream and cry all you want. There's nobody to hear you and nobody to help. It's about time I taught you a little respect. Now get your ass up."

Max lifted her to her feet and she felt another powerful punch to her upper arm. No longer coherent, blood dribbled down her chin from the split in her lip. She could hear the baby crying, and felt a last hard kick to her thigh before dropping to the floor for a second time.

"I brought you some tea."

Alexis tried to open her eyes, but one of them was swollen shut. Her head ached unbearably as the morning sunshine came through the open windows of the bedroom. As she tried to speak, the blood began to seep from her cracked lower lip.

"Why the hell did you make me do that to you?" Max asked.

She didn't answer, but tried to sit up without success. Her left arm and leg were huge and swollen black and blue. Jordan sat on the bed looking at his mother. Now sixteen months old, he was too young to know what had happened, but could sense something was wrong. He crawled over to his mother, lifted her shirt and began to nurse. She cried in pain as he bumped her arm. Finally Max arranged some pillows to support the baby's weight.

"You shouldn't make me that angry, *Ntombi*. I don't like to hurt you."

"What do you want me to do?" Alexis mumbled through puffy lips. "Tell you I'm sorry again? Apologize for pissing you off?"

"I don't know," he said, contrite at last. "You make me crazy sometimes. I don't know why or how, but you always manage to push my buttons."

"I don't want to push your buttons," she mumbled in pain. "Maybe you can help me recognize what they are in advance so I don't do it."

* * * *

Alexis kept her thoughts to herself as they got in the truck to go to Belize City. Max got in the driver's seat. He squeezed her knee and smiled.

"Boy, it's really a beautiful day, isn't it, *Ntombi*? The mud's drying up; the sun's out. Tell you what. As a special treat I'll take you to a nice restaurant today. Would you like that?"

"Sure, that would be great," she replied in a monotone. In her private mindset, she found his cheerfulness was as oppressive as his anger.

"You're not still mad at me? That was two weeks ago."

"No," she lied. Unbelievable, she thought to herself. He is still seeking my approval.

Her mind drifted back to earlier that morning when they'd had sex; it couldn't be called lovemaking. He never tried to pleasure her sexually, and she no longer cared. She hated his touch, the sound of his voice as he grunted and sweated on top of her like a pig; she hated the look on his face when he reached climax. Sex was now nothing more than submission. It was something she endured because she had no choice.

Anyway, none of it mattered anymore. The cruelty, the jibes, the constant badgering – they had all taken their toll. Alexis didn't want to leave Belize; the land was beautiful; she would miss the jungle and the new friends she'd made, but it was over. I'm out of here, she thought. I can't live like this any more. She focused on her plans; today she would make her escape. She intended on inventing some excuse to stay in the van while Max went to make purchases. Then she'd take Jordan to the airline ticket office and grab a fast taxi to the airport. Hopefully, they'd be out of Belize before Max had time to track them down.

In the end, the attempt proved to be a miserable failure. As Alexis had gathered a small bag of clothes and diapers from the van, Max returned unexpectedly and confronted her. She sought the help of a policeman passing by, but he refused to interfere when he discovered it was merely a domestic squabble.

"It's okay, Officer. My wife has just been under a lot of stress lately. I'll take care of her." As the policeman left, Max turned to Alexis with a clenched fist and steely eyes. "What is the meaning of this?"

"I'm afraid to live with you anymore," she cried. "I don't want to go back into the bush and be alone with you."

"You're married to me. You made a commitment to live with me for a lifetime. We've bonded. That's my son you have there." His face was terrifying as he hovered over her.

"Maybe we never should have had a child. You don't like my mothering. You don't like my – anything. Nothing I do is ever good enough. You say you love me, but you don't even like me. You told me you fell in love with me because I was vivacious and spirited, and you've condemned me for the same qualities ever since. Now you spend every ounce of energy trying to change me into someone else. What is it you really want from me, Max?"

"I want a woman who will be a credit to me, a good mother for my children, a dutiful wife who will grace my side like a lady. What do you want?"

"I want you to be kind to me," she cried. "I want you to treat me like a person who has merit and worth, whose thoughts and feelings are valid. I want a man I can love and respect."

"I knew it," Max said triumphantly. "You don't respect me!"

"Respect and fear are two different emotions. A husband should be a supporter, a defender. It's not right for a woman to fear her husband."

"And it's not right for you to humiliate your husband in public," he interrupted.

"You asked me a question," she said, vehemently. "Now you won't even let me answer. I want to respect you without having to be afraid of you. I want to be the gracious woman you're talking about. I want to be a good partner, to share life's experiences, and still take time to smell the roses."

"Let's get something to eat." Max seemed to be relaxing a little. "Then we'll get out of the city and go home. You don't need to be afraid. We'll talk some more once we get back, and we'll work it out. I promise."

That night, back at the house on the river, Max embraced Alexis as they lay in bed together. He caressed her body gently and then ran his hand up to the hollow of her neck. Without warning, he tightened his grip around her neck, cutting off her air supply. She tore at his hand, fighting for breath.

"That's twice you've tried to walk out on me, once on Owen's farm, and now again here in Belize. So you listen and listen well. If you ever do leave me, you'll go alone. No baby. Do you understand? Absolutely alone. And if you ever try to take my child away from me again, I'll fucking kill you."

EMOYENI

chapter 9

For seventy years, Joshua Harrison had paddled up-river in his dory. His patience was that of the river itself. In the treacherous shallows he would navigate with a pole, and as he passed through the clear emerald eddies, he would deftly switch to his paddle in one fluid movement. At the age of seventy-six, the old black man was well-acquainted with both joy and pain. Life was always hard, but sweet, and with patience all things eventually came to pass. This year his bumper crop of watermelons had ripened, crisp and sweet, at the very peak of perfection, and had yielded him more money than any other season in his memory. So, Joshua had rewarded himself by investing in a little five-horsepower outboard motor.

Now, with a battered straw hat pulled low over his brow, old Joshua steered upstream in the old mahogany dory, staring into the deep green river. Although his eyes were rheumy, he could still make out the shape of the large tarpon as it glided beneath him. They had much in common. The tarpon had swum upstream from the sea for over a hundred miles, and like Joshua, it had fought the current every step of the way in the failing strength of old age. Soon the fish would spawn in the fresh mountain water; then it would die. But for Joshua, things would be easier now. His callused black hand was steady on the rudder as he listened contentedly to the hum of the machine.

Joshua could not know that he was destined to outlive his outboard motor. Twelve years would pass, the machine would die, crops would fail, and he would find himself paddling upstream once again. But even then, the old man would never complain, or give any thought to the irony. He was a river man, not a philosopher.

As much as Max and Alexis begged Mrs. Whitmore, she refused to sell them Michael's land, just as Rick had said. It was 1977, Chinese Year of the Snake, and the smart old woman knew that in a few more years the riverfront piece would have a tremendous resale value. She would bide her time and wait for bigger profits.

The couple looked for other properties along the river but came across the same situation over and over. Typically, land was owned by a Belizean family that had been divided among perhaps a dozen children after the parents' death. In most cases it was impossible to track down all the brothers and sisters, especially since more than half of them might be living in Houston or Los Angeles. And even if all family members could be accounted for, there were always one or two siblings who didn't want to sell.

The new generation of Belizeans identified themselves as either bush-people or town-people. Bush-people stayed on the land, grew their own food, and stayed out of trouble. Their lives were simple, but there was always fresh food and open air. However, most of the younger crowd preferred to live in town where the action was, even if the action meant nothing more than getting drunk on a bottle of One Barrel Rum at the Blue Angels Disco Club on a Saturday night. And neither the bush-people nor the town-people could understand the desire of the crazy *gringos* to buy a piece of land that was *back-a-bush*.

One Saturday evening, Max returned from a solo trip to the market with some astounding news. Joshua Harrison's son, Renaldo, wanted to sell his forty acres. Reynaldo was nearly sixty years old himself and he had little interest in the place, nor did any of his children or grandchildren. They all thought the place was too far upstream from Cayo.

"Of course, it's not prime land," Max told Alexis, as they sat on the front verandah facing the river. "It's high and rocky and the frontage is steep, but it is on the river. It's a couple of miles further south, upstream, past Mrs. Whitmore's land, and just opposite the Del Fuego property. I asked Reynaldo what he wanted for it. He said three thousand Belizean dollars, but I think he'd take a few hundred less."

Alexis' eyes grew wide. "Really? Are we going to go look at it?" she asked excitedly.

"You bet," he said sincerely. Max was a happy guy. "I have to repair the tie-rod ends on the Land Cruiser. Then we could go tomorrow before it gets too hot."

Max had sold the old '59 Ford step-van to a Mexican potato chip vendor in a comical transaction. As in many third world countries, Belizean currency came in different colors, depending upon the denomination. The one-dollar bills were green, the twos were purple, the fives were red, the tens were black, and the twenties were brown, and there weren't any more. That was it. No fifties, no hundreds. So when the van sold for cash, the stack of twenties on the table was several inches high. Alexis joked that perhaps they could have just measured it with a ruler instead of counting it.

Getting a ride to Spanish Lookout that same day, Max had purchased a Toyota Land Cruiser with a partial body from the same Mennonite who owned the junkyard. The transmission had four speeds, plus a high and low range. With his help, the two created a hodgepodge body out of several other junked Land Cruisers on the lot. The resultant vehicle was a mish-mash of lime green quarter-panels and white doors. There was no windshield, but it didn't matter much since the vehicle had no roof. After a bit more scrounging, the two men came up with an ill-fitting fiberglass white shell top with a scratched plastic windshield which they bolted onto the body. With luck, it might keep out some of the rain. Unfortunately, the alternator was non-functional, but Max came up with the simple solution – routinely parking it on top of a small Mayan mound on Michael's property, and jump-starting it on the way down. Max figured he'd put big knobbly mud tires on it, and, with the right person driving, it would be a real tortoise in the mud. As it turned out, the machine's durability would only be surpassed by the burning heat through the floorboards, the noxious fumes from the broken manifold, and the irritating clap-banging of the bolted-on roof and mismatched body panels.

As they drove south on the *Cristo Rey* Road toward Reynaldo's property, Alexis sat in the truck, lurching in the heat with the heavy baby on her lap, wondering again where her life was going. Max had been calmer in recent months, but she'd learned to always be careful. His temper was unpredictable and she never knew what small thing might set him off again. Sometimes he was affectionate, even sweet, but it never paid to let her hair down – not anymore. Walking on eggs had become part of her lifestyle. Suddenly, Jordan struggled to stand in her lap, and pointed vigorously out the window. "Moo cows?" he said.

"Yes, Jordan, those are cows," said Alexis. "See the big moo-cows?"

The toddler stared at the animals again, and mimicked his mother.

"Moo," he repeated, smiling. "Moo cows."

"Here we are," Max said a few minutes later as he pulled over to the side of the road. "This is where the driveway will be if we buy the place. But for now, we'll park here and walk in." He lifted Jordan into the baby backpack and hoisted it on Alexis' back. "Be sure to watch where you're walking. Keep your eyes open."

Although it was not high bush, the *wamill* had grown to a height of eight to ten feet. This was no tame pasture surrounded by predictable fencing and routinely trampled by cows. Max made as much noise as possible and whistled as he swung the machete right and left, an old Zulu practice designed to scare away anything that might be lurking in the underbrush. Alexis expected to break into a clearing surrounding the house itself, but there was no clearing; the grasses had swallowed it. All of a sudden the house was there in front of Max's machete.

"Not much from the outside, is it?" said Alexis, in a carefully controlled tone.

It was obvious that the shack had been abandoned for years. It was a simple rectangular house, twenty-six by sixteen feet, with two windows on each of the four sides. The structure was raised a few feet off the ground on crude concrete pilings. The cedar siding was an ugly sun-bleached gray, and paper wasps had made a dozen nests under the eaves. Old tin cans, boards, plastics, broken glass, and other assorted trash lay everywhere. Max kept chopping until they reached the three stair front entry. One wooden step was missing and the others sagged forlornly. Only the view was spectacular. Max was trying not to cringe.

"Okay, let's go inside. Maybe it won't be so bad."

It was bad. In fact, the inside was a horror show. Separating the living room and kitchen area from the rest of the house, the press-board partitions created two more rooms. But, like the rest of the walls, they were covered by a chalky white dust. Several windows were broken, and an acrid odor filled the house. A huge hairy tarantula, as big as a salad plate, lay dead on the floor amidst the shattered glass.

"Not much from the inside either. What is all this white stuff everywhere? It stinks like some kind of chemical." Carefully, Max walked around the room and extended the machete to poke gingerly behind the door. A small document gave him the answer.

"Oh shit," said Max. "The *Aedes Egypti* Eradication Service. That's DDT on the walls."

"Poison!" Alexis cried. "We left the States to avoid chemical pollution and then we end up in a room of wall-to-wall DDT? That's it. Let's get Jordan out of here."

Max agreed instantly. "I'm right behind you."

Once outside, she shivered in spite of the heat. "That was horrible. Are we going back to the truck now?"

"Not yet. I still want to check out the river frontage. If it's more than eighty feet to the water, we'll have to get a piston pump. The centrifugal pump would be useless if the gradient's too steep."

"You're still considering buying this dump?" Inside, Alexis was screaming. Outside, she was barely in control. "You can't be serious."

"We've got to get our money invested somewhere. We can't just keep spending it on rent. We could pay somebody to scrub this place clean, fix it up, and put in some plants. But water is the crucial issue. I've got to check out how close the river is. Are you going to come with me or stay here?" It wasn't much of a choice. Alexis could stand here with the baby in the hot sun, wait in the house with the DDT, sit in the hot smelly truck, or go with Max and cool off in the river. She went with Max.

Finding the river was easier said than done. There was no established route to the bottom. Max spotted a faint passage that animals used and began to blaze a trail with his machete, following the path of least resistance. Throughout the year they'd been in Belize, Alexis had gotten much stronger physically, but now she struggled to maintain a foothold on the rugged terrain with the baby on her back. Unlike the flat on top of the hill, the slope to the river was not *wamill* grass, but dense tropical vegetation.

"There's the water," Max said suddenly. The jungle was so thick they could not proceed any further anyway, but it was close enough for Max to do his calculations. "See it sparkling through the trees down there? Looks like a little beach there too. Boy, this is some hill all right. It must be four hundred feet of distance and a two hundred foot head – three times the height and distance of Michael's place."

"Can the water even be pumped that far?" asked Alexis.

"With a positive displacement piston pump it can. Here's the high water line. It doesn't look like the floods ever go above this point. This is where we would put the storage shed for the pump and the outboard motor."

"The outboard motor…?"

"If we live on the river, we'd have to have a dory," Max said.

"So let me get this straight. You're saying that you'd mount the pump way up here on the hillside? And the suction hose would work from fifty feet away?"

"No, we'll store the pump up here fifty feet away when it's not in use. Then I'll throw a small cement slab at the river's edge and set upright bolts into it. We'll carry the pump down the hill whenever we need water, bolt it in place, pump the water, and then carry it back to the pump house."

"You're talking as though we've already bought the place."

"Maybe I already have."

Alexis sighed. She hadn't really expected him to say anything else.

The capital of Belmopan was a long ride from back-a-bush, yet Minister Moran didn't even have the courtesy to look at the young people. He continued to hold the newspaper in front of his face while he spoke.

"So you want to buy a piece of land?" he said. "Tell me, what interest do you really have in Belize? Americans come here for only two reasons – either you want to grow marijuana, or you're land speculators."

"With all due respect, we don't have any interest in either one," said Max. "We just want to live here and have a little place to call our own."

The Minister put down the paper and leaned across the table, looking at them for the first time.

"I don't believe that for one red-hot minute. Let me tell you something. I'm not like these local buffoons in Public Offices. People don't come to Belize just to eat mangoes. So, here's your answer. I haven't decided yet. Maybe I will give you the land permit, and maybe I won't. Just remember that we Belizeans can do whatever we want here. You cannot."

"I assure you–" Alexis began.

"You may go now," he interrupted. "Come back in ten days. I'll give you my answer at that time." Max could barely wait to get out of earshot to make his comment.

"What an officious asshole," he said, as they walked back to the truck. "This is our third trip to Belmopan and they're still giving us a hard time."

Alexis agreed emphatically. "We've done everything they've told us to do: fingerprints, police records, putting up a bond, green card, work permit, Belizean sponsor, and the five-year development plan. What more do they want? Every time, it's 'come back next week.'"

"If the stupid phones worked in this country maybe we could just call the jerk to see if he's made up his mind yet. This Alien Landholding Act stuff is pure crap."

On the way home, Alexis had a brainstorm.

"Max, you know what? I'm going to write a song and sing it for that idiotic minister. I'll write about our attempt to buy the land and I'll sing it in Creole. Either this guy will think we're crazy and kick us out, or he'll think we're crazy and we fit right in. Either way, at least it will be over and we'll be able to get on with our lives."

At first Max was skeptical, but the more he thought about it, the more he supported her idea. No time like the present, she thought, pulling out a pen and paper. She began to write, pausing from time to time to ask him a question or two. "When we went south and checked out Punta Gorda, didn't we hear people calling it by its initials?"

"Yeah, they just call it P.G.," Max replied.

"Good. Okay. And what's the prime minister's name?"

"George Price." By the time they were home, Alexis' song was complete.

Ten days later they made what they hoped would be the final trip to the capital. True to her word, she took along Max's old guitar.

"You're going to play a song for me?" Minister Moran asked, looking uncomfortable.

"Yes, I am," Alexis answered, "and it's in Creole too."

"*Yu know fu talk Creole*? Well you're going to have to play it for Mr. Archibald. I will get him for you. I have to...uh...get a drink of water." Quickly, he ushered Alexis into the office next door.

"Neville! Come here. I want you to listen to the lady's song."

Out in the hall, Max sat on the bench, shaking his head in amazement. Meanwhile many officials became curious. Even Minister Moran returned after his supposed trip to the drinking fountain, and sat inside his office. He was clearly not comfortable. Meanwhile, Neville Archibald was loving the spectacle. Alexis had drawn quite a crowd.

> *Oh Belmopan, Belmopan,*
> *Seems like yu no help us, but we know yu can.*
> *We just lookin fu, one small helpin' hand,*
> *We just wan to buy, one lee piece of land.*

We look in El Cayo, we look in P.G.
Border de Guatemala to de edge of de sea.
No mind steep or rocky, or full lone high trees,
We just wan to buy one lee piece of Belize.

Do farmin in de daytime, play music all night,
We won do anything now, that yu wouldn like.
And only yu can help to rescue us from our plight,
We wan peace and love, mon, we don wan to fight.

And then if we get it, it will be so nice...
We'll say thank yu, Mr. Moran, thank yu, Mr. Price.

Without exception, everyone in the hallway broke into a round of applause and Alexis bowed graciously. She beamed at the minister until even he had to laugh. Ten minutes later Minister Moran presented the couple with the permit to buy the land, and two days later they purchased the property from Renaldo Harrison for twenty-seven hundred BZ. Max named it *Emoyeni,* Zulu for "place of the wind."

The Year of the Horse would be grueling. Even before Max and Alexis could move in, certain things had to be done to make *Emoyeni* livable. First, the area had to be reclaimed from the tall grasses. Four hired hands from Cayo came to the farm, and under Max's direction, they widened the path to the river and hauled water up the hill by hand in five-gallon buckets. Heating the water in a large vat over an open fire, Max added a strong disinfectant and set them to work with rubber gloves and brushes, scrubbing the DDT off the walls from top to bottom. The guttering was the next priority, and Max realized they would need to build another heavy wooden stand so the tank they already owned on Michael's property could be transported. With these things in place, it would be possible to catch the last few rains before the dry season began.

As the only woman, Alexis found that her entire day now consisted of conventional women's work. She cooked large quantities of food for the workers, did the dishes, cared for Jordan, and washed the clothes and diapers in the river. It wasn't easy work and, worse yet, it was menial. The men, on the other hand, did the impressive work; you could see their progress daily. They dug postholes for fencing, felled big trees, chopped bush, and strung wire. Unlike her endeavors, their effort produced tangible results. After three days, she'd had enough.

"Max, I'm sick of stirring pots and washing dishes. How about letting me have a go at some of those postholes?"

"A fresh pair of hands? Sure. By all means, take a turn," said Max. "But you better wear gloves. Check this out," he said, showing her his hands. Hard yellow calluses and raw torn blisters covered his palms and fingers. Alexis didn't care. Even if her hands didn't last long, she'd be able to get out of the house for a while.

"Go for it," Max said quickly, before she could change her mind. "I'll take care of Jordan."

On the southern boundary, the workers were trying to sink holes into solid white *marl*. The posthole digger was useless, so they were using a pointed iron bar to chip through the hard limestone, a fraction at a time. Alexis joined their efforts, and in no time, sweat poured off her forehead in rivulets and plastered her ponytail to the back of her neck. The sun beat down mercilessly, and in a little over three hours, she no longer had the strength to even lift the bar.

Through the experience, Alexis discovered an important factor about life in the third world: men's work and woman's work fell along traditional lines for good reason. Women's work in Belize was tough and demanding, but men's work was truly rugged. It required a physical ability beyond the strength and endurance of even the hardiest woman. Let the tough-girl women's libbers come to Belize if they wanted to be equal to men, thought Alexis. Maybe stirring the pots wasn't so bad after all.

Somewhere far to the north in another world, people sat in their cars in five o'clock rush-hour traffic. The Dow Jones industrial average rose and fell on Wall Street as fortunes were won and lost. Luke Skywalker battled the forces of the Dark Side on the silver screen. Winos and the homeless died in the streets. Prostitution flourished in the red-light districts of big cities, and cocaine surpassed marijuana as the elite drug of the affluent. Factories continued to belch poison into the atmosphere. Huge holes appeared in the ozone layer. Crooked politicians took bribes, broke promises to their constituents, and rented fancier penthouses for their mistresses. Scholars at Harvard graduated Summa Cum Laude. Bored housewives gossiped, and talked over coffee about who shot J.R. Hippies cut their hair. Lawyers got richer. And the beat went on.

Life on *Emoyeni* was indeed hard, but sweet. Everyday, the young couple was busy from dawn to dusk with goats, chickens, gardening, cooking, washing, mending, fencing, and ongoing vehicle repairs. Max was almost finished with the pump house near the river, and they had already taken their first ride in the newly purchased dory, complete with outboard motor. But, as the months passed, Alexis realized that life was becoming nothing more than one long stream of chores. A crucial element was missing: contact. With no outside stimulus and no one with whom to share new ideas, she felt she was losing touch with the real world. There were a few Belizean families within a mile or two, and as long as the conversation centered on crops or babies, there was plenty of common ground. But Alexis couldn't discuss black holes in space, philosophy, computer technology, or the hottest new rock group. Her physical world had expanded while her intellectual sphere diminished.

Alexis had been working on a new craft idea as a surprise, and now, holding up the necklace of malachite and silver beads, she was feeling quite pleased with the finished product. Just then, Max walked in from feeding the chickens.

"I'm trying a new style of jewelry. What do you think?" she said happily, honestly wanting his approval. "I had the idea to try this a long time ago. See? I set the semi-precious stones about an inch apart across the front, and centered in the middle. Then I connected them with handmade silver links and made more around the back. We still have quite a few beads left from the Harrisburg project. I bet these would sell."

Max looked interested, even intrigued. "To whom?" he said, as he came across the room and picked up the piece.

"The British Army soldiers. Heck, they fly over the farm in helicopters all the time. I bet if we could persuade them to land, they'd buy stuff to take back to England as souvenirs. I could make up a bunch of these necklaces, with earrings and bracelets to match, and pin them up on a nice display board. Then we could chop a big 'H' landing pad on the knoll and invite the pilots for four o'clock tea. Besides, it would be nice to talk to somebody who speaks English again. If I spend much more time speaking Creole, I'm going to lose my vocabulary altogether."

"Wow, *Ntombi*. You sound like me when I first suggested the grand *heishi* scheme. I suppose it might be a good market. Do you think it will work?"

"Is that a challenge?" Alexis flashed him a winning smile. She could hardly believe that he was not opposed in some way. Her ideas were rarely greeted with such enthusiasm.

"Hey, I'll support your efforts if you want to try," Max said, with uncharacteristic warmth. "A money-making cottage industry would be great. Go ahead if you think you can make it happen."

She looked down at the tray of beads, and smiled again. "Watch me."

Matthew Richardson tied the chicken by its feet to the low-hanging branch. As he cut off its head, blood splattered on the grass and the disembodied clucking sound still came forth from its severed neck. *"It neva good to let the chicken run round wit no head. Too much blood stay inna de body,"* he explained to Alexis. *"Dis way, alla de blood come out."* After the bird had stopped flapping, he dipped it into scalding water. It had to be hot, but not boiling. Then Alexis helped him pluck out the wet feathers. The next step was gutting and, when he saw the look on her face, he offered to do the next step as well. She was relieved. In the States, chicken had always come in a plastic wrapper. *"It okay, Miss Alexis, I do it. The main ting is for no cut de gut. Odderwise, de meat wan spoil."*

"Thanks, Matthew," she said, gratefully. "I'll get Jordan. It sounds like he's waking up from his nap."

Alexis and Max had invited the river man to have Sunday dinner with them at *Emoyeni*. He had reciprocated by insisting on bringing the main course. The little blond boy was almost two and half now and slept in his own small bed with light removable wooden railings that kept him from falling out. Now he looked up at his mother and smiled, stretching out his arms to her. Although he had taken longer than usual to begin talking, there was no doubt he was bright. Jordan had two unusual qualities for a child: he had extreme persistence, and the ability to occupy himself. This was a child who had never played on a swing set and never seen a television. But if you gave him two sticks and a rock, he was happy. She picked him up and carried him outside to where Matthew was finishing the poultry preparation.

"Dat baby mighty sweet," said Matthew. *"Betta watch de Dwendes no ketch him. Do yu know the dwendes, Miss Alexis? Dey are de small peoples who live inna de bush,* he said. *"Yu scarcely ever see dem."*

Intrigued by the local legend, Alexis encouraged him. "No, I've never heard of the *dwendes*. What do they look like? Are they evil?"

"Well, de Dwendes, dem bout t'ree feet tall. Dere faces are round and flat, and dey wear a big sombrero. Dere feet is put on backway. Dat is to confuse yu, fu mek yu no track dem. And dere heels have points on de bottoms. People say diff-rent tings bout the Dwendes. Dey no really bad. More like mischievous. Dey like to steal

babies, dat's true. But alla dem play de guitar. If a man wan to learn to play guitar so he could win de heart of a lady, den he go to de Dwendes. Dey will teach him to play, but dey trade fu his soul. Dat's de ketch."

"Are there other creatures in the bush too?" Alexis asked. She would not dishonor him by making light of his beliefs.

"Oh yes, ma'am. In Guatemala dey have de Sisimite. But we no got dat in Belize, and dat's a lucky ting. Dey is very dangerous and big, 'bout maybe eight or nine feet. Dem tall and hairy. If a man see one, he die. If a woman see one, she live forever. Course de Sisimite is worser dan de Dwendes. Dey likes to carry off women. Beg pardon, Miss Alexis, carry off women fu breed wit."

Again respectful, she replied, "Well, I'm glad you warned me, in case I go to Guatemala. But how can I avoid the Dwendes here in Belize?"

"Just don go walkin in de moonlight alone, Miss Alexis. Dat is de time de Dwendes come out. Especially if yu hear de sound of dere guitar."

Alexis knew better than to laugh. Matthew lived alone in a thatched hut beside his banana plantation near Macaw Bank, another half-mile or so upstream. Ever since his wife and young son had died in an automobile accident years before, he had lived a solitary life. Part of a superstitious culture, Matthew Richardson held beliefs common to many of the local people. A black cat at the crossroads at three o'clock in the afternoon on a Friday was a sure sign of evil. *Obeah* makers, purveyors of black magic and witchcraft, put curses on people, gave them strange fevers, or made them blind by sewing a toad's eyelid shut with black thread. There was no doubt that Matthew was a believer. The stories had been taught to him by his grandmother from the time he was a child.

That same night, Matthew awoke from a nightmare in a cold sweat. Hot fingers clutched his throat and squeezed his heart like a vise. His chest heaved in pain as he tried to draw breath, and as the room closed in, he could feel the presence of the recurring *obeah* curse of a jilted lover from long ago. Suddenly, the beast was before him, sitting on his chest, its crimson face glowing with malevolence, the whites of its eyes gleaming in the flickering lamplight.

The simple river man never once suspected that the layers of white DDT, sprayed yearly on his walls by the Malaria Eradication Service, were slowly poisoning him.

One morning, Alexis saw a man at the front gate. Standing in the doorway, she couldn't tell who it was but it looked like one of the villagers from Cristo Rey. She called to Max, who was working in the far corner of the distant garden. "Max, there's a man out front."

"Yeah, I recognize him," he shouted. "Hang on. I'll go see what he wants."

Alexis watched as Max went to the gate and led the man into the yard toward the house. He was acting strangely nervous and kept looking behind him.

"Alexis, this is Chico. Chico, this is my wife, Alexis."

"Buenos tardes, Señora. I have someting to show yu." Again, the man looked behind him nervously. *"Well, really, I no have it here. It is back inna de village."*

"All right, the next time we pass by the village we'll stop by your house," she said.

"Well, really, my brother have it. He inna de bush outside."

Like pulling teeth, Alexis thought. "So bring him in."

By now the man was sweating profusely, and he motioned to another man hidden in the bushes alongside the house, who had apparently been there all along. The two men entered cautiously. Alexis and Max couldn't imagine why. Here they were, out in the middle of nowhere, ten miles from the nearest town, and a mile away from any other living human being.

As they lifted a burlap bag on to Alexis' kitchen table, she could tell it was heavy. There were three parcels inside, each wrapped in layers of burlap. The man opened the first one, and Alexis saw the black stone figurine of a woman in a crouching position. The figure was badly scratched and not particularly impressive. Next, he opened up a smaller bundle, and this time they were amazed at the sight of a Mayan necklace of jade. It was obvious that the piece had been restrung by an amateur, a collection of mismatched jade beads varying in size, shape, and color. Included in the strand were some flared convex pieces with a pea-sized hole in the middle that Alexis recognized as ear ornaments. There was no doubt that they were authentic. She knew from pictures that the flared piece fit through a large hole in the earlobe, and another small cylindrical piece fit through the back of the ear like a plug to hold the piece in place.

Then Alexis' eyes widened as Chico opened the third parcel and a huge green stone came into view. Max inhaled sharply. There, on the table before them, lay a tablet of solid jade, a death mask, carved in the likeness of an old Maya woman. The nose jutted out below the stylized headdress of stone feathers and the impassive face confirmed her nobility. No doubt, it was a grand lady of royal prominence, now venerated in death.

"Yu wan buy dese Maya tings?" the man asked simply.

"How much?" Max choked. As for Alexis, she couldn't even talk.

The one brother looked at the other and nodded. *"Three hundred Belize dollahs."*
"Each?"

"No. Fu everyting." Max looked at his wife. Given the exchange rate, the man wanted fifty U.S. dollars apiece for these priceless artifacts.

Ironically, the young family now lived on the edge of poverty themselves. The new piston pump, dory, and outboard motor had cost them what little cash they'd had on hand. The garden was still young; it was subsistence farming at best; they had enough to eat and no more. Each week they might splurge on either peanut butter or jelly, but not both in the same week. Their only dessert was cold rice with goat's milk and brown sugar. They couldn't afford Mayan treasures. Now part of the Belizean culture, they were no better off than the poor villagers who were offering them priceless antiquities.

The thumping of the rotor blades could be heard long before the helicopter came into view. Max was on his way up the hill from the river, and sprinted for the house. Alexis leaned out the back door and called to him, "Hurry, Max, this is it. Here they come. I'll go get the sign." Alexis dashed for the sign in the spare room while little Jordan ran to the front door.

"Biti Jammy, Biti Jammy," Jordan cried, pointing to the sky. It took Alexis a moment to figure out that he was saying; she smiled in amused indulgence when she realized he was saying "British Army."

"C'mon, Jordan," she said, taking the little boy by the hand. "Let's go out and wave to the soldiers." Just then Max caught up and together they ran out of the house, across the yard and up to the grassy knoll. Alexis held up the large piece of cardboard with the capital T written on it, hoping they would understand the invitation.

"It's working. They're circling a second time. I think they're going to land."

For a moment it looked like the men in the chopper had changed their minds. The aircraft rose above the height of the western ridge where it hovered for a few minutes, then made the approach to the H shaped landing pad. The noise and wind were tremendous as the whirling blades came closer to the ground and flattened the tall grass.

"Hello," said the very English voice as the man jumped out of the helicopter. "Allow me to introduce myself. I'm Captain Tony Martin, Army Air Corps, Worcester and Sherwood Foresters. How do you do?"

"Alexis Lord," she replied, extending her hand. "This is my husband, Max, and my son, Jordan. Nice of you to drop in."

"We saw your sign and, quite frankly, we were charmed by your thoughtfulness as well as your innovative invitation. This is my copilot, Lieutenant Hugh Worthington."

"See, Max?" Alexis said radiantly. "I told you they'd get it."

From that time on the Lord family became good friends with Her Majesty's Forces. The pilots not only stopped for tea, they indeed bought the jewelry that Alexis made, grateful for something original to take home to England. Alexis had always assumed the English were very proper, but she quickly found out that they were quite fun with a wonderful dry sense of humor.

Soon the British began to come on a regular basis. They arrived in helicopters or Army jeeps on a Sunday afternoon, sometimes six or eight at a time, bringing their friends or wives to socialize or go swimming in the river. The officers were not only great guests, they brought copious quantities of steaks, hamburgers, and legs of lamb, complete with mint sauce, beer, twelve-year-old Scotch, and chocolate bars. After spending over two years in Belize, Max and Alexis had long ago given up vegetarianism; the repetitive diet had taught them to be grateful for any kind of variety. On one such visit Captain Martin brought a special gift for Alexis. It looked like the thin branch of a tree with a hard white material encrusted on the surface.

"It's called black coral," Tony said. "Apparently it's not a true calcium carbonate coral, but more like a dense underwater wood, and it grows only in very deep water. The local chaps out on Ambergris Caye use it to make jewelry." Handing it to her, Alexis examined the piece minutely and showed it to Max. "I realize it doesn't look like much now," he continued. "But when it's sanded and polished, it becomes black and lustrous. They make beads with it and carve it into sharks and dolphins and crosses. Some of their stuff is lovely. I just thought maybe you'd like to try working with it."

"That's very kind of you to think of me. I'd love to experiment and see what I can come up with. Thanks, Tony."

Her creative mind was already racing with possibilities.

* * * *

The afternoon turned nasty as gray clouds lay heavy on the horizon and a capricious wind began to blow. Alexis was busy polishing her very first black coral carving and half-dozen hand-made black coral beads. She was pleased at her growing stockpile of artistry, as her jewelry business now involved selling trips to hotel gift shops in Belize City, as well as the primary British Army base just fifteen miles beyond, on the Northern Highway. Suddenly, a particularly strong gust tore loose one of the shutters and banged on the window frame. Securing it, she decided to turn on the radio. Maybe a storm was coming.

"...and as you just heard in our latest update, Hurricane Greta is due to make landfall in Belize at approximately five o'clock this evening."

Jordan looked up from his toys in surprise as his mother leaped off her stool and flew out the front door. "Max!" Alexis yelled at the top of her lungs. "A hurricane is coming. Come quick. It's on the radio!"

"...also we urge you once again to stock up on nonperishable foods, candles, and first aid supplies..."

Hearing her cry, Max came running down the path from the goat house. In his haste, he had spilled half the milk from the bucket, and arrived breathless at the door. "Did you say what I think you said?"

"Quick! Yes, a hurricane! Listen!"

"...Don't forget that any loose objects in your yard can become projectiles in the high winds," the weatherman cautioned, "and if your house has a tin roof, be sure to throw ropes over the top and stake them into the ground. Remember to leave a window open opposite the blast of the wind. This will prevent implosion. Make sure all your family members have a piece of plastic or raincoat for cover. Keep plenty of dry clothes on hand, wrapped in plastic, and be sure to prepare some food in advance. The hurricane is packing winds of up to one hundred and twenty miles per hour, and is expected to lose very little strength when it makes landfall near the town of Dangriga. Play it safe and don't take chances. This Hurricane Greta advisory comes to you on Radio Belize, courtesy of the Caribbean Weather Service."

Max's face contorted with worry. "I wonder how long they've been warning people already. Maybe it's been on its way for a long time and we only just found out." Later, his suspicion would prove correct. The rest of the world had known of the direct threat for over eight hours. Being out of touch was only part of the darker side of paradise.

Max and Alexis did everything possible to prepare for the storm that would arrive in a matter of hours. Jordan was aware that a big wind was coming, but he was more excited than afraid. He watched his father secure the wooden shutters over the glass windows, throw ropes over the house, pound stakes into the ground, and then helped drive the goats and chickens into their respective sides of the thatched coop duplex. Such buildings were able to withstand high winds because they allowed the air to circulate through the open eaves, and often stood a better chance than conventional housing. But it was anybody's guess. The hut was twenty years old. It would either stand or fall.

Just shortly after five-thirty, the rains began in earnest, the first hard gusts coming from the southeast. As darkness fell, the gale force hit the house so hard, the water seeped through the tongue-and-groove siding and dripped inside the house. By the time the hurricane winds rotated to the southwest, a fine spray was blasting into the room, right through the walls. In the flickering lamplight, Max was forced to drag the newly-built double-bed into the center of the living room and began to shove their plastic-wrapped possessions beneath it.

Alexis held Jordan as he screamed and cried with fear, as the roaring wind rose to a terrifying level. Conversation became impossible. Large branches and other debris began to tear loose from the surrounding jungle and crash against the sides of the house. The monster storm continued its circular motion, and by eight-thirty the rain was driving from the northwest, rattling the sheets of tin on the roof as they tried to work their way loose from the nails that secured them to the rafters.

"Do you think the roof will hold?" Alexis shouted anxiously.

"I don't know," Max yelled back. "But if one corner goes, the wind will peel off the rest like the top of a tin can."

Outside the blast was in full fury, and the entire house rocked with the violence of the storm. Just when Alexis thought the wind couldn't blow any harder, another malevolent blast roared at a previously unsurpassed level. Huge limbs crashed against the house. They could hear the tin roof creaking, and any moment they expected it to tear off and collapse the walls on top of them. Suddenly the spitting water hit the kerosene lamp, shattering the glass and snuffing the flame. The little house was plunged into darkness. Jordan screamed and buried his face between his mother's breasts. Fearing for their lives, the young family dropped to the floor and crawled under the bed.

"It's okay, baby," Alexis said soothingly. "Everything's going to be all right." But her voice and body language betrayed her. She trembled. Max put a firm arm around both of them and didn't say a word. Now it would be a waiting game.

The next morning an ashen sunrise crept slowly over the wind-torn river valley, and the morning sky was veiled in weird hues of yellow, brown, green, and gray. The force of the hurricane had begun to weaken around midnight. It had diminished through the early hours of the morning, and by dawn, the storm was over. When there was finally enough light to make out the familiar view, it was difficult to focus on what they saw. Nothing looked the same. As Alexis and Max rubbed their tired eyes, they couldn't believe what lay before them. The spectacle of destruction was beyond comprehension.

"The river," Max whispered in awe. "My God. Look at the river."

Never before had the Macal been able to be seen from *Emoyeni*; the valley was two hundred feet deep. Yet beyond simply rising and spilling its banks, the engorged waterway had spread to a width of more than half a mile, and dominated the entire landscape to the southwest, west, and northwest. No longer a mere river, it appeared to be nothing less than a silvery-brown inland sea of unimaginable proportion.

The property damage was beyond comprehension. The outhouse roof had been flung into the trees, well beyond the fenced yard, and its walls had totally collapsed over the wooden box that had served as the seat. The old chicken and goat house still stood, but half the thatching was gone and two of the walls were listing badly. The Nubians were unharmed, although they seemed highly indignant at having gotten thoroughly soaked. Some of the chickens were missing, and those that had not been blown away looked bedraggled in their sodden feathers. The custard apple tree was gone. Once towering over sixty feet, the enormous tree had born the sweetest *anona* fruit in the valley. Now it lay on the ground in tangled confusion.

Toppled by the storm, it had fallen right on top of their largest lime tree, as well as a huge stretch of the new fencing. Everywhere they looked was awesome destruction. The high jungle was mangled and crushed, looking like it had been chewed up and spat out by dinosaurs. Much of the smaller bush was flattened. Branches and limbs, leaves and palm fronds trashed the entire hilltop area. Huge trees had snapped in half and lay on the ground beside white splintered trunks.

But somehow their house had survived. Upon closer inspection, one corner of the tin roof was curled upward; Max estimated that the sheet metal couldn't have held more than a few minutes more when the storm had started to subside. One wooden shutter and its glass window beneath had been broken by an enormous tree limb and many household items had gotten wet. But all in all, they were lucky. Nobody had been injured. Although shaken, they were all alive and well.

"I'm going down to the river," Max said.

"Please wait a little while. With all the rain in the mountains upstream, I'm sure the river hasn't finished rising yet. There could be flash floods."

"The water level must be awfully close to the pump house," he stated. "I've got to get the machinery out of there before the water goes any higher. Besides, if the dory line got tangled in the bush as the river rose, then the boat's either on the bottom or washed somewhere downstream. I've got to check the line and free it if I can."

"But Jordan's asleep," protested Alexis. "I can't go with you. He's so exhausted, it's not likely he'll wake up for at least four or five hours, but I don't want to leave him here alone."

"I'll go down and check things out. Then I'll come back and get you if I need to."

"Be careful. Take the machete with you. The path is probably blocked with bush, and there are bound to be snakes coming up the hill to get away from the flood."

Taking her suggestion, Max started down the path. Slipping and sliding, the mud mixed with the shale made a deadly combination. Four times he had to cut his way through fallen bush on what used to be a path. Then, only two-thirds of the way down the hill, the river was suddenly at his feet; he gasped in awe.

The pump house was nowhere in sight. The flood had consumed it. Max took a bearing on some large trees and tried to estimate where the pump house might be, if indeed, it still existed at all. Wading into the water, he took a deep breath and submerged himself. He repeated the process over and over, groping blindly among the submerged bushes in the filthy brown water, at last finding the corner of the roof. Ascertaining its whereabouts, he surfaced, and made his way slowly up the path again to the house.

Meanwhile, Alexis paced nervously in the yard, keeping an ear out for Jordan to awake, and an eye out for Max's return. She couldn't conceive of what he might be facing down at the river's edge, and an errant thought made her vaguely consider what might happen if her husband simply failed to return altogether. Even though only about forty minutes had passed, it seemed like a lifetime before he finally re-emerged out of the bush at the top of the hill. He was soaked and filthy with muddy water from head to foot.

"This flood must be the highest in anyone's memory. It's completely covered the pump house." Max was maintaining his calm. Having handled many natural disasters in Africa, Alexis had to admit he was a good man in a crisis, and was determined to step up to the same level of self-control. "As far as I can tell the structure is still in one piece, so the two machines are probably still inside, right there under the water. I'm going down with some rope and see if I can fish them out." Concentrating on his non-emotional focus, Alexis asked him if he wanted her to come with him. "Not yet," he replied. "Wait about a half hour, and then come down. I should have the machines out of the water and on the bank by that time. You can help me bring them up the hill. If Jordan's awake, you'll have to bring him with you. We won't have a choice."

"I understand," she said, evenly. "Be careful."

Sliding down the hill once more, Max made his way to the water's edge. He tied one end of the rope to a nearby tree and the other around his waist. Fighting his own buoyancy, it took six attempts to locate the door of the pump house and several more to get the key into the padlock while underwater. Pushing his lungs beyond capacity, he nearly drowned himself trying to force the door open, but it was crucial to retrieve the engines and strip them promptly. With a superhuman strength born out of necessity, he finally wrestled the outboard motor from the water, hoisted it to his shoulder, and carried it up the slippery bank.

Alexis met him at the top of the hill.

"Jordan is still sleeping. Do you want me to come help you get the other one?"

"Yes. We'll have to take a chance," he replied. "The pump is much heavier than the outboard; I won't be able to carry it alone."

The runoff from the distant mountains continued to funnel into the Macal. The great river was still rising, and Alexis was shocked when she came to the edge of the brown swirling torrent.

"It's okay," said Max. "You don't have to go in. I've already done this a bunch of times. You stay here and watch the rope. This time I'm going to tie it on to the pump, rather than myself. When you feel me tug twice, start hauling. You'll be pulling the pump and I'll be pushing it, so keep this end wrapped around the tree. It will act as a winch so it won't backslide. We'll be out of here in five minutes." He paused. "Are you scared?"

"I'm worried about Jordan waking up in the house alone. And I'm worried about flash floods," she said. "Look at the current out there. I know you'll be close to the edge, but this time you won't even be tied to the rope."

"We don't have a choice, so let's get it over with."

Once freed from the water, getting the heavy waterlogged piston pump back up the hill was one of the hardest physical efforts Alexis had ever made in her life. Four times she and Max stumbled and fell with the heavy piece of machinery. Once she slipped off the trail and would have disappeared over the bank if she hadn't latched onto a sturdy vine. When they finally reached the house, providence was on their side; Jordan was still asleep.

Immediately they launched into the next phase. There was no time to waste. Max started to strip the pump, and simultaneously coached Alexis on how to do the same with the outboard. Every minute out of the water compounded the likelihood of irreparable corrosion in the circuitry. When Jordan finally awoke three hours later, they were close to finishing, and although Max couldn't be absolutely sure the machines were in working order until he had the opportunity to test them, it appeared that they had, most likely, averted any permanent damage.

By noon the next day, the river had receded enough to expose the pump house. Finding the end of the dory line still attached to a previously submerged tree, Max followed it, searching the riverbank until he located the craft. The swift water had carried the dugout to the full length of its long rope, the backwater eddies causing it to edge over and finally come to rest high in a bramble of thorny bamboo. Almost impossible to reach from any angle, Max hacked away with the machete until he could seize the heavy craft. Dragging it to the water's edge until it was free-floating, he went back to the pump house and hauled the rope hand-over-hand, until he was able to finally secure the dory beside the pump house. Then, determining that it was time to mount it on the boat for a test, Max hiked back to the house, picked up the motor and started to carry it back down the hill. Suddenly his foot slipped and, as he fell, the outboard shaft hit a rock and bounced up into his face, knocking out the center portion of his two front teeth, adding another element of horror.

It took a full twenty-four hours before Radio Belize came back on the air and only then did Max and Alexis begin to understand the enormity of the nationwide destruction. Listening to the reports of damage and death in the urban areas, the young family realized that, in many ways, they had been safer in the bush. At least they were self-contained and did not depend on public utilities. Taking stock of their situation, Alexis realized they had a full tank of rain water, butane for the stove, their own generator for electricity, and plenty of beans and flour. In addition, they had a good supply of fresh produce: a windfall of limes, hot peppers, and all the avocados they could eat. The best plan would be to sit tight for a few weeks until the rest of the country had a chance to recover.

In the town of San Ignacio, the aftermath of the hurricane was appalling. Floodwaters from the Macal River had risen so high that even the main streets were inundated with up to nine feet of water. The river had rushed through the lower stories of houses and shops, across backyards, and into the outhouse pits, and the water supply was contaminated with sewage and the bodies of dead animals. Power failure was widespread. Families huddled around candles in the darkness at night. Grocery stores on higher ground ran out of dry goods and staple foods immediately. Fresh fruits and vegetables were scarce as farmers found themselves with damaged crops, or the inability to transport their produce into town from outlying villages.

Seventy-five miles away on the east coast, the hurricane had created widespread havoc in low-lying Belize City. Amid gusting winds, a tidal wave had swept over the sea wall and demolished flimsy buildings of wood and cheap cinderblock. Huge trees, torn out by their roots, lay broken amidst the wreckage of walls, roofing, overturned cars, and power lines. Over a period of days, the water receded and a vile stench rose from the stinking carpet of saltwater mud left on the streets and the lower levels of buildings spared by the storm.

* * * *

It had been a full month since Alexis had visited the city. As she stepped out into the courtyard from the Fort George Hotel, she breathed a sigh of relief. Just previous to the hurricane, jewelry sales had been brisk, and the buyer still needed to replenish his stock. Max had built her a beautiful jewelry display case, which helped to improve her presentation. The rich red velvet inside the case set off the black coral and silver to perfection. Tucking the money carefully inside a special inner pocket, she hailed the green Chevy Impala taxi in front of the hotel. As she got in the back, Alexis recognized the driver. Unlike the young black troublemakers who roamed the city streets, he was a gentleman, one of the "old school," raised in respectable British colonial tradition.

"Joseph?" she asked politely. "You're Joseph, aren't you?"

"Yes Miss, dat's me. How yu know me?"

"I rode with you before. Remember? The jewelry lady?"

"Oh yes, yes, of course. Good to see yu again, Miss. From Cayo, no true? Yu should ride wit me every time yu come to Belize. My car is in good repair, and I am a safe driver."

"I appreciate that Joseph."

"So which part of de city yu wan go today, Miss?"

"Please take me out to Airport Camp. Time to sell to the soldiers."

"Let's refresh the lady's drink, Derek," said Captain Pearson, as they all sat in the Officers' Mess that evening. "We may be starved for entertainment, but let's not be rude."

"May I see this necklace, Alexis?" said a young flight lieutenant.

"Just a minute, I'm buying her the drink," Captain Pearson said as he handed her the glass, "so I get to monopolize her time for a moment. How much is that black coral dolphin please?"

Alexis settled back in the chair and smiled. The Officers' Mess was not fancy, but it was clean and comfortable, a pleasant change from the farm. She was glad they had invited her to come on a regular basis. Far away from the land of Greenwich Meantime, the officers rarely had the opportunity to enjoy the company of a white woman. Like school boys, it seemed, they all competed for her attention, making Alexis feel like Scarlett O'Hara at the Twelve Oaks barbecue.

The trips were not only fun but profitable, and it was turning into quite a trade since the officers had begun asking Alexis for custom carvings. A challenge to her artistic ability, it was becoming her favorite aspect of the business.

She arrived back at the ranch late, and when she walked in the door, Max was not amused. "Where the hell have you been? I expected you home hours ago. I had to do all the evening chores, cook dinner, and give Jordan his bath. It would be nice if you could make it home in time to take care of your responsibilities." With a three-day growth of beard and an inverted "V" in his two front teeth, Max looked horrible. Although he had made an appointment for the repair the following week, he had yet to see the dentist.

"I've been selling in Belize City since yesterday. I was at the army base last night. Then I picked up supplies in town this morning, and established a new wholesale outlet this afternoon. By the time I got to Cayo it was already dark. Then I had trouble getting the truck up Monkey Fall Hill by *Cristo Rey*. That road is becoming impossible. I had to rev it at the bottom to get enough speed to get up the hill, and I nearly tore the bottom out, high clearance and all."

"You bloody liar."

"You've been drinking," said Alexis in surprise.

"So what if I have? You're still a liar."

"Whiskey. I can smell it – the twelve-year-old scotch the soldiers left behind, no doubt. Why do you drink it, Max? It doesn't agree with you."

"No, you're the one who doesn't agree with me. I'll drink if I feel like it. Who do you think you are anyway? My fuckin' mother?"

Alexis tried to distract him. "Is Jordan sleeping?"

"I asked you a question," he persisted.

"Please, I don't want to fight. I'm exhausted. I just don't think you should drink alone. It's not good for you."

"I'll tell you what's not good for me. You're not good for me. You've been screwing soldiers, haven't you?"

"Of course not." Alexis almost laughed at the absurdity, but checked herself in time. "Here, look at this money. I sold eight hundred dollars worth."

"And I need to know if you made the money lying on your back."

"What? That's crazy. Why are you quarrelling with me? We've been making good money for the first time since we've been in Belize. It sure beats the hell out of selling tomatoes. At first it was every six weeks, then once a month. Now I'm going down every two weeks, and I'm knocking myself out making the jewelry in between. After all, you encouraged me."

"Oh, so it's my fault then?"

"No. OK, let me word this more carefully – it's what we agreed on."

"I don't like it," Max growled. "You're putting yourself in a position to be tempted."

"I don't desire other men." Of course, by this time, she had no desire for Max either. "The only thing I enjoy is the fact that they're nice to me."

"Quite a contrast to life with me, isn't it?" Max leered at her, purposefully, with his grotesque broken teeth. Alexis knew the situation was getting dangerous, and started to move to the bedroom where Jordan lay sleeping.

"Stay away from that kid. Get your ass outside. Now!"

It was too late. Alexis knew what was coming. A horrible sickening sensation came over her as Max came behind and shoved her roughly out the door. The smell of whiskey was strong and sour. She stood facing the full moonlight. Given the circumstances, it could have been a romantic evening. He stood behind her breathing heavily.

"Please don't overreact," she said, turning to face him. Couldn't we just–" With one powerful blow, he buried his fist into her solar plexus. She collapsed; her lungs unable to draw the next breath.

"Fuckin' slut," he mumbled, as he walked back into the house.

Alexis lay there and gasped for air, unable to breathe. The bitter taste of bile rose in her throat and she retched in the dirt. Her mind cried out to God, to the sky, to the moon, to anyone. But there was no answer. All she could feel was the cold ground under her body. She felt utterly helpless and alone. Her only comfort was that this abuse had been short-lived. After perhaps twenty minutes of recovery, she was able to get up and go into the house. Max was in the bedroom lying down in bed. She walked into the room and took off her clothes.

"You're not going to be lying down tonight."

"Please. I'm hurt and I'm tired. I need to sleep."

"You're not going to lie down here or anywhere else. Or sleep. You're going to stand right there and do absolutely nothing."

Alexis started to cry. "Please, Max! What do you want from me? I'm begging you. Let me lie down. At least let me sit down."

"Stand there and stop your blubbering. If you don't shut up, you'll wake the baby." Alexis stood there for several minutes in silence, and then began to put her clothes back on.

"Leave your clothes off."

"But I'm getting chilled and I have to pee."

"Good. Uncomfortable, isn't it?"

It was almost two hours later when Max let Alexis lie down beside him, demanding that she first perform fellatio. Within one minute of his climax, he passed out. Alexis lay down beside him and cried herself to sleep.

CAYO

chapter 10_____

As a child, Alexis had loved holidays and the family traditions surrounding them. Every year, she was in the Nativity pageant, and later she participated in the church's musical presentations with the youth group. Frank put up the lights on the house and Liz baked cookies and made decorations out of *papier-mâché*. On Christmas Eve, instead of watching TV, the family played cards or board games together while listening to carols on the hi-fi. On Christmas morning, Frank presided over the opening the presents, one by one. Later, Grandma and Grandpa arrived and the wonderful smells of turkey and pumpkin pies filled the air.

Of course, in her rebellious teenage years, Alexis had gone through a stage when the family environment had become too square; she wanted to spend Christmas or Easter with her friends. But her father had insisted that those holidays were reserved for family. He had said that, in the future, the friends would be all but forgotten, while family would remain.

"Family is the only thing that counts; the only thing that lasts," Frank had said. "Only your family really loves you." How wise Dad had been on that count, she thought.

In those days of young innocence, when Alexis had dreamed of the future, she had imagined herself to be the kind of wife and mother Liz had been, and her husband would be like her father, funny and caring, kind and giving. Max was none of these things. Instead, he had become the enemy, the opponent. Anti-love, anti-trust, anti-laughter. Now she dreaded the holidays. There was no tradition, no cohesion in the family, and the contrast to her childhood made the pain greater.

Compounding the problem was the radically different climate in Belize; it was virtually impossible to create a typical holiday ambiance. There were none of the usual props. No grandparents were due to arrive from over-the-river-and-through-the-woods. There was no church pageant, and no snow. During the previous Christmas, Alexis had made a trip to the Pine Ridge and cut a scraggly long-needled pine, but then she had fretted that there were no decorations. So she'd strung some popcorn and hung it on the tree, only to find that, by morning, ants had invaded the house and eaten it. Chicken was abundant in Belize, but turkey was scarce. Orange pumpkins were unknown, and even if Alexis had been able to obtain such delicacies, she had no oven in which to cook them.

Now it was Easter, and Alexis wanted to show Jordan some of the traditions she had enjoyed as a child. She searched the shops in Cayo to find an Easter basket, jelly beans, and a chocolate rabbit, but found nothing. Colored dye for Easter eggs was unheard of; no one even knew what she was talking about. Disheartened, she went home and put some eggs on the stove to hard-boil. Then, while Jordan was napping, she looked through his toy box for some crayons. The art work would be crude, but she would do her best. But, of course, Max took issue with her.

"What the hell are you doing?" he said, as he saw the tray of eggs with Crayola faces.

"I just wanted to do something for Jordan for Easter. I thought it would be fun to have an egg hunt."

"That's stupid," Max said, unequivocally. "All that holiday stuff you're so attached to is pointless."

It seemed that everything had become either pointless or stupid to Max, unless it revolved around him, or directly related to making money. Alexis felt utterly invalidated by his contempt, and it extended to anything she held sacred or meaningful. But it wasn't just the holidays. It was more far-reaching than that.

Gradually, Alexis' image of what family life should be was fading into a charade. Except for her son, and the beauty of the verdant jungle around her, life had become colorless. The dream of a utopian farm had degenerated into a jaded monotony of daily chores. Alexis felt her horizons shrinking. She was lonesome for human companionship. Fear and boredom directed her wooden movements as her verbal creativity became first stifled, then crushed. She no longer wrote poetry. She hadn't kept a journal for years. Life was no longer an open book, full of promise. Max was unbearable and hounded her like a drill sergeant. He cross-examined her every word, thought, and deed, then nit-picked her answers. When she spoke, he wanted to know what she was insinuating, instead of taking her word at face value.

Sadly, Alexis learned one very valuable lesson: that a plausible falsehood was often more useful than an unworkable truth. She wasn't a dishonest person, but it simply became more practical to tell the man whatever he wanted to hear. If openness and honesty were the trademarks of a healthy marriage, then Max had effectively educated her on the value of deception. He'd taught her to become a liar by making the truth a punishable offense.

Inside the fenced-in garden perimeter, the family began the arduous task of preparing the hard-packed ground for planting vegetables. Max had found an old abandoned single-share plow on the property, so he borrowed a draft horse, horse collar, and harness from a neighboring farmer, and began to break up the stubborn earth. Guiding the horse to hug the edge of the broken ground, he forced it to plow in straight even furrows, and even Alexis had taken a turn at the reins. Now, the clods of earth, matted deep with grass roots, had been baked in the hot sun to the consistency of bricks, and since they had no disc harrow attachment, the next step had to be done by hand. Alexis hacked at the clods and pulled the heavy hoe until her stomach muscles burned. Encrusted with dirt from head to toe, insect bites made her itch, and the salty sweat streamed down her body, burning the red scratches on her bare legs left behind by the tall harsh grasses.

"I can't do this anymore," Alexis told him at last. "I'm exhausted. I'm itchy and tired and dirty. I've just got to quit. I feel like I'm on the verge of passing out."

"It's soil, not dirt," Max corrected her, "and you give up too easily. When you feel like you can't go on, that's exactly when you've got to keep going. Only when you've felt that way ten times over, can you feel righteous about stopping. It's good training; it'll make you tough and will teach you not to give up. But go ahead and take a break for five minutes, sit in the shade, and drink some water. Then get back to work. I suggest you draw on your inner *chi*; make your inner strength work for you. You need to learn some work ethic. Don't be a wimp. Let's see you endure a little."

Alexis was so angry and frustrated at his lack of compassion, she didn't even notice that he was manipulating her. Max had shamed her into it, and her humiliation served him well. Attacking the job with renewed vigor, she chopped at the stubborn chunks. I'll show him.

Soil, my ass, she thought. It was freakin' dirt.

Outside the garden, they had used machetes to clear a large acreage for corn. Refusing to victimize the virgin forest, Max and Alexis had elected instead to tackle a section of shorter bush and *wamill*. The chopped vegetation had lain on the ground since early April, and now the torrid heat had dried it into a hardened tangle. For the first time Alexis understood why Belizeans resorted to burning. If they didn't, the new growth of weeds and grasses would simply grow up through the dried-out snarl and create a permanently impenetrable barrier.

Burning was a job best done in the heat of the day, and with the rain clouds gathering on the horizon, they could see that the distant neighbors were already laying fire to their plantations. The smoky dry season haze drifted lazily over the Macal river valley, creating a strangely-colored sky that was more pink than blue. No one wanted to take a chance on missing a clean burn before the June rains. So, with the wind at his back, Max lit a match at the far corner of the field, and together, the couple watched as the blaze began to sparkle and snap, fueled by the steady breeze. But, unlike the locals, they were careful to keep this fire within the perimeter of the chopped area, so it did not run wild. Steadily, the blaze crept along the ground, burning everything in its path, consuming the smaller branches until it reached the heaped piles of thicker limbs and underbrush. As the open areas burned out, they consolidated the brush piles using two fresh-cut green poles as levers.

It was already ninety-five degrees in the shade. In the sun, temperatures were over one hundred. But even that seemed insignificant compared to the scorching fire. It was so hot near the flames that when Alexis stepped back and merely stood in the sun, it felt like shade. Working close to the inferno, she adjusted the wet bandanna that protected her hair from catching fire, but her arms and legs still burned red in the heat. Sweat poured from her face as she wedged the pole under the burning brush and boosted it, little by little, toward the flames. Suddenly, a large limb burned through and the entire pile shifted. Out of nowhere, the tip of a hot poker sprang forward and touched lightly on Alexis' face just below her left temple, narrowly missing her eye. The skin hissed as she felt the hot sting and smelled her own burning flesh. Screaming, she jumped backwards.

"What happened, *Ntombi*?" said Max as he ran toward her. Within seconds, a blister the size of a nickel had formed. "Are you OK? It looks bad! Go into the house right away and put a wet cloth on it, as cold as you can get it. I'll be right in."

As Alexis ran towards the house for relief, she realized that, although the tiny butane refrigerator was cool enough to preserve goats' milk for a day or two, it did not provide the luxury of ice. Anxiously, she drew water from the tank, but it was tepid at best. She wet a cloth and laid it on her blistered face. It did nothing for the pain.

Jordan had been watching from the front steps, his little face full of concern. "What happened, Mommy?" asked Jordan. "Fire burn you?"

"Yes, honey. Come give Mommy a hug."

The little boy crawled up into her lap. For the moment he was the big man, the comforter. "Sorry, Mommy," he said, patting her. "Kiss and make better?"

"Thank you, sweetie," murmured Alexis. She dipped the rag again, bitterly. Living in the jungle, the most basic therapy for burns was simply unavailable.

Thousands of miles separated Alexis from her family in the U.S., but they kept in touch through the post office in San Ignacio and the occasional phone call made from the local Belize Telecommunications Authority. On the next trip to town, Alexis received the news that her grandparents' estate was breaking up in order to allow the old folks to enter a Senior Living Facility, and she had some inheritance coming. It was a badly-needed windfall.

"Well, I think we ought to use the money to get some more jewelry equipment and supplies for you," said Max. "Then we ought to use the rest to buy another vehicle."

Alexis' mouth twisted. "But it's my inheritance. They're my grandparents." She knew she was taking a chance by voicing her opinion.

"So what's your objection to using it for something worthwhile?" he asked sarcastically. "I suppose you want to put it into a bank account and let it earn some interest, right? Well, that's just more crap your parents put into your head. Work a job, put it in the bank, the only life they know. Self-employed people don't save money for a rainy day, they invest it. When you're in business for yourself, you can't let money sit around in a bank account. You have to turn it over. Banks are for people who don't know how to invest their money; they get the bank to do it for them. Do you know how many times we could invest and reinvest within a few years?"

"I understand what you're saying." She was on dangerous ground. "But I still think I should have some—"

"Oh. So what's yours is yours, and what's mine is ours, huh? Well, guess what, Mama? I'm running this show. You don't have a choice. I'm the brains in this outfit, and I'm going to tell you what's going to happen. I'm going to take that money, fly to the States, buy a new vehicle, get some more jewelry supplies for your army business, then drive back down. I'll be gone about ten days. That ought to be enough time. If you have any objections, then I suggest, in the best interests of your continued health and well-being, that you keep them to yourself."

June arrived during Max's absence, and the renewing rains of *Yum Kax*, the Mayan god of spring, brought forth the greening of the land. Overnight, the flowering trees burst forth in their tropical rendition of spring. Royal Poincianas opened their flame-red flowers among the feathery mimosa-like leaves. Giant Crepe Myrtle bloomed in flowers of lacy purple, and *bukut* trees opened their tiny delicate blossoms of the palest mauve.

Jordan was turning into a robust little boy. Almost four now, he was intelligent and strong. He had learned to swim almost before he learned to walk and had quickly developed sturdy leg muscles from hikes to the river. Basically, Jordan was a happy child. The only dark cloud in his young mind was the friction he felt between his parents. He loved both of them, but was hurt and confused by the constant strife. Often he heard them when they thought he was asleep and, somehow, felt it was his fault. He thought that if he could be a really good boy, they would stop arguing.

While Max was gone, Alexis thought she might feel lonely or afraid, but instead she found herself having a wonderful time with her young son. Every day, from morning until night, they worked and played together. It was a time of discovery for both. Jordan helped her feed the chickens, milk the goats, cook the meals, and clean the house. He carried the basket from the chicken coop when they collected eggs, and helped her hang the clothes on the line. Later, in the cool of the evening when day was done, Alexis and Jordan sat together on the back step overlooking the river valley and she sang to him. He laid his head in her lap while she stroked his platinum hair and ran her finger over the outline of his ear. To Jordan, there was no sweeter sound than his mother's singing.

Alexis' friend, Anita, surprised her by catching a ride on a passing dory to *Emoyeni* for a visit. It was a rare opportunity to speak openly with another woman without Max's presence. She found herself telling Anita things she had never admitted to anyone. They sat together on the back steps, facing the green majestic river valley. Alexis talked and Anita listened sympathetically.

"I'm scared to death to let anyone know," said Alexis. "Max threatened me. Says it's nobody's business but ours. He's always careful to beat me where the bruises won't show. I don't understand how our relationship has degenerated into this."

"I don't know what to tell you," Anita replied. "I'm shocked. Don Elijio says that sometimes people are possessed."

"Possessed? By evil spirits? Like Matthew's *dwendes* and *sisimite*?"

"Perhaps the two worlds are not so far apart. Even in contemporary theory, it has been suggested that some people become victims – providing fertile ground for evil manifestations. Is there something in his past that made him so belligerent?"

"It's possible," Alexis said thoughtfully. "His girlfriend back in Africa left him for his best friend. His mother was a tough disciplinarian; she was really hard on him. Is that enough to turn a man into a monster?"

"Maybe he holds a grudge against all women; maybe he isn't even conscious of it. But, to tell you the truth, it's hard for me to see any of this in Max. He always seemed like a decent guy to me, and I've never heard anything different from anyone else. Don't get me wrong; I believe you. Max is obviously very good at keeping his other side hidden."

"He is, believe me. I know the image he projects to Rick and Suzy and our other friends back at Baron's Creek," Alexis agreed. "I see it all the time. But when we're home alone, he's somebody else."

Anita put her hand on Alexis' shoulder. "You still love him, don't you?"

"Yes," she replied. "That's why it hurts. If I didn't care, it wouldn't matter. I remember who he used to be. I just can't accept that this is the way life was meant to be for us. And I don't mean the lifestyle, or the isolation. If Max and I were cooperating as a team, living here would still be the realization of our dream. It's the conflict that eats me up inside. We're not living happily-ever-after inside the Garden of Eden; this isn't how the story is supposed to go. I hold on to the past because I want to believe that one day that same man will come back to me."

"Have you ever considered leaving him?"

"I've left him twice already," said Alexis, "once before Jordan was born and again when we were living in Michael Whitmore's house. The first time I invited him back. The second time I took Jordan with me. Max found me before I could get away and threatened that if I ever left again, it would be without my son."

"The longer you stay together, the greater the investment." Anita shook her head sadly. "You've had six years together and now you have Jordan as well. At what point do you cut your losses?"

"That's why I hang on. I just have to believe that, one day, things will come right again."

"And if they don't?"

Alexis shook her head. Tears came to her eyes. "The alternatives are unthinkable."

"Daddy!" cried Jordan. "Mummy, look! Daddy's home!"

They both heard the honking of the horn and watched as the new little Chevy Luv headed up the long driveway toward the house. Jordan went running happily to his father. Alexis gave Max a dutiful hug and kiss.

"Hi, you guys. Boy, I missed you. Well, this is our new truck. Do you like it?"

"I wanna drive, Daddy! Let me drive it!" Max put Jordan on the driver's side. The little boy wrenched the wheel back and forth and made truck noises.

"It's real cute," said Alexis. "You must be exhausted."

"I'll sleep well tonight, that's for sure, but first things first. Give me a hand taking in all the goodies from the truck. I brought presents for everybody and some very good news."

It was a treat to see all the store-bought items from the States. Max brought a portable cassette player and some new tapes of their favorite artists. He gave Jordan a pair of Oshkosh overalls and a big yellow Tonka bulldozer with a backhoe. Alexis got an elegant rust-colored skirt, a pretty frilly blouse, and a stylish pair of leather shoes. Max had an uncanny knack for picking out beautiful things that fit.

"Those are for your army trips, Alexis, so you can look good, and make lots of money. And here's your jewelry stuff. I got you a rotary unit with a flexible shaft. Here's an assortment of burrs and bits, mostly dentist-type stuff, and a bunch of fine-grade sandpaper, buffing wheel, and jeweler's rouge."

"That's fantastic," Alexis said. She really was pleased. So far the black coral had been completely handmade. Now she would be able to work the raw material much faster.

"Now for the real surprise." Max was grinning as he gave Alexis another small box to unwrap. She opened the tissue paper and found the lovely teardrop of crystal. As she lifted it to the light, she saw that it hung inside a crescent-shaped moon made out of wood.

"It's lovely. What is it? A window ornament?"

"Exactly. The wooden moon catches the breeze and turns it in the wind. The crystal reflects the light and throws rainbows on the walls. I met a guy named John who markets these wholesale." Alexis thought of Mark with his crystals so long ago. Berkeley now belonged to another lifetime.

"There's more." Max opened the two large boxes. "This is a band saw, and this is a router," he said. "With them comes an order from a man named John for one thousand crescent moons made out of Belizean mahogany. We are now in the crescent moon business, and I'm the 'moon man.'"

Max's mood was expansive that night as they lay in bed together.

"It's a whole new ball game. This is just the break we needed. With a financial link to the U.S. we can live here in Belize and still enjoy the best of both worlds."

"Are you going to run this moon operation here on the farm?"

"Why not? We've got the generator. That way, you can use the electricity for your black coral work at the same time. We'll have the new little truck for comfort and the old Toyota for the rough stuff. Tomorrow I'll check the lumber mill for prices on one-inch mahogany. Generally, 'shorts' are no good for construction anyway. I'm sure I can get them cheap." He paused. "Alexis? Did you miss me while I was gone?"

She paused, perhaps a fraction too long. "Yes, I missed you."

"I've been rough on you lately. I guess I can be a real bastard sometimes."

She held her breath, not daring to say anything. This was as close as Max had ever gotten to an apology.

"Come here, *Ntombi*," he said gently, reaching for her. "Let's make love."

Over the course of the next few months, the manufacture of the wooden moons became a successful venture. Back in the States, the man named John received the first order and was so pleased with the workmanship, he placed a second order immediately, creating the need for Max to streamline production. Eventually, he realized that the only way to improve and maintain production would be to have a constant source of 110-volt current. Jordan would also need to start school soon. He discussed the situation with Alexis, and together they decided to put *Emoyeni* for sale and move into San Ignacio as soon as possible.

At this point, Alexis was doing an outstanding business with the British Army. Between wholesale and retail, she was bringing home anywhere from a thousand to fifteen hundred Belize dollars per trip. On each visit, she sold first to the Officers' Mess, then the Sergeants' Mess. Then, if she had enough nerve to withstand the brazen catcalls, she went to the Corporals' Mess. She drew a line at catering to the "lads" however. Because the Privates obviously didn't see many white women, she felt too much like meat on the block. If they wanted her jewelry, they could buy it from the old Sri Lankan shopkeeper at the gift shop on the base, who was also her customer.

Surprisingly enough, the farm sold within a month. A group of five young Swiss expressed their interest and, for perhaps the only time in Belizean history, a rapid transaction took place. Max encouraged the Swiss to buy the machinery that was an integral part of bush living, and although Hans, Franz, Moritz, and the rest of the gang were smart enough to take the piston pump, they refused to buy the lawnmower.

"You don't understand," Max told them. "You'll need this lawnmower to keep back the bush. You have no idea how fast it grows."

Moritz spoke for all of them when he made chopping motions with his hand and smiled good-naturedly.

"No, it's okay," he said. "We will use machete. We like, we make, we chop."

Max nodded cheerfully to Alexis as the Swiss people drove away after making the down payment. "They bloody well better 'we like, we make, we chop.' When they get out here, and they have no lawnmower, they'll be doing precious little else. By the way, *Ntombi*, I found a house for us to rent in Cayo, better than the one I was looking at originally. Up on the hill going out toward Benque Viejo. Not far from the San Ignacio Hotel. A guy at the lumber mill told me about it."

"That's fantastic, Max! Is anybody living there now?"

"No. An old woman named Miss Carmen was living there, but she died and now her nephew wants to rent it out. It's a two-story frame building with a living room, kitchen, two bedrooms, and a work room for your jewelry. We can put the woodworking shop downstairs. I guess it was a mess while the old lady was living there, but the landlord's got it all cleaned up now. He'll even repaint it before we move in."

"Did she die in the house?"

"Yeah, I guess so. So what? She had to die somewhere. But it's perfect, and the landlord only wants a hundred Belize a month. We'll have a flush toilet, with water and electricity twenty-four hours a day. Won't that be great?"

It did sound great. In fact, life was feeling pretty good again. Money was coming in from the moon manufacturing and the jewelry. The Swiss paid the balance for *Emoyeni* in cash and on time; they were ready to move in as soon as the Lord family moved out. Even the weather had been reasonable. During the past year, they had experienced a dry wet season and a wet dry season, striking a pleasant and temperate balance. Once again, Max had made good his promise. There were still periods when he mistreated her, and fell into black moods, but overall, things were improving. It was an answered prayer for Alexis.

A paragon of superstition, the old woman had lived alone for years in the house on the hill in San Ignacio. Even on the brightest days, she'd kept the boarded windows shut tight against the forces of the Evil One. The spirits were coming for her, she knew. It was just a matter of time. Ever since her son's funeral, she no longer left the house, not even to shop for provisions. If it hadn't been for the daily meals left at her door by her daughter-in-law, Carlita, she would have starved.

Two months before, her son had died a gruesome death. A freak accident at the lumber mill had occurred when the workmen were squaring a large rosewood log. The six-inch-wide blade on the huge band saw became lodged in the cut. The resistance of the wood broke the welded seam, and the fifteen-foot blade had sprung from the carriage. It coiled like a serpent around the man's body, cutting off anything protruding beyond its wicked teeth. Within five minutes the man had bled to death.

Life was already over for old Miss Carmen as she sat and waited for the demons of the darkness to come and take her. She rarely ate, she did not sleep, and the only word she spoke was her dead son's name. "Emil. Emil."

On the hill in San Ignacio, not far from the hotel, a little Spanish boy hesitated before he climbed the back steps of the old two-story frame house. The tin can he held contained a fat toad and his friend, Juan, watched from the soccer field behind the house to see if the dare would be carried out. On the landing at the top, Julio stopped and drew a deep breath. He pushed hard on the lower corner where the wood was rotten, and shoved the toad through the triangular opening. As the door sprung back into position, the toad's rear leg was caught and crushed. The boy ran away laughing.

Miss Carmen was familiar with the sounds of the kitchen, the cockroaches and scuttling rats. Now the mutilated toad, its one leg dragging, crabbed into the darkened room where the woman sat. She heard soft plopping noises and the scratching of tiny feet. Cold terror gripped her. She tried to focus her failing vision on the demon but could not see it. Suddenly the slimy body dragged itself across her bare foot. The old woman clutched her chest and something clamped down on her heart and lungs like a vise. She could not breathe.

"Emil, Emil," she cried as she lurched sideways and fell to the floor.

The next morning Carlita discovered the food still outside. She opened the door and called out, but heard no answer. The house was a tomb of stale air, further befouled by urine, lard, and human sweat. Cautiously, she entered the kitchen and opened a window. A beam of sunlight fell on the long forgotten dishes, scummy with thick mold. Pots encrusted with spoiled food squirmed with white wormy maggots. Steeling herself, Carlita walked across the living room floor stepping over heaps of filthy rags, soft drink bottles, wire hangers, papers, and trash. Flinging open another window, cruel daylight streamed in on the prostrate body of the woman. Miss Carmen had been scared to death. The hungry rats and cockroaches had eaten away most of her face.

As Alexis carried the large box of clothing upstairs, she noticed Miss Carmen's primitive Jesus painting still hanging on the wall of the living room. The blue eyes of the conspicuously Caucasian face stared oddly from the flat canvas, and his steady gaze seemed to follow her around the room. Not only had the Belizean artist fallen short of divine inspiration, the painting was almost a caricature. With the bleeding heart and eternal flame superimposed over Jesus' chest, it was creepy-looking, and Alexis was at a loss as to what she should do with it. Somehow, she couldn't just throw it in the trash. It was too corny to give away, too awful to leave in view. Finally, she slipped the painting behind a cabinet against a wall and forgot about it.

The house wasn't spacious, but it was adequate. Upstairs there were two bedrooms, the jewelry room, kitchen, and living room, and the whole lower story would serve as a woodworking shop. There was a toilet all right, but it had been starkly installed, *sans* privacy, in the corner of what was now the jewelry room. There was no actual bathroom, so Max built two little dividing walls, one with a door. Most people in Cayo still had an outhouse in the backyard. Indoor plumbing was just starting to become fashionable for some of the more affluent townspeople. In Miss Carmen's last years, her son had bought her the flush toilet and tied it into the town's new sewer system. Had it been on the first floor, the city water pressure might have been sufficient to fill the toilet's four gallon tank, but on the second floor, there was no chance. So, as in every other place they'd lived, one of Max's first jobs was to buy a water tank and build a tank stand above the level of the second floor. By diverting the rainwater from the roof into the tank, he created a secondary water supply to make up for the deficiency in pressure. Rising to the occasion always brought out the best in him.

In the backyard was a rickety structure of rotting wood that served as a bath house, but it was nothing more than a wooden floor surrounded by four walls and no roof. Max made a few improvements by repairing some of the existing wood and adding a soap and shampoo rack. Still, there was no running water in the stall itself.

For the next year and a half, the routine would remain the same. To bathe, Alexis had to fill a white plastic bucket of water at the foot of the stairs and then carry it to the stall in the backyard. Once inside, she used a coffee can to dip into the bucket and pour the cold water over her body.

Alexis rapidly learned that living in San Ignacio didn't mean that public utilities such as water, electricity, and sewers were more sophisticated. It simply meant that instead of being within their control, she and Max would now be subjected to all the inadequacies and inconsistencies of town life in the third world.

 **STATESIDE**

chapter 11

The magnificent barrier reef lay off the eastern coast of Belize, extending almost two hundred miles from its northern end to the southernmost tip. The reef varied in width from several hundred yards to just a few feet wide. In some areas, pinnacles pierced the surface among the thrashing breakers. In other places, it lay below the surface by eighty feet or more, where vicious riptides and turbulence created massive ravines and canyons. Consisting of calcium carbonate and trace minerals, the hulking reef had been created through infinite eons of time, as billions of coral organisms added their skeletons to the myriad formations on the ocean floor. There, marine life was bountiful. Nestled within the cradle of life, the living coral reef was a microcosm of the ocean as a whole, a stage upon which the drama of life and death was played out. From the tiniest plankton to the giant goliath grouper, the reef provided for each species to feed on the weak and inferior in the presence of superior predators, all in accordance with survival of the fittest.

Like sparkling jewels flung across the sea, a chain of tiny tropical islands sheltered inside the barrier of protected waters. Fine white coral sand glistened on the windswept beaches, while borders of coconut palms guarded the salt marshes of the mangrove interior. Most of the *cayes* were inhabited solely by thousands of seabirds: brown pelicans, gulls, frigate birds, cormorants, sandpipers, and red-footed boobies. Only a few islands supported human habitation.

The northernmost island, Ambergris Caye, boasted unspoiled miles of windward beaches and a small fishing village of perhaps two hundred people. The islanders were proud of their heritage, and they enjoyed a financial stability superior to that of the mainland, even in the early days before *gringo* tourists made their debut. Their success was due to a rich fishing industry and the San Pedro Co-op, which had enabled them to export fish, shrimp, and lobster to the United States.

The sea was their life. Once a year, the villagers held a somber celebration to St. Peter, the patron saint of fisherman. The midnight mass continued long into the night and ended with a silent procession to the beached boats. In the last hours of darkness, each boat was blessed with a votive candle and fervent prayers were offered for the safe return of the fishermen. As dawn broke on the horizon, the candles were blown out and the men paddled into the pink misted dawn.

"I can't believe we're going to do this," said Alexis, happily. "Actually taking a vacation." Compared to the old Land Cruiser, the little Chevy truck allowed them to ride in unparalleled air-conditioned comfort as they headed east towards Belize City.

"Hey, why not," said Max, magnanimously. "We've been working hard and deserve a break. Besides, after hearing about San Pedro for all this time, it's ridiculous that we've never been there. Lots of tourists think Ambergris Caye is Belize. Many of them never come to the mainland at all."

"Where are we going to stay? The hotels are expensive."

"I don't think it will be a problem. Eric told me about a guy named Raul, who has a nice hotel for tourists, but also some little *cabañas* that he rents to locals for cheap.

"Are we considered 'locals'?"

"I would think anybody who's living here on the Belizean economy would qualify, and your jewelry business with the army is what's supporting us. Speaking of which, we'll buy some more raw black coral while we're in San Pedro. Also, we'll take the bulk silver wire and other findings, just in case any of the island artisans are interested in components. That way we can combine business and pleasure." It made sense, of course, but somehow Alexis was disappointed that their trip wouldn't be a business-free vacation. But it would still be a break, and she decided not to make an issue of it.

"Are we going by boat or by plane?" she asked, instead.

Jordan looked up from his picture book as he heard the magic word. He had always loved to watch the helicopters flying over *Emoyeni*. Now he ran over with excitement.

"Airplane, Daddy! I wanna go on the airplane!"

"Could we Max?" Alexis pleaded. "Just this once? I know the boat is much cheaper but it also takes five hours to get there; the plane takes fifteen minutes."

Max thought about it. "Okay," he conceded. "We'll take the plane. Just for you, Jordan."

Arriving at the tiny municipal airstrip in Belize City, the single-engine Cherokee was a five-seater, the tiniest plane Alexis had ever seen. It shuddered and shook down the potholed runway, threatening to lose its wheels before getting up enough speed for takeoff. A little nervous, Alexis thought it was like flying in a Volkswagen with wings, but Jordan wiggled with excitement, his nose pressed hard against the window. As the small craft gave a final bounce and vaulted into the air, he cried out with exhilaration. In seconds, the aircraft was across the open ocean, beginning the climb to its cruising altitude of a thousand feet. Belize City had never looked so beautiful, and, far above the squalor, it was easy to believe that below them lay a shining city of cleanliness, charm, and grace. As the minutes passed, the city faded in the distance and the little plane continued on its northeasterly bearing.

"Look, Mummy, the houses are so small," said Jordan. "We're really flying." Max and Alexis smiled indulgently and their eyes met. Things had been good between them and this break from routine felt like the beginning of a new phase. Alexis gazed down on the brilliance of the sunlight reflecting on the Caribbean. Small cumulus clouds floated beneath her, and beyond them, the sea, in deep shades of cobalt, turquoise, and aquamarine, brought back memories of the *Déjà Vu*.

Ten minutes later, the island came into view, the palms shading a string of red-roofed houses and the odd rustic hotel. Expertly, the young pilot manipulated the rudders to compensate for the crosswinds, and the wheels touched down lightly. Jordan was first out of the plane, and he skipped around in eager anticipation as Max and Alexis retrieved the luggage.

There were only fourteen vehicles on the island, and Raul was the proud owner of the newest. He had driven his pickup to the airstrip to save his guests the mile-long walk back to his hotel. As a budding middle-aged entrepreneur, Raul had the beginnings of a beer belly and a delightfully casual manner. Business on the island was so informal and relaxed that most of Raul's transactions were conducted from a hammock strung under the palms. One of his daughter's had playfully pinned a sign on the hammock that read: **Office**.

Elevated on short four-foot stilts, Raul's *cabañas* were constructed of *tasíste* stalks and finger-leaf bay palm brought over from the mainland. The room was simple, lacking in artistic flair, but it was clean and adequate to their needs. There was a double-bed and a single portable cot, sink, shower, and twenty-four hour electricity. Alexis lifted the suitcase onto the bed, but before she could unpack, Jordan stripped himself naked and dashed for the water. Laughing, Max ran after him, tiny bathing suit in hand, explaining to the youngster that, although he didn't have to wear much clothing in San Pedro, minimal decorum was still required, and no peeing in the bush.

That evening, after a delicious meal of lobster bisque, rice, and baked grouper, Alexis tucked the tired and sun-browned little boy into bed. Kissing him tenderly, she walked back out on the beach under the stars. Meanwhile, Max was on his way to the bar, and returned a few minutes later with two piña coladas. Reclining in the lounge chair in the sand just outside the cabaña, Alexis settled herself in his arms. It felt like the old days.

"Look at those stars," she said, softly. "There are so many of them, like a blanket, more stars than sky. In fact, the sky looks like it did when I was a little girl. Not so many years ago in Key West, I remember thinking that maybe there weren't as many stars as there used to be. But now I know it was only the pollution. Belize has its faults, but the air is absolutely pure."

"That's one of the reasons we came here, to provide a clean environment for our children," said Max. Alexis sensed something in his tone. "I want another baby," he admitted, quietly. Instantly, a thousand thoughts raced through Alexis' mind. No longer naive, she knew what was involved in child bearing and rearing. Max had made tremendous demands on her during Jordan's infancy. She thought of the long heavy pregnancy, the pain of childbirth, the rewards of giving life, the burden and joy of responsibility for a brand-new human being.

"You know I don't believe in people having irresponsible numbers of children," he continued. "The focus should be quality, not quantity. We already have a fine son, and I would love to have a beautiful daughter. She would be a miniature of you, a little girl to spoil and love – someone for Jordan to play with. Haven't you ever thought about having a little girl?"

Of course she had. In her early childhood, Alexis loved her dolls and had spent hours of make-believe as their mother. She had bathed them and fed them, changed them and cuddled them when they pretend-cried. And of course, during the fifties, all dolls were girl-dolls. What little girl didn't want a real live baby girl when she grew up?

"You don't want Jordan to be an only child," he added. "Do you?"

"No. But it's a big decision. I'd need some time to think it over."

"That's fine, *Ntombi*. We don't have to rush into it."

That night, Max made love to Alexis with a tenderness she never thought possible. That night he was the man with whom she'd fallen in love, and when the sound of seagulls awoke her the next morning, she stretched like a sleepy cat, still caught in the spell of the magic the night before. Max sat framed in the open doorway, looking out on the ocean, the yellow orange sunrise behind him.

"Jordan's out here playing in the sand," he said. "Want some tea? I've got two cups here"

"Perfect. I'd love some."

She sat up and Max propped two pillows behind her as he handed her the steaming mug. "So what's on the agenda for today?" asked Alexis.

"Swim in the ocean, get a tan, scope out the town in general, and see what we can buy and sell," Max answered, smiling. "I'd like to try to meet some of the *gringos* that live on the island. There aren't many, but a few have started up some partnerships with the San Pedranos. I'm sure they could give us some insight into what's happening out here."

As they talked, Alexis suddenly became aware how normal and unstilted their conversation was. For the first time in years, she had let her guard down; they were talking like regular people. What was a common occurrence for most couples was a rare moment for her, and she wondered if this trip could be more than a new start, maybe a complete renewal of their relationship. Whatever it was, it was great, and she didn't want it to end.

They made many new friends and business associates during the course of the next few days. They swam and snorkeled inside the reef, went for boat rides, and Jordan caught his first fish. After a life of relative solitude on the farm, the little boy knocked himself out playing from dawn to dusk with dozens of children and the next morning surprised both his parents by speaking a few words of Spanish. Alexis met many of the hotel owners and sold some of her finished products. She also sold wholesale silver wire, chains, and other findings to the local craftsmen, exchanged valuable carving tips, and bought a pound of raw black coral from local divers. Max also made the rounds of the village, getting new ideas for other wood products that might be saleable on the local or international market. On the third day, he was breathless with excitement.

"*Ntombi*, you won't believe what I found. You've got to come and see."

"What is it?"

"It's a chair," he said happily. "In fact, it's THE chair – a chair that is going to take us down the road to success. It's a great design. It's wood, it folds, and we've got almost everything we need to manufacture it. I bought one as a sample to take back to Cayo. We'll take it apart, improve the design, and turn it into a first class product." Ceremoniously, he led her into their *cabaña* with his hands over her eyes. "There it is. What do you think?"

Uniquely designed, the chair was made of mahogany slats. Each individual slat had been drilled and cleverly sandwiched with the others to form a comfortably contoured seat. The slats were held together with hidden pieces of heavy-gauge wire, and the overall effect was that of a pair of inverted hands folded in prayer with four slats extending beyond the main body to form the legs. Of course, this inelegant prototype had been made by a Mennonite or San Pedrano using limited tools; it was short, stumpy, and rough. But its weight and low center of gravity made it the ideal deck chair. Alexis understood Max's excitement. He was right; the chair definitely had major possibilities.

* * * *

In the months that followed, the home-based business in San Ignacio began to boom for Alexis. Many of the visitors to the jewelry room gift shop in Miss Carmen's house were young British soldiers, lonely for company and anxious to find a keepsake for their girlfriends back home. Belizeans came to buy occasionally, but most of the visitors to the Lost Gringo Trading Company were young wide-eyed Americans and Europeans on vacation. Although tourism was still in its infancy, recent interest had grown after a feature story in National Geographic, and as a result, a few hardy souls were venturing inland to visit the Mayan ruins. With them came their U.S. dollars, money which was happily spent on black coral souvenirs

Other visitors had a different look – shady characters with dark eyes and obscure backgrounds. On the run from authorities, some were drug smugglers looking for pilots, suppliers, and middlemen; others were corrupt opportunists and speculators, drawn to small *gringo*-owned businesses in the same manner as a vulture is attracted to dead meat.

Even before he opened his mouth, Alexis took a dislike to the tall man standing in her doorway. With his large nose jutting out beneath hooded eyes and shaved head, Alexis noticed the shiny scar above his eyebrow. The man sniffed perpetually and his stance and attitude gave clear warning signals.

"I'm here to see Maximilian. My name's Brad Tongas. Is he here?"

"No, he's not. May I help you with something?"

"Are you Mrs. Maximilian?"

"Max is his first name. Max Lord. I am his wife, Alexis Lord. Are you a friend of his? Or are you looking to buy something?"

The corner of his mouth rose up further, as if he were about to make a smart remark and then thought the better of it.

"Not exactly," he said. "He and I have a mutual friend. His name is Perez." The name was familiar, and Alexis couldn't place it where she'd heard it.

"Max is right down the road at the San Ignacio Hotel having a beer if you want to go look for him. Otherwise, you can come back later. He should be back in an hour or so."

"Okay thanks." Without another word, the man turned abruptly. As he walked away, Alexis noticed a slight bulge under his shirt at his waistline. Then it struck her. The man was concealing a gun.

Alexis could hardly keep up with the volume of jewelry sales at the Lost Gringo Trading Company. Sometimes the steady stream of customers prevented her from making any headway at all on her daily quota, so she hired a local girl named Lupita to help with the household chores and Jordan, and assist her in black coral production. In the beginning, she had made black coral beads, pendants, and earrings from polished branches. But, as her skill progressed, she had perfected three-dimensional carvings of sharks, sailboats, and porpoises. Now, more interesting and unusual challenges were arising from Her Majesty's contingent. An officer stopped into her shop one afternoon with one such request.

"I say, Alexis, do you think you could make a miniature black coral helicopter? Not one of those little Scouts or Gazelles, mind you. Those are Army Air Corps. I'm RAF, Royal Air Force, and we fly Pumas. Are you familiar with them?"

"Not really," she replied. "But if I had a line drawing of one, front view, side view, rear view, I could probably carve it for you."

The end result was a precise miniature of the Puma with authentic air intakes of inlaid silver and tiny hammered silver blades and rotor. The RAF officer was overjoyed. He paid Alexis more than what she asked and took the small treasure back to Airport Camp. Within a few days, she found herself swamped with custom orders.

Several officers were interested in larger works of art. Through experimentation Alexis had learned that black coral could be bonded and joined by a special process. The only real limitation was the size of the raw stock. So when an officer asked if she could make a sailfish large enough for a tabletop conversation piece, she was thrilled with the challenge. By using seventeen individual pieces of black coral, Alexis carved, bonded, and shaped an eleven-inch sailfish with a narrow bill and graceful arching sail. She mounted the finished product on a piece of teak and sold it for a hundred and fifty dollars.

After that, the sky was the limit. One after another, the requests for elaborate custom projects came rolling in. Another RAF officer commissioned her to make a five-inch Harrier jet fighter which she mounted on a piece of rosewood. A wealthy Belizean woman asked her to carve the torso of a pregnant woman for her obstetrician to use as a paperweight. For another customer, she made an African woman of black coral, naked to the waist, with a basket balanced on her head. At last, Alexis had found a market for her creative talent and it was making money for her.

Not only was the jewelry going well, but the furniture division of the Lost Gringo Trading Company was also on the move, and Max hired a crew of four woodworkers. Although the prototype of the improved deck chair had turned out beautifully, he was still discontent with the amount of time it took to make each one. Unable to fabricate the crescent moon and develop the chairs at the same time, Max hired two more employees dedicated to the exclusive production of John's orders. Further preoccupied with efficiency and materials projections, he began to spend a lot of time at the hotel talking with local businessmen.

"*Ntombi*, I have got to find a way to make these chairs faster so we can bring down production costs. I think the key to the whole thing would be to buy two more machines: a double-sided planer and a bell saw. First, the wide planks would get run through the planer which grinds both sides smooth in one process. After that, the plank would go through the bell saw, which makes multiple cuts. This would create instantly workable slats, already cut to size. Then all we'd have to do is drill and route the edges and wire them up. I'm thinking we could produce thirty percent more chairs and reduce costs by almost twenty percent."

"Are machines like that available here in Belize?"

"No way. Somebody would need to go to the States again. I went the last time; I was thinking maybe you'd like to go this time."

The States. It had been so long since Alexis had been there; she couldn't even imagine what it would be like. After five years, many things were sure to be different. In a way the prospect excited her, but in other ways she didn't know if she had the nerve. She wasn't used to life in any lane any more, let alone the fast one.

"Of course, it wouldn't just be a buying trip," Max continued. "We can't afford any dead-heading. I'll arrange for you to take a shipment of 'moons' with you and you can deliver them to John. Also, while you're in Miami, you can buy more bulk silver."

"And you're comfortable with me handling the arrangements for shipping back the machines?" she asked tenuously.

"Sure *Ntombi*. We'll go over all that stuff in detail before you leave. I have the name of a contact in Miami who will be able to help you find a Rockwell machinery dealer in the area. We can call him before you go. His name is Sid, and he's a friend of a guy I met recently at the hotel. I think you met him here at the house one day – a big tall guy named Brad Tongas."

The sun had been down for two hours when Alexis finally pulled into the driveway a few days later. It had been a long selling trip to Belize City and she was dog-tired. Gathering the jewelry display board and the jumble of packages, she started up the stairs of the house. Max and Brad Tongas were sitting around the coffee table, involved in an animated discussion. In front of them was a small plastic bag, dusty with white powder, a mirror, and a razor blade. Long white lines were laid out and a rolled-up U.S. hundred dollar bill lay beside it. Max was laughing.

"Hey Alexis, just in time. You remember Brad."

"Yes, I do," she said, coolly. "Max, can I see you in the bedroom for a moment, please?"

He walked in behind her as she threw the stuff down on the bed. "That was a little bit rude. What's the deal?"

"Where is Jordan? Is he in bed?" she demanded.

"Yeah, he went to sleep about an hour ago."

"And suppose he should wake up? You've got drugs lying on the coffee table."

"He's just a little kid. He'd be half asleep and wouldn't know what was going on anyway. Boy, are you uptight. Why don't you come out and do a line or two?"

"Why do you have that man in the house?" Alexis persisted. "I don't want him here."

"Don't take that fucking tone with me," he snapped. "He's my guest. I invited him." She looked into Max's eyes. He was sky-high; his eyes shone wildly and were as black as two pee holes in the snow.

Alexis backed off immediately; it was wise to pick her battles when it came to Max. "I'm sorry. It's just that the guy makes me very nervous. A little smoke in the house is one thing, but cocaine is something else. Did you know he carries a gun? I saw the bulge in his shirt on the first day met him."

"I'm sure you're wrong," Max argued.

"I saw it."

He paused, then changed the subject. "So, did you get your airline ticket?"

"Yes. I'm booked for Wednesday on the morning flight."

"Good," said Max, beginning to relax again. "Now come on out and sit with us for a while. Have a snort or two. I know you're probably tired, but this will wake you up."

"I don't want to wake up. I want to go to sleep." She kissed him on the cheek. "Goodnight."

When the 767 wide-body jet had taken off from Belize International Airport and, as it ascended, only the tiny terminal amidst the broad expanse of jungle gave testimony to the presence of man. Beyond that, the river snaked through the vast expanse of knobby green bush, clumped together like so many heads of broccoli. An hour and forty-five minutes later, the plane began its descent over the silver and white metropolis of Miami. How strange to see the creations of man dominating the landscape again, the bumper-to-bumper traffic crawling on the freeways like army ants. It was only then that Alexis realized she was returning to a previous world that was now as foreign as a planet inhabited by aliens.

From that very moment onward, everything was different: the sights, the sounds, even the smells. People talked fast and moved with purpose. The claustrophobic gangway, the neon lights in the concourse, and colorful advertisements on the walls all contributed to the feeling of unreality. Not knowing where to go, Alexis was carried along by the surge of the crowd. To the extreme right, she saw an aisle reserved for returning American citizens. Feeling privileged, she sauntered through Immigration, the officer barely glancing her way. In the other lines, hundreds of Costa Ricans, Colombians, Bolivians, and Chileans stood in line to have their passports stamped. Moving to the Customs area brought a marked change in ambiance. Because Miami was a major entry point for illegal drugs, the tension was evident. Although she saw no specific indications, Alexis knew that plainclothes police mingled with the crowd. Customs officials asked pointed questions as they searched baggage. They looked directly into the eyes of passengers, and watched for nervousness or tell-tale body language, especially for those who fit the smugglers' profile.

After that, a sense of playful wonder overcame Alexis. She began to feel like a kid at Disney World. Seeing a TV set was bizarre. After so many years, Alexis wasn't used to cathode rays, and it was impossible to look at the screen for more than a few seconds. The flickering light and the rapid changes in camera shots hurt her eyes. She rode an escalator, and marveled at the clean designs of space-age architecture in the contemporary terminal. Everything was so shiny and sterile, so functional, orderly, and purposeful. However, the encounter at the car rental turned out to be neither functional nor orderly. It took almost as long to rent a car as it had taken to fly from Belize to the U.S.

"Pardon me? Did you say you don't have a credit card?"

"No Ma'am. I've been living outside the U.S. for several years now. I've never even owned a credit card before and I don't own one now. But if you need a security deposit, I have cash."

The woman, flustered by the unprecedented situation, spent nearly an hour going back and forth from the front counter to a rear office. Several phone calls were made back and forth before Alexis finally received the go-ahead on the transaction.

At last, with keys in hand, Alexis sat in the driver's seat of a little Plymouth Horizon. Unlike the Land Cruiser or the Chevy Luv, it had low clearance, an FM radio, good speakers, and powerful air-conditioning. It was comfortable, clean, and quiet. Confidently, Alexis turned the key and pulled slowly out of the parking area.

The heady feeling didn't last long. Within three minutes of getting behind the wheel, Alexis was confronted with the whirlwind of the Florida freeway. In Belize, speed limits were governed by how fast one could pass over the potholes and washboard surfaces. Now, far away from the land of *mañana*, she would have to drive fast, think fast, watch for exits, change lanes, and keep up with the fanatical speed of a modern city in a hell of a hurry.

First, I must get to the bank, she thought.

Alexis checked the map and laid out a course to Southeast First National in downtown Miami. Taking her place with the other army ants on the freeway, she maneuvered through the traffic, cars zipping in and out on all sides. Finally arriving on Biscayne Boulevard, she entered a parking ramp next to the bank, spiraled to the very top, and pulled into an empty space. Now it was time to face the new world of people, tarmac, and concrete. Squaring her shoulders and taking a deep breath, Alexis grabbed the keys in the ignition to remove them, and found they wouldn't budge. At first, it was annoying. But after a full minute, it had become a real dilemma. She couldn't get the keys out of the ignition. Her stream of consciousness ran amok.

What will I do now? I can't leave the car without locking it and taking the key. Here I am in the middle of downtown Miami and I can't get my key out of the ignition. It must be a new safety feature. Maybe I have to push and turn at the same time. Nope, that doesn't work either. I'm actually going to have to ask someone. If I had skin of a different color, or had an accent, then maybe people wouldn't expect me to know how to do things. But I look American. I'm supposed to know how to do stuff like this.

A few minutes later, an elderly Cuban, who spoke only Spanish, showed Alexis the small release button on the column. The keys came right out.

The buildings, made of thousands of panes of glass, winked in the afternoon sunlight. Downtown Miami looked different; architecture seemed to have come a long way in just a few years. The enormous bank was very new, very stylish. Looking for the entrance, Alexis walked down the long side of the bank searching for the doors. Doors were easy to recognize, of course, because of the large brown rubber mats that extended outside. Everybody knew it was necessary to step on the mat to open the doors. Hmmm, no mats, no doors.

After walking the entire length of the bank, she paused, and then walked its width as well. She could see people inside the bank, so obviously there had to be a way to get in. At that moment, a Chinese man approached the side of the building. Although he looked like he was on a collision course, the wall opened like magic at the last second to admit him. Whoosh – just like Star Trek. Amazing. No mats outside the doors; the doors looked like part of the glass wall. Quickly, Alexis followed behind the Asian, trying to act like she'd known where the doors were all along. It was too late for pretense, she thought, chagrinned; people had been watched her pacing the perimeter of the bank building for the last five minutes.

The United States was different; everything had changed. Convenience stores were different. Cash registers and checkout counters had changed. Pay phones cost more money and had different instructions and functions. Alexis' continuing culture shock would be ongoing, the humiliation complete when she went to the bank drive-in later that day.

Drive-in banks were not a new concept but, like everything else, they had changed. Years back, when Alexis used the drive-in services, she had simply driven up to the side of the building. The teller, visible through the glass, would speak through a microphone, and the transaction would be done through a drawer. But now the bank building was far away; the drive-in was ten lanes wide and drivers waited in line to pull up to some kind of individual station beside their lane. Having no idea what to expect, Alexis was startled at her station when a drawer suddenly flew out and extended a tubular object toward her. OK, no live teller. Staring at the tube, she finally figured that this thing was used for transactions. Oops, too late. Hesitating a fraction too long, the drawer pulled the cylinder back inside and swallowed it. Uh-oh, thought Alexis. I just know this machine is going to talk to me.

"Ahhh, you didn't put anything inside the carrier, Ma'am."

Alexis had had enough. She was an American but couldn't function like one. It was time to firmly establish her identity as a foreigner. So, in her finest Creole pidgin, she replied, *"Well look hyah, Mummy. Yu neva give me one chance, mon. Yu done take de t'ing back too quick."* When the vacuum tube was returned, Alexis seized it immediately. But, unfortunately, then she didn't know how to open it.

The second day she delivered the order of mahogany moons to John. Uninterested in contacting anyone or anything having to do with that Brad character, Alexis used the Yellow Pages to locate industrial machine manufacturers, and then shopped for the best deal and made the order through the distributor in Atlanta. On the third day, she dragged her sample chair in and out of every import showroom and warehouse in the greater Miami area. On the fourth day, she visited furniture retailers who specialized in unfinished or 'naked' furniture. Everybody liked the chairs, but nobody wanted to buy them in quantity.

"It's a very nice product," one importer told her, "and at twenty-five U.S dollars, FOB Miami, please understand, it's not that it's overpriced, it's just that it's overbuilt. We'd want something light and easy to transport, landed here in Miami for around six bucks, so it can retail for nineteen ninety-five. This deck chair is beautiful, but even folded, it's still bulky and hard to transport. After all, it's made of solid mahogany and it must weigh at least ten pounds. You get the price down, and I'll see about ordering some."

Alexis knew it would never happen. Instead, she had some professional pictures taken of the chair to use in future promotions and then sold her sample to the photographer for fifty bucks. There were other priorities that demanded her attention. Alexis would still have to buy the jewelry supplies, but that was something that should be done at the end of her trip, so she wasn't carrying valuable silver all around town.

Once the machinery arrives from Atlanta, she thought, I'll have to arrange to get it shipped to Belize, air freight. But that won't be for a few more days. Meanwhile, what would be the best use of my time? I still have some samples of crystal moons and black coral jewelry. Maybe if there were some head shops around here, like the ones that used to be in Key West...

Key West. She recalled the reflection of a face, and fragments of sleeping memories. Key West was only a hundred and fifty miles from Miami, a three and a half hour drive down the long skinny highway that spanned the island chain. Suddenly, she had to go there. The magic was drawing her back.

Key Largo, Islamorada, Bahia Honda. The names rolled over her tongue like fine wine. In a trance, she took Truman Avenue into the heart of Key West, turned right onto Duval Street, and arrived at Mallory Pier just before sunset. Alexis stood on the quay, watching in silence from the sidelines, this time an observer rather than a participant. Young people enjoyed the spectacle of sun and sea in their glad-rags and patched jeans – the dogs, the kids, and the babies, just like before. But, lacking the spirit of an earlier era, they all seemed to be pale impersonations of the colorful characters Alexis had once known, and there was not one familiar face.

The next morning, Alexis went to a gift shop in Old Town and found that luck was with her. The buyer bought all the crystals and almost every piece of black coral jewelry she had. A half hour later, she had cash in her pocket and stepped out into the late morning sunshine, almost colliding with a handsome young man of Mediterranean descent.

"Eddie? From the Hialeah Gallery?"

"Alexis? Wow, what a surprise! When did you get back in Florida? Gosh, how long has it been? Seven years? Eight?"

Together, the old acquaintances went to a local cafe and ordered Cuban coffee. Eddie told her that he and his boyfriend had broken up when the gallery sold some years back. He had then purchased a boat and endured a harrowing adventure on the high seas that ended up beaching him on the Virgin Islands for a over a year.

"I've still got the boat but I'm fixing her up for sale. It's been anchored on Bahia Honda where I've been living. I only came to Key West today to meet a potential buyer and drive him up there."

Talking about good times, Alexis elaborated about Max, Jordan, and Belize, and they reminisced about Marcy and others they had known. "I know of one person who's here, someone very special to you, if I recall. Indian Ron. He's here in Key West."

Ron. Of all people. Silently, her heart swelled with joy. Choked with emotion, she could barely say the words.

"Where is Ron?"

"He's living over on Whitehead Street, not far from the old Hemmingway house. I can take you there if you want."

"Oh yes, please! This is why I was meant to come back. It must be fate."

"Perhaps more than you know," said Eddie, cryptically.

"What do you mean?"

He hesitated. "Ron is dying. He's got lung cancer. It's terminal."

"Take me to him, please," she whispered hoarsely, taking his arm."

They took Simonton to Eaton and down Whitehead. Within a few blocks, Eddie pointed out the large white house. It was a classic wood-frame Key West house, complete with widow's walk and gingerbread trim on the verandas and eaves.

"That's the house. Good luck. I've got to go meet my buyer. Besides, I'm sure you'd like to see Ron in private."

"Thanks for everything, Eddie. It was so wonderful to see you. Maybe we'll meet again on the shores of Belize." She hugged him, and then turned to face the house, squaring her shoulders.

The house was shady, surrounded by large palms and a towering Spanish lime tree. Gardens of pink and white oleanders and peach-colored bougainvillea lined the walkway. Music came from around the back of the house, and the thought struck her that perhaps Ron lived alone, or was bedridden, unable to answer. So she walked around the back and peered through the sliding glass doors. It was a comfortable space, painted in soothing greens and blues, with houseplants of all kinds and a waterbed in the corner. A hand-painted mural of an island seascape adorned the far wall, and a lovely arrangement of fresh flowers graced the room.

Alexis knocked on the glass door gently and slid it open just a little. Immediately, she sensed the fragrance of sandalwood.

"Ron?"

"Just a minute," came the muted reply from the bathroom. "I'll be right there."

Alexis' heart beat wildly at the thought of seeing him again. Instead of taking a chair, she knelt on the soft carpeting, not knowing exactly why. Bowing her head quietly, she waited for him. The frail figure entered the room slowly, as she raised her head. He was recognizable, but just barely. It was hard to say which of them was more startled.

"Alexis? Is it really you?" he said, throwing his arms wide. "My darling girl."

Alexis couldn't speak. With a kaleidoscopic mind of color and poetry, Ron had been her teacher of life and living. She loved him for his high ideals, as well as his human weaknesses and inconsistencies. Lifting her chin to look into her eyes, he spoke softly.

"Somebody told you, didn't they?"

She nodded. "Yes."

Ron started to talk, but then turned aside and began to cough. Hacking loudly, he doubled over as his tiny frame was racked by the spasm. She supported him and gently helped him back to the waterbed.

"I hate this," he said, wincing in pain, "and I'm still vain enough to not want you to see me like this."

"You wouldn't say that if you knew how happy I am to see you again." She paused. "Is there any hope?"

"My dear." He smiled, regaining stability as the spasm left him. "There is always hope. As long as man draws breath, there is hope."

"You're not living alone here, are you?"

"Oh no, thank God. There are people who love me still. I have a good woman named Sarah. "She is at work right now, but will be home shortly. Her younger brother lives with us too. He is helpful during bad spells."

Alexis touched Ron's thin face. "You still have your hair. You haven't been doing chemotherapy?"

"No, I am treating myself with the Max Gerson diet. Are you familiar with that?"

"*Death Be Not Proud*. The John Gunther Jr. story. I read it as a child."

"Most people aren't familiar with it. I eat fresh organic vegetables and fruits, especially apples and carrots. I also have to do coffee enemas three times a day to draw out the tars and toxins."

"An enema? Using coffee?"

At this point, the tension was broken as Ron started to laugh. "You remember how much I used to love my Cuban coffee. Well, now I just ingest it in a different way."

"Oh Ron!" Alexis was laughing too. It was comic relief, a release of tension.

"All those cigarettes you used to smoke…"

"I smoked more than two packs a day for thirty-five years. It was my one great sin against myself. I never respected the temple of my body. Now I'm paying the price."

"You were worried about your health the last time I saw you. Wasn't that just before you went to New York for testing?"

"Yes. We have a lot of catching up to do."

They spoke for hours until the light began to dim and the apricot sky blended with the dusky violet. Finally, Ron made a suggestion. "Let's go out on the veranda and smoke a doobie," he said, with the old familiar twinkle in his eye.

"Smoke? You can't be serious. Smoke is what's killing you."

"Cigarettes, not pot. This will be the last time I'll ever see you. One more joint won't make a difference. I'm dying anyway."

"Don't say that."

"Let me finish. Sarah doesn't know it, but for over a year I have saved one good bud of Colombian for such an occasion. Marijuana has been my sacrament for these many years. I want to share the spirit with you for one last time. Indulge me. It will be a moment for us to remember."

"You're never far from me Ron. I will always carry you in my heart."

Alexis stayed with Ron and Sarah that night in a quiet guest room overlooking the vegetable garden. Sarah was a lovely woman, cultured, caring, and artistic. The next morning, Alexis awoke feeling refreshed, and sat with Sarah on the front porch swing. They sipped their tea while Ron was busy with his morning treatment.

"I'm so grateful that you're here for him," Alexis said.

"How could I not be? That's just the kind of man he is," she replied. "Many women have loved him. I'm just lucky to be one of them. I know you are too. I appreciate and respect your closeness to him. He told me about you many times."

"Thank you for letting me stay the night. I'll be heading back to Miami this morning."

"And I'll be off to work in a minute. Help me bring Ron out here into the sitting room before I go."

After Sarah left, Alexis walked around the back of Ron's chair and began to massage his neck. She could feel his frailty. "I'm afraid it's time for me to leave as well, Ron. I wish I could stay and take care of you."

"That's sweet, darling. But you have your own life now and your own husband and son to take care of. So much has happened. Tell me, do you still have those dreams, Alexis?"

"It's funny you should mention it. It's been about a year ago since the last time I dreamed about that beach again – the wind and gray and the cold seaweed under my feet. And sometimes I still have those dreams where the demon is chasing me."

"I, too, run from the demon. But, of course, I know the name of mine." He paused. "You are so beautiful my dear, so young and strong. Your face glows. Come close, and let me look at you again." She came close, and smiled at him, her eyes bright with emotion. "Closer. I want to see something."

Ron looked in her eyes carefully. Then he reached down and touched her abdomen. "There is life inside you," he said. "You are going to have a baby. A daughter this time."

"What? I'm pregnant? Are you sure?"

"Yes. She will be the light of your life, with golden hair, and eyes like yours. God's cycle continues. Life moves on. His justice is perfect – a life for a life. I am the brown leaf that withers and dies. But the fresh green growth of springtime carries the everlasting promise of renewal. With this new baby, my place on this earth is filled by another." He touched her face gently as he leaned forward to kiss her one last time. "Now I can truly tell you not to cry for me."

 **JESSICA**

chapteR 12_____

The return flight to Belize was such a stormy nightmare of bumps and squalls that Alexis was ready to kiss the earth when the wheels touched down. Home sweet jungle home. Within minutes, the familiar damp heat penetrated her clothes and skin. After passing through Immigration and Customs, she scanned the crowd and saw Max's unsmiling face. Oddly enough, she didn't see Jordan.

"Hi Alexis," he said brusquely, ushering her out of the airport. "Let's go."

"What's the matter? Where's Jordan?"

"Get in the car."

Max was silent as he loaded the baggage into the Land Cruiser and a terrible fear crept over Alexis. Something was dreadfully wrong. He drove away from the airport, turned down a side road, and parked in the shade of a tree. Then he began to question her.

"I want to clear the air right away. I want to know who you slept with when you were in the States. You fucked around with somebody. I know you did. Who was it? Brad's friend?"

"What are you talking about? Is that how you're going to greet me after I've been working my ass off in the States? You know what I was doing up there. My every move was orchestrated by you before I left."

"Your ass is exactly what I'm talking about. What's his name? Brad's friend? Did you go to see the contact guy about the machinery?"

"His name was Sid. And no, I didn't see him. I used the Yellow Pages and let my fingers do the walking. What's gotten into you, Max? Where did you get such a crazy idea?"

"After you left, Brad started talking about what a letch Sid is. He said he'd have you in bed within two hours."

"If that was true, then why did Brad advise that I look him up in the first place? Why didn't he share that juicy tidbit with you before I left? Don't you see what a shit-stirrer Brad is? Even if the guy did try to hit on me, wouldn't you trust me to refuse him?"

"I don't know," said Max, his hands shaking. "We were snorting a few lines and I got freaked out. Brad created a mental picture of you screwing this guy and enjoying it. Ever since then, I haven't been able to shake the feeling."

"When we got married we made a deal. I've kept my word. I have never been involved with another man." The statement was a bad move on Alexis' part. It served to remind Max that the reverse was not true. The memory of Katrina was still vivid, and instead of defusing the situation, her comments made his anger burn hotter. He glared at her, scrutinizing her face for anything that might betray her words.

"Maybe not in the past, but this time you fucked somebody else. I can sense it."

Continuing homeward, they drove in silence for the next hour and a half. When Max and Alexis arrived at the house, he took her into the bedroom immediately.

"Where's Jordan?" she asked.

"Playing at the neighbors' house. Take your clothes off."

"What?"

He struck her in the face with the flat of his hand and Alexis' mind exploded in shock. "Don't fuck with me. I said take your clothes off. Do what you're told. I know you screwed around and I intend to find the evidence."

Stunned by the blow, terror shook her as she undressed. Max was somebody else again, somebody she didn't know. Anger and humiliation rose until she thought she would choke on it. Naked, Max made her lie down on the bed. Then he removed his own clothing and began to examine her body slowly, his breathing heavy and his voice coarse. She could feel his excitement as he ran his hands over her. He probed her breasts, neck, thighs, and pubic area, looking for any indications of red marks, swelling, or recent sexual activity.

"Okay," he said. "So your lover was careful and didn't leave any marks on you. That's more than you'll be able to say for me. I'm taking back what is mine." Gripping her upper arms, his fingers bruised her flesh. Her scream was suppressed by a savage kiss. Then he forced her legs apart, and took her brutally. It took three weeks before Alexis had the nerve to tell her husband she was pregnant.

During her first trimester, Alexis slept ten hours every night and still took a two-hour nap in the afternoon. She felt perpetually tired, and unlike her first pregnancy, suffered with morning sickness. From the relative calm of the previous months, Max had reverted to his old ways. Luckily, he was gone a great deal of the time and Alexis was thankful for his absence.

Max had been spending a lot of time with Brad and his white powder, ever since Alexis' return from the States. First, they had met regularly at the house. Then, uncharacteristically, Alexis put her foot down and said no more and, just as surprisingly, Max had yielded.

"If you insist on hanging out with this guy, then please arrange to meet him at the hotel. I'm pregnant, and I'm trying to stay calm and healthy for the baby's sake," said Alexis. "I've made it plain that I don't like the guy hanging around this house. What is it that you talk about all the time anyway?"

"Don't push me," Max lashed back. "You've got a lot of nerve telling me where I can and can't meet my friends. As for our venture, you will be informed on a need-to-know basis. And right now, you don't need to know."

The fall of 1979 would be remembered by many as the worst rainy season in a decade. Tropical showers were expected to be frequent and heavy in the months of September, October, and November, but this year malevolent storms raged, one after the other. The heavens opened and raindrops the size of golf balls smacked the ground. Puddles became ponds, ponds became lakes, and lakes began to creep across the lowlands. In the high country, rivulets became streams, then creeks, and finally roaring rivers in full spate. The water flowed from the mountains into the Sibun and Belize Rivers until they overflowed their banks and spread across the flats of scrub and saw-palmetto east of Belmopan, eventually covering the highway that connected east with west.

Alexis looked out the window despondently. Normally, the term 'rainy season' didn't mean it rained all the time. It was simply the time of year when it was expected to rain, unless of course, it didn't. But this was like Bangladesh during the monsoons. The idea of trying to conduct business in Belize City with all this rain was ludicrous. She was tired, but she knew she must make another army selling trip before Christmas. The soldiers would be buying like crazy. Also, if she didn't go, she'd be stuck trying to buy presents for Jordan in Cayo, and there was nothing to buy. The rain persisted and finally she could put it off no longer. Alexis gave some last minute instructions to Lupita and kissed Jordan goodbye. Max handed her an additional list of needs for the wood shop.

"And if Augusto Quan's doesn't have that yellow wood glue, go to the Lebanese shop on Basra Street. But for God's sake, don't come back without it. Production will come to a halt if we don't have wood glue."

"Anything else?"

"Yeah. Make sales. Don't let anything get in your way. Just get the money, Alexis. That's the main thing. Just get the money."

The rain was ceaseless. As Alexis left Cayo and drove east, she began to see the standing water. Usually she could only catch a glimpse of the distant rivers, but now they filled the valleys, brown and swollen, spilling their banks. The flooding was extensive, but she didn't realize exactly how extensive until she stopped at the edge of the newly-formed inland sea just east of the junction to Belmopan. Directly in front of her the highway disappeared; there was water as far as she could see. About sixty feet out, she saw an overturned bus, and a Land Rover, drowning in the current.

For several days, vehicles such as British Army Land Rovers, Unimogs, and busses had continued to brave the short stretches of water that breached the road. But when the water was so high it seeped in under the doors, even high-clearance vehicles had to give up. For another day or two, buses had driven to the edge of the water and discharged passengers into dories to be ferried to other buses waiting on the other side. But at last the water became too high, the distance too great. The current over the road began to sweep the dories off course, endangering the occupants. The watery gap widened, and finally all transportation between east and west came to a halt. It was an impasse; Alexis was not going anywhere. She turned around and drove home.

"What the hell are you doing back here?"

"I couldn't get through, Max. The road's flooded. The lowlands between Belmopan and Hattieville are completely underwater. Traffic is totally cut off."

"You're making up this bullshit because you don't want to go to Belize City. The water couldn't have been that high. We've slogged through before. You know how to do it; just drive slowly so the water doesn't splash on the spark plugs."

"It wasn't a matter of splashing. The whole vehicle would have been submerged!"

"Damn it, there had to be a way. It couldn't have been that deep. You could have left the truck with somebody and hitched a ride with one of those one-ton high-clearance Land Rovers the army has. Haven't I taught you anything about ingenuity? Where there's a will, there's a way. You just didn't want to get through. You're too damn lazy. All you want to do is hang out at home with your feet up."

"Stop it! Just stop it! That's not fair! Yes, I've been tired lately. Yes, it's been an effort to motivate myself. I'm pregnant. But I need to go. I've got a million things to take care of. I've got wholesale accounts I need to see, Christmas presents to buy."

"Christmas again," he spat in disgust. "You and your fucking Christmas bullshit."

"Stop criticizing me!" Alexis finally shouted. "I'm your wife! Does it never end with you? The yelling, the badgering, the lists, the rules, the detailed reports of everything? Can't you ever just believe in me and trust what I say?"

"How dare you raise your voice to me like that?" Max yelled back at her. His face was black with rage as he knocked her back against the mahogany bureau. Her head hit the sharp corner with a crack. Blood poured from a inch-long gash above her ear and streamed down her neck and shoulder. He walked away in disgust. "Bitch."

In mid-March, Max received the letter from his mother saying that Guy had died of a massive heart attack. Ellie had written that he had awakened one morning, "feeling buggered" was how he'd put it, and asked if she'd like a quick tennis game "to get the kinks out." Preparing for the serve, Guy bounced the ball a few times and tossed it into the air. The chest pain hit him in mid-swing and he collapsed on the hard-packed surface.

The next two hours had been a blur to the old woman. In all the years on Good Faith, there had always been people around, children, grandchildren, and servants. Yet, coincidentally, on that particular day, there was no one nearby. Ellie tried in vain to resuscitate her husband, then cradled Guy's head in her arms and held him until his body turned cold. A soft rain began to fall. Finally, Ellie managed to drag him into the house, phoned the police, and nearly got herself jailed for moving the body.

"Can you imagine?" she had written. "What was I supposed to do? Leave him out there in the rain?" Guy had wanted much from life and had received bountifully. Of death, he had made only three demands: that God let him die before his wife, to go quickly without suffering, and to die on the tractor wearing his boots, or the tennis court wearing his sneakers. "Lucky devil," Ellie had written. "He got every last wish."

Max took the news fairly well, but Alexis mourned her father-in-law. Although she had known him only through his wonderful letters and a few photographs, she had loved his warmth and humanity. To Alexis, Guy seemed to be the best part of Max, and now he would never see Jordan, or his new unborn grandchild. Alexis' thoughts turned to her own parents. She began to see clearly now that the move to Central America had been a selfish act, one that had impacted many lives besides her own. She started to realize how much she had cheated her family; Frank and Liz deserved Jordan and the new baby, the children deserved their grandparents. She was beginning to realize she had cheated herself as well.

The dry season was in full force as May arrived. Every time a big truck passed their house in town, more white silt blew through the air and into the house. Eight months pregnant, the ninety-seven degree temperature was stifling, and Alexis longed for the river. The Macal was most beautiful at this time of year. It was when the waters receded into deep bottle-green pools and iguanas, fat with eggs, lay prone on the lowest branches of the trees, ready to plop into the cool river at the slightest disturbance.

It was hard to concentrate on her jewelry business. Alexis had hoped she could decrease her trips to Belize City, but Max disagreed with the logic. He said it made more sense for her to press hard now while she still could. Once the baby was born, there would be a long delay before she could go again.

There was another reason for her reluctance. There had been two shootings in Belize City over the last two months, and authorities believed them to be drug-related. Many thought that Belize had become a stopover for Colombian drug-running and that Lear jets had been landing offshore for refueling. Although the local population of unemployed indigents had always drunk One Barrel Rum, and some indulged in smoking marijuana, now there was a source of contraband cocaine, and the city-dwellers were learning to cook it into free-base.

In reaction to the incident, Max's solution was to buy Alexis a twenty-two caliber semi-automatic pistol. She not only disliked the weapon, she refused to carry it. Guns were for people who had the mind-set to use them, and in spite of the incident, Alexis wasn't sure if she would use a gun if a similar situation arose. If a gun were involved in a confrontation, it was more likely that she might be its victim. Nevertheless, Max schooled her in the basic use of the pistol. And now, pregnant or not, he insisted that she carry the weapon, and continue her trips to Belize City. Resistance was futile.

Her selling trips stopped abruptly in mid-June when Alexis went into labor, and by coincidence, it seemed that nearly everyone she knew happened to be in Cayo on that particular Thursday. When the word went out that the baby was on its way, more and more friends arrived to wait out the home delivery, and the gathering in the next room turned into a party.

Even Maggie Davis happened to be in town that day. A former obstetrics nurse from Texas, she and Alexis had become good friends through the years. Maggie had offered to help deliver Alexis' baby, if good fortune allowed her to be nearby at the critical time, and she turned out to be a godsend. As the labor progressed, she could hear the talking and laughter from the other room, and every time she screamed, somebody simply turned up the volume on the record player. Although torment racked her body, it was not as intense as the first time, and when the contractions were less than one minute apart, Maggie held her hand and told her to push.

At four minutes after eight o'clock, Jessica Lord was born, bright-red and howling, weighing in at seven pounds, two ounces. Even at birth she was beautiful, and Alexis experienced one of the proudest moments in her life when Maggie laid the newborn child across her bare chest. The baby began to nurse even before the umbilical cord was cut.

Alexis' recovery rate was phenomenal. Forty-five minutes after delivery, Maggie helped her walk down the back stairs and take a shower. An hour later, she was able to join her friends in the living room and show off the tiny infant. Max was happy-drunk and wept for joy. Jordan danced around the room wearing a straw hat, and playing his toy ukulele, but he wasn't really sure what had happened until his father sat him down on the couch and put his infant sister in his arms. Then Jordan's little face lit up with pride and delight.

A few weeks after Jessica's birth, Max went on a buying trip to Mexico. He was convinced that their next step should be to offer a less expensive line of costume jewelry and found a good source in Taxco. With Lupita's help, and the help of a local woodworker named Ernesto to manage the woodshop, things could pretty well run without Max for a week or two.

During Max's absence, Eric came to visit Alexis at the house. He was one of the few who hadn't been in town on Jessica's birthday, and was sorry he'd missed the big event.

"Aw, she's gorgeous," said Eric softly, as he peeked into the crib and saw the head full of thick dark-gold hair. "She looks like you."

"She was a raisin-face at birth," Alexis teased, pulling the light cotton cover over the sleeping infant. "But she's my beautiful baby girl now. Let's go sit on the front porch outside, if you like, and you can give me the low-down on valley life."

"And plenty of low-down there is," said Eric. "Wait 'til you hear what's been going on. First of all, Joel and Kirsten are adjusting to life back in the States. Kirsten thinks she has a good job lined up and Joel's going to go back to school at Texas A & M. I guess they are trying to buy a house in College Station."

"It's just as well. I don't think they were ever really cut out for Belize," said Alexis.

"A lot of people came around the same time we did and a lot of them have already gone back. This lifestyle is too hard, especially on women. I don't know how much longer Maggie and Tim will be staying either. It sounds like they're going back to San Antonio. You know how it is. In the beginning, it's all fun and games, a fantasy lifestyle in the jungle. But then the reality of chopping wood and carrying water kills the magic. To tell you the truth, my marriage with Sheila is on the rocks for the same reason. She's just plain tired of working so hard. Can I blame her? Since when have I made money here in Belize? I made a little working with Richard Foster and the Belize Zoo people on the nature movies. Then I did all right on the exploratory oil rigs down south. But I've never had a consistent income as long as I've lived here. It's a hard life for Sheila. She's fed up with spiders, scorpions, ants, and now with this malaria going around..."

"Malaria?" said Alexis, alarmed. "Who's got malaria?"

"You didn't know? It started off with a couple of the Mennonites downstream, but then the Fernandez family got it, and I think a couple of *gringos* too. Everybody's dosed themselves with quinine and I guess they're doing all right now. Nobody died. But then again nobody knows if it's the recurring strain or not. Not yet, anyway."

"That's terrible."

"Yeah, well I've got a lot more medical news." He pulled the bandanna from his head. "See? My forehead finally scarred over from the *leishmaniasis*."

"The heavy metal injections worked?"

"Yep," Eric continued. "That's what finally cured me. But the antidote is quite poisonous; the shots made me violently sick the whole time. And let's see? What else? Oh, I speared my foot on a piece of cohune last week. What an idiot! I was splitting the ribs barefoot, and a big splinter went right into my foot and broke off. The British Army doctor got out most of it, but he said the smaller splinters will have to work their way out, little by little. So every time another one gets near the surface, I get Maggie to come over and remove it surgically. It still hurts though."

Belize is definitely not a good place for the accident-prone, Alexis thought.

"And the biggest news is that I finally took my long-anticipated excursion into Nohoch Sayab. You might remember that an archaeologist wandered into the valley last year and expressed interest in exploring the water cave. Yeah, right. Every *gringo* to ever visit Baron's Creek talks about doing that. But this guy, Carl, and his buddy George, actually showed up about six or eight weeks ago with a specially outfitted canoe, lights, ropes, dried rations and all the supplies necessary for a three man expedition." Eric's eyes glowed with excitement as he told the story.

After extensive preparation, the three men had entered the mouth of the huge cavern and paddled into the darkness of the underworld. As home to countless tens of thousands of bats, the smell of *guano* permeated the chamber, and flocks of swiftlets had flitted in and out of the enormous cavern, their nests high in the crags of jagged limestone. At first, there were river otters and other signs of life, but as the river twisted and curved up into the belly of the mountain, their carbon torch headlamps illuminated an ancient cavern that was completely devoid of animal life, but revealed spectacular geological form and color previously hidden in the blackness.

For the first several hours the enormous tunnel maintained its size. Shining their headlamps, they could see that the water was stunningly clear, with a clean sandy bottom that was rarely deeper than six feet. But as they went further, the tunnel widened into an amphitheater of unimaginable proportion. Low clay banks were studded with stalagmites, and their upper counterparts hung like massive spears from the lofty arches. There were pillars of limestone the size of giant sequoias and a vaulted ceiling that extended far beyond the range of the lamps. Eric and George were tempted to land the craft and explore, but Carl reminded them that the primary directive was to go as far into the cave as possible.

As the expedition pressed on, the current became stronger. The walls closed in and the ceiling dropped dramatically. Sitting in the bow, Eric could clearly see a narrow fissure ahead where white water gushed toward them with terrific force. Although the three men were in peak condition, they had been paddling constantly for hours and the effort was beginning to show. The waves hit the bow and splashed over the gunwales, but no one wanted to turn back. Slick with sweat, Eric and George pushed against the slippery rocks with short sticks while Carl sat astern and used the paddle as a rudder. Fighting to keep the boat's nose headed stubbornly upstream was dangerous work. To capsize could be fatal; lost in the black waters, survival would be unlikely. To make matters worse, the fissure was not only narrow, it was long. With tremendous effort, the men finally reached the top of the rapids. Once they had broken free of the white water they found themselves in another spectacular cavern with calm gentle water.

"It's nighttime somewhere out there," said George, cheerfully.

"Dark outside, dark inside. When you're in a cave, it doesn't matter what time it is," Carl replied.

Eric shined his torch lamp into the vastness. "Wow, look at this place. Let's park this thing for a while. I'm exhausted."

The river hugged the rock wall on the right side, but on the left was a great humping bank of dun-colored sand. Beaching the canoe on the point, the men got out and stretched painfully. They had already been gone for seven hours. Except for the dripping water echoing hollowly beyond the shadows, they heard only the sounds of silence.

The next few hours were among the most exciting of Eric's life. To the rear of the sandy bay, he climbed above to a wide terrace of rock and found nine human skeletons, all laid out in a row. Nine was the sacred number of the Maya and the flattened foreheads on the skulls revealed their nobility. They were obviously chieftains, as bits of colored thread and particles of feathers still clung to their bones. Also, several clay pots had survived; some still contained petrified *cacao* beans, once used by the Maya as currency. One of the pots was decorated with colorful pigments and depicted captives being humiliated and tortured before a victorious king. Near the body of the seventh chieftain, Eric spied a narrow tube of clay half-buried in the sand. He washed it carefully in the river, discovering that it was a small open-hole flute about six inches in length. Holding it to his pursed lips, he blew into the instrument and heard the soft resonance of the note.

Meanwhile, Carl had made another discovery. Thirty yards away he found a mat of fibers. Between the layers was a complete set of ceremonial knives made of obsidian. Some were as small as razor blades, and others large enough to cut out a human heart or dismember a human body.

Eric knelt beside the second skeleton and tried to envision the burial scene. Nine lords of the night, he thought. What would it have been like to see the long procession of boats, illuminated only by torches of corn cob and pitch pine? He plucked absent-mindedly at a tuft of cord in the sand as his thoughts wandered. A second later, he pulled out a large strand of jade beads varying in size from a small pea to the size of a man's thumb. The centerpiece contained the face of Chaac, the Rain God. The remote cavern had surrendered archaeological treasures beyond their wildest hopes.

The threesome decided to continue farther upstream, but the journey became anti-climactic. From that point onward, the size of the tunnel dwindled. There were no more chambers, just more rushing water and narrowing passages. The ceiling became lower and lower. Finally the men needed to lie down below the gunwales just to get through. It was enough.

"This is as far as we can go," said Eric, "and it's just as well, 'cause I just had a horrible thought."

"What's the matter?" asked Carl.

"Well, I know it's only mid-May, but what if it should happen to rain in the Maya Mountains? This cave would fill up. If the water level would rise after we passed through even one of these low-ceiling keyholes, we would be trapped until the water level went down enough for our boat to pass through. If we didn't drown or starve." It was an appalling thought. Instantly, the decision was made, and the tired team turned back and began the easy float downstream.

Alexis took a deep breath as Eric concluded the incredible story. "Did you keep any of the stuff from the cave?" she asked.

"Oh no," Eric said, with a mysterious smile. "That would have been illegal." He pressed an object into her palm. "But I do have something for you. Congratulations on your new baby." Alexis looked down and saw, in her palm, a dark jade bead the size of a small marble.

In Mayan culture and custom, four colors represented the four cardinal directions: north was black, east was red, south was white, and west was blue. Green was the Mayan color that represented the center of it all, the here and now; it was symbolic of the place where a person was, at any given moment. Jade was green – the color of being.

* * * *

Max kept unusual hours after Jessica's birth. He went out in the middle of the night and made unexplained trips during the day. Alexis tried to ignore her suspicions about his involvement with Brad until she overheard the wood-working crew talking.

Apparently, a man named Perez had been growing weed for shipment to the United States. When the crop was harvested, with a plane and a pilot waiting, Brad had shown up on the farmer's doorstep in an old Ford step-side pick-up truck. Apparently, he had explained, a problem had occurred with the money for the shipment. Apologizing for the mix up, Brad had offered Perez the gift of two shotguns, as well as the truck, as a good faith partial payment towards the balance of the money he promised to bring on the next trip. Perez knew the big *gringo* had conned him and he was angry. But he still needed to get rid of the crop. Brad had the advantage and the local man knew it; he couldn't just leave the stuff sitting around the *ranchito* getting moldy inside the plastic garbage bags. Perez had no choice, and had handed over the goods.

Two days later, Max drove a huge Dodge recreational vehicle into the driveway. Although it did not seem to have any direct correlation to the story Alexis had heard, she was more than suspicious. Sure enough, Max said that it had been a gift from Brad and would be ideal for hauling chairs to Belize City for international export, or local retail sale.

Brad spent hours in secret conference with Max and his other cronies. Ensconced in their secret hidey-hole in San Ignacio, they smoked, drank coffee, and schemed on their future millions. Brad conned others, but never Max. Instead, he gave him the van and kept him high. Max was useful to Brad, and besides, the van was stolen anyway. And things were going well. Another crop was already in the ground, being tended by another Belizean farmer Brad had blackmailed, and the police were being well-paid to look the other way.

Max's illegitimate business was also booming. By making trips to Mexico, buying finished silver jewelry, and smuggling it into Belize using the cheap costume jewelry as a cover, he was turning a good profit. And taking that hot little Creole girl with him the last time had been delicious. She wasn't a prostitute, just the sister of his Belizean mechanic. The girl had only wanted a little joy ride in a nice vehicle, a good meal, and a little spending cash. So Max took her over the northern border to Chetumal, fed her, fucked her, financed her to the tune of ten dollars, and put her back on the bus to Belize City. Both legally and morally, Max considered himself above the law. He was a heavy dude. There was no remorse.

 **ADVENT**

chapter 13_____

From her earliest days in Belize, Alexis had made a personal crusade to bring birth control to the native women. There were too many children, little professional medical attention, and even less nutritional knowledge. The strong influence of the Catholic Church made it impossible for these women to have any career but motherhood, and the government's only interest was to produce as many Belizeans as possible. The infant mortality rate was appalling. Many babies died of simple dehydration.

Alexis had had a talk with Lupita early in her employment, explaining that, without birth control, she would never have the opportunity for any life beyond the stereotypical barefoot-and-pregnant village girl. She would chop wood, carry water, cook for her husband, have a baby every year, and be old by the time she was thirty. In spite of her simple upbringing in *Cristo Rey*, Lupita was a bright and perceptive girl, and often talked about how much she would like to break away from Belize and have the opportunity to know other places. In the States, a woman could have a career, or a family, or both. Women didn't have much of a future in Belize.

"Tell me, do you have a boyfriend?" Alexis inquired delicately.

Blushing a little, Lupita had answered. *"Yes, but we don' do dose t'ings."*

"Well, if you don't now, you certainly will before long. Why don't you let me help you out? I'll take you to the doctor and get you some birth control pills."

"But my ma would lash me, and my pa would knock me 'cross de room."

"They don't have to know about it," Alexis reassured her. "This is your life, not theirs. No matter what happens later, if you're tied down with a baby, you won't be able to take advantage of anything that might come your way."

Lupita had decided to take Alexis' advice, and now, almost two years later, her oldest sister had invited her to come and live in Los Angeles. There was a job opening, and Lupita would have the chance to attend classes at the university. In a few weeks, Alexis knew she would have to say goodbye to her employee and friend, but she was pleased at having played a small part in Lupita's efforts to better herself and expand her horizons.

A woman named Bertha interviewed for Lupita's job. At sixty-two years old, her gray wooly hair was tinged yellow from wood smoke, and her eyes shone blue with cataracts. The old black hands were gnarled and callused, the nails yellow and horny. Although hard work had long since robbed her of youth and beauty, Alexis felt this was the type of employee that would last. Bertha was the grandmotherly type who could cook and clean; she would be devoted to the children and rule the house with love and a firm hand. Alexis was all set to hire her when Max threw a wrench in the works.

"I want you to interview one more girl for the maid position," said Max.

"But Bertha has already given notice at her old job. I can't back out on the deal now."

"There's a young Salvadorian woman who's looking for work. She comes highly recommended, and I think she would be a better match. Besides, she is willing to live in. That would be a distinct advantage."

"But I don't want to go back on my word."

"I'm sure Bertha could get her old job back at the hospital," Max suggested. "All I'm asking is that you talk to this girl, *Ntombi*. Maybe she won't be right for the job anyway. She lives just up the street from the post office."

"Have you met her already?"

"No," he replied, "but the bartender at the hotel said she'd be perfect. He sent a little boy to her house as a runner. It's all arranged. I would like you to go pick her up."

"Now?"

"Yeah, now. Then we can both interview her, and then we'll take it from there."

"Okay Max, if that's what you really want."

When Alexis knocked at the door on Minerva St., a petite young woman in a blue dress answered. She was barefoot, carried her shoes in her hand, and looked to be perhaps twenty-one at the most. Astonishingly beautiful, she had the clear unblemished skin called *café con leche* by the Spanish. Her eyes were dark and almond-shaped, sweeping upward at the outside corners. Her lips were sensuous, the teeth perfect, and her features were framed within a halo of luxuriant dark ringlets. She had no guile, and her sincerity was evident from the start. Her name was Angelina, and she was twenty-two years old. Seemingly nervous at first, the girl relaxed as they started to drive up the hill past the hotel and on to the house.

"So what makes you think you'd like to work for us?"

"Dey say yu are a nice lady and yu treat your workers good."

"I am fair and I treat my employees with respect. If you work well, you will be paid well. The job involves washing, cleaning, some cooking, and minding the baby. My husband runs a furniture business. I have a jewelry business that I run from our home."

"I love leetle babies, Miss Alexis. I have a son too. Jaime. He also has six years."

"That's wonderful. Maybe our boys could play together. Aren't you very young to have a child of that age?"

Angelina turned and looked at Alexis sincerely. Her beautiful face was troubled and she spoke apologetically.

"Miss Alexis? I wan' tell yu somet'ing 'bout me. Den if yu no wan' me, we could be done wit' dis right now. When I was fifteen, I get pregnant. My ma gave me one bad time wit' dat. She mek me leave Salvador for sake of shame. Den, because I came from Salvador to live wit' my Tia – how yu say – my auntie, and how I had dis baby so young, peoples in Cayo – dey no like me at all. Dey say I a bad woman and call me bad names. Dat's why I really want de job wit' yu. I no wan' live dere. I can' stand to live 'round dis badness any more."

Suddenly Alexis felt protective of this girl. She knew from her own experience what it was like to be labeled and criticized. The heartfelt plea made her want to give Angelina a chance. Besides, she was young and energetic. "You know, I thought I'd already found the right person for this job, but now I think I was wrong."

"Yu already have somebody?"

"Not exactly." Alexis smiled. "I want you to meet my husband and children, Angelina. You need an opportunity, and I'd like to help."

It didn't take long for Angelina to become part of the family. She was nanny to Jordan, friend to Alexis, nursemaid to Jessica, and waitress to Max. Through the next six months, the house was clean, the laundry was spotless, and meals were served on time, regardless of the work load. Angelina slept in the bedroom with the children, and kept track of the house and its contents as if they were her own.

Within that time frame, Max made trips to Mexico much more frequently, and with each passing venture, he seemed to get more agitated. In some cases, he was planning and mandating the next phase before he came in the door – before he'd even unpacked.

"Whoa! Take it easy. You just got home," said Alexis. "You still have Mexican dust in your hair. Why don't you relax a little while? Then we can talk."

"Oh, don't worry. I'm going to take my shower, have a whiskey or three, and wind down," Max said hurriedly. "I just want you to know, in advance, that you should plan on a major trip to Belize City in the next few days. Besides the Fort George, your soldier retail at Airport Camp, and your Sri Lankan buyer, I know of three more businesses in Belize City that are interested in carrying our line."

Shortly thereafter, the family adjourned to the back yard to watch the sun go down. Max lay in the hammock, sipping his drink, while Alexis sat in one of the slatted chairs holding Jessica on her lap. An errant chicken, belonging to a neighbor, wandered into the yard, and Jordan, always boisterous and energetic, poked it with a stick, evoking a loud squawk.

"I've been thinking more about this business trip, and I will want you to fly out to San Pedro as well." Max's tone was preemptory. "You can turn a quick profit on the silver I just bought, and buy more raw black coral from the divers."

Alexis didn't answer right away, but warning signals were going off in her head. "If I go alone with a huge agenda like that, I'd be gone at least four days. Jessica's weaned, but still, I don't like the idea of being gone for so long."

"Oh, get over it!" he snapped. "Your jewelry business is what justifies your domestic help. Besides, we need the money."

"But I'm in the jewelry shop all day long as it is," Alexis protested. "I'd like to be spending more time with the children."

"You work at home. What more do you want?" Max argued. "In fact, you're always home except for these selling trips. Don't worry. While you're gone, I'll watch over Ernesto and the woodshop, plus spend some time redecorating the gift shop. We need to create a more professional appearance and I brought back some bark paintings and other artwork. It'll look nice. Besides, someone needs to be here for walk-ins. I was also thinking of teaching Angelina how to handle a sale. Lupita became quite good at it. It's a shame we had to lose her, but she was lucky to get the chance to go to the States." Max paused reflectively, and then continued in a softer tone. "You know, you really helped by getting Lupita birth control. Now she can have a life, no matter where she is. It's nice that you've done that for so many local women. Speaking of which, maybe you could arrange to help out Angelina too." Thinking the remark was crafty, his intent was blatantly obvious.

Life with Max had become unbearable. He criticized absolutely everything she did, ridiculous things, from the way she folded towels, to the way she brushed her hair, what she ate, and the amount of toothpaste she used. He bedeviled her in every way possible, berating her in front of Angelina and the children, and no matter what she said in her own defense, he would only get angrier. Trying a different tack, Alexis began to admit to her mistakes and inadequacies, hoping her lack of denial might cool his anger, but that didn't work either. Arguments started over nothing at all, and encounters didn't end until Max hit her. Beatings had grown closer together until she found herself freshly bruised almost every two weeks.

There were only two explanations in Alexis' own mind: either she was truly at fault for everything, or Max had become a vindictive monster bent on destroying her, mentally and physically. Because Max didn't seem insane about anything else, she began to believe she must indeed be the source of the problem. She had always had a strong personality; she had been confidant and secure within herself. Now all self-esteem disappeared. Desperation was her constant companion, and Alexis couldn't imagine continuing to live this way. Nor could she imagine leaving, not with her children hanging in the balance.

Silvery slashes of lightning flashed against the backdrop of darkening clouds on the western horizon like an evil omen. The late afternoon sun dropped into obscurity and the rain bucketed down, plastering the windshield with water. Alexis was tempted to pull over and wait for better visibility, but with no road shoulder, and no painted lines on the roadway, it would have been madness to stop. Something nagged at Alexis; she had been gone for four days and wanted to get home badly. From a monetary standpoint, the trip to Belize City and San Pedro had gone well. Max would be pleased at the twenty-five hundred dollars bulging in her purse. Although it had actually been a relief to get away from him, it bothered her to be away from the children for so long. How much did she love them? Words couldn't begin to say. When Jordan was born, Alexis learned that the love between spouses was insignificant compared to maternal love. Then, when she gave birth to Jessica, she thought her heart would burst at the love she felt for her little girl. With her children, she finally understood the meaning of "unconditional love." Jordan and Jessica were the only reasons she stayed with Max. Otherwise she'd have been long gone.

When Alexis got home, Jordan was playing in the backyard under Angelina's supervision and Jessica was taking her afternoon nap, so there was nothing to prevent her from speaking to Max immediately. It was a lucky coincidence – as Alexis was in a state that allowed no pretense. Not even a conscious thought before she spoke it, the remark came directly from her gut.

"So you're having an affair with Angelina, aren't you?"

Max looked surprised, but his response was composed. "What do you mean? Is this something you know? Or something you think you know?"

Alexis closed her eyes. She hadn't known, but his not-so-sly answer had said it all, and the pain hit her as solidly as his physical blows. It was true.

"Well, NOW I know."

At that moment Angelina walked into the room. With one look, she knew what had transpired, and even from across the room, Alexis could see the blood drain from her face.

"Sorry to disturb," she said softly, backing out of the room and closing the door. *"I will go check on de children."*

At first, Max didn't say anything. Like the minutes during the Guatemalan earthquake of '76, Alexis waited for her world to collapse. When Max spoke at last, his words proved worse than the silence that had preceded them.

"Well, OK. I guess now that it's in the open, I don't have to hide it anymore."

"You don't have to hide it anymore?" cried Alexis. "That's all? Aren't you ashamed? Don't you regret your actions? Aren't you going to tell me 'I won't do it again'?"

"No, why should I?" Max fired back. Actually, it was starting to feel like a huge relief. "You don't enjoy having sex with me anyway. I'm a man. I need a little variety. The Zulus have the right idea – when one wife's 'on the rag,' they've still got the other."

"That's disgusting. How can you talk like that? What the hell did you tell her to convince her to have sex with you?"

"What makes you think she didn't come to me, begging for it?"

"I just know she didn't," Alexis hissed. "She's not like that. I know you, and you're the one that made the approach. You convinced her. Or blackmailed her. What did you say?"

"I told her that it was okay with you, that you and I talked about it and decided to open up the marriage and get involved with different partners to spice things up. We did have that discussion, if you'll recall."

"It wasn't a discussion, it was a monologue, and you planned the whole thing. I never agreed to anything. You brought up the idea because you intended to do it anyway." It was too much; Alexis broke down and cried. "This is totally destructive! What are you doing to us? We used to be proud of our monogamous relationship. Is nothing sacred anymore?"

"It doesn't mean I don't care for you," said Max, reaching for her arm. "You're still my wife."

She shoved it away rudely. "A fact which obviously means absolutely nothing."

"Ntombi—"

"Don't '*Ntombi'* me."

"How about someone for you? So we're even?"

"No. I don't want to be even, I want to be happy! If this doesn't stop now it'll ruin our lives and our children's lives. Listen to me. It will destroy us all."

"You're hysterical. I'm going to have a whiskey."

"I'm not hysterical! And have six whiskeys for all I care."

Alexis grabbed her bags, ran into the bedroom, and shut the door. Crying as she changed her clothes, she heard a diminutive knock. Jordan looked up from the open doorway saw a funny look on his mother's face. "What's the matter, Mummy?"

"I'm just tired, sweetheart. It was a long trip and now I don't feel very well. Where's your sister?"

"She just woke up from her nap," said Jordan.

Just then the little girl appeared in the doorway. "Mama!"

"Hi Jess. How's my baby?" Alexis hunkered down as the toddler ran to her mother. Drying her tears, and encircling each of them with an arm, she said, "I missed you, my darlings, and I brought you each a little present."

"Oh goody, goody," said Jordan. What is it?"

"Goo-dy? Mama?" Jessica chimed in.

"Over there on top of my overnight bag. There's one for each of you."

The two children ran over and opened the brown paper packets. Inside were two beautiful Salvadoran terry cloth robes with bold Mayan designs around the border. Jordan's was green and Jessie's was orange. Beautiful gifts were scarce in Belize but Alexis had gotten these from her Sri Lankan buyer at the army gift shop.

"They're pretty," said Jordan. "Thanks, Mummy."

"Pret-ty," little Jessica echoed.

"I thought you'd like them. Tell you what, after your bath tonight you can try them on so we can see how they fit. Now run along and go play. I need to take care of a few things."

Angelina was making tortillas when Alexis walked into the kitchen. Through the window she could see Max was lying in the hammock under the plum tree and the children climbing up in his lap.

"Angelina?" said Alexis.

"I know. Now I have to go away. OK. But I tell yu dis truth. Mista Max tol' me dat yu di'n't care. I know he treats yu bad. I shoulda neva listen to him. He done tol' me a lie, no true?"

"Yes Angelina. It was a big lie, but I'm not really angry with you. I'm angry at him. He's good at making people believe anything he says. I know how convincing he can be."

"But I shoulda kno' betta."

"Yes, you should have, but I can't blame you. When he is bad to me, he still manages to convince me it's my own fault."

"If yu let me stay, I no will let dat happen again. But I will go dis minute if yu want."

"No, you don't have to go. At least not now. I need to think a while. I'm going to go out and take a walk. I'll be alongside the creek heading out towards the river. I won't be gone too long."

"Miss Alexis?" Angelina looked up and wiped a floured hand under her eyes, leaving white streaks. *"I'm so sorry. To God, I sorry. Yu have been good to me. I neva mean to hurt yu."*

Most of the afternoon's intense heat had already dissipated by the time Alexis reached the sandy beach at the edge of the creek. She waded across the shallows to the opposite bank and followed the stream. In sharp contrast to the arid pasture lands scorched by the dry season, there were tall shade trees along the creek and thickets of lush fern and big bamboo. The sky was bright sapphire and the sun bathed the bush in golden light, as Alexis saw a huge snowy falcon come to rest in the branches of a giant ceiba tree. But today, she had no eye for the natural beauty surrounding her. She couldn't think and she couldn't feel. Her mind could neither focus on the situation at hand, nor could she begin to grasp the choices she might be forced to make. Torn between the love for her children and the hate for a man who had become a monster, there were no answers, only more questions. In a quandary of doubt, she walked until she reached the point where the creek emptied into the river. Alexis sat down on its edge and rested against the large stump of a tree.

Over and over she tried to make sense of it all, debating the wisdom of quick action, versus the slow death of inaction. One thing was certain. She couldn't keep on like this. More and more, the children were beginning to see it happen. Jordan was old enough to know that even Mommy wasn't clumsy enough to have so many bruises. In his subconscious mind, the abuse was something he had known about for quite some time, although his young mind could not accept it. His devotion to both parents was profound; Jordan was unable to love one and despise the other. Even Jessica looked at her mother in a funny way some times. There was fear in the little girl's eyes when her father shouted at Mama and called her bad names. Other couples fought, but most people had the good sense to hide it from their children. With Max, it seemed like he enjoyed verbally degrading Alexis in front of them, as though their young minds had the ability to follow his logic and endorse his actions. That was typical of Max, of his psychological makeup, of his need for an audience.

Alexis knew she had to get away from him; that was clear. But she couldn't leave with the children, and she couldn't leave without them. Max had taught her that long ago. His words still rang clearly in her head. He would kill her if she ever tried to take them away. Even if she could leave, what method could she use? Fifty ways to leave your lover. But it wasn't so easy. If she left him, how would she live? She would need money, and with the exception of her selling trips, Max had always kept her in the dark about finances. In fact, unbeknownst to her, he had carefully hedged his bets for years and protected his own personal interests in every way. The land, the vehicles, the house, everything was in his name. Without him, Alexis would be destitute.

Minutes passed into hours and suddenly she realized the sun had already set. Twilight was coming quickly and she didn't want to get caught in the bush after dark. She washed her face in the river to try to regain her composure and turned back towards the house. It would be a bumpy night.

When she was about a half-mile from the house, she heard Max calling her name. At first the inflection in his voice sounded like concern for her well-being. But as she got closer, she realized it was a tone of anger.

"*Ntombi eyami*!"

"Over here. I'm coming." She couldn't see him yet but she walked faster heading towards the direction of his voice. "Here Max. Hang on, I'm coming."

At last she saw him ahead through the trees. He stood on the side of the creek with something in his hand. Alexis stopped dead in her tracks. His face was full of rage.

"*Ntombi*! Get your fuckin' ass over here right now! Double time! Run, you bitch! Do you hear me? I want you to run. Run! Get over here now!"

Numb with fear, Alexis saw that Max brandished a stout stick in his hand. At least an inch in diameter, he smacked the rod into his palm like a drill sergeant as she ran up to him.

"Max, don't!"

"About time you got back. Where the hell have you been? Is this your revenge? Worrying me like this? By going for hours, and not telling anyone where you were?"

"I told Angelina where I was—Jesus, don't hit me. Not with that stick Max, for God's sake."

"Yeah, you better be on good terms with God, because you're going to be calling his name in a minute. I guarantee it. Now bend your ass over."

"Max, don't. Not with a stick!"

"Bend over and brace yourself on this log. You're going to need the support."

When she hesitated, he screamed, "Bend over, God damn you, before I take a swing at your head instead."

There was nothing left; Alexis obeyed and bent over. Max took the rod in both hands and swung it full force into her buttocks as if he was hitting a home run with a baseball bat. The shattering pain made Alexis' vision go black. Stars swam dizzily before her eyes. Without the log in front of her, the force of the blow would have driven her into the ground. The pain was indescribable, beyond anything she'd ever experienced.

"That's one," said Max. Again, the stick whistled through the air and cracked against her buttocks. "That's two." With the third and final blow, Alexis passed out. Max revived her by throwing handfuls of cold water from the creek into her face.

"Now get up, you lazy cunt, and start walking."

Alexis staggered to get up, her rubbery legs refusing to support the weight of her body. The pain was so great, she was sure her pelvic bones were cracked.

"Get up, you stupid ass. Move, before I hit you again."

Through sheer force of will, Alexis made her reluctant body take a step at a time. For the rest of the way home, Max kept up a steady stream of invective. He insulted every facet of her life: personal habits, lineage, heritage, nationality, and culture. None of it mattered. She kept moving to avoid another blow; that was all that counted.

"And I will also remind you, you ugly horse-faced bitch, that you will tell no one of what just happened, or by God I'll come down on you three times as heavy. When we get home you will go directly into the shower, get cleaned up, and make yourself look presentable. You will come into the house and have a nice normal dinner. You will eat with an appetite and cheerfully participate in family conversation at the table. You will sit on your swollen red ass and you will show no signs of pain or crying. Do you understand?"

"Yes, Max."

As soon as the children were asleep that evening, Alexis excused herself and went to bed, but she did not sleep. The throbbing pain in her buttocks was unbearable. She could hardly move. Finally she rose from the bed in agony and went to the full length mirror. Looking back over her shoulder, she saw this was no mere swollen red ass with a couple of whip marks across it, but an injury of grievous proportion. The massive black and purple hematoma was six inches wide and extended full breadth of her buttocks. Not just a bruise, it was an enormous lumpy blue-black mass that had stretched the skin taut and shiny. Because of its sheer size, it was far worse than the horse kick, so long ago.

It was well after midnight when Max came to bed. As he slid between the covers, Alexis could smell the scotch on his breath. Soon he began snoring thickly. As quietly as she could, Alexis crept out of bed, went into the kitchen, and returned to the bedroom with a large cast-iron skillet in her hand. In the future, she would never be able to recollect how long she had stood with it raised over his head. Her anger consumed her. She was determined to kill him, to smash his skull and see his brains splatter across the pillows.

Wait. There was a better way. Crossing the floor, she opened the locked box containing the .25 automatic pistol. Again, she stood over Max, this time with the gun pointed at his head. Now, do it now. In anguish, Alexis tried to force herself to squeeze the trigger.

Then, in a flash of self-loathing, she turned the gun on herself, pointing it to her temple. Sweating profusely, her hands trembled violently. Wait. No. More sure. Alexis put the gun in her mouth, her finger ready on the trigger. Squeeze. Goddammit, squeeze!

It was no use. Tears of rage streamed down her cheeks, but she knew she couldn't follow through. Alexis was no murderer, no matter how much she hated Max. She couldn't leave her children motherless, any more than she could leave them fatherless, and she didn't want to die. More than anything, she wanted to live. Alexis locked the gun away and crawled back into bed beside Max. Instinctively, he rolled over in his sleep and threw his arm around her. How strange that, not so long ago, the unconscious gesture had thrilled her. Now instead, revulsion filled her, and she shuddered at his touch. Alexis lay there, unmoving, until the first light of dawn.

The next morning when Max awoke, he found the bed empty beside him, still warm with the scent of her body and the imprint of her head on the pillow.

My God, he thought. What have I done?

He found Alexis standing in the kitchen window, drinking tea and looking out into the yard. "*Ntombi*," said Max.

"Yes?" she replied quietly, still facing away from him.

"Let me see your backside."

As she turned to face him, Max realized that this woman looked nothing like the young girl he'd married nine years before. Alexis' face was drawn and tired, her complexion muddy. With dark circles etched under dull eyes, she looked older than her thirty years, her shoulders postured in defeat. Without protest, Alexis untied the belt, turned away from Max again and accommodated him by dropping the terry-cloth robe to the floor.

This time, even Maximilian Lord was shocked. He gasped aloud when he saw the results of his uncontrolled rage, admitting, even to himself, that this was beyond discipline in any sense of the word. This was brutality. He was suddenly frightened at the creature he'd become. Tears sprang to his eyes when he saw the lumps of blue and purple that protruded from the distended mass of misshapen flesh.

"My God, *Ntombi*. Oh Jesus. I'm sorry. God, you're really hurt. Shit, what have I done?"

"I'll tell you, if you really want to know. You punished me because I didn't react well to the fact that you were having an affair." Her voice was monotone.

"I'm so sorry. Jesus, I'm sorry. I didn't mean it."

"But you did mean it. You did it." This time, Alexis didn't care about what she said, or how it came out. "What good is it to be sorry afterward? You still did it. I don't want you to be sorry. Do you hear what I'm saying? I'd prefer that you felt justified in beating me. Otherwise, it means the punishment was meted out for nothing, and that is far worse. Why can't you be sorry before the fact, instead of after it? Be sorry in the beginning, so it will prevent you from doing it in the first place."

"It's done now. I said I'm sorry. It's over. I can't take it back. What else is there but to move on?"

"I want to take a vacation." said Alexis. She gathered her nerve. "I want to go away for a while, take a break, maybe go out to San Pedro, and take some time to sort out my feelings."

"What's that supposed to mean?"

"Which word didn't you understand?" Alexis asked sarcastically. She was taking chances but she had nothing left to lose. "I want to take a vacation. I want to get away from you. I need some time to sort out the way I feel. I want to take a break, alone."

"You don't want to take the kids?"

Alexis smirked. "You mean you'd allow me to take them?"

"No." Max paused. "Is this break you want supposed to result in some kind of conclusion?"

"Yes, it is. I need to make a determination of whether I can continue to live with you. I need to have some space and time to think about it."

"You're not going anywhere," Max said, his fury mounting again. "Not with or without the kids. You're my wife and you'll stay here."

"Yes, *here*. What other opinion could I possibly expect you to have? Let's talk about *here*. *Here*, where I provide the primary income that supports your budding furniture business. *Here*, at home, where I'm not, for two days a week, because I'm out there selling. *Here*, in this house, where you also happen to live, fucking your concubine *here* under my own roof, a mistress who also lives *here*, in the same house where our children sleep. Of course you want me to stay *here*. *Here*, where I'm nothing more than a jewelry-making machine. *Here*, where you beat me like clockwork. *Here*, where you beat me carefully, only hitting the parts of my body that will be hidden by clothing, so very careful not to mark my face. *Here*, where I have to hide my bruises and my terrible secret from Jordan and Jessica, a charade of happiness and normalcy. *Here*, where I read my children stories, and pretend we're one big happy family. *Here*, where I can never let on to a solitary soul what really happens *here* because I must protect the children from forces that they can't possibly understand. *Here*, where I am on the verge of a mental breakdown because I can't live like this anymore. Yet you tell me that I must stay *here*."

True to his ways, Max found a solution that resolved absolutely nothing. He decided to give Alexis the break and grant her the vacation. However, it would be ultimately conditional, as everything was, structured, not to be conducive to Alexis' needs, but to his own.

"We'll all go to San Pedro. We all need the break."

"Really, Dad?" Jordan piped up in delight as he walked into the room. "We're going to go to the Cayes for a while?"

"You bet, son. Not just for a few days either. We're going to go there and stay out there for a while."

"All right!" he yelled joyfully. Alexis could hear him shouting outside. "Jessie! Guess what? We're going to San Pedro! Come on! Let's go tell Angelina."

"Angelina's going too?" asked Alexis.

"Be reasonable. Somebody still needs to cook and clean while we're out there. Don't worry. It was just a little fling, purely physical. It's over. Ernesto can manage the wood shop and you can still do your jewelry business from right there in San Pedro. We'll rent a small apartment and I'll set up a nice little jewelry worktable for you. Maybe we could even rent a retail shop for a while. We'll enroll Jordan in San Pedro School temporarily. It'll be fun. You know, just what we need, a healing experience. We'll all go out and take a break for a few months."

"You're missing the point," she said tiredly. "That defeats the entire purpose. I don't need to be away from the kids, I need to be away from you. I can't accomplish anything if I don't have the time and space. And now you've told the kids we're going. What a brilliant tactician you are. I can't fight that, and you know it. Don't you understand a cry for help? I am looking out for the best interests of the family, namely, keeping it together. There are no mental health professionals here. I have no one to help me work through this. If we were in the States I would have my parents. Or we could go to a marriage counselor."

"And hang out our dirty laundry for other people to see? It's just like you to suggest some bullshit thing like that. That's not even a real science. Besides you don't need anybody else to talk to. You can talk to me about anything."

She looked at him. It was over. It had been over before it started. Max was a consummate artist when it came to getting what he wanted, and had gotten his way once again. She was beaten and she knew it.

"Whatever you say, Max. Let's all go to San Pedro."

Something changed inside Alexis on that day. Max had refused to recognize the warning signs, and now it was too late. So she retaliated by using the one weapon she had left: Alexis made a conscious decision to stop loving him. The ultimate weapon in a war of emotion, Max could delegate her body, but not her mind. It was over. He would never be able to make Alexis love him again.

MEXICO

chapteR 14

The family vacation in San Pedro had proved a fiasco. Max had rented a cramped and overpriced apartment on the beach. Designed for double occupancy, with five of them, the space was overcrowded. After only two weeks, Max had become restless and bored with island life. He worried constantly about the wood shop, sure that Ernesto or one of the other workers was stealing from him. Subconsciously, he blamed Alexis for taking him away from his responsibilities on the mainland, and they quarreled. Before long, Max began to spend more time at the bar than at the apartment.

For the children, island life was a dream come true. Happy to reject the school uniform of Cayo, Jordan wore a white short-sleeved shirt, khaki shorts, and went barefoot. After school, he played basketball or soccer, or went fishing or snorkeling with his new-found buddies. For Jessica, San Pedro was a new world of people and things to do, a wonderful contrast from her secluded life in the western uplands. The charming village was a magical place. Of course, Jessica was too young for school, but she loved playing in the sand or in the park with the other toddlers.

A not-so-subtle change had come over Angelina. She did not act like a maid anymore. She sounded like a wife, and treated Max with a casual off-handedness that suggested lingering intimacy. Angelina seemed constantly annoyed; she complained about everything in the apartment. Nothing worked the way it was supposed to and the apartment lacked the comforts of home. Fresh vegetables and fruits were hard to get, the stove and fridge were too small, the pipes leaked, the water pressure was terrible, and the torn screens admitted bugs.

Jordan and Jessica were the only joys in Alexis' life. She watched as they played on the beaches of San Pedro, building castles in the sand. She grimaced at the irony. But not even her love for them could mitigate the need to get away from Max and his abuse. Getting out had become an obsession, and Alexis couldn't think happy thoughts about her children without imagining what it would be like to leave them. First, the emotion would take over, the hand-wringing and despair – then the calm, the rational thinking, the ability to reason and weigh the difficult choices. But just as a plan began to formulate, Alexis' heart would betray her and the cycle started all over.

Jordan was now seven and a half, tall and tanned with sun-bleached hair. He was a good student and loved sports and mechanical things. Although he loved his mother very much, Jordan was his father's son and always had been. Jessica had strawberry-blond hair and dark green eyes. True to the sign of Cancer the crab, she was soft and vulnerable one minute, tough and stubborn the next. Jessica was a generous child, always willing to share her toys or candy. But even at age three, she was fiercely independent with a mind of her own. As Indian Ron had predicted, Jessica was her mother's little girl, the light of her life.

How could I ever leave without them? she thought. How can I continue to stay here? Should I go to my parents? Go back to the States? How could I hope to resolve this from so far away? How could I fight a legal battle in Belize if I lived in the States? No. I would have to find refuge, some place close by like Mexico where I could keep tabs on things without being directly involved. What about money? Oh God. How can I even think of money? Leave the children? My babies? What if I left and then Max took them away somewhere? I might never see them again.

Once upon a time she had loved Max wholly. Through the years, she had learned to fear him. Now there was nothing left but hate, and it burned white hot. And not just the man himself. She hated his clothes, his profile, his voice, his accent, his inflections. She hated the verbal expressions he used over and over to describe his delusions of grandeur. She hated his handwriting. She hated his sandals because they exposed the long black hairs on his big square toe with its big square toenail, which she also hated. And she hated his name.

Max Lord = Maximum God
Max Lord = Maximum Supreme Being
Max Augustus Lord = Maximum Venerable Lord

Lord? God? More like the demon of her dreams; his face was certainly similar. Already tanned dark by the sun, it seemed to crunch towards the center as his rage increased, turning it black. She knew the look well; it was the face she saw before each beating began.

Because of the feeling of impending doom, Alexis spent as much time with the children as she could. She read them stories, played with them. They took long walks together on the beach. Jordan and Jessica were both gifted children. They were bright and healthy. They didn't deserve to come from a broken home. The thought tormented her day and night.

But they don't deserve to see the way their father treats me either, she argued with herself. They deserve a nurturing home life. The shouting, the beatings – they're both old enough to know right from wrong. When their father ridicules me in front of them, pointing out that Mummy is clumsy or stupid or ugly, what will these things do to them in the long term? Will they be scarred forever? I can't let them grow up believing that that's the way husbands are supposed to treat wives. Will they watch their mother sink lower and lower? To become a non-entity, a slave, a doormat? Watch me slowly go insane while Angelina becomes wife and replaces me as mother? And yet, what memories of childhood will become their cornerstones if I do leave? Oh God, Alexis pleaded for the thousandth time, please don't force me to make this decision. Why does Max have to be so blind?

One afternoon in early January, Alexis walked back towards the apartment after a PTA meeting at the elementary school. Jordan was still at the schoolyard playing soccer. She waived to him as she passed by. Jessica would be waking up from her nap shortly and Alexis planned to take both kids to the playground after dinner. She turned the knob on the door. It was locked.

That's funny, she thought. Angelina should be here with Jessie, unless she woke up and they already went to the store. But even so, Max should be back by now. She used her key and opened the door. A radio was on, but Alexis could hear muffled voices coming from the bedroom. Fighting a sinking feeling and fearing the worst, Alexis tiptoed to the bedroom door and looked in.

Angelina was naked on her hands and knees, braced to accept the driving motion of the man behind her, her black hair tumbling over her back and shoulders. The whiteness of Max's body contrasted with Angelina's light brown skin. Alexis watched as his loins smacked hard against the girl's flesh. Unaware of Alexis' presence, Max reached around and slid his finger into the cleft of black pubic hair and listened to the girl moan with pleasure. He kneaded her breast, working the large dark nipple between his fingers. He pumped harder, thrusting, as his hands slid back along her flanks and gripped her buttocks. He was close now, Alexis could tell, and she watched as Max reached climax. Spent at last, he collapsed. Angelina sighed and cuddled next to him.

"Was it good for you Angelina?" Alexis asked.

The two lovers sprang apart in shock and hastily clothed themselves.

"No, let me guess," Alexis continued, unabated. "Angelina's never had an actual orgasm herself, so she makes the perfect lover. Isn't that right Max? You don't have to worry about pleasuring her, do you? The perfect little sperm receptacle? Such a good housekeeper she is, requiring nothing for herself, and only living to serve her master. How very Christian of you."

"Lay off her, Alexis," growled Max.

"Interesting choice of words. You and all your bullshit about having stopped the affair. What am I, some kind of an idiot? You've never stopped messing around, have you? It's always been one woman or another. First there was Katrina, then your girlfriend in Washington DC, You didn't know that I knew about that one, did you? And then the Creole girl from Santa Elena, your mechanic's sister. Shame, shame. I'm sure your very white family in South Africa would never approve. Imagine, taking her home to meet your mother."

"God damn it! Shut your fucking trap. I've had enough of your shit."

"*No Max, don'*," Angelina pouted. "*I tol' yu—*"

"Be quiet, Angelina, it's all right. There's a way we can work this out." He composed himself. "Alexis. Come over here, and I will overlook those last remarks. Why don't you come over and join us?"

"Go fuck yourself! Go to hell. You and your multiple wife fantasies, you sick *ménage à trois* perversionist. It's a good thing you have your Spanish mistress here because you're going to need her. I wouldn't let you touch me again if you were the last man on the face of the earth." Alexis's face reddened as her hatred burned hotter. Nothing could stop her now. "You're disgusting. I can't believe I married you, that I bore you two beautiful children. I can't believe what you've done. You took our holy matrimony and turned it into a – a circus of horrors. I would rather – I would rather rut with a farm animal than join you and your slut. Do you understand what I'm saying? Bestiality would be preferable to having sex with you again. I'd rather fuck a pig."

With a speed Alexis didn't think possible, Max was out of bed and across the room. "You goddamn filthy cunt! This time I'm gonna tear you a new asshole."

Just then Jessica awoke. "Mama?" she cried out. "Mama, come here."

Alexis stood riveted to the floor. "Just a minute, honey. I'll be right there," she croaked.

"Angelina," Max barked, as he put on a pair of shorts. "Throw on some clothes and go tend to Jessie. Take her outside and go for a walk."

A moment later Alexis watched as the Salvadoran girl took her daughter outside, and with her, any chance of escape. Now there would be no stopping Max. Slowly he walked towards where she stood pressed against the wall. With daggers in his eyes, Max brought his face close until it was all she could see. Inches away, he pressed his nose against her nose in an ultimate gesture of intimidation.

"So you would rather fuck a pig, my lovely wife? Such a colorful thought. Perhaps that could be arranged. But until then I intend to teach you some respect, once and for all."

Then Max Lord began to beat his wife, slowly, methodically, and deliberately. She offered no resistance, knowing it was futile. He punched her arms and shoulders, knocked her to the ground, and cursed her. Max kicked her, directing blows to her thighs, head, face, shoulders. This time he had no regard whether the bruises showed.

"You have no respect for me, do you? Stand your ass up. Come on stand up, you goddam bitch. I'll teach you both fear and respect." With those words, Max swung his fist and the blow caught Alexis squarely in the left side of the face. She heard the crunch of bone and broken teeth and felt warm blood spurt inside her mouth.

"Daddy! No! Stop!" cried Jordan.

Alexis looked up through the blinding pain and saw her young son standing in the doorway, still holding his soccer ball. She tried to speak, but no words came out. Blood dribbled from the corner of her mouth.

If a doctor had seen Alexis during the next few days, he would have diagnosed her with severe contusions and a concussion. But no doctor had been called. She lay in a daze of pain and wrestled with strange fevers that seemed to come and go with the rising and setting of the sun. The swelling in her brain would not allow coherent thoughts; the relativity of time and space were lost. She saw images of people going about their lives, but none of it had meaning. They seemed to glide instead of walk. When they spoke, their lips moved but no sound came out. Or they stood in front of her, whispering and pointing, as if she were a freak in a side show. It was over now, just a matter of time. Even the children were distant and afraid. They looked at her wide-eyed from across the room and hardly spoke. God only knew what Max had told them.

When the moment came nine days later, there was no emotion at all. There was only a quiet decision born of the realization that Alexis must first save her own life if she were to live to be a mother to anyone. It was survival, a sacrifice beyond sacrifice, a decision made for the sake of the children and their future. She was packing a suitcase when Max walked into the room.

"I'm leaving you."

For once, it was Max who now felt the pain strike his heart. He had heard the words before, but this time he knew it was real.

"You're not taking these kids anywhere."

"I know," she said flatly. "You told me many times that you'd never let me take them. So I'm going alone."

"Then who are you going with? Who is helping you?"

"No one. I could never do this leaning on someone else's strength. It's a decision I'm making on my own. The only way it could be."

"I don't believe you. You don't have the guts."

"Watch me."

"I won't give you any money."

"I don't care," she replied simply. "I'll go without money."

"No jewelry either, nothing to sell, no way to support yourself."

"It doesn't matter." Her voice was cold.

Max put himself between Alexis and the suitcase. "I won't let you go."

"You won't let me go? You won't stop me, Max. This time you have no choice. This time I am leaving no matter what. I'll go without children, I'll go without money. I'll go with nothing. I am leaving you. I'll stowaway on a boat if I can't get on a plane. I'll leave without a suitcase. I'll leave without clothes, but I will go. Unless you tie me up and chain me to the wall, you will not stop me. If I have to, I will go naked in the middle of the night and swim to the mainland. But this time, I am leaving you."

Fear shook Max to the very core of his being. His face went white. This time he knew it was real. There was no ammunition left. He went into the bathroom and vomited. Upon his return, Alexis listened dispassionately and kept on packing.

"Oh *Ntombi*, for God's sake please don't go. I can change, I swear I can. Don't leave me now. I'll say what I've never said before – I was wrong, and I'm sorry. All I ever wanted was to have you love and understand me, to be a mother to my kids, and be my lady. I'll turn over a new leaf. I swear I will. I'll be so different. I'll send Angelina away forever. It will be just like it used to be in the old days. Oh God, please don't do this, Alexis. Please don't leave me."

"It would be foolish to send Angelina away. You've already trained her so well. Besides, you're going to need a mother for the children you have turned against me. What have you told them to make Jordan and Jessica so distant? Did you tell them I had gone crazy?"

His answer was obvious as he turned his head in shame.

"I figured as much."

"I'm sorry—"

"It's too late. Much too late. You should have let me come to San Pedro by myself. I told you I needed time and space to sort out how I felt. But you didn't listen. It's gone far beyond that now. You see, I truly do not love you anymore. Are you listening? I do not love you anymore. Ten years. I spent ten years with you, and during that time, you've turned over more new leaves than a jungle in the wet season. But it's always the same. You'll never be any different. You'll never change."

Losing ground, Max changed to the lowest tactic of all. He called for Angelina, Jessica, and Jordan who were outside on the beach, and announced to the children that their mother was abandoning them. Angelina wrung her hands in dismay. Jessica cried and ran to Alexis, holding on her mother's legs. Jordan screamed and pleaded. The crying seemed to go on and on, an eternity of anxiety, one that would scar all of them forever. Agony tore at Alexis. Perhaps Jordan and Jessica would never understand. But her decision spelled survival, nothing less. She could not stop now. If she stayed, she knew Max would kill her. Either that or she would kill him in self-defense. She kept on packing. Max threw some money on the bed.

"Here's four hundred dollars. Take it. At least it'll keep you off the street."

"I don't want your money. I don't want anything that will give you an excuse to follow me."

"Then go, goddam it!" he said angrily, "and take all your shit with you. Don't just take one suitcase. Take everything. Take every single thing that belongs to you. Get to hell away from me. Don't leave any of your junk for me to deal with. Here's a duffel bag. Here. Take this and this, and here – take this stuff too!" His logic told him if she had too much to carry, she wouldn't go.

"Forget it, Max. Those are only material things. I'll just drop them off at the airstrip or on the beach. If I can walk away from my kids, do you think a duffel bag full of stuff will stop me?"

"Christ! Then for the children's sake, Alexis, don't go. Look at these little faces. How can you leave them?"

Tears streamed down her face as she stooped down to hold them. She held her children close for a last time. Everyone was crying and screaming.

"It is because of them that I go. I can't be their mother if I'm not alive. It's the hardest thing I've ever done." Alexis sobbed openly and kissed the crying children. "I have to leave you, my little loves. I know you don't understand. Maybe you will understand someday. Maybe not. Either way, I have to go away for a while."

"Don't go!" sobbed Jordan. "Daddy said you'd gone crazy."

She looked up at Max. "Daddy didn't tell you the truth. No, I'm not crazy. I must go because Daddy does bad things to me. I can't have you thinking that daddies are supposed to treat mommies that way. I love you my darlings."

"I don't think anything, Mummy. Please don't go away."

"*Ntombi*. Please."

"Take care of my children, Angelina. Regardless of what has happened, I have never questioned your devotion to them. For God's sake, take care of my babies. Love them for me. Goodbye, my sweet babies."

Alexis picked up her suitcase, turned her back on Max, and left him. For the last time.

* * * *

The sea-green walls of the cheap hotel room were meant to impart a feeling of tropical ambiance. But, with the shades drawn, the room felt ice-cold, more like an institution or a prison. Alexis shivered as she lay on the bed staring at nothing, staring through the walls, through the miles beyond nothing, and into outer space. Cold was the only sensation she could feel. Outside, Mexican ranchero music played in the streets of Cozumel. Sometimes she could smell the aroma of roasting peppers and corn tortillas. But no force was strong enough to lure her into the outside world. It simply didn't matter anymore. Nothing did.

Alexis couldn't remember the last time she'd taken any nourishment. A week? Maybe more. Nor had she slept at all. She had lost the ability to be hungry and the urge to be sated. On the few occasions when she tried to eat, her throat had closed up. She was unable to salivate or swallow. Shunning food and human contact, Alexis had lain there now, day after day, alone in the Mexican hotel room. Awake, unmoving, uncaring.

In the light of late afternoon, a ray of sun peeped through the cracks and fell across her legs. The huge bruises on her thighs had lightened to greenish-yellow. She stared apathetically, then roused herself to go look in the mirror. The black eye was almost gone, as were most of the marks on her face with the exception of the lump on her jaw. The face she saw was that of a stranger – an old hag, thin and pale, mouth pinched, eyes devoid of expression. Alexis lay down on the bed again and tried to recall the days since her departure.

Some memories were blocked out by the compassionate nature of subconscious denial. Others lurked beneath the gray veil, and when she dared to peek cautiously beneath that shroud of darkness, vivid nightmares were exhumed. Her head throbbed as a thousand little monsters assaulted her, pricking her eyeballs with hot needles. The legions of doom had been there all along, waiting, hiding – their evil faces painted in blackened blood, in terrifying illusions of smoke and mirrors. A silent scream died in her throat as she saw her children just beyond reach of her outstretched arms. She watched helplessly as they drifted towards a distant horizon. Her empty heart ceased to beat as a cold tide washed over her unholy corpse.

Homeless now, she had left behind the last hope of her survival. Now there was no life. Now there was nothing. The vigil was not a choice. Instead, it was a trial by fire to determine her destiny. Alexis had lost the strength to make the conscious choice between life and death. Now her inner spirit would decide which force would succeed. Either she would stay alive, or drift into a coma and die. Time was running out.

Alexis had very little recollection of how she had actually reached Cozumel. She must have taken the money, as she vaguely remembered Chetumal, and a short puddle-jumper flight from Playa del Carmen, but the details were lost. In a forgotten dream, there had been a taxi ride from the Cozumel airport into its only town, San Miguel, and the payment of a week's rent for a room in the cheap hotel near the main square.

Still in a state of shock, Alexis managed to go through the motions of being human. Just before sunset, she showered, washed her hair, and put on a fresh change of clothes. Then she stepped out on the balcony and watched the twinkling lights of the village flickering in the dusky afterglow. That evening, as she walked the streets, the gravity of her decision seemed to sink in at last. Along every street were happy tourists eating and drinking, toasting each other in the spirit of camaraderie. Young couples walked hand in hand, laughing and talking. She saw old withered grandfathers leaning on their canes and heard Mexican mothers chastising their children. She smelled the aroma of tantalizing culinary delights and listened to the music of the *mariachis* as they played in the square. Alexis watched as the boats furled their sails and docked in their slips for the night. It was here that they snuggled safely on the lee shore, away from the blustering force of the windward side. All around her were the sounds and sights of life, love, and laughter. Like a sleepwalker, she returned to the sea-green hotel room and lay down numbly on the bed. Then her spirit died. What was left behind was a mere shell of a living being, a mortal coil depleted of its soul and its humanity.

Only God knows what effected the dramatic reversal that saved Alexis' life. Perhaps it was a voice that spoke to her from afar. Maybe a vision of the future. It could have been a waking dream, or the power of God answering the tearful prayers of her parents or children. But whatever it was, something caused Alexis to rise from what would otherwise have become her deathbed. In a trance, she moved to the window and looked out on the world below. It was all still there, the skies bright with sunshine, the blue waters of the Caribbean. A fog seemed to lift from her mind. Life came into focus once more. Alexis opened the windows and took a deep breath, feeling the sunlight and fresh air flood the room.

"*La playa, por favor,*" Alexis said to the taxi driver. "To the beach, please."

Which beach was irrelevant; her needs were simple. Still afflicted by intense cold, maybe the sunlight could bring her back. After the devastating withdrawal, she must find a way to be hungry again – for food, for laughter, for life. But there would be families on the beach, and the thought of seeing children was a raw wound. Alexis would have to control her emotions. If she couldn't learn to be an observer, how could she ever again become a participant?

The taxi drove south along the rocky western side of Cozumel until Alexis saw a stunning tropical hotel with a white crystalline beach. She paid the driver and stepped into the brilliant sunlight. Careful to circumvent the lively crowd of well-oiled tourists, she looked for a quiet corner where she could be alone. Conversation was unimaginable. Even if she could speak to someone, what would she say?

Hello, my name is Alexis. I've just escaped a brutal husband. Now he has my kids, and I'm in exile. I can't go back. I can't survive alone. I'm dying inside. How are you enjoying your vacation in Mexico so far?

No. Not a good way to make friends.

The savory aroma of roasting meat wafted from the open-air grill. Alexis walked until she saw a group of lounge chairs, partially shaded by a huge hedge of red hibiscus. No one else was there; it was perfect. She lay down and looked at her bikini-clad body for the first time. Her skin was sallow. Her rounded breasts had all but disappeared, every rib was visible, and her belly was as sunken as a greyhound's. Even her ankles and calves were emaciated. But being outdoors was a beginning; the warmth was seeping in. For the next half hour, Alexis lay in the sun, listening to the waves and the wind. She heard live music, a man's voice accompanied by a steel-string guitar, beautifully amplified, with some light percussion in the background.

The young man sat on a high stool behind the bar of the little thatched *palápa* with his guitar. He was tall for a Mexican, with dark good looks, and a voice that was deep and honey-smooth, with a gentle tremolo. The artist played several Mexican ballads, followed by some popular contemporary American selections in English, and for a few blessed moments, Alexis actually forgot everything and lost herself in the music. His pitch was superb and his interpretation, flawless. He reached out to his listeners and she was not the only one touched with emotion. After his last set, he thanked his audience and began to pack his gear. She walked over and spoke to him.

"*Su música es medicina para mi alma,*" Alexis said, sincerely. "Your music is medicine to my soul."

"*Muchisimas gracias, Señorita.* You are most kind. *Me llamo Bishara Simone,* at your service."

"*Me llamo* Alexis Lord.*" She shook his hand. *"Mucho gusto."*

They struck up an easy conversation. His English was only a little better than her Spanish, but the overlap made it work. Music was an area of common ground, and blessedly so, as it was unaffiliated, in any way, with her identity or circumstance. Bishara learned that she sang, played flute, and had a natural ear. Alexis learned that it was a relief just being able to talk with another human being after so long a silence.

Bishara invited her to join him for dinner, but she hesitated in answering, knowing the anorexia would not allow her to eat. She cringed at the thought of his asking why, as then she'd be forced to make a response. So far, the conversation had been limited to music. Perhaps the truth would alienate him, but if she didn't tell him, they would never establish a friendship.

But, as it turned out, Bishara confessed to a recent and bitter divorce of his own. The ink was barely dry on the papers. His ex-wife had kept their young son and, like Alexis, his emotional scars ran deep. So they took a taxi to a little restaurant and found a table in the far corner. As expected, Alexis barely nibbled, but wisely, he did not push. Originally from the Yucatan peninsula, Bishara had grown up as a home-town boy, and even though he'd spent three years at the Music Conservatory in Mexico City, and another two in Los Angeles, his *Yucatéco* heart always brought him back to Mérida. But when his divorce had been made final, he had struck out in a new direction. Putting together a repertoire of music as a solo act, he had invested in a new guitar and moved to Cozumel to play and sing professionally.

"...then when I've finished playing all the venues here, I'll go to Cancun; there are dozens of places in the *Zona Hotelera*," Bishara explained. "So, I am curious. Why did you choose to come to Cozumel rather than somewhere else?"

"I don't know exactly," Alexis mused. "It just seemed like a good place to hide until I could decide what to do."

"Then it is very much a coincidence, if you know the history of this island," Bishara said, with a whimsical smile. "Maya women have been coming here for thousands of years. The ruins of *Ix-chel* are here. She is the goddess of hearth, health, and childbearing, and the patron goddess of women. It is the place for *refujeras*, women like you, seeking refuge."

The next day, Alexis arranged to meet Bishara at the same beach after his last music set. She brought her old flute from Berkeley, and showed it to him. It was one of the few personal items she'd managed to grab in her escape from San Pedro.

"It's glazed ceramic, baked clay. I used to sell these in California ten years ago. It's note-perfect. Chromatics are a bit difficult because I have to half-hole the openings. But straight scales are easy."

Bishara's face lit up. "Would you be interested in jamming with me a little?"

Alexis looked down demurely, and then lifted her eyes to meet his. She was overwhelmed. "I feel privileged to be asked, and I would love to. Since this whole thing began, listening to you has been the only thing that has been able to make me forget, even for a few moments. It has provided me with the only peace I've known."

From the start, it was music that brought Bishara and Alexis together. There was a natural camaraderie and deep rapport. They shared a taxi back to his apartment and, for the rest of the evening, he demonstrated his favorite solos, guitar riffs, and harmony lines, and then showed her all the different effects he could get with his equipment. Next thing they knew it was one-thirty in the morning.

"Let's go eat," said Bishara. "I'm going to take you to a place where the *frijoles charros* melt in your mouth, and the *carne asada* and *guacamole* are the best in Mexico. It's so *delicioso*, you will eat like a little pig."

Alexis wanted to eat. A psychologist would have probably told her that she had "swallowed" all she could with Max, and her body had merely manifested the condition. She'd lost a lot of weight; her clothes were all huge. "Do you have a scale?" she asked, looking around the room.

"Si. It's right there in the *baño.* It shows both pounds and kilos."

Alexis came out of the bathroom a moment later, looking pale. "The scale said forty-three kilos. I have gone from a hundred and twenty-two, to ninety-five pounds."

Bishara held out his hand; he did not judge her. "Let's go eat, Alexis. *Vamos.*"

El Foco, the Lightbulb, stood out as one of the island's only all-nighter restaurants. Alive with people, colored lights inside and out, and ranchero music, *aficionados* of Mexican cuisine were lured inside by meaty aromas from the open grill. Bishara ordered for both of them, and Alexis made a substantial effort, managing to eat a little of her old favorite – refried beans and hot sauce on corn tortillas. But the *cebollitas chambray*, large green spring onions brushed with butter, grilled on an open flame, and sprinkled generously with lime juice and a little salt, were a revelation. The moment would mark the beginning of her recovery.

The waiter came and Bishara paid the bill.

"So where do we go now?" he asked. They got up from the table and stepped out into the warm night air. "Are you going back to your hotel?"

Alexis hesitated. "I guess."

"Would you like to stay in my apartment with me tonight? It's more convenient than walking back or taking a taxi."

"Are you asking me to sleep with you?"

"No. I am not so insensitive, but I would like to help you in any way I can. Perhaps just the comfort of another person..." Bishara put an arm around her shoulders gently. "It's okay. I'll give you my bed; I will sleep on the couch."

"It's very kind of you, but I'll take the couch. I don't sleep anyway."

Alexis lay on the couch and prepared for another sleepless night. Bishara turned out the light and climbed into bed on then other side of the room. Yet, thirty minutes later, his mellow voice came softly through the darkness. He sensed she was still awake.

"Alexis? I want to take you to Mérida tomorrow. We should buy you a silver flute so you have a professional instrument. You'll also need your own microphone and a microphone stand. I want you to be my partner. With a temporary membership as an *extranjera* in the Musician's Union, we will practice hard and get very good together, very professional. Then we'll go to Cancun and play the big clubs, at least until you know what is happening, and where your life is going."

"But I'm not good enough," Alexis protested.

"I disagree. We could learn a lot from each other."

Although he couldn't see her face, she was now smiling. She hadn't smiled in weeks. "I'd love to be your partner."

As the roosters crowed in the early dawn, Alexis continued to lie awake on the hard couch. The ancient upholstery smelled musty and the coil springs poked rudely into her ribs. Still intensely cold, she thought she'd never be warm again. Even under the blanket, her feet and her hands were like ice, and she shivered so violently it caused physical exhaustion, and yet, sleep still eluded her. The forces of heaven and hell seemed to wage a battle inside her brain, never arriving at a clear victory or defeat. Like an injured animal seeking warmth, Alexis finally walked across the room and stood beside Bishara's bed. In the pale light, she could just make out his face. He was awake, and silently, he threw back the covers to receive her. Alexis lay down next to his warmth and he wrapped his arms around her. Within a few minutes, she slept, for the first time in weeks.

Three days later, they returned to the Cozumel apartment with Alexis' new musical equipment. Bishara had been so sure of a prosperous musical future that he'd staked her against future earnings. And thus began Alexis' career as a professional musician in Mexico, first in Cozumel, then in Cancun. The phase would last only six months, but the twist of fate would give her the opportunity to do something she never would have done otherwise. A new force awakened inside her, a high level of creative musical energy, one that had been born out of the desire to survive. Pragmatic now, she became focused again. The only way to see her children again was to stay alive. To live, she needed money. Only money would buy her power for the inevitable fight, no matter the format, circumstances, or time-line. Moreover, the music provided the necessary creative outlet to release her emotion. Practicing long hours every day, she used her sorrow to reach new heights of accomplishment.

As Alexis studied Bishara's repertoire, she gradually performed more and more songs with him. When they weren't performing, they spent nearly every waking moment studying music and teaching each other Spanish and English. At first, Alexis sang the Spanish songs phonetically, not knowing all the meanings of the words. Bishara did the same with the songs that were sung in English, so they often sat together and translated for each other. There was one particular song that seemed to express all she was feeling. It was called *Adiós Triesteza,* Goodbye Sadness.

"*Poco a poco se va triesteza?*" she asked.

"'Little by little the sadness goes,'" he answered.

"*Haciendo por su pena poco de miel.*"

"'Taking, for your pain, a little honey.'"

Intrigued by this song, and similar ballads, Alexis discovered the beauty and clarity of the Spanish language. It was clean and unencumbered, so different from her native tongue with its pointless auxiliary verbs and clumsy conjugations. Lyrical and fluid, it bespoke her deepest emotions.

> I go with the tides, with the sadness.
> Like a bird, a swallow, that the wind has carried away,
> I go because of a love that could never be.
> Like one more star in the coming of the night,
> Goodbye sadness.
>
> I take with me, my life; I leave to you my childhood,
> And all the years that I gave to you.
> I take with me, the moon,
> And the dreams we dreamed together,
> But I don't want, to want you, anymore, goodbye.

Inside of two weeks, Bishara and Alexis were playing and singing together with dynamic professionalism. With the flute, guitar, rhythm, lead, and vocal harmony, the resultant sound was that of an entire band. Bishara had progressive tastes and, through careful selection, they drew their repertoire from jazz, ballads, popular American artists, and even Brazilian sambas, with Alexis also learning the Portuguese phonetically. Apparently, her performance was convincing, especially when guests began to ask if she was from Ipanema, Brazil, where blond hair and blue eyes were not uncommon.

On one of their days off, Bishara surprised Alexis by taking her on a tour of Cozumel, renting a small motorbike for the day. They took off from San Miguel, heading due east across the interior, and visited the ruins of Ix-Chel, then drove to the windward side of the island. Unlike the western lee shore, the east coast was untamed and huge waves lashed the shore. Long wide stretches of boulders made access to the water difficult, until they suddenly gave way to wide expanses of sandy beach. Here, there were no people, only the coastal wilderness of windblown dunes. Moved by the beauty of the seascape, Bishara and Alexis parked the motorbike, and ran into the ocean, but not too far. The power was awesome, and a vicious undertow surged and sucked at their feet. For a few brief moments, Alexis again forgot her anxiety, glorying in a moment of oneness with nature. Again, she felt the watery embrace, the wind in her hair, and her bare toes squishing in the sand. Once again, ever so briefly, future and past held no meaning – an eternity compressed in a timeless moment.

Continuing south, they reached Punta Celerain where the old lighthouse had stood guard over the southern tip of Cozumel since 1934, although the remains of an even earlier lighthouse were still visible. Through the cycles of the seasons, the lighthouse had illuminated the stormy waters with its brilliant shining eye, and warned sailors of hidden shoals and reefs. Now the edifice was decrepit, with sweaty walls and peeling paint. Undaunted by the smell of sea rot and bird dung, Alexis and Bishara climbed the spiraling stairway to the top. From the lookout, they saw a landscape of magnificent desolation. Empty of trees, the jutting peninsula was pocketed with stagnant salt pools, groundcover succulents, and sea grapes. Beyond the promontory, the waters of the Caribbean faded into a reflective haze that obscured the horizon, while a solitary seabird wheeled on the air currents. Alexis closed her eyes and projected herself into the bird, feeling the familiar thrill of flight from her dreams, as she looked down through its eyes.

There was a restaurant of sorts at the base of the lighthouse. It was only a small *palapa*, and the kitchen consisted of an open fire surrounded by four large hearthstones, over which a crude metal mesh had been placed. On top was half of a fifty-five gallon drum full of boiling oil. The proprietor served fried fish. No menu, no choices – that was it. He simply gutted the fish, gave it a cursory scaling, and threw it into the drum of boiling oil. Once fried, the fish was salted and served whole on a piece of newspaper. Customers ate standing up. She looked at the eye of the fish as it stared back at her, all yellow and gooey and crispy. Gross, Alexis thought.

Bishara laughed when he saw the look on her face. "You don't like the head?"

"It's the eye. I don't like the idea of eating anything that's looking back at me. In Belize, the locals like the eye. They say it's the best part, along with the cheek."

"Here too," Bishara replied. "Just like the worm in the bottle. In the beginning, it looks disgusting, but by the time the men drink all that mescal, they fight over who gets to eat the worm."

"Well, they can have it; and the fish eye as well," she laughed. "You know, Bishara, when I first went to Belize, I ate something called *bollos*; it's similar to *tamales*. On my third bite, I found a chicken foot inside. Not the leg, mind you, but the foot, with the little yellow toes and toenails and everything. I thought it was a joke, or there was some special meaning to it, like finding the silver dollar in the wedding cake."

"Like the toy surprise in the box of Crackerjack I had in L.A.?" They both laughed.

"When I was in college," Alexis began, "I was taking a course in North African literature, and the professor decided to serve a North African dinner for the students. I ate six or seven little round things that were being served as appetizers before somebody told me they were goat's eyes. I barely made it to the bathroom in time."

"You also didn't care for the octopus tacos we ate in Mérida," Bishara added, with a smile.

"You mean 'you ate.' Little pink rubbery suction cups on a bed of lettuce? Not on my taco!" Alexis laughed. "I should have known better when I saw 'served in its own ink.'"

"But I like to watch Americans when they order '*al tinte*'..."

They were both laughing now; it was good medicine. He put his arm around her shoulders. "I like you like this, Alexita, happy and making jokes. It's much better than seeing you cry for your children."

"I think, so far, my favorite Spanish word is '*sobrevivir*', to 'survive.' Literally translated, it means to 'over-live.' I like that. I'm going to over-live this situation, and you are a part of it."

"You are doing very well," said Bishara, sincerely. "Many people would have gone *loco*."

"I almost did, but I can't afford to," replied Alexis. "I have to keep it together *para sobrevivir*. You saved my life by helping me eat again; I owe it to you to be as easy to get along with as possible. If I allow myself to be weak, or go crazy, or act impossible, then how could we work together and live in the same space? I have to focus on some kind of goal, and so do you. I am using my anger and frustration as a source of strength. It's a survival technique that I'm inventing as I go along."

"You are a strong woman."

"No, not strong. I just refuse to be a victim anymore."

Per his original plan, Bishara and Alexis continued to play in clubs and beach resorts in Cozumel, and then agreed to go to Cancun where the market for musicians was virtually unlimited. With a minimum of hassle, Bishara and Alexis took a quick trip across the channel and found a modest house for rent in Cancun. They signed an agreement with the landlord, and moved in a week later.

Cancun was a unique place. Only fifteen years before, there had been no city, only a swamp full of mosquitoes and caimans on the northeastern tip of Quintana Roo. Arching into the Caribbean, a thin peninsula in the shape of an orchestral harp jutted from the mainland, encircling a central lagoon. Although most cities throughout the world evolved through time, starting first as small hamlets, then villages, and then cities, Cancun was conceived in advance. The layout of the entire region was to be structured to the last detail in accordance with the tastes and needs of the visitors who would eventually flock there by the tens of thousands. More than an entertainment attraction and vacation spot, Cancun was to be a modern showcase of the future. The city planners had been both artistic and meticulous. Every hotel in the *Zona Hotelera* was of unique design. One featured the look of a Mayan temple; another had a roof with the triangular silhouettes of windsurfers. Even more impressive was the fact that each hotel on the strip was positioned so absolutely every view, from every hotel room on the peninsula was unspoiled by the presence of any other structure.

Alexis and Bishara established a wonderful working relationship and became great friends through the months to follow. Yet, strangely enough, only a small part of it was sexual. Bishara had served with the Hari Krishnas in California, and had practiced celibacy for several years. So, although he enjoyed sex, it was not an obsession, and their mutual lack of physical desire turned out to be a part of their compatibility. But they took great comfort in the other person's presence and warmth. Above all else, music was their primary source of joy and strength.

A time-sharing condo complex called Club International provided their first musical gig in Cancun. It wasn't much, just playing the cocktail hour outside near the pool. But word got around and soon they found themselves playing at Carlos and Charley's, Camino Real, and Pier 66. They played Club Fandango at the Miramar Mission, did a gig at the Krystal, and later at the Sheraton. Finally, Bishara and Alexis were offered a lucrative two-month contract at the Exelaris Hyatt, playing for the dinner hour. With the peso valued at one hundred and forty seven to one with the American dollar, Alexis was soon making three hundred and fifty U.S. per week.

Now, night after night, week after week, she played and sang songs of love and yearning. Somehow, each one seemed to speak to her circumstance – songs about love, the nature of love, falling in love, needing love, being in love, losing in love. In Alexis' mind, the songs of lost loves were not for a man, but for her children. Yet, in spite of it all, she maintained her professional demeanor for the audience. No one could imagine how hard it was to keep her voice clear and strong when so many of the lyrics revealed her own deepest emotions. Like Pagliacchi, she never let the audience see the tears behind the smile, and every night she put aside her private hell and performed for her listeners.

How strange that my life should take another twist of fate, thought Alexis. Now, because of it, I have become a professional musician, a career I never would have pursued under normal circumstances. If I could have chosen between this and my kids, I would have chosen my children. But there was no choice. And now, because of the hand I've been dealt, I find myself wearing another hat, involved in yet another occupation. Is being a musician worth the price I paid? No, never. But, because this is the hand I was dealt, is it worth trying to enjoy what I am doing? Yes, absolutely. I will find the rose among the thorns, and hold on to it.

Part of the goodness that Alexis discovered was that of a new type of love. During her life, she had experienced many kinds of love – familial love, emotional love, sexual love, and spiritual love. Performing before the crowds, love took on a whole new form, a reciprocal love resulting from the music. It was called applause.

Applause. Alexis did not love applause because it fed her ego, or made her feel special, or better than other people. Rather, she loved the feeling of giving when she sang for them; she was serving them in the most intimate way. The overall effect was stunningly sensual, as though she were making love to all of them. She felt their ebb and flow as she pleasured them, stroked them, coaxed their emotions, tugged at their heartstrings. And they gave it all back through their applause. Applause was a portrayal of giving and receiving in its purest form, freely spontaneous and undeniably genuine. Within a large crowd, it started as gently as a nervous lover's first caress, and then, rippling across the room, the response built in tempo and volume. Within seconds, applause became a thundering crescendo of warm emotion that washed over her like waves of love.

Through the hotel gigs, Bishara and Alexis met many talented musicians. After work, they went to Friday Lopez, and listened to other jazz and pop groups. It always amazed her that the musicians were so friendly and clean-living. Not one of them drank or took drugs. Many had attended the Conservatory in Mexico City; all of them were serious musicians in pursuit of the highest standards. Music was their life, and their dedication to their art was absolute. The weeks had become months. Although her life had stabilized, Alexis was still no closer to a final resolve. Nightly, she watched the skies, following the phases of the moon, crying every time it waxed full – the symbol of another month away from her precious children. No words could explain the emotional roller-coaster of anxiety and despondency. It was also inevitable that, at some point, she would have to go back to Belize and face Max again.

"You know I would do anything to help you," offered Bishara. "But in this problem I am nothing, only a friend. Why you don't see if your mother or father can come here? They already offered on the phone. We can take some time off, rent a car, and drive to Belize."

"The three of us?"

"*Si, como no.* Why not?"

It had been difficult to call her parents when she had first made her escape. Alexis had been hiding, afraid they'd tell her to go back, and of course, she should have known better. It only took one phone call from Alexis for her mother to book her ticket to Cancun.

Liz DuBois arrived at the International Airport in Cancun on Mother's Day in 1983, and with an orchid on her lapel, she waved to Alexis from the other side of Customs. Minutes later, they shared a tearful embrace.

"Are you all right, honey?" Liz asked, holding her daughter tight. "You look so thin. You're not sick, are you?"

"I'm okay. I was a lot thinner before. I gained back ten pounds already." Alexis gently broke the embrace. "Mom, this is my friend and partner, Bishara Simone."

"I'm so grateful to you," said Liz, shaking his hand, and then spontaneously hugging him. "I hardly know what to say. Thank you for helping Alexis. Her father and I owe you a debt of gratitude."

"*A su servicio, Señora.* It is my pleasure to help. It has been very difficult, but Alexita is doing much better now. She never told me that her mother is so young and pretty."

"Alexis told me about your Latin charm." Liz smiled. "I see she was not exaggerating."

Arriving back at the house, Liz got to the heart of the matter. "The first thing to decide is what you really want. Do you want to get back with Max? Or do you want to be apart? Unless you've made a decision on separation or reconciliation, there's not much I can do to help you."

"There's no question," Alexis said, without hesitation. "It's over. Max tries to change, but it'll never be any different. Now that I've had the chance to stand away from the situation, I have gained perspective. I know now how blind I really was. I see clearly again, what is right and wrong. I could never go back to that kind of life."

Liz sighed. It would be a tough road.

There were many emotional moments as the three prepared for the drive to Belize. Tension ran high and then vented itself in unexpected ways. At one point, Liz showed Alexis a nightgown she had brought for Jessica. At the sight of the tiny garment, she broke into tears. Already, she had missed out on five months of her children's lives.

It was Alexis who did all the driving as the little rented car flew down the highway south to Belize. With her foot to the floor, she drove obsessively. Liz rode in the passenger side. She was nervous from the dizzying speed, but neither she nor Bishara had the heart to complain. Although they may have genuflected in their minds, they too, trusted God that this was not their time to die. Alexis had no such fears. Invulnerable now, she was bouncing back, rising to the challenge. She had power, money, and people who cared about her – cared enough to take up her cause, and lend her strength.

Death may come tomorrow, she thought, or next week, or next month, but I will not die today. I know this to be true, because today, before the sun sets, I will see my children.

Alexis agonized all over again at the confusion and fright the children had endured in the past few months. She wondered if Jordan would hate her for deserting him, and wondered if Jessica would even remember her. Alexis touched the jade bead around her neck, her Mayan bead, the color of her being. Beyond her spiritual torment, she endured a physical ache as well, an intense maternal yearning, an abiding need to hold her children again, to give comfort, and in turn, be comforted by their nearness. She needed to rock them, sniff their delicate scent, for even at age eight and three, Jordan and Jessica still had that same baby sweetness when they lay sleeping.

Although Liz suffered for her daughter's sake, she could not grasp what Alexis was going through. But her presence would be critical in the emotional negotiations, as her degree in guidance and counseling allowed her to be objective, and still wear a variety of hats – mother, counselor, grandmother, and friend.

There had been no point in Frank's coming to Belize. This was women's ground, and even he had admitted he was too emotional. Alexis needed her mother this time, and Frank's contribution had been to let her go. As he paced the living room of the Dubois home in Pennsylvania, he had never felt so impotent in his life. He was sick with worry about his daughter, and he missed his wife. Throughout Alexis' childhood and teenage years, Frank had been her hero. He was the daddy who could make the hurt go away by kissing her bruised knee. He was the daddy who bought her ice cream and took her to play miniature golf. He was the daddy who devoted long hours on Christmas Eve assembling her new toy – one with impossibly confusing instructions in which every paragraph began with the word "simply." He was the daddy who could fix. Yet somehow his precious daughter had become the victim of a cruel and vindictive husband, torn from her home and children. She was most certainly unstable, and possibly even suicidal. This time, Frank was absolutely powerless to do anything. This time, Daddy couldn't fix.

Passing Belmopan, the tension became unbearable. It was only a few more miles. Nobody spoke. There was nothing to say. Alexis thought for the hundredth time what it must have been like after she left San Pedro. How long had Max, Angelina, and the kids stayed on the island before returning to Cayo? Were they home at all? What if he had taken the children back to South Africa?

As they crested the hill, the Lord house came into sight. It looked different. There were rose trellises and ivy and impatiens and coleus planted everywhere. As they pulled into the driveway, Alexis saw the blond boy riding his bike in the front yard. She opened the door and called out.

"Jordan!"

"Mummy? Is that you, Mummy? MUMMY!!" he shouted. "EVERYBODY! MUMMY'S HOME!" The boy ran to his mother, arms open wide and flung them around her, crying for happiness. Angelina came out of the house, the three-year old girl clinging to her skirts.

"Welcome home, Miss Alexis," she said, formally.

Unable to focus on anything but her children, Alexis dropped down on one knee, still holding Jordan tightly. Only fifteen feet separated Alexis from her daughter, yet it seemed to be a huge chasm.

"Jessica. Come here, honey." Shyly, the little girl smiled and started to walk slowly toward her mother with a quizzical look on her face. "I know you," said Jessica, sweetly. "You're Alexis. They talk about you all the time."

"This is our Mummy, Jess," said Jordan.

"Yes, my darlings," said Alexis, as she flung her arms around Jessica as well. "I am your mother, and I love you more than you could ever know."

Hearing the commotion, Max stepped out of the house.

"Hi Alexis," he said "Hello Mum. Nice to see you again." Liz nodded coolly but made no move. He was immediately disadvantaged by her presence.

"Max, this is Bishara," Alexis said, "my musical partner from Cancun." Max extended his hand, and Bishara shook it. They all stood in the yard awkwardly.

"So, now you are back," said Max. "Have you come home?"

"Not to stay," Alexis replied.

"No!" cried Jordan, throwing his arms around her a second time. "Mummy, you have to stay. You can't leave again."

"Don't get upset, sweetie, please," she said, comforting him. "I'm here now, and we'll spend plenty of time talking about whatever is on your mind. I have many things to explain."

Max didn't know whether to be happy or angry. His mind was searching for answers. If Alexis stayed, it would spell disaster; if she left again, it would spell disaster. "So why did you bother to come back again if you're not going to stay?"

"I couldn't stay away from the kids any longer. My heart has been breaking for them."

"But not for me, I suppose?" he inquired, belligerently. Max was already up for a fight.

"Do you really want to get into this? Here? Now?"

He sighed, softening.

"No. Come in the house where it's cool and sit down. Angelina will make us something to drink."

After making lemonade for the three guests, Angelina left through the back door. She didn't want to be a part of the conversation. Her destiny would be determined by Max, as everything was. When it was over, he would dictate his decision.

At first, everyone sat in the living room together, and Liz and Bishara attempted to make polite small talk. It was awkward. Alexis sat silent, content just to hold Jordan and Jessica in her lap, to kiss them, and touch them. But it was anathema being in the same room with Max. After all, she hadn't come back to see him, talk to him, or reconcile anything. Her purpose was to see Jordan and Jessica. Being near Max again was a necessary evil, part of the price that had to be paid.

After a few minutes, Alexis couldn't stand any more. She excused herself and took the children outside to swing in the hammock under the plum tree. Bishara, feeling like a fifth wheel, followed them.

Liz remained inside and listened patiently to Max as he explained how much he'd changed. It was true that he seemed different, almost soft, and his words were straightforward. He explained how much he'd suffered, how he'd done his penance, and now sought ultimate pardon.

"I'm trying to tell you," Max began, "I am truly a changed man. I have spent months in mourning, reflecting on my own shortcomings. I have had a difficult time learning to forgive myself for what I did. And I made a promise to both myself and the kids that if Alexis came back, she and I would wipe the slate clean and we'd start a new life together."

"I understand. But it takes two to make a new beginning, and Alexis hasn't come back with that in mind. She has come back to end the marriage. She doesn't love you anymore. It sounds like it's too late."

"I don't believe it," said Max, shaking his head. "No. We have too many positive things going for us – the children, and the many years we've invested together. Alexis needed the time away, but now she has got to come back. It's time to move forward again. I don't believe she would throw away everything we had."

"Everybody has their limits," Liz cautioned.

"I still don't believe it. I'm going to call her back inside. If it's true, she has to tell me to my face." He went to the door and asked Alexis to join them.

"Is it okay if I stay out here with the kids?" Bishara called out. "I'll look after them." The tension was rising, and he could sense that the confrontation was about to begin.

"Sure, good idea," said Max. "Jordan, why don't you and your sister show our guest the new puppies?"

"Okay Dad."

Liz readied herself to play the part of referee. Alexis came in and sat down beside her mother, across from Max. She braced herself; this was it.

"*Ntombi*, your mother says that you don't want to get back together. I can't believe that's true. Now that you've had your break and your time away, surely you're ready to stop this nonsense. It's time to come back to your family and assume your responsibilities."

His words and his tone were presumptuous, superior, reprimanding her for misbehavior. In one simple sentence, the familiar uneasiness returned, putting her on the defensive. If Alexis had ever doubted her decision, she now knew, with certainty, what had to be done.

"I came back to see Jordan and Jessie. That's all. Seeing you is extraneous. I told you before I left that I don't love you anymore. I still don't. You killed that in me. It's gone forever."

"But you can't separate your love for the kids and your love for the man who created them with you," Max protested.

"That's the most naive statement I've ever heard," Alexis scoffed. "Many women love their kids and not their husbands; that's why people get divorced. If a woman is raped and becomes pregnant, she may end up loving the child, but she will never love the man who raped her."

"But you were gone for five months. That was a long time. You missed the kids. Didn't you miss me while you were away?"

"No," she said with finality.

"Not at all? Not even a little?"

"No. I was glad to be away from you."

He absorbed the comment and continued. "But you said you just needed a break, so you could sort out your feelings. You were supposed to come back refreshed and renewed and ready to put things back together again."

"You can't delegate emotion, Max. It's not for you to say what I am supposed to feel. I told you I needed to distance myself from you so I could see reality, and what I found out surprised me. First of all, I discovered I wasn't a bad person at all. I found out that my feelings and beliefs were valid, and amazingly enough, I found new friends who really liked me for who I am. I saw families loving and caring for each other. In comparison, our life together was a sham. I lived in constant fear, and where there is fear, there can be no trust. Where there is no trust, there can be no love. All of that has made it crystal clear that we have irreconcilable differences. I know now I could never live with you again."

"Not even for the sake of the kids?"

"No. Even if we could manage to put aside our anger and hurt, the kids would grow up one day and be gone. Then it would still be you and me. The chasm between us is too deep. You are a fire sign, and I am air. You would continue to consume me, and use me up, just as you have always done. You were always insanely jealous of any facet of my life that didn't revolve around you. That's why my artistic talent died – my writing, my music. Birds don't sing in caves. You never allowed me to be myself. You fell in love with me because of my spirit, my spark. Then you spent the next ten years trying to crush it. That's not what it's all about. Your love for me has always been conditional."

"But through all these years in spite of everything, I have loved you."

"Then why were you so cruel to me?" Alexis challenged.

"I guess because you acted crazy," Max countered.

"You made me crazy by being so cruel to me."

"Well, I guess we have a problem then."

"Not really. There's no problem. It's over," she said, matter-of-factly. "We had a lousy marriage; maybe we can have a good divorce. All we need is a mutually acceptable arrangement concerning the children, the money, our property, and personal effects."

"No way. I'm not prepared to deal with any of that. You have to come back. I am the lion; I mate for life. I did my time alone, and now I want you back."

"You weren't alone. You had Angelina. Speaking of which, if I did come back to stay, what would you do with her? Kick her out?"

"I don't know. Give her some money and send her on her way, I guess."

Alexis attacked him. "Just throw her out? After she's stuck by your side through all of this?"

"What do you want me to say?" Max cried. "I'm damned if I do, and damned if I don't."

"He's right, Alexis," interjected Liz. "Don't corner him like that. It's not fair."

She backed down. "Okay, you're right. But it doesn't matter about Angelina either way. The marriage is over."

Max didn't speak for a moment, but when he did, the anger surfaced. "Why don't you tell me the truth? You never wanted kids in the first place, and now that you've gotten a taste of the single life again, there's no turning back. I know you were playing music in Cancun, running around at all hours of the night, hanging out in smoky clubs and screwing every good-looking guitar player around."

"Max!" Liz spoke again. She'd called Alexis on her *faux pas*, and now was calling Max on his. After all, fair was fair. "That kind of remark is totally uncalled for. You can't possibly comprehend what Alexis went through after she left."

"Apparently not near enough, or she would have come to her goddamn senses by now." Max was changing before their eyes. He darkened, and his temples began to throb. His voice became vehement as he cranked up to a full-blown tirade, punctuating his remarks with his fists.

"You don't know anything about your own daughter," he shouted. "Did you know that she had affairs with soldiers every time she went to Belize City to sell jewelry? You think she has suffered? Are you aware of the mental agony I have suffered by being with her? It started the day before our wedding when she was flirting with a naked guy on the Yuba."

"Enough, Max!" Liz stood up and cut him off, matching his volume and intensity in righteous indignation. "Just look at yourself! How many times have you told that story? How can you ever let go of the recent past, if you're still holding a grudge for something from ten years ago? Maximilian Lord, you haven't changed at all. You're no different than you ever were, standing there shouting at the top of your lungs, with your eyes flashing, pounding your fists. If I weren't here, those fists would probably be working her over by now. You know, for a few minutes, you almost had me fooled. If you'd have been able to keep up that charade for much longer, I would have been prepared to suggest that Alexis reconsider her decision. But not now. She was right all along. You'll never change, and you just proved it. You can hide behind a thin veneer of decorum in your better moments, but that old animosity is always just under the surface, just dying to get out. Alexis was right. Leaving you was an act of self-preservation on her part. You're a violent man who lives on the edge, and I wouldn't try to change her mind now for anything in the world."

Further discussion was pointless. He finally understood that Alexis' only motive was maternal. Through his mother-in-law's insistence, Max eventually agreed to let Jordan and Jessica go with Alexis, Liz, and Bishara to spend the night at the hotel. At first, he was certain that Alexis planned to flee with the children, but he couldn't deny that Liz was an honorable woman, and she had given him her word. Besides, Alexis had no intention of escape; she never doubted that Max would make good his threats of pursuit.

During Alexis' absence, Max had informed everyone in San Ignacio that his wife had abandoned her children, running off to play music in Mexico for no plausible reason. He spread rumors that she had been unfaithful to him, concocting stories, so his retaliatory actions would appear justified. So when they checked-in, and then waited in the main lounge for their room to be ready, the hotel personnel looked on surreptitiously.

"Mummy? Can I go over there to the arcade room while you are talking?" asked Jordan, politely. "They have video games. I'll take Jess with me and watch her if you want."

Alexis looked at her son fondly. Jordan's simple world had righted itself quickly and, comforted with his mother's return, he was ready to move on. As if Liz could read her mind, she reached out for Alexis' hand. "Let them go play for a while, honey. Then we can all take a swim together in the pool."

"All right," said Alexis to her son, "but stay where I can see you."

"Okay, Mummy," he promised. "I'm so glad you're back. I love you."

When the children were out of earshot, Bishara posed a question. "How is it that Belize allows women to be abused by their husbands? I still don't understand."

"The problem is that, as long as I'm married to him, the English 'rule of thumb' still applies," Alexis explained. "Most people don't know what that means, but according to English law, a husband is allowed to beat his wife once a week with a stick no larger than his thumb. It's archaic, but it's still actual law. Belize is not exactly a country that sticks up for women's rights, and the local authorities couldn't care less. This law means I'd have to be officially divorced from Max before I could feel safe. I'd need the assurance that he couldn't touch me physically, legally. Maybe then we could work it out."

"But you'd have to work it out for him to agree to a divorce in the first place," said Bishara.

"He will never agree to a divorce," Liz interjected. "It's a vicious circle."

They hadn't been talking for more than ten minutes when Max walked into the hotel; he'd followed them almost immediately after they'd driven away. "Unbelievable," Bishara whispered. "You were right. The man cannot leave you in peace."

"I'll handle this," said Liz quietly. "You two go take Jordan and Jessica to the pool. I'll talk to him." Max saw Alexis and Bishara taking the children away, but made no attempt to go after them. Instead, he sat down with Liz and ordered a beer from the server. "You just couldn't stay away, could you?" she said, with uncharacteristic irritation. "Didn't you think you could trust me either?"

"I don't know who to trust." In this moment, he was again submissive, wounded, and vulnerable. "You saw me back at the house. I can't even trust myself."

Liz leaned towards him and peered into her son-in-law's eyes.

"Tell me why Max. Just between you and me. Right here. Right now. Why did you do it? Why did you beat her?"

He answered slowly, sincerely.

"I don't know, Mum. I really don't know. I never treated another woman like that in my life." Although it was not an answer, it was as close as anyone would ever come to knowing the truth.

The house in Cancun was never quite the same after their return. Liz flew back to Pennsylvania. Alexis had seen the children again, and established her position with Max, but nothing had really changed. He still wanted her back. She still loathed him, and vowed never to return as his wife.

Bishara, always the gentleman, said he would be supportive either way. The music had effected a healing for him as well, and he would never forget her. A few weeks later, Alexis decided to return to Belize to face the inevitable divorce. It had been a good relationship. Bishara and Alexis had learned much from each other, and they parted friends.

 ISLAND

chapter 15

Alexis knew better than to live on the mainland within Max's immediate circle of influence so she settled on the island and San Pedro. But she had underestimated his reach. The people had been kind to her in Cancun; she had been taken at face value, even loved. Here, Alexis found herself snubbed by the San Pedranos. Max always hedged his bets, and before leaving, he had made sure all the islanders knew of her desertion.

Her time of healing began to slip into memory, and reality struck hard when she found herself living in a small dingy apartment in San Pedro village. Now, several months later, Alexis realized she had begun to miss Mexico from the moment she crossed the border. Aside from the emotional aspects, there was also a physical reality. With a small nest egg of a few thousand dollars, there was only enough money to last a few more months, provided she lived frugally and continued to forage from the sea. She went to the bar a few times, but the nightly crowd of tourists, drunks, and hopeless womanizers created an insufferable loneliness, and once more the cobwebs of dark depression began to curl around the edges of her mind.

One afternoon, Alexis found herself walking along the cold deserted beach. She touched the little jade bead around her neck, but this time it did nothing to soothe her soul. The wind itself seemed to utter a harsh reproach, and her spirit cried for vindication. The beach was empty as she walked north along the shore. A strong breeze blew from the east, off the water. The sky was ugly and gray and so was the ocean...*the seaweed and sand are cold and wet under my bare feet. I feel an aching grief, too heavy to bear. There's a hopeless desperation, one that nothing can resolve. It's as though I've lost something terribly important and I don't know what it is. The wind has an evil sound. It accuses me over and over saying, "unworthy, unworthy..."* The long forgotten premonition overwhelmed her. Beyond the fulfillment of prophecy, Alexis tasted the bitterness of irony. Once again, the destiny of visions past had been fulfilled.

Without the stability of friends, Alexis soon stopped worrying about what other people thought. It didn't seem to matter anyway. The rumor mill on San Pedro, always a source of colorful depravity, churned out exaggerated stories which quickly filtered back to Max in Cayo. Alexis was supposedly consuming cases of tequila and engaging in bizarre sexual escapades.

At first, Max allowed Jordan and Jessica to fly to San Pedro to visit their mother. But now, due to the rumors, he called off the visits entirely. Phoning Alexis several times a week, he insisted on talking to her for senseless hours, spending hundreds of dollars in the process. All conversations were in vain; hostility and recriminations were never-ending. Max insisted that Alexis come back as his wife, but always under his terms of unconditional surrender. She held firm, but implored him to allow the children's visits to resume. He refused, insisting that if she wanted to see the children, she must come to his territory – endless circles, with never a minor compromise, let alone a resolve. There was only one compromise with Max: giving in and doing it his way.

Finally, he tried a different tactic on the phone.

"I want to invite you to join the kids and me on a vacation to Mexico. No business. Just a restful relaxing vacation."

Alexis resisted immediately. "You've never made a pure pleasure trip in your life. It's always buy-and-sell. You never do any dead-heading."

"Not this time. I swear it," said Max, sincerely. "All you have to do is enjoy yourself on a family vacation that we should have taken years ago. No conditions, no strings. I'll foot the whole bill. And you don't have to sleep with me either. I won't even ask."

"And no innuendoes? No lusting after me when I change my clothes, or take a shower?"

"I can't help what I feel inside, but I promise I won't let it show. No pressure, sexual or otherwise. I swear it."

"What's Angelina going to do?" said Alexis belligerently. "Come with us again?"

"Absolutely not. She's going to stay, and take care of the jewelry shop here at the house."

"She must love this idea. Are you telling me that she has agreed to 'mind the store' while you try to reconstruct our relationship? Possibly resulting in the termination of her way of life with you? What a saint! She's either incredibly devoted, or incredibly stupid."

"I don't love her, Alexis," he persisted. "All this time, I've just been marking time, waiting for us to get back together. You're still the only woman for me. So will you come with us to Mexico, *Ntombi eyami*? We'll go to Playa del Carmen. It will be perfect."

"If I went, I'd only be going to be with the kids, not with you. I will not let you touch me. I won't sleep in the same bed with you. And you'll pay for everything, right?"

"Right."

"Okay, I'll go. But only because of the kids. Don't expect much." She hung up.

The trip to Playa del Carmen turned out to be an exquisite paradox of pleasure and torture – a pleasure to play on the beaches with Jessica and Jordan, torture in the moments late at night after the kids were asleep, when Alexis was forced to discourse with the devil. Max tried his best to play the romantic. For the first time in his life, he wanted to smell the roses with Alexis, to walk in the moonlight. He put love songs on the tape player, explaining how this one, or that one, spoke to his heart. He tried to get her to take off her wedding ring, so he could cleverly slip it back on her finger with vows of renewed love. None of it warmed her soul. His overtures were repugnant to her; the gestures left her cold. This was the man that had vanquished her spirit, brutalized her, physically and emotionally.

"It's dead in me," Alexis said, with finality. "I told you that."

"I thought I could bring it back. We used to have so much together. Remember California? Santa Cruz?"

"It was another lifetime. A million years ago. Perhaps if your cruelty hadn't been so consistent throughout the years, there might have been a chance. But it went too far – much too far – far beyond too far. I don't love you. I could never love you again."

"If you would only let me make love to you one more time, I could bring back the magic."

"Max!" Alexis accused. "You said you wouldn't even ask. I knew you couldn't keep your promise."

"But I love you, and you look so beautiful tonight. I know I promised, but look at those precious children sleeping there. They are the products of our love. You mean you wouldn't try it just once more? Not for my sake, but theirs? Did you ever consider that making love with me one last time might re-kindle our feelings for each other? What if this turned out to be the final opportunity for reconciliation as a family, and you passed it by?"

Damn, he was good. Alexis couldn't dispute the logic, no matter how loathsome the thought. For the children, she repeated over and over. Against every grain, fighting every instinct of heart, mind, and body, she lay on the bed, prepared to submit to his intimacies one last time.

Once an enjoyable lover, Max's caresses now felt awkward and offensive. His lips brushed hers lightly, but she made no move to return the kiss. His repulsive hot breath on her neck chilled her body with goose flesh as he moved his face steadily downward. He licked her breast and he seized her nipple sensuously, moaning softly with animal lust. Alexis continued to lay rigid under his touch, subjecting herself to the vile mating ritual. At last, with quiet determination, Max began stroking the skin of her inner thigh in a futile attempt to excite her, but found no warm wet welcome. Nevertheless, he lowered himself between her legs and began to thrust into her unforgiving body...

Alexis awoke with a scream that died in the silence of the night as she came to full consciousness. The ivory moonlight streamed in from the window and she saw the sleeping form of her small daughter in bed beside her. They were still in the beach hotel room in Playa del Carmen.

"What is it?" mumbled Max. He was in the other bed on the far side of the room next to where Jordan slept.

"Nothing. A bad dream," said Alexis.

The doubting was over, forever.

Max dropped her off at the municipal airstrip on the outskirts of Belize City so she could catch her flight back to San Pedro. She thanked Max for the trip, kissed the children, and waved goodbye. As soon as they left, she postponed her flight and took a taxi back into Belize City.

Alexis went straight to the office of Geoffrey Goodman, the same attorney she and Max had once used for their property transactions. Paying for the initial consultation, the lawyer advised her, that according to English law, there were only three valid grounds for divorce: adultery, abuse, and desertion. Since Max was guilty of two out of three, Alexis was fairly confident about her chances in court.

"Thank you for your advice, Geoff. Please go ahead and prepare the papers. I'll send you a deposit from San Pedro as a retainer."

* * * *

"Tom!" Alexis called, from across the bar at the Barrier Reef Hotel. "Tom McDowell. Is that you?"

The young man's face split into a wide grin of recognition, as she rounded the corner and sat on the stool beside him. Tom was a well-known American bicyclist who competed every year in the Belize Bicycle Race on the day before Easter, racing from Belize City to San Ignacio and back.

"What are you doing out here on the island?" he said, giving her a friendly kiss on the cheek. "Where's Max?"

Her expression changed.

"Not a good subject. I guess you haven't heard yet. Max and I have been separated for almost a year now. It's over. I don't know what's going to happen with my kids. Do you mind if we don't dwell on it?"

"No problem," said Tom, kindly. "I just got in this afternoon. How about letting me buy you a drink?"

"Thanks. A White Russian, please. So how's it going? Win any lately? I missed seeing you in the last Holy Saturday race. Do you still compete here in Belize, or are you only doing U.S. races these days?"

"Oh, I'm still hooked on Belize. I've competed in cross-country for six years in a row. But lately there has been talk of making the race exclusively for Belizean nationals. Closing the race to *gringos* would be the only thing that would prevent my entering. But this time I'm here for some serious scuba diving."

"Diving's awesome," said Alexis. "I've been living in an apartment here since late last summer, and I've been diving for my dinner, pretty much, ever since. I took my safety course a few months ago, and got my PADI certification. So who do you dive with when you're here? Jerry's guys from the Paradise?"

"Sometimes, but mostly I go with Jorge and Luis Fordham from the Tackle Box. They're old friends from years back, and they give me the best price. But the last time I went diving here, I went with Sean from Mañana Beach Resort."

"I met him a few weeks ago. Great diver." Alexis remembered the attractive well-built blond. It was said that when Sean shaved close and wore his hair short, times were bad. But when he looked like a pirate, letting his hair and mustache grow long, he was laughing all the way to the bank.

"Yeah, he's a good guy," Tom agreed. "He's a good shot underwater. Before spear guns were outlawed on the reef, he was deadly accurate with a triple-bander. All we can use now is a stupid Hawaiian sling. Hey, we're going out tomorrow morning at nine. Would you like to join us? If you've got your own rubber gear, I'll buy your air for you. The boat's already paid for."

"Really? I'd love to," Alexis replied, happy at the prospect. "I have a regulator, backpack, and BC vest. It's all used gear, cast-offs really, but it's safe and well-tested. The tank would be all I'd need."

"It's a date," said Tom. "Listen, I've got to run right now to meet some people. I'll see you tomorrow at the Tackle Box pier at nine sharp. Okay?"

"You bet. Thanks for the drink. I'll be there."

After a small breakfast, Alexis made a thorough check of her gear before heading to the pier. Once before, she had been on a dive, completely ready and prepared to fall over the side, only to find a malfunction in her regulator which forced her to stay in the boat and sit it out. She put on her bathing suit and looked at her body, pleased with the improvement in her physique. The extensive swimming had toned and firmed her legs and developed the muscles in her arms and back. She had more overall strength than ever before, and in spite of emotional distress, Alexis was beginning to look better than she had in years.

Scuba diving was a sport that Alexis had wanted to learn since childhood because it was as close to flying as any human being could achieve. What other medium on earth provided the ability to propel oneself with total freedom through a world of neutral buoyancy? Her snorkeling experiences in Key West had been exciting, but they had only whetted her appetite. Diving was the real thing. Never content to observe from the surface, Alexis wanted to go deep, to swim with the sea creatures, and become one with them. Now, living on Ambergris Caye, diving had become her new passion.

The Tackle Box was the most unique drinking establishment on the island. At the end of the pier beyond the Fordham's Dive Shop, it perched above the water on pilings buried deep in the sand. Inside the thatched hut, the bar had been crafted from the deck of an old mahogany boat, the rich dark grain polished to a high luster. The bottom of the craft had been cut out, and the bartender stood within its perimeter. Drinks were served on the boat's wide gunwales, bow, and transom. However, the Tackle Box was most famous for its fish *kraal*, a circular wall that acted as a giant saltwater aquarium, featuring dozens of species, such as amberjack, leopard rays, barracuda, parrot fish, green turtles, and sharks.

Tom was on the pier with the Fordham boys by the time Alexis got there at nine o'clock. The gear was already loaded except for one last tank still connected to the compressor. She glanced at the gauge and saw that it had almost reached the optimum: twenty seven hundred pounds of pressure.

"Hi Alexis. It's going to be a flawless day," said Tom, excitedly. "Perfect diving weather."

"And the water has been especially clear lately," she added, "with infinite visibility as deep as ninety feet."

Soon they were underway and, turning hard-to-port into the channel, the skipper slowed the boat at the outside corner of the barrier reef, and then sped north for several miles. Alexis thrilled to the feel of the boat skimming the surface, and the sound of the hull smacking hard on the waves. Jorge Fordham was an excellent skipper and guide. His brother, Luis, was a Master Dive Instructor for tours that came to Ambergris during the winter months. Together, the four divers had finalized their plan, agreeing to do both a morning and afternoon dive. Because of the risk of nitrogen buildup, they would do the deeper dive first. At ninety-five feet, bottom time was restricted to only twenty-five minutes, but at that depth, they also had a good chance of seeing the giants of the marine world – goliath grouper, moray eels, or sleeping nurse sharks. Because the tidal surge was strong, Jorge decided not to anchor during the dive. Instead, he would cruise the surface in the same direction as the current, following the bubbles as the divers swam the outer edge of the reef, and he would troll for fish as he motored.

Tom liked to dive with minimal equipment whenever possible, whereas, even in tropical waters, Alexis preferred protection against hypothermia and the sting of sharp coral. After dunking her neoprene suit, booties, and fins into the water to make them slippery, she pulled them on, and secured the weight belt around her waist. Checking her regulator, she strapped the sheathed diving knife on her calf, the depth gauge to her wrist, and put on her diving gloves. Then Tom helped load the heavy tank on her back.

When Tom and Luis were similarly outfitted, all three divers opened their air lines and checked the pressure gauges. Next, they each smeared a little saliva inside their masks and rinsed it out with sea water, a preventive measure to reduce fogging. While they balanced on the gunwales, Jorge made sure the divers were clear. Then each dumped over backwards, falling tank-first into the ocean. For people who have never experienced scuba diving, the image of a tropical reef is difficult to envision. Contrary to the mental picture of a thin curtain of coral standing vertically in the water, the barrier reef was a gargantuan hulking structure, hundreds of yards wide and over a hundred feet tall. Containing billions upon billions of tons of coral, it was the great sea mother, born in the dawn of prehistory. Unlike the whitened and broken skeletons of lifeless coral littering the ocean floor off the Florida Keys, this grand reef was alive with vibrant colors and configurations of every description, an entity supporting astounding diversity, a grand organism teeming with life.

As the bubbles foamed around her, Alexis entered the world of aquatic flight. She saw Tom and Luis looking for eye contact, and confirmed her readiness with the OK signal. The divers made a steady descent to the depth of almost four atmospheres, and the silent watery underworld unveiled itself, as strange and far-removed from the surface as a distant planet. Even at that great depth, the azure water was amazingly clear. From the base of the reef, Alexis could see the coral bulwark extending south as far as her eyes could focus. Below her, the base of the reef connected with a broad sandy shelf. With a sparse smattering of dusky aquatic plants, it extended for perhaps thirty or forty yards before reaching the drop-off where the shelf slipped into the navy-black darkness of the abyss.

The men had left their Hawaiian slings on the boat, as they would be of no value against sizeable game fish. The second dive would be in shallower waters where smaller fish were plentiful, and the spears would be far more useful. Luckily, Alexis had still brought her diving bag, and now she was glad to see a sandy ravine ahead with dozens of large conchs on the ocean floor. Signaling to the others, she pointed and swam downward, and proceeded to stuff six or seven of the mollusks into her net. Closing the wire mouth and clipping it securely, Alexis inflated the bag's bladder with a small amount of compressed air and released it. The bag rose slowly to the surface where Jorge could retrieve it with a gaff.

Rejoining the others, the divers continued swimming beside the barrier reef, and Alexis was again overcome by the mysterious beauty in this world of perpetual motion. Purple sea fans swayed gracefully while schools of sergeant fish, wrasses, spadefish, and hog snapper swam close by. Four spotted leopard rays emerged from beyond a distant coral ridge, and in perfect formation, their undulating wings rippled through the water with fluid elegance. A large silvery barracuda appeared from nowhere. Motionless, he stared at them, the fearsome teeth and elongated jaw giving him an evil appearance. Alexis turned her head, and in the blink of an eye, the barracuda disappeared. A dark oval shadow caught her attention, and she looked up in time to see a huge loggerhead turtle pass just overhead. Alexis and the others watched excitedly as the reptile wheeled, using his front flippers to steer and his stubby tail as a rudder. Oblivious to the divers, the turtle continued to patrol the area in a circular motion. She had heard plenty of diver's stories involving petting sharks, feeding moray eels, or catching rides on porpoises or turtles, but never imagined it could actually be done. Swimming in hard pursuit, Luis reached the slow-moving turtle first, but he was unable to get a firm grip, and the sharp barnacles on the shell forced him to let go after a few seconds. Tom intercepted the turtle next and his hand grabbed its rear foot. Taking care to avoid the long slashing claws, he was towed in the opposite direction.

Disappointedly, Alexis could not hope to catch up until the loggerhead surprised everyone by turning sharply. Tom was shaken off. Then, against all odds, the creature made a beeline towards Alexis, angling upwards at the last moment and turning his back on her. Grateful for her heavy-duty power fins and gloves, she seized the opportunity and kicked forcefully, latching on to the upper lip of the shell with both hands. Immediately, the turtle turned its head and gave her a baleful look. Alexis nearly let go as she saw the curved beak snap in irritation, but held on doggedly. She stole a quick glance at the depth gauge on her wrist, keeping in mind that if the turtle went too deep, she would have to let go, or risk embolism. But somehow, the loggerhead stayed on a nearly level plane and, for a few seconds, Alexis experienced a once-in-a-lifetime thrill.

After regrouping in the boat, she doffed her equipment and wetsuit, and they cruised north, passing Mañana Beach Resort, and two more channels. Besides Alexis' conchs, Jorge's trolling efforts had yielded several yellowtail snapper. As skipper, he took a bearing, turned hard to port, and angled through another narrow break in the reef. The boat was about thirty feet offshore when he cut the engine. Luis jumped out and grabbed the bowline and the others followed suit. Together, they beached the small craft, taking care to haul the boat well above the high-tide mark.

A dilapidated thatched hut stood near the tree line, partially protected by the shelter of the palms. Inside was an elevated hearth. Using coconut husks as briquettes, Jorge built a fire while Tom and Luis cleaned the fish; playfully tossing the entrails up where the waiting frigate birds swooped down to catch them in mid-air. Before long, Jorge was wrapping clean white filets in foil, and adding his own special sauce, and laying them among the coals.

Alexis was preparing her own contribution. First, she found a smooth flat plank of driftwood and laid it at the edge of the water as a cutting board. She had brought a bowl, a bag of limes and other ingredients, a small hatchet, a fishing knife, and two of her conchs from the boat. After carefully selecting the exact spot between the third and fourth spiral on the conch shell directly opposite the opening, she chipped a hole with the hatchet and slipped the knife under the connecting membrane that held the conch securely inside. Effortlessly, the animal slid out on to the wooden board. After repeating the process with a second conch, she cleaned away the inedible portions and pounded the sea snail with the back of the hatchet to tenderize it, then chopped the meat into tiny pieces. Taking out a dozen fresh limes, she saturated the conch with juice, adding chopped onion, tomato, *habañero*, salt, black pepper, and cilantro. The acidic limes would soon cook the seafood and transform it into *ceviche de caracol*, a mouth-watering delight she had first tasted with Bishara on Playa Chaac Mool in Cancun. It was a delicacy that was, without a doubt, her favorite food on earth. Served in a communal bowl with corn tortilla chips, along with the baked fish, the feast was suitable for Neptune himself.

After lunch and a brief siesta, they checked the diving charts and concluded that residual nitrogen would not be a factor; the second dive would be shallow. Luis offered to trade positions with his brother to allow him a chance to dive. But this time, instead of motoring behind the divers, they would anchor in the channel itself, taking care to secure the both boat fore and aft.

The weather was still flawless as Luis steered the outboard towards the cut in the reef. The tide had come in, and the water had a surreal crystalline clarity, heaving and swelling under the deck like rolling liquid glass. As they cruised back south, Alexis saw the rounded heads of brain coral, and huge racks of golden staghorn below the surface. They opened into another channel, and on either side of the narrow throat, there were spires of bright red coral that thrust above the breakers, glinting sharply in the sunlight. Luis cut back the engine, threw out the fore and aft anchors, and waited until the boat stabilized. Conscientiously, the divers went through the usual drill, checking and rechecking their equipment. Then, outfitted with fresh tanks and Hawaiian slings, they adjusted their masks and plunged over the side.

When the bubbles cleared from Alexis' vision, the water thrashed in a frenzy of activity. When the turbulence subsided, she saw a school of baby sharks and became unnerved as a half dozen of them headed straight towards her. But before she could react, they changed direction, and she could see the sucker-like mouths on their undersides. She felt silly; they were just little cobia. But Tom had been amused, and even with his mask on and the regulator in his mouth, Alexis could see his eyes were laughing.

The water in the channel was vastly different from the cerulean depths outside the reef. Here, the light was brilliant, illuminating the white sandy bottom, refracting in crisscross patterns of palest turquoise. In these relative shallows, schools of fish, grunts, and yellowtails swam in the tens of thousands. Tiny tropical fish, like shy flamboyant jewels no more than an inch long, hid in the small crevices between the coral heads, while others secreted themselves among the sea grass, or nestled smugly between the vicious barbs of sea urchins. Enchanted with these tiny treasures, she found herself peering over the tops of the coral heads, inverting her body vertically to seek out the dazzling gems in flaming vermilion, deep teal, or emerald.

Suddenly, she heard a chinking sound, the tapping on an air tank, and turned to respond to the signal. Tom was pointing towards Jorge who had speared a sizable sea bass with his sling. It had been a clean shot between the eyes, and the fish had died instantly. Jorge slid the fish off the spear and put it in the diving bag hanging from his belt on a long tether. Alexis gave an OK of approval and nodded vigorously. Then she turned back to pursue another tiny fish, this one in bright fuchsia with a silvery stripe down its side.

Jorge was now far off on Alexis' left, fairly close to the boat where his brother waited patiently on the surface. Tom was alone, far off to the right, almost at the outside of the channel. It appeared that he too had just speared a fish, but his shot had not been clean. Even from a distance, Alexis could see that the fish was still flailing and bleeding. Tom carried the fish midway down the haft of the spear between his two outstretched hands where it continued to flop around as blood trickled from its flank. As he began to swim toward Jorge and the boat, heading across the field of Alexis' vision, she could see him looking purposefully from side to side. It wasn't the best situation, and she knew he was watching for sharks. His head swung back and forth with every few kicks, looking first over his right shoulder and then over his left. He should get that fish off the Hawaiian sling, Alexis thought. Stab in the forehead and kill it.

Suddenly Alexis' eyes went wide and she screamed into her regulator, sending a long stream of bubbles to the surface. Unknown to Tom, an immense gray leviathan was only a heartbeat away, approaching him diagonally from the far side of the channel. As the young man swung his head again from his left shoulder to his right, he found himself face to face with a tiger shark; its great serrated teeth already clamped over Tom's right forearm. She screamed again but there was nothing she could do except watch in horror. She took out her diving knife and banged it hard on her tank to draw Jorge's attention. He turned at the sound and saw the shark attacking, but both divers were powerless to make any move to defend Tom. The evil predator shook him back and forth as if he were a rag doll, and Alexis watched helplessly as the sea around him clouded with scarlet. Heroically, Tom swung at the shark with a fierce left hook, punching him in the nose, the sandpapery leather tearing the skin of his knuckles. The shark seemed temporarily stunned and let go. Tom back-pedaled on to the reef behind him and found footing on some brain coral near the surface. The tiger shark circled and lingered, plotting the best route for his comeback. Huge gouts of blood came from the wound on Tom's arm and it was only a matter of seconds before more sharks would come in for the kill. In a true feeding frenzy, Alexis knew that both she and Jorge would also be in imminent danger. From his vantage point topside, Luis had seen the billowing red and Tom's hasty retreat, and had reacted by pulling up the first anchor. Jorge pushed the limits of a safe ascent and broke the surface quickly. Swimming to the boat and climbing in, he helped Luis pull up the second anchor, and then seize the ripcord on the motor. The outboard roared to life.

Extensive studies on shark behavior have led to only one conclusion: they are among the most unpredictable creatures on Earth. But, for some reason, at the sound of the engine, the predator decided that retreat might be the best course of action. One moment the man-eater still circled the area, intent on his would-be meal. The next moment he had vanished, and miraculously, no other sharks appeared.

Alexis used the quick-release to ditch her weight belt and tank. Time was critical, the equipment insignificant. She made a long continual exhale, trying to stay below her bubbles. But like Jorge, her ascent was still too fast. Now, as she swam on the surface towards Tom, she could hear his screams for the first time. Kicking with powerful strokes, she reached him moments before the boat arrived. Climbing on the coral head beside him, she grabbed his butchered arm and applied firm pressure to the brachial artery. When pressure wasn't enough, she dropped any pretense of modesty, took off her bikini top, and used it as a tourniquet.

Still holding the pressure point, they somehow got him into the boat. Luis tossed his bandanna over to replace the bikini top, and it was only then that Alexis got her first real look at the appalling wound. The enormous curved bite had shredded and torn away the entire musculature of the outer forearm, leaving the cracked bones of the radius and ulna exposed. Strips of fleshy skin, sinew, and muscle still hung in tatters from the ruined limb, and the underside was cruelly lacerated with an arc of jagged triangular incisions. Tom's screams subsided into moans as he visibly weakened. His skin was pale and waxy. She felt for the pulse on other wrist but couldn't find the beat. Frightened for his life, she pressed her fingers on the carotid artery in his neck and then probed his groin with the other hand, searching for the femoral pulse. The beat was palpable, but rapid and weak, his breathing shallow and irregular.

"We have to keep him warm," Alexis cried out. "He's going into shock. What do we have on board that's dry?" The two Fordham boys were looking almost as pale as Tom, in spite of their deeply tanned skins. They were both good divers and boat men, but in a serious medical emergency such as this, Alexis knew it was up to her.

"Luis, check under the bow and pull out all the towels. Lay the damp ones flat on the deck and make a pad so we can lay him down. Then help me get my wetsuit under and around him. We can pile any dry towels we have on top."

"Where are we heading, Miss Alexis?" said Jorge, allowing her to take charge. "All the way back to the village?"

"No way," she asserted. "He'll never make it. Turn into the next channel and head into Mañana Beach Resort. We'll get Sean to radio the British Army and tell them to get a chopper out here, *pronto*. We've got to get Tom some medical attention immediately."

The towels and small wetsuit did little to hold in the heat and Tom shivered uncontrollably. In desperation, she finally lay down on top of him, trying to transmit as much of her own body heat as possible.

"Talk to me, Tom," she cried. His lips moved as he tried to speak but no words came out. He was barely conscious and still losing blood. Shaking with fear, she continued to cover his body with her own and her hands gripped his shoulders as she sobbed. "Please don't die. Hang on, Tom. You can make it. Oh, God. Please don't let him die."

Alexis sat on the end of the Sean's pier, leaning forward, continuing to hold her head in her hands. She could still hear the faint echoes of the chopper as it sped towards Airport Camp with the wounded diver safely in its hold. Sean came up behind her and sat down wordlessly and put his arm around Alexis' shoulders.

"Is he going to live?" she asked. Her eyes were red and she wiped her nose awkwardly with the back of her hand.

"They've got him hooked up to a bottle of Lactated Ringer's, massive antibiotics, and the bleeding is under control. The medic told me they've got several pints of fresh blood waiting for him at the army base, and a Lear jet ready to take him to Miami. He'll be in a U.S. hospital within an hour. I think he'll make it. You did a good job, Alexis. You acted like a first rate medic. How did you know what to do?"

"I don't know. I took basic First Aid when I was a teenager. The rest was just instinct. Oh Sean! There was so much blood. I've never been so terrified in my life. I'm a wreck. This is a hell of a way to get to know you better."

"Well, you may have saved Tom's life. That's a pretty shaky experience. How about a drink at the bar? You look like you could use something to calm you down."

"Where are the boys?" said Alexis suddenly, looking up. "I don't see their boat."

"They needed to get back to the village, so I told them to go ahead without you. I rinsed your diving gear in fresh water; it's already loaded on my skiff. There's a full moon tonight. If we stay inside the reef, there'll be enough light to take you back later whenever you're ready."

She looked at him gratefully. "Thanks, Sean. You're a prince."

They walked to the main building and climbed the stairs to the wide veranda that edged the second story bar. Most of the employees who worked at Mañana Beach had returned to the village for the slow season, so the resort was pleasantly deserted. Alexis was glad. She was feeling positively fragile.

The sun was sinking slowly in the west behind the island. It glimmered softly on the sea to the east in darkening shades of royal blue and navy. It was hard to believe that this was the same tranquil ocean that had played host to the life and death drama she had just witnessed. Alexis watched as Sean poured her a drink and handed it to her. They sat for a while, sipping their drinks, and Alexis began to relax.

"It's all the same to the ocean, isn't it? Life. Death. The ocean doesn't care," Sean said, quietly. "All part of the circle of life."

"How did you know what I was thinking?" she asked.

"It's written on your face. I understand what you went through today," said Sean, gently. "When I was in Vietnam, I saw so much death, so much blood, and so much senseless pain. I saw my friend trying to stuff his own intestines back inside his belly. I watched others die right beside me. I saw them get their heads blown off, or shrapnel rip through them. Yet every day when the fighting was over, the moon still rose in the night sky. The next day, the sun still fulfilled its role in shining brightly over the jungle. The grass still grew, and flowers bloomed, in the same soil nourished by the blood of friend and foe alike. Nature doesn't care. Life, death, it's all the same to her. It's all part of the plan, her creative and destructive ambivalence."

"That's beautiful. I had no idea you were a philosopher."

"I just lived through it, that's all. And what survivor doesn't philosophize? Back then, I was just a naive seventeen-year-old. A stupid kid in a stupid war on the other side of the world. War makes you grow up fast. Suffering does too."

"Yes," Alexis reflected, thinking of her own experience. "I didn't realize we shared so much common ground."

He sipped his drink pensively. "I also know about Max."

"I'm sure you do." Her mouth twisted. "The whole village knows. And what they don't know, they make up. But they don't know the truth."

"No, but I do. You're not hard-hearted, and you're not devious," Sean said simply. "Therefore, I suspect that innocence is on your side."

"You're amazing me again."

"If you don't mind my asking, was Tom your lover??"

"Good heavens, no," she laughed. "We're just friends. I don't really even know him that well. I met him years ago through the former Vice Consul at the American Embassy and used to watch him in the bicycle races. Of course, he's gorgeous – I'm not blind. He could put his boots under my bed any time. How about you?"

Sean grinned. "Sure, I'd like to put my boots under your bed, too." He laughed. "Sorry. I couldn't resist. No, I don't know Tom that well either. We went diving a couple of times together. And because I'm a body builder, I admire his dedication to physical fitness. He runs, he bicycles. He's in great shape. Speaking of which, his excellent physical condition will help to get him through this."

"They won't amputate his arm, will they?" she asked, suddenly horrified at the thought.

"Don't torture yourself. You did what you could. It's out of your hands."

"Yeah, I guess." Alexis took another sip. "Do you ever worry about sharks when you dive?"

"No. For me, it's just like the war. Somehow, I knew that I would come out of Vietnam unscathed, even when my friends were getting hit. You see, I've always known how I'm going to die – some irate husband is going to shoot me in the back as I'm escaping out the window."

"You're something else," she said, smiling indulgently. "You're married, aren't you?"

"Well, sort of. Not officially. I guess you'd have to say that Karen's my common-law wife. But it's an off-and-on relationship, which is why she's not here right now. Most of the time, she'd rather be somewhere else. It used to be a great relationship, but we've been together a long time. Now she loves me with all the possessiveness of a wife, but she doesn't enjoy being a woman to me anymore. She worries about me having affairs and is jealous as hell of any woman I talk to. Yet she won't allow me to make love to her anymore."

"So, all the negatives and none of the positives: a jaded marriage, like everyone else's. Why is it that all relationships seem to go that way in the end?"

"I don't know," said Sean. "But I guess that's the reason I could never be true to just one woman. Like the song says, it would be like drinking only one kind of wine. I love the whirlwind passion and the madness."

"Being happily and crazily in love? I can barely remember what that's like. It's been a long time since I felt that way. Of course, I fantasize but, like most women, my fantasies are more romantic than sexual. Men's fantasies are usually hard-core porn."

"Not always. Not all men," he cautioned. "Sure, sex is part of it. But some men also love the wild romance. I know I do."

Sean and Alexis' conversation continued easily as they spoke. They talked of feelings, the past, the future, the war, of time, and misspent youth. They spoke about marriages, politics, love, children, and growing up. As the hours passed, the sun dipped behind the island's western tree line and gave way to the tropical night. Crickets sang, and they could hear fish jumping. At last, a mystic beauty revealed itself as the yellow moon rose over the sea.

By nine-thirty, they realized it was time to get underway, and together, they walked to the end of the pier. For a moment Sean stood away from her, facing the full moon with his hands on his hips. She could hear him breathe a soft sigh. Then he turned and knelt to loosen the mooring.

"I want to thank you for tonight," said Alexis. "It's been so meaningful to talk like this. With all the things we've said, I feel like a burden has been lifted from me. We've become friends in a very short time."

"Destiny, maybe?" Sean replied. Alexis swallowed hard and watched Sean's long hair fall forward over his bare brown muscular shoulders. He was beautiful and sexy, this blond wild man with the drooping mustache. Suddenly, she didn't want to go back to her lonely little apartment in the village. She wanted to stay with Sean, to be swept off her feet in a flight of fancy. As though he had read her mind, he secured the rope again and stood tall again, looking down at her face.

"Alexis," he said, his words echoing her thoughts. "Stay the night with me. Let's ride the illusion of romance; let it take wing. Stay with me tonight and let's pretend we're madly in love."

Perhaps it had been the gruesome scene, the shark, the blood, and mortal fear that triggered her need for closeness and quickened her desire. Whether it was love or lust, Alexis needed to feel some semblance of passion, even if it wasn't real. Without another word, she gave herself to the moment, and fell into his embrace. Sean picked her up in his big arms, as if she were a child, and carried her across the threshold of a dream.

At first, every moment spent with Sean was nothing more than escape. She wasn't in love with him, but rather with the image he represented. Sean was rugged and energetic. He had a winning attitude, was positive and self-assured, yet unpretentious. She saw him as gallant cavalier, the poet warrior. Sean and Alexis spent their time walking along the shore, sunbathing naked on the open beach, and then pumping iron back at the resort until their bodies were hard and glistening. They went scuba diving every day, speared fish, gathered lobster and conch, and drank coconut water. At first, it was like a game, being in love with love, living a fantasy for fantasy's sake. But through the weeks, a deeper feeling began, changing to something of substance. They both fought against it because the relationship could not possibly endure. It was inevitable that their time together would soon come to a close. Even if Sean had been willing to share her life, Alexis had vowed that she would never again live with a man who couldn't be true to her alone. Sean had loved many women, all women, and would always love them. He had admitted that he would never change. Karen was expecting to meet with him in Houston soon, and he would have to leave for the States. Then Karen would return to Belize with him. The escape from the real world was nearly over. Soon Alexis would have to go back to her lonely life and face the next turning point.

One morning, as suddenly as it began, it was over. Carrying a flight bag for his trip to the States, Sean and Alexis cruised back to the village of San Pedro in the skiff. They spoke little. Sean docked at Fordham's Pier and helped Alexis carry her things to her apartment.

"I guess this is it," she said. "I always knew there was no future, but I don't regret the time. I'll always treasure the memory. I'm grateful for the sharing. I think I had almost lost the ability to be close to another human being again, getting so hardened and cynical. You broke through that somehow. Because of you, I might actually be able to love someone again, someday."

"We don't have to say goodbye right this minute. I need to do a couple things for about an hour before the Cherokee takes off for International Airport. I'll stop back when I'm on my way to the strip."

"Okay," she said.

It was a compassionate lie, and she knew it. He wouldn't be back. They embraced and kissed, and she watched Sean walk out of her life.

* * * *

With Sean gone and Max still refusing to let her see the children, Alexis felt the darkness begin to creep over her again. But she never knew how bad things could get until she called Geoff Goodman in Belize City to inquire about the status of the divorce proceedings. She picked up the receiver and dialed the number. His response was confusing.

"I beg your pardon, Mrs. Lord," said Geoff, "but it was my understanding that the nature of things had changed dramatically since last we spoke."

"I don't understand." Alexis was puzzled. "Didn't you receive the money order?"

"No, I did not," he replied. "But moreover, I have come to understand that you are conceding your rights in this divorce issue, and allowing Mr. Lord to sue you on grounds of desertion. You see, shortly after our last conversation, your husband contacted me. He has since presented me with a document – grounds for a no-contest divorce. It is a statement, signed by you, in which you admit to deserting the domestic household. By law, that is all that is needed to validate proceedings under his claim."

Immediately, Alexis could feel fear beginning to escalate. "But I don't understand. I sent you a retainer fee of three hundred dollars a few weeks ago along with instructions to serve the papers on Max immediately on the grounds of adultery and abuse."

Geoff cleared his throat uncomfortably. "I'm sorry. But I never received your retainer. In the meantime, Mr. Lord has hired me to represent him. Therefore, if it is still your intention to pursue the case, I cannot also represent you. A conflict of interest, you understand."

"No, I absolutely do not understand." Gripping the phone tightly and fighting for control, she continued. "I mailed you a valid postal money order. And how could Max try to sue me? He's got no grounds."

"Apparently he does. As I said, Mr. Lord is suing you for desertion."

"Desertion?" Alexis exclaimed. "I never deserted! I distanced myself from the man who was abusing me. It was a period of separation, that's all, enough time to be sure that I could no longer be married to him."

"I'm sorry, Mrs. Lord," Geoff replied. "But what you are saying does not fit with the documentation your husband gave me."

"I don't know what you're talking about! And stop calling me Mrs. Lord! My name is Alexis, and I've never seen such a document, let alone signed one. Whatever you've got in your hands is a fake. Even if it was authentic, what possible motive could I have to authorize such nonsense?"

"It's not my place to–" he began.

"God damn it, Geoff! Stop being an attorney for a minute and be a human being. Why would I sign such a thing?"

He paused briefly. "Actually, I must admit, it did seem a bit strange at the time. Especially since you had been so adamant about your valid grounds for the suit. So I asked him that same question. He told me you had reconsidered, that you'd agreed not to contest, for reasons of your own. He said you needed a quick divorce to feel safe. Something about the `rule of thumb.'"

"That bastard. That fucking bastard," Alexis sobbed. "He knew that was on my mind and he used it as a plausible excuse. It's a lie."

"I don't know what to tell you." It was hard to know if Geoff's sympathy was real, or merely part of his professional demeanor.

"But on the grounds of desertion, isn't there a time period that has to pass first?"

"Yes, the deserter has to have been gone for three years."

"Three years? Even you know I was around for all but the last year or so. According to that time frame, it means I would have left...," Alexis sniffed and wiped her nose, making a quick calculation, "...that I would have left when Jessica was only three months old. Sure, we were in San Pedro for a few months. And there was the separation period when I was in Mexico. But that was less than six months."

"Mr. Lord's explanation was that you yourself had contrived the idea of fudging on the time frame because you needed the divorce to feel safe."

"It's a lie! It's total bullshit!" she cried. "I never signed anything of the sort. There are dozens of witnesses that could back up the fact that I didn't leave three years ago."

"Would your witnesses testify?"

Alexis couldn't respond. She knew some people in Cayo would succumb to Max's bribes and the rest wouldn't want to get involved. When she considered the situation, there probably wasn't one Belizean that would be willing to jeopardize themselves by coming forward on her behalf. If their *gringo* friends were forced to choose sides, it was unlikely any of them would risk crossing Max – after all, they still had to live there. No one could come out unscathed. Max was the one with the money, the influence, and the legal and political connections. Who would side with the loser? The victim? The so-called deserter? Even if someone did side with her, it would be their word against Max's.

"What else did Max say?" asked Alexis. "What are his terms?"

"There are no terms," said Geoff. "He is offering no settlement, and according to the document, you are in full consensus."

"No. Oh, my God, no. This just can't be! What should I do?"

"I'm sorry, Mrs. Lord – I mean, Alexis. It's really not my place to advise you. The point is that I can no longer represent you. I suggest you seek good legal counsel immediately."

"I did seek legal counsel," Alexis cried. "I came to you. I sent three hundred dollars. That was my only nest egg. Where is my money? I have no more money to initiate a counter-suit. How can I offer to pay an attorney out of a settlement that I may not receive?"

"I realize this must be a terrible shock," he sympathized. "There's nothing more I can tell you."

"And the children? What will happen to my children?"

"As it stands right now, the case will be considered 'no contest.' The signed document indicates you deserted the family home. In doing so, you effectively conceded all custodial rights regarding the children. Mr. Lord will therefore gain full custody of both children unless you can prove to the courts, beyond a shadow of a doubt, that the document is false, and can provide witnesses to attest to the same."

Alexis was trembling and she could not speak. It was a terrifying scenario of loss and hopelessness.

"And visitation?" she choked back the tears.

"Mr. Lord is not mandated by the courts to cede visitation rights unless he wishes to do so out of his own generosity."

"This is a frame. He did this to me. He intercepted the money, falsified the document. You've got to believe me! For God's sake, I need help. I have no one to turn to. Max is holding all the cards, and I am the one who has been victimized. What will I do?"

"Again, Mrs. Lord, I extend my sympathy to your situation. I will send you a copy of the document, but I assure you the signature is identical to the one used on the land transaction I did for you in 1977. I advise that you get good legal counsel and do so quickly."

Desperate now, Alexis called her parents immediately, making arrangements to have money wired to retain another attorney for a counter-suit. She began to make phone inquiries to various lawyers and set up appointments. Flying into Belize City on one of the little island-hopper planes, she held conferences with each one, with identical results. The last lawyer on her list was Daryl Bannister. She turned the corner on Regent St., went through the wrought-iron gate, entered the foyer, spoke to the receptionist, and waited to be called. It was a typical interior for a building in the old colonial section of town, with dark polished wood, uncomfortable Victorian chairs, and the requisite photo of the British Royal Family. After waiting twenty minutes, he called her into his office, and introduced himself.

"My esteemed colleague, Mr. Goodman, tells me that your husband has provided a document stating that you left the matrimonial home some three years ago," said Daryl. "Do you have a copy of that document?"

"Yes. Right here." Alexis placed the paper on his desk and he picked it up. It was the photocopy from Geoff, a single typewritten page, signed and dated at the bottom.

"Is this your signature?" he asked.

"I never signed that thing."

"Yes, I understand. But is this your signature?" he insisted. "If I checked valid signatures, say at the Registry of Land or the Birth Registry when your daughter was born, would the signature look like this?"

Alexis sighed. "It is an excellent reproduction, but I did not sign it."

"I see. Let's put that aside for a moment and examine the other aspects then. So you wish to initiate a counter-suit against your husband based on physical abuse and adultery." Daryl began taking notes. "Let's start with the adultery charge. With whom did your husband commit adultery?"

"With our maid, Angelina," she replied. "I asked him and he told me."

"Mr. Lord admitted he was committing adultery with the maid?"

"Yes. I know it sounds strange, but he was proud of it. Max is from Zululand, South Africa. He liked the idea of having several wives, like the *Bantu*."

"He was proud of his affair with another woman? And did you approve of it?"

Alexis shook her head vigorously. "No, of course not."

"Was she a willing partner?"

"I don't think she was at first, but Max is a very convincing man. He made her believe that it was all right with me, and she complied."

"So how do you know for sure that he wasn't making up this affair?" Daryl asked. "Perhaps it wasn't real. A jealousy tactic maybe?"

"No, it was real. A few months later I caught them together."

"Ah, you caught them *en flagrante delicto*. Good, we can use that. Now, do you have any physical proof to enter into evidence for the court proceedings? Photographs? Other witnesses? Anything solid to document the allegations?"

She shook her head again. "No, nothing at all."

"Hmmm. Not good. Okay, let's put that thought on hold for a moment and explore the other possibility. Let's look at the question of abuse. You claim that you were a battered wife? How long did the abuse go on?"

"On and off throughout the last six or seven years, but especially during the last three."

"Did your husband beat you with his hands, or did he use some other means?"

"His hands mostly, open-hand slaps at first, but later on with closed fists. Once he beat me with a stick, and several times he slammed me up against walls or furniture." Alexis squirmed in her chair. The admissions were embarrassing.

"Were the blows of sufficient strength to make marks on you?"

"Oh yes. Many of the beatings were extremely violent. I suffered terrible bruises and, on several occasions, I bled from head wounds."

"So the beatings were severe enough to warrant medical attention?"

"Oh yes, definitely."

"Good. Now we're getting somewhere," Daryl smiled and clapped his hands together. "So you have the medical records from doctors and hospitals to corroborate the injuries?"

"No. I never went to a doctor or a hospital."

He frowned. "You never went? Why not?"

"You've got to understand, I was under dire threat not to expose what happened – not to anyone," she despaired. "I couldn't just go to the doctor or a hospital. Also, in most cases, I was up river in the jungle, and hurt too badly to drive anywhere."

"Hmmm. This is not going well," repeated Daryl, shaking his head. "So again, you have no documentation. How about witnesses? Did anyone ever see the bruises? Friends, relatives? Is there anyone who can back up your claims? Surely you must have shown the bruises or injuries to someone."

Alexis hung her head as she answered. "No, no one saw them. Max was always careful to beat me where it wouldn't show, at least until the end when he didn't care anymore. Besides, I was ashamed. He maintained the illusion that we were the perfect couple. I couldn't bear the thought of exposing his cruelties to anyone. They would think it was my fault; they would judge me guilty of causing the abuse in the first place. I kept praying that things would get better, that he would stop, that everything would be all right. It all sounds so foolish now. But you can't imagine what it was like. So much shame, so much guilt. He had me convinced that my own actions were to blame, that his punishments were justified."

"So you're quite sure that no one ever saw anything? Neither the beatings as they were happening, nor the physical evidence afterwards?

"The only one who really saw anything was Angelina," Alexis offered. "She saw plenty."

"Angelina? The same maid he was sleeping with?" Daryl threw up his hand in despair. "Mrs. Lord, you are not giving me anything I can use. We can't go to court and even have a hope of winning on a collection of unsubstantiated allegations. We need proof. Real proof. Right now, you have absolutely nothing to go on."

"But what happened is a reality," she insisted. "These things did occur. I've been victimized in the cruelest sense of the word. If I told you some of the other things he did to me..."

"Nevertheless," Daryl insisted. "You have not made one claim that can substantiate abuse or adultery. In the eyes of the court, you have absolutely no proof. Is there nothing else you can tell me, nothing you can offer?"

"I guess not. The truth is all I have, and it appears that the truth means nothing."

"I'm sorry. But I'm afraid I can't do anything for you," said Daryl, shaking his head. "If I agreed to take your case, you'd be wasting your money on something you can't possibly win. I am an attorney, but contrary to public opinion, I am not unprincipled. Under the circumstances, you have no case. Therefore, I cannot agree to represent you."

Alexis shook his hand.

"Thank you for your candor, Mr. Bannister. I won't take up any more of your valuable time."

The *mañana* factor had always been a plague to the *gringos* who had chosen Belize as their country of residence. It was a third-world country, a banana republic where nothing ever happened quickly. "Soon come," was the national expression, just as "right now" meant "later" or "in a little while." Actually, it could mean anything from tomorrow, to next week, to never. It was commonly called "the Belize factor." Yet, the one time when Alexis pleaded for the wheels of injustice to turn slowly, the court case was over before she knew it.

Max Lord divorced Alexis Lord in early 1984, and was awarded full custody of both children. No authoritative body ever deemed her to be unfit; there was no social service organization to determine the best interests of the children. Worse yet, Alexis was not even advised of the actual date of the case in Belize City, so she never even had the option to appear. She simply received a phone call one day from a clerk in some government office, advising her of the court's decision. Alexis had been cheated out of Jordan and Jessica, just as the children were cheated out of their mother. No concessions were made for visitation rights. Without her presence in the courtroom, the issue of visitation had never even been addressed. Nor did she receive a settlement of any kind. For Alexis there would be no money, no car, no home, not even a token for the investment and commitment she'd made in two children, two businesses, and a marriage of ten years. When it was all said and done, she was left destitute. Still there was more. Besides her own guilt and shame, the termination of Alexis' legal rights meant the termination of the rights of her loved ones. Through her, Liz and Frank had lost their grandchildren, just as the children had lost their grandparents. Jordan and Jessica were innocent victims, punished for her sins. For the rest of her life, Alexis would carry the burden of their suffering as well as her own.

With no one beside her, her darkest hour had arrived, and with it, a sadness too great to be born. Out of options and spiritual strength, Alexis berated herself for thinking that it would all work out somehow, for thinking that good could possibly win over evil. She started to believe that Max may have been right all along, that perhaps she was undeserving of family, earthly rewards, or even the barest amount of normalcy in her life. The dreary little apartment in San Pedro became her cave and her prison. Day after day, she sat on the bed and stared at the walls. Her senses cried out for fulfillment, love, and a future. She wanted something steadfast and solid, to have a life, to win back her children, to be loved by a man, to accomplish something worthwhile. She tried to listen to music or concentrate on reading cheap paperbacks, anything that would help pass the meaningless time, and prevent her from going insane. The world was convoluting rapidly once more, and she began to think of death. Wouldn't it be nice to go diving and just keep going deeper and deeper forever? What a peaceful, nonviolent way to die. Deeper and deeper, until the narcosis took hold. Deeper and deeper, until she just didn't know and didn't care. And then, nothing. Beautiful nothing.

The telephone rang at the little apartment, and Alexis jumped at the noise, startled.

"Hello, Alexis? This is Anita. I'm in Chicago. I know we haven't talked in a long time. I've been up here working on my degree in naprapathic healing, and don't expect to be back in Belize for quite some time. But I just heard that Max raked you over the coals, took your kids, and left you with virtually no options. I was worried about you. Are you OK?"

"No, I'm not," she said honestly.

"Well, your luck's about to change. I've got a rich doctor friend from here in Chicago who owns a beautiful ranch up in the Mountain Pine Ridge, and he needs somebody to mind the place. Are you interested in caretaking?

"That's so kind of you," Alexis choked. "But it's all too weird. You wouldn't want to get involved."

"Look, some people who care about you don't listen to vicious rumors. I want to help you and Ted does too. Don't say another word. He's going to come out to San Pedro to meet with you. If you hit it off, he'll take you up to his ranch to see the place. What have you got to lose?"

 **HORSES**

chapteR 16_____

When Ted Vaughn got off the plane in San Pedro, Alexis knew immediately that she was going to like him. He was in his early forties, tall and lanky, and walked with an easy stride. Beneath the curly mop of brown hair, Alexis saw a sparkle in the man's eyes, and his handshake was warm and friendly.

"It's so nice to meet you," said Alexis. "I can't thank you enough for this opportunity."

"Same here," said Ted. "Since my wife and I had our twins, we just can't seem to get down here often enough." He turned to pick up his bag from the tarmac, and together they began walking down the sandy street to Alexis' apartment.

"Anita tells me you're a doctor," said Alexis.

"Yes, I'm a pediatrician."

"Oh, a children's doctor."

"Hey, you're better than average. Most people think that makes me a foot surgeon." Ted laughed. "But I'm not practicing medicine right now. Our kids have arrived relatively late in life, and I decided to take a few years off to be a full-time father and husband, and part-time gentleman rancher."

As they drove west from Belize City the following day in the rented Land Rover, Alexis tried not to think about the fact that, when she got to Cayo District, she would be within fifteen miles of Jordan and Jessica. This was not the time for a spontaneous visit. It would be a mission to discover if she had a future on Ted's ranch. If things worked out, there would be plenty of time to arrange some unofficial visitation, provided Max's attitude softened. And even if it didn't, at least she would be living closer to the kids.

It was dark by the time they drove the eight miles up the Mountain Pine Ridge Road and turned into the mile-long driveway leading to the property. As Ted drove, Alexis dozed and tried to envision the house. She wasn't expecting anything beyond the usual thatched hut with stick walls, or maybe a metal roof, if she was lucky.

"Time to wake up," said Ted, nudging her gently. "This is the place."

Alexis raised her head sleepily, and looked beyond the shadows of the citrus orchard to the hill beyond. There, in the twinkling lights, the enormous six-sided hardwood and glass house, perched on the side of the hill, glittered like a fairy castle. It dawned on her then that her new potential residence would be a real home, with generated electricity and gravity-fed running water; here she could live in an atmosphere beyond rustic comfort, and near-elegance. It was beautiful beyond anything she'd imagined. Like something out of a story book.

In the morning, Alexis awoke in a vision of Eden. From where she lay in the spare bedroom, she could see the morning sunlight glinting on the cave-pocked white cliffs to the south, framed by the magnificent backdrop of the Maya

Mountains. Drawn by the spectacular vista, she draped a brightly colored sarong around her, and stepped out through the sliding glass doors onto the wide second-floor veranda that encircled the entire house. The surrounding jungle and tropical exotics sparkled in the morning dew, and she could feel the cool air blending with the rising warmth of the coming day. It was then that she saw the enormous *llora sangre* tree on the western flat below. She blinked twice; it couldn't be real. A monstrous bromeliad was suspended from a large upper branch, dangling on a coarse brown grapevine that looked to be as thick as Alexis' arm. Over one hundred feet separated the tree's rich crown of foliage from the magnificent air plant that swayed heavily in the breeze of early morning. It took her breath away. Just then, Ted stepped out of the master bedroom door to join her outside.

"Good morning. I hope you slept well." He smiled and stretched his arms overhead. "And if you're wondering why I didn't tell you about the tree before, it's because it's hard to describe, and even then, words still don't do it justice. I thought I'd let you see it."

"How did you ever manage to hang the bromeliad? It must weigh a half a ton."

"No human could have done that. When I first arrived, the plant was wedged in the fork, way up there," said Ted, pointing to the tree. "One afternoon, there was an incredibly vicious storm. Thunder shook the whole house; there was lightening all over the place. I was standing right here on the balcony when a tremendous bolt struck the tree, and I watched the bromeliad fall. But it never hit the ground. A long length of grapevine went with it, so the plant fell short by about ten feet. It's been hanging there, suspended like that, ever since."

Throughout the ten years he'd owned the place, Ted had turned the grounds around the house into a vision of landscaped beauty. He'd planted beds, and trellises, and flowering arbors of all types. There were cannas and ginger lilies, royal poincianas, continental palms, rubber banyans, lobster-claw lilies, and the corkscrew-like pandanus tree. He had also put in variegated aralias, fragrant dracaenas, pink and white oleanders, poor-man's orchid, sweet-scented frangipani, and bright bougainvilleas. But the *llora sangre* with its hanging bromeliad was the showcase.

Ted was proud of his farm, but because of its remote location, and the four big black German shepherds who stood constant guard, few people had ever seen it. Nibbling the fruit of the *akee* tree, he gave Alexis the tour of the chicken house, generator house, tool shed, and the beautiful blue artesian spring under the *llora sangre* tree, an *ojo de agua* that had given forth life and sustenance since the days of the Maya.

They walked the pastures, looked at the twenty-odd cattle and four horses, made friends with the dogs, and then hiked to the top of the hill on the north end of the property. From there, Alexis could see the abundance of pineapples, avocados, *maumee*, yucca, *sapote*, bananas, and the green expanse of citrus trees bordered by the watershed jungle. Hiking down the western face, Ted took her to a little thatched hut on the edge of the property and introduced her to Tsamuel, his live-in foreman.

Tsam Tzul was pure Maya with the classic features of his ancestors atop a small frame which he bore with dignity. A hard and loyal worker, Tsam had been with Ted from the beginning. As foreman, he was in charge of the pastures, citrus orchard, banana and pineapple plantation, and vegetable garden. He maintained the old Ford pickup, as well as the generator, jet pump, and the two-way radio communication towers. The one-hundred-fifty acre ranch took a lot of management and Tsam was an integral part of its success. Tsam would be there, on the property, should she need any assistance.

The entire scenario was perfect. Alexis would live in the house. Ted would cover her personal and ranch expenses, and give her a small stipend. Within two hours, they were sitting at the dining table, drawing up a contract.

Three days later, Alexis drove in tandem with Ted back to Belize International, he in the rented Land Rover, and she in the Ford pickup that lived on the ranch. Seeing him off with a handshake, followed by a grateful hug, she made a quick round-trip flight to San Pedro to gather her things, then drove back to the Mountain Pine Ridge and moved into Ted's house.

Although Alexis was alone, the days and nights passed quickly. Far from the eyes of the world, she lived in her own private jungle paradise. A time to heal once again, she found solace in solitude, and enjoyed the magic of sunlit days that gave way to nights spirited with flowers and moon dance.

After moving in, Alexis made only one attempt to visit Jordan and Jessica. She went to Max's home with the idea of proposing regular visits on a civilized weekly basis. They were divorced, so she knew she was physically safe. Nevertheless, the results had been disastrous. Alexis had been so frightened by Max's violent reaction that, once back on the ranch, she became reclusive and, for the next six months, she never left the farm. Tsam continued to be supportive; he kept the generator running, ran to town for provisions, and got whatever she needed. But Alexis was at her wit's end to find something to resolve the situation. She couldn't go on hiding, with the kids never seeing their mother, and Max holding all the cards. Alexis wrote to her mother for advice and received a letter a few weeks later.

Dearest Alexis,

When you requested that the children visit every weekend or so, Max still had to find a way to remain in control. He may eventually allow you some type of visitation, but you can be sure it won't be regular. If it ever happens, surely he will dictate when you can have them and for how long. He will keep you a victim. Only when it suits his purpose will he permit you to have the children. That way, you will be unable to pinpoint any fault on his part, and it will appear as though he's cooperating if the authorities get involved later on, which brings me to the next point.

You spoke about going back to court. As for taking the whole situation to an attorney, you will have to decide whether you really have anything to gain by doing so. I'm inclined to agree that time and patience may eventually change your situation to the point where Max may mellow, once he sees you are not a threat. And although Max would like to be rid of you, his options are limited. He can't go back to the States and Angelina can't go to South Africa. I'm no seer, but I think he will stay there and keep on trying to hold the upper hand between you and the children, just enough to keep you in line, using the kids to punish you.

Another point to consider is that Max is legally, in the eyes of the law, the sole custodian of Jordan and Jessica. Their future is in his hands. Unfortunately, as things are right now, he can do what he pleases and you don't have a legal leg to stand on. Therefore, if you want to have a say in what happens in the long term, then you must let the law determine it. It may be a visitation suit or a custody suit, either of which may create a difference in Max's behavior.

Only God knows the answers, certainly not Dad or I. But I will say that in your present situation, it would not be a good idea to have the children full time anyhow. You have a whole new set of responsibilities with the ranch, and you couldn't handle it right now. You have to have time to get rid of the ghosts, build new confidence, and create a new life. All of that takes time.

I don't know if any of this helps. By the time you get this letter, something may have happened and my advice will mean nothing. Things change when distances like ours have to be spanned. Regardless, always know that we love you and will continue to support your cause all the way. We are here if you need us.

I love you,
Mom

Little by little as the months passed, Max did start to allow Jordan and Jessica to visit the ranch for an occasional weekend. Eventually, he became comfortable with Alexis' proximity, and began to appreciate the convenience of a free baby-sitting arrangement. But just as Liz had predicted, Max manipulated the timing, often giving little or no advance warning. He also changed plans on a whim, thereby forcing her to forfeit her visit at the last minute. And of course, he refused to share the responsibility of picking up or delivering the kids. His attitude was that if Alexis wanted to see Jordan and Jessica, the burden of transportation was solely hers.

* * * *

The idea came to her slowly over a period of several days; first a vague thought, then a potentially brilliant concept, and eventually a solid business plan, wrested down to earth and grounded in confidence, opportunity, and common sense. She started with the facts. First, Alexis knew she needed to come up with a money-making strategy in order to make another attempt at legal action. Secondly, Ted's ranch was at the base of the National Forest Reserve, a protected area of government lands, rich with tropical flora and fauna. Thirdly, the ranch was not presently profitable; it produced limited fruits and veggies, and some beef cattle. How could all these factors be aligned to bear something profitable? The following Saturday she drove to Central Station to call Ted. It was the nearest phone.

"I suppose every *gringo* who ever came to Belize probably thought about doing horseback tours at some point or other," Alexis admitted. "And since Belize has a serious lack of infrastructure, there would be many challenges. But I think that between you, Tsam, and me, we might have everything that's necessary."

"OK, I'm listening," said Ted.

"First, we need someone who can ride, guide, host the guests, handle the business, create the advertising, and do the sales and marketing locally. That's me. Second, we need someone to mastermind the stateside liaison, coordinate the communications and marketing on that end, and finance the entire operation. That's you. Third, we've got Tsam Tzul. He knows this area. We can sell the cattle and use the money to buy more horses. Tsam knows where to get them and how to train them. He knows the bush, the plants, and will be critical helping design the trails.

We simply tell him the kinds of features we're looking for – waterfalls, caves, or unusual rock formations, and then hire some of his *compadres* to cut the trails. We've got the Ford pickup truck to haul the bags of feed from Spanish Lookout. And I know someone who's got access to cavalry saddles made by a leather worker in Costa Rica. Cavalry saddles would be ideal for mountain riding, as they have a high rise in front, high cantle in back, and stirrup covers. Best of all, we've got the one thing that no one else has – close proximity to the edge of the National Forest Reserve in the Maya Mountains. What more could we ask for?"

Ted considered her thoughts carefully. He would love to make money from the ranch, and Alexis just might be the one to pull it off. But there was still one major consideration.

"We're still talking about chopping trails through government property. That means permission from Belmopan, and what if they say no?"

Alexis had considered that obstacle, and now she proposed a bold, if not risky, solution.

"That's why we cut the trails first, then go to the government later and explain how inland tourism would benefit national revenue. After all, the trails will be only ten feet wide and twelve feet tall; we're not talking about chopping down huge tracts of land. What better way to utilize the forest and still preserve it? When the government officials hear our logic, I believe they'll say yes. But in this case, it's better to ask for forgiveness, rather than permission."

"Would you take responsibility for that part of the equation?" asked Ted gravely. "It would have to be your sale, not mine. It's a major gamble. Think you could handle it?"

"No sweat," Alexis said, confidently.

The reference to sweat had been prophetic, as the long arduous months ahead would require a great deal of it. Alexis decided that there should be a minimum of two full-day and two half-day trails to allow enough variety for clients who might ride several days in a row. Each trail must have several worthwhile features, and an ultimate destination. An activity needed to be associated with that destination as well, preferably swimming, and all riders would need to be fed. Ideally, the return trail should be via a different route to provide variation, and preferably, it should be less strenuous. Studying the topographical maps provided by the Ministry of Natural Resources, Alexis and Tsam spread them out on the dining room table, scrutinizing the lay of the land and logistics, trying to assess what areas would serve as suitable destinations.

"Okay," said Alexis, pointing to the map. "We're aiming towards this big waterfall over here. If we follow this ridge, it looks like we might be able to skirt this valley and end up with a nice view on this promontory. It looks promising as a good picture-taking spot, at least on paper."

"*I try dat way already, Miss Alexis,*" said Tsam. "*But de whole area is lone rocks.*"

"OK, what if we ride straight up this steep incline here and then around the south end?"

"*Maybe. If we no come too close to de wall here and the horses can still fit der feet between de cliff and de creek. But if the creek in flood, it can't work. Even in de dry season de rocks be wet and slipp'ry. Check out lines 'pon de map. Dey're so tight, it look like dat cliff goes maybe 'bout six hun'red feet, straight up.*"

Each grueling day Tsam and his co-worker, Uberto, rode the two mares to the far extent of the previous day's work. Then they would tie the horses and push through the next stretch on foot with sharpened *machetes* in hand. Sometimes the day's work ended in frustration when a promising trail dwindled into a cul-de-sac or a sheer drop-off. Other times Tsam returned, glowing with excitement, over a newly-discovered waterfall or hidden cave. It was dangerous work involving frequent skirmishes with thorns, scorpions, and tiger ants. A close call with an aggressive fer-de-lance, the deadly *barba amarillo*, reminded them to stay vigilant. After killing the snake, Tsam insisted on decapitating it and impaling the head on a stick, jaws agape, to prevent someone's stepping on the lethal fangs. The species was just as deadly after-the-fact.

The jungles of Belize had many faces. In the primary forest, under the high canopy, ground cover was sparse and relatively easy to walk through. *Wamill*, tertiary growth, was an unlovely and virtually impenetrable barrier of tall weeds. Secondary growth featured both high trees and choking undergrowth. Sometimes high canopy trees were so tangled in vines that, when cut, they didn't even fall – they merely sagged and creaked and then hung there in the snarl of rattan, strangler fig, and *mata palo*.

Every few days, Alexis accompanied Tsam on one of the geldings to inspect the progress and evaluate the trail as to natural beauty, gradient, and practicality. Only then could they judge if the route was worthy of further attention. As a child, Alexis had always imagined the jungle as a fantasy of exotic plant life and wild animals. With hard work, these trails would eventually resemble that vision, once they were beaten back, tamed, and manicured. But right now, the passage through the bush was claustrophobic, the trails less than half the width and height they would be in their finished state. The growth was dense, confining, and Alexis passed through the tunnel with no safe margin. Sagging half-broken vines festooned from above, and the chopped harvest of tangled plants and splintered wood from Tsam's machete lay in mounds along the narrow path.

On one particular occasion, Alexis had been forced to ride with her head down on the horse's neck, her belly to the saddle, in order to pass under a long section of thick foliage concealing biting insects and needle-like thorns. She ducked and dodged the debris while keeping Tsam's horse in sight. Finally, the bush opened, and Alexis was relieved to be able to sit upright in the saddle again. Ahead, through the vegetation, she caught a glimpse of the distant lookout and the magnificent view beyond. But just at that moment, Tsam's horse stepped awkwardly over a branch, catching its rear leg on a vine. Instantaneously, a twelve-foot pole, its tip slashed cleanly at forty-five degrees, angled upward between the horse's neck and the reins, and came directly towards Alexis' stomach. Too late to swerve or avoid its thrust, only her quick reflexes saved her. Sucking in her belly, and pulling the reins with all her strength, she forced the horse to a dead halt with split-second timing. The sharpened tip of the gruesome spear stabbed through the material of her shirt, and grazed her flesh. In another second, Alexis would have been skewered like a piece of meat.

Purchases to outfit the horses warranted a trip to the U.S. It had been five years since Alexis had passed through the immaculate portals of Miami International Airport and now, once again, the sterile environment seemed totally alien. The neon lights cast an unearthly glow as she saw her own face distorted in the stainless-steel panels of the escalator. After years of fresh air and the unadulterated scents of natural living, the airport terminal was a strange fusion of foreign smells. New carpeting, industrial cleaning fluids, and room deodorizers all blended strangely with the odor of hot dogs, coffee, perfume, popcorn, and aftershave. Feeling like a stranger in a strange land, Alexis passed through Immigration, rode the moving sidewalk, and then waited for her suitcase to arrive in the baggage claim area. Now that the Belize Government had approved the project after the fact, Ted was providing ample funding for the horseback riding business, and she planned to spend four or five days buying outfitting equipment. Military surplus stores were a good source for water canteens, mess kits, rain ponchos, headlamps, khaki shirts, and other survival necessities. A western shop would provide saddle blankets, cantle bags, nylon bridles and halters, and a pair of flat-heeled women's riding boots. The other priority item was to get the brochure printed. Alexis was still not satisfied with the wording. It had to be catchy and to-the-point. She hoped to get a better idea of the layout and text when she saw developed photographs. The baggage seemed to be taking forever; the conveyor was moving, but she still didn't see any suitcases from her plane.

"It's 'hurry up and wait' with these things, isn't it?" said the young man standing next to Alexis. He was in his mid-thirties, with a kind face, thinning blond hair, and a pleasant manner.

"Yeah, I guess," she responded, casually. "But I really don't have anything to compare it too. It's been a long time since I was in the States. I've lived in Belize for almost nine years."

The young man had been on the same flight from Belize, and they struck up a conversation to pass the time. He was fascinated with Alexis' new horseback project. His name was Adam Kent, and the more she spoke, the more animated he became.

"... So now the trails are being chopped, the saddles have been ordered and we're in the process of buying more horses," Alexis explained. "There's a *cantina* under construction and the crew is working on a corral and a stable. So the only real critical element left is the advertising brochure."

"You know, there's somebody that you should meet here in Miami," said Adam. His name is Jack Madera, and he's been to Belize dozens of times. I'm sure he could help you with the brochure."

"Does he have printing contacts?" asked Alexis.

"Sure, but that's not the half of it. He's a world-famous photographer and writer. His whole life has been advertising, not to mention he's one of the most colorful people you could ever imagine. Jack's an expert on travel writing, and has hundreds of worthwhile contacts. I'm sure his input would be invaluable to you."

"I really appreciate your suggestion, but what would make your friend want to help me? He doesn't even know me. I can't just call him up as a total stranger."

"Sure you can," said Adam, as he smiled. "He's retired from corporate life. Now he just goes on writing assignments whenever something takes his fancy. Jack thrives on helping people with all kinds of interesting projects. I used to date his daughter. Just tell him you met me. He'll welcome you like family. That's just the kind of guy he is. Here's his card. Give him a call."

Just as Adam had promised, the voice on the phone was friendly and receptive. Jack listened attentively as Alexis spoke, and without hesitation, he invited her to come to his home in Miami. The house was nestled among gnarled trees, so entangled in green growing things that it was difficult to see where the trees ended and the house began. Scattered beds of wandering jew and creeping vetch gave way to blossoms and gardens of impatiens and lilies, all shaded beneath burly-armed giants laden with bromeliads and flowering orchids. There was a special feeling about the place, and Alexis felt a curious connection to whatever lay beyond the mahogany doors magnificently carved in Mayan motif. She rang the bell.

"Hello!" said the man, smiling enthusiastically. "You must be Alexis. Come on in. I'm always happy to meet people from Belize."

Alexis' first look at Jack Madera was a revelation. It was an extraordinary face with smooth tanned skin and soft creases like fine leather. His black eyebrows arched sharply in pointed peaks over the laughing eyes that seemed as blue as the sea and twice as deep. He was perhaps in his mid-sixties, yet the aura that surrounded him suggested a youth and vibrancy rare in a person of any age. It was an expressive face, whose features reflected a lifetime of adventure under ten-thousand foreign suns. It was a face that revealed a wealth of insight and experience, a face that would live forever in Alexis' memory and in her heart.

The house was full of relics, a veritable art gallery and museum of treasures from distant cultures. There were paintings in oil and water colors, richly-colored oriental rugs, statues of stone, and carvings in ebony and ziricote. A glass display case contained an astonishing variety of rare and perfect seashells. A large articulated metal fish, green with the patina of aged copper, dominated a low Japanese table of dark teakwood. Adorning the walls were dozens of photographs of Jack standing shoulder-to-shoulder with primitive-looking natives in various states of undress, and in the doorway to Jack's private studio stood an Indonesian fertility god with an enormous phallus. There were crudely carved wooden fishhooks and aboriginal knives with wicked serrated edges, long feathered arrows from South America, a Zulu *assegai* and shield of black and white cowhide, colorful beadwork from Swaziland and Lesotho, and a *coco de mere* from the Seychelles. Everywhere Alexis looked she saw anthropological curios and artifacts from Mongolia to New Zealand, from the Amazon to Zambia, from India to Tierra del Fuego. Towards the rear of the living room was an upright grand piano beside an ample drafting table covered with sketches and photographs. Beyond that were sliding glass doors leading to a large exterior screen-room with an oval-shaped swimming pool and hundreds of hanging orchids in bloom.

A tall slender lady in her late fifties came through the back entrance. She wore a pair of jeans three sizes too big, a khaki work shirt, a red bandanna around her neck, a large floppy sunhat, and a pair of soiled gardening gloves. Nevertheless, it was plain from her graceful bearing that she was a lady of culture and elegance.

"Ah, my dear," Jack said tenderly, taking her arm. "Meet my new friend, Alexis. This is my wife, Marina."

Over the course of the next few days, Jack and Alexis spent many hours cutting and clipping and pasting. Together, they wrote and rewrote the text, bolded certain parts and italicized others, then threw out the changes and started over. Using his darkroom to develop her photographs, most of the exposures were too light to be usable, and there were only three or four good ones. But again, Jack was able to help out by donating a few of the thousands of pictures he'd taken in Belize over the years. After three days of intensive labor, the brochure was ready to print.

Now from her window seat, Alexis could see the afternoon sun slanting across the tops of the clouds, creating dimpled pockets of delicate peach and carnation pink. The plane skirted the west coast of Cuba, and every once in a while she caught a glimpse of curving land mass and blue ocean. She picked up the brochure and looked it over again, pleased at the professionalism of the operation now called Belize-By-Horseback. On the front cover was the large horseshoe waterfall surrounded by bush with a cluster of orchids in the foreground. Another picture below featured a group of riders on a mountainside staring towards the distant valley. Inside were more color photos depicting caves, creeks, rivers, and vistas. The descriptions were brief: options for half-day or full-day, what would be provided, what riders should bring and wear, including 'supportive undergarments' for both genders. Any body part that was capable of bouncing up and down should either be strapped up or strapped in.

Jack Madera. She thought of him again, savoring the memory. The man seemed to radiate, and Alexis was drawn to him. She had invited him to visit the ranch, and wished they could have spent more time together.

"Of course I'll come," Jack had told her. "I go to Belize at least every couple of years, and now that I have a new adventure to check out, I'll be sure to take you up on your generous offer."

Alexis hoped it would be sooner rather than later. The man fascinated her.

Buying horses for the trail riding business was a long-term endeavor, as Belize did not offer an abundance of the particular crossbreed ideal for their purposes. Quarter horse blood provided the necessary size and strength to carry big-bodied Americans; local blood gave the animals their stamina and resistance to infection. But, similar to searching for good used cars, good horses were rarely for sale. For that reason Alexis bought mostly young, unbroken animals, purchasing two and three year olds as they became available.

Genaro, Uberto's brother, was hired as a horse trainer. His methods were both inventive and effective. Generally, he blindfolded the horse and led him, by road, all the way back to Baron's Creek, seven miles away. Then he removed the blindfold, mounted the horse bareback, and let it thrash around in six feet of water until it was exhausted. After a brief rest, Genaro re-tied the blindfold, loaded two hundred pounds of corn on the horse's back, and walked it out of the valley via the back route, taking the switchbacks through the high bush, up the six-hundred foot hill.

The Mennonites proved to be the best source of good horses. They were plain folks who could be trusted in an honest trade. Cornelius Troyer had originally purchased the big gray gelding to be a cart horse, but he kicked the cart into pieces and then stood quietly amidst the wreckage waiting to be released from the traces. No matter. Cornelius had patience and perseverance, as well as faith. So he led the big gray to another cart and harnessed him in position. After another few minutes, the horse again stood calmly among the rubble of splintered wood. That was enough. Whether the hint was from God or the devil, Cornelius wasn't sure, but either way, he was running out of carts. Alexis purchased the horse for three hundred Belize dollars and named him Ash. An animal of incomparable endurance,

Ash soon established himself as the number one lead-horse on the ranch. From the beginning, he would be the undisputed head honcho of the herd.

Harvey Kratzer belonged to the modern Red Creek Mennonites. With his farm, acres of crops, herds of livestock, lumber interests, and farm machinery rental business, his reputation made him one of the most respected and influential men in the area. Young for a patriarch, Harvey's wife had given birth to their firstborn son when they were both eighteen. Now his eleven grown children were married, with children of their own, and all were involved in a variety of commercial ventures. Alexis and Tsam leaned on Harvey's corral in the bright morning sunshine, making their choices. One filly was dark and spirited, putting up a fight when the lasso was thrown around her neck. Tsam liked her. She had a good head and straight back with long slender legs, and Alexis knew instinctively that the filly would be a fast runner and a prime choice. Tsam was also partial to a feisty strawberry roan, half-brother to the filly by a different dam. They also chose the clay dun, a blue roan, two more mahogany bays, and a palomino mare. There were more horses that looked like good candidates, but none of them made a lasting impression on Alexis until she saw the sorrel chestnut. She asked Harvey's cowboys to run the herd around the corral once more so she could watch the colt move. Sired by the same Quarter horse stallion as the dark filly, the sorrel was almost sixteen hands, big for a three-year-old. His coat shone like burnished copper. With the same striking head as his sister, he had a big dished jaw, small neat ears, dark round eyes, large nostrils, and a white star on his forehead. The horse's confirmation was exceptional in every regard. The angle of the shoulder blades was perfect, his back, straight and broad, leading to huge solid hindquarters. The hams were thick and well-muscled, and the legs tapered gradually to strong narrow fetlocks and finely-shaped hooves. But his most singular feature was his gait. With a buttery trot and a canter like a prayer, the sorrel was grace on the hoof and poetry in motion. It was love at first sight. Alexis had found Cisco.

THE BUSH – 1987

chapter 17_____

It rained again that night. Before the advent of the trail-ride business, Alexis had enjoyed the sound of rain on the roof. It made for great sleeping-in weather. But now the sound prodded her rudely with visions of muddy trails and slippery hillsides. The drizzle had stopped just before dawn. There would be no reprieve today. The group of tourists would ride, rain or shine. She savored the comfort of the sheets for a few seconds longer, watching as the sky began to clear. From her pillow, she could see beyond the *vega* to the magnificent white cliffs above Len's old valley. The caves there remained forever aloof, inaccessible, except to the birds of prey. But there were hundreds of caves that could be reached without wings.

Spelunking had become her passion. Throughout the first year of the tour business, her fascination had gradually replaced her fear and, with each caving excursion, she had become a little bolder, gone a little deeper. Yesterday, Tsam had told her about a new cave, virtually untouched. Apparently, it had a difficult entry, and that was good – the more intimidating the hole, the more exciting the find. But, as the new cave was northeast of the ranch, and today they were going southwest, Alexis had decided to keep it on reserve for another day.

She dressed in a sleeveless khaki shirt, army pants, and two pairs of thick socks. Her khaki riding hat, a gift from a grateful tourist, sat next to the cantle-bag containing the first aid kit. Her riding boots were cleaned and polished after every ride. The shine didn't last long, but keeping the leather well-conditioned paid off. It was like the old adage about horses: no hoof, no horse. The jungle was no joke, and Alexis needed her feet.

The preparation for a day of trail riding was the hardest part of the job and people seemed to hold a common misconception as to what was involved. For some reason, tourists had a mental picture of a string of dispassionate horses tied to a railing twenty-four hours a day, already saddled, waiting patiently for riders to show up. Maybe it was true at the circus, but not in real life. The tour operation did not accept walk-ins. Instead, Alexis had established a handful of commissioned agents in Belize City who took deposits and used the two-way radios to call in reservations. A crucial part of the information was the height, weight, and riding experience of each guest. This enabled Alexis and Tsam to match the right horse to the right rider. Saddling the animals was laborious. During the rainy season, the horses came from the pasture plastered with mud and had to be hosed off, curried, washed down, and toweled dried before saddling could begin.

The preparation of food was also no easy task. Without ready-made foods from grocery stores, there were no convenient lunches of cold cuts and packaged bread. On half-day rides, guests and guides returned to the *cantina* around noon for barbecued chicken or steak, fire-roasted potatoes, coleslaw, tortillas, and dessert. On full-day rides, Alexis served lunch at the waterfall, a Mexican Fiesta of boneless seasoned chicken, refried beans, chopped onions, tomatoes, lettuce, grated cheese, homemade salsa, and tortillas. Guests drank lemonade or iced tea, depending on the bearing season of the citrus trees. For dessert, there was either banana cake or brownies. All foods were prepared from scratch and much of it was grown right there on the ranch. Pre-packing meals for the rides was an engineering feat that had taken Alexis months to perfect. Deciding what to serve for lunch was one factor, but having the food arrive in an edible condition after banging on the sides of a horse for four hours, was something else. Guests always raved about the food. Perhaps it was the waterfall setting, or the fact that their hunger had been piqued by hours of hard riding. Regardless, the horseback tour business had a reputation, not only for riding, but for having some of the best food in the country.

"*Buenos dias*, Tsam. I've got some coffee here for you," said Alexis, as he came in the door of the kitchen.

"*Thank yu, Miss Alexis. It look like P.J. gwine be out for one lee while. He got a big wire cut under his eye. Uberto's gwine walk de fence today, an' see if he could fin' de break.*"

She had given him the details for the ride yesterday. There were two couples from California – Chuck and Sandy, and Ross and Jenny, who were all fairly experienced riders, and Alexis had chosen Ali, Champagne, Jah, and Ginger. Tsam would be on Chani, and Alexis was riding Ash, as he was better in the mud. Everybody was staying at Rick and Suzy's, so the guests would be ferried across the river in canoes, and would meet the taxi driver from San Ignacio on this side, who would then bring them to the ranch. Finally, she was getting this transportation thing sorted out. With a little luck, the guests should be here on time.

Rick and Suzy had worked hard to develop the nicest bush resort in the area. Years before, they'd purchased the property opposite Mrs. Whitmore's, next to Anita's, and established Tarpon Run. Now, individual cottages of white stucco with colorful curtains and thatched roofs dotted the hillside. The large round dining room with its huge cone of palm thatching created an ambience of rustic elegance. Meals were served on real china, with real silverware and linen napkins. Rick and Suzy were gracious hosts, and their high standards were paying off. Because Alexis couldn't offer accommodations on the ranch, she had to depend on Tarpon Run's operation to deliver the clientele promptly. Timing was a crucial element for a full day's ride. There were a defined number of miles in the daily route. If the riders got a late start, other delays created a snowball effect. So far, she had never been forced to spend the night in the jungle with a group of hungry tourists, but the possibility was always there.

"*Yu neva believe what happened dis mawning,*" said Tsam. "*A big female jaguar done cross de driveway, right front of me. She had t'ree good-sized cubs wit' her. Look like she gwine up to de Pine Ridge.*"

"That's fantastic. I've only seen two of them in my life, other than the Belize Zoo," said Alexis. "Once, at night, as I was coming back late from Belize City. The other time was with you when we were chopping fence line."

"*Dey say de jaguars makin' a comeback—*"

"There's the taxi van coming in from the road now," Alexis interrupted, looking out the window. "I'll go down and do orientation. What's our timing?"

"Bout ten minutes. Uberto and Genaro just finishing de saddling when I came here to de house."

"Okay, great. Here's the lemonade for after the ride," said Alexis, handing Tsam the jug. "Can you take it down to the cantina, along with the food saddlebags? I'll bring the rain ponchos and the emergency bag with the first aid kit. I'm glad we've got experienced riders today. There's too much mud for novices. See you in few minutes."

After welcoming the guests and introducing herself, Alexis began the orientation. She spoke about handling the horses, trail etiquette, and safety procedures. Guests were advised not to pick orchids or take stalactites or pieces of pottery from caves. Smoking was not allowed on the trail but would be permitted at rest stops, providing all butts were field-stripped and buried deep in the humus. Alexis made it clear that, although the purpose of the ride was to have a good time, trail procedures were to be followed without exception. After the guests were mounted on the horses, Alexis took the lead position and the group rode single-file into the forest.

It was a good group today, and she was grateful. Any trail ride was rigorous enough without babysitting a herd of whiners. Of course, even towards the end of the day, most guests, hurting and exhausted, still maintained a positive attitude. Perhaps it was because adventure was what they had paid for, and real adventure is rarely comfortable. Or perhaps it was because, once on the trail, the tourists were simply at the mercy of the elements, and depended on the guides to deliver them back to civilization. Or maybe they were just wary of anyone with a big *machete*.

Under Alexis' supervision, Tsam and the crew had spent the better part of a year chopping approximately fifty miles of trails for the horseback tours. Some trails went south to the mountains, others led east into the valley behind the ranch, or northeast toward Lazzaro and Baron's Creek. In the open areas in the Mountain Pine Ridge, paths were developed by simply making blazes with a *machete* on the trunks of pine trees. In those areas, the short grasses parted naturally after the horses passed over them a few times. But where the trails led through heavy jungle, pathways had to be chopped regularly due to constant encroachment, and sometimes there were miles of trails that were not even open to the sun's rays. They were more like tall tunnels through the bush. Tsam and Alexis made a habit of swinging their *machetes* as they rode, hacking off any branches that had dropped. The routine helped maintain adequate width and height for horses and riders. The guests would tease Alexis, saying that one day her horse would come home with only one ear. But it never happened. She was good with the blade.

"So here we have all the houseplants you ever tried to grow," Alexis began her narrative. "The only difference is that these are sixty feet tall. The indigenous palm of this area is the 'cohune' palm, also known as the American Oil Palm. The leaf can be used for thatching, but it's not as durable as this ladyfinger bay leaf. This is what's used on your cottage at Tarpon Run."

Suddenly, as if on cue, an iridescent butterfly flew across the trail in front of Alexis. "Look, a blue morpho!"

"I can't believe how beautiful it is. I've seen pictures of them but they are so much more colorful in real life. Are there lots of animals here?" asked Ross.

"Oh yes," said Alexis. "We have deer and fox, porcupines, and opossum, but there are also many animals you've never heard of. We have a small earless rabbit called an *agouti*. And there are *peccary, coatimundi, kinkajou,* and a cute furry rodent called a *gibnut*. There are wild cats too. The smallest is a margay, but there are also ocelot, cougar and jaguar. We have great howler monkeys with huge throat sacks that make the most horrendous noise. The first time you hear it, you'd think it was a jaguar."

"Tsam told us that you do a great howler imitation," said Jenny.

"It's not that good," Alexis protested. "It's not loud enough. I haven't got the throat sack for it."

"Don' listen to no excuse, Miss Jenny." Tsam laughed. *"Miss Alexis know to mek de sound real good. One time she get de howler to answer."*

"Is that true?" said Sandy.

"Yeah," Alexis laughed. "And our guest was the Prime Minister of Belize, along with his wife and kids and bodyguards. A big howler was up in a tree, so I tried out my monkey roar. When the howler roared back at me, I started to worry about exactly what I had said!"

Ash was irritated. With each step, his feet sank to his fetlocks in the deep mud. He twitched his ears and looked accusingly at Alexis. The horse had slogged through the mud for months. Sometimes it was so deep it sucked the shoes right off his feet. Both horse and rider would be happy to see the dry season again.

"Look at the thorns on that tree," Jenny commented.

"That's called 'Give and Take,'" said Alexis. "Those spikes can give you a nasty wound, but its roots are used to suppress blood flow. So you get the injury and the cure from the same plant. It is also useful for stick walls, once the spikes are cut off, of course. Again, this is what they use at Tarpon Run. The trunk can be handled if it's done with care. You just slide your hand down in the same direction the spikes grow, like you'd hold a catfish. Preferably with gloves on."

"No thanks. I'm a builder from the first world. I'll stick to my own construction materials," said Chuck.

"Ideally, it's not a good idea to touch anything in the bush," Alexis advised. "There are many trees and plants with spikes or sharp spines. We've got some really nasty ants too. There are devil thorns, also called 'cockspur,' and fluffy white caterpillars that the locals call 'hairy worm.' They can give you a horrible weeping rash. So dodge, duck, and avoid everything you can."

"You don't need to tell me twice," said Chuck.

"Almost paradise," said Alexis. "When paradise doesn't have bugs and snakes and thorns, then it'll truly be paradise."

"Do you see snakes often?" Ross asked.

"'See' is the operative word. They're out here, but we only see a small percentage of them. It's funny. If a horse sees a piece of black PVC pipe that looks like a snake, it'll jump. But when a real snake slithers right between their legs, they don't even notice."

"Are there poisonous ones?" asked Sandy.

"Oh yes. The *barba amarillo,* or 'yellow jaw' is a fer-de-lance. Hemotoxic. Very nasty snake. We also have coral snakes, but they are passive unless you step on one or disturb its nest. They say there are rattlesnakes in the Pine Ridge too, but I've never seen one. Tsam hates all snakes and kills them whenever he can, no matter what kind. We saw a bright emerald tree-snake back by Slate Creek a few days ago.

It must have been nine or ten feet long. It just watched us for a long time then slithered away."

"I read a book a few years ago about a woman who was going to South America," Sandy continued. "The woman was going to buy some of those leg-guards but the salesperson told her not to bother. She said, 'Any snake that's half-trying can bite you above the knees. Besides, they drop from trees.'"

Alexis laughed. "I don't know if that's true, but it makes for good copy."

"Speaking of good copy, you're the one who should write a book," said Ross. "Preserve all of this for future generations. Make a hell of a story for your grandchildren."

As the trail rose in elevation, the soil became drier. The vegetation changed and the trees became thinner and taller. The sun had come out of the clouds and the patches of blue were a welcome sight. The riders rode along the edge of a ravine, and sunlight flickered on the brown leaves and lichen-covered rocks. Suddenly, Alexis held up her hand to halt the riders. She sensed something – a murmur, or buzzing, something she could feel, rather than hear. Then a deep chuffing sound came from ahead and the hair prickled on the back of her neck.

Tsam slid the *machete* from its scabbard and dismounted. Without a word, the little Maya crept around the horses, ascending into the underbrush and disappearing. Alexis twisted around on Ash, and put a finger to her lips, motioning the guests to stay silent. It was an unnecessary gesture. Seeing their faces, she realized they were too scared to say anything.

Standing out of sight behind the saw-palmetto, Tsam stared down at the bleeding animal. The young tapir had been shot in the gut and left to die a slow painful death. Flies had already gathered on the wounds, and vicious ants were eating his flesh while he still lived. Tsam wished he had a rifle to put a clean shot into its head. A machete was a messy way. With regret, he thrust his long blade between the tapir's ribs and into its heart. The beast gave one last shudder and expired.

"It okay, Miss Alexis," Tsam called out. *"It was just a danto. Look like somebody shoot it. It was sufferin' bad. I finish him. He done dead already."*

After wiping the bloody *machete* on the ground, Tsam shoved it into his scabbard and walked back into view where the riders waited in anticipation. Out of the corner of his eye, he caught a glint of brass and blue plastic. Picking up the spent cartridge, he carried it to where Ash stood and tossed it to Alexis.

"Twelve gauge," said Tsam.

"Zander," she leveled her reply. They understood each other perfectly.

"Have to be Zander. He de only one who got de twelve gauge shotgun around here."

Alexis felt a hot flash of anger but knew she had to keep cool in front of her guests. As Tsam remounted his horse, she started the tour moving again. "I'm sorry for the delay, everyone. It seems that someone has been using the trails for purposes other than sightseeing."

"Somebody shot an animal? I thought this was a National Forest Reserve," said Chuck.

"It's a Reserve, but unfortunately, not a Preserve," said Alexis. "That's an important distinction to the government. In a Reserve, you can still get a permit to do virtually anything you want, like logging, or even hunting."

Taking the next switchback up the hill, the trail passed within view of the dead beast. Like most Americans, these tourists were animal lovers and ardent conservationists. The crude scene of the animal lying in a pool of blood disturbed them. Above the tops of the trees, vultures circled overhead. Soon they would be gorging on the feast.

"What kind of animal is it?" said Jenny. "I've never seen anything like it before."

"Most Americans haven't. They don't look like any other animal. The locals call it a 'mountain cow' or 'danto,' but the real name is tapir. Looks like a cross between a pig and a small hornless rhino, but it's actually a distant relative of the horse. They're herbivores with a prehensile snout, and they're completely harmless. Jaguars are their only natural enemy, other than man. This poor thing was barely a teenager, maybe a year and a half old, probably about three hundred pounds. Full grown they weigh around six hundred."

"Why was it shot?"

"A local guy has been chopping down a piece of high bush every year so he can plant his corn and beans. Since the high bush is all but gone around the perimeter, he's starting to intrude on the National Forest itself. The tapir is the Belizean National Animal and this one was killed inside the boundaries of its own National Forest. Zander probably shot it because it was trampling his bean patch. Then he didn't even bother to use the meat or hide. He just left it to rot."

"That's sick," said Chuck. "This Zander guy, he's a Belizean? The one who shot it?"

"Yes," Tsam answered. *"He de one who shoot it. He is Creole, not Maya like me, and he got one bad attitude. He no like de gringos coming in here, makin' de money. Plenty a people no understand dat de bush is what Belize got for bring tourists. Zander only want to chop it down fu plant his corn. He got no mind for de future. Zander used to be a friend, but he change plenty."*

"That's right. When we first opened the trails, Zander worked for us," said Alexis. "Later, we offered him a job as a guide. But as soon as we depended on him to be here on time, he was late, or didn't show up at all. I told him if he didn't want to be a guide, he could still take advantage of the tourist trade on his own. I suggested that his wife could make lemonade and meet our riders on the trail, and charge for drinks. Or get his kids to paint cohune nuts, or carve souvenirs. Instead, he chose to make life difficult. Sometimes he even chops down trees maliciously, just to block our trails."

Zander had done that, and much worse. About a half mile inside the National Forest was a spectacular sinkhole. Unlike artesian springs whose water gathers on the surface, a sinkhole is just the opposite, serving as a drain for the surrounding jungle. In this case, one side of the sinkhole formation was a gigantic semi-circular rock face of limestone, adorned with huge feathery ferns. The other side was a sloping hill bisected by a small rivulet. In heavy rains, the water rushed down the bank and disappeared into a cave-like hole at the bottom. Topside, above the rock face, tall hardwoods shaded the entire region. Ten degrees cooler at the mouth, the sinkhole was alive with tropical orchids and bromeliads. Often, riders had seen peccary or *coatimundi* there, and even the rare white morpho butterfly. Aside from the waterfalls and spectacular caves farther south and east, the sinkhole was one of the most beautiful features on the trails. Zander had chopped it all down. The bare rock formation lay raped and denuded under the harsh tropical sun. Then he had burned the area to a charred ruin and planted his corn.

"Sorry about the tapir, everybody," Alexis apologized. "Adventure mixes the good with the bad. Didn't mean to bum you out. But, as they say, it's a jungle out here. Tell you what," she continued, trying to improve morale. "There's an area ahead where we can go for a little run. Remember to shorten the reins and keep substantial distance between your horses. Don't allow your animal to overrun the horse in front of you. And remember to watch for my signal to slow down."

A few seconds later, Alexis gave Ash a squeeze with her legs and the big grey took off, the other horses following suit. The sun was bright now and sparkled on the giant ferns as they cut through the grassy uplands. The air tasted delicious as the riders laughed and cantered up the trail bordered by the southern white pine and thickets of mountain laurel.

"What's that noise?" said Sandy, as they all slowed their horses to a walk.

"Dat de waterfall," said Tsam. *"Yu will see. Yu will like dis place plenty."*

"You can dismount just ahead, and tie your horses. Just pick a tree. Tsam will come and re-tie the ropes anyway." Alexis grinned at Tsam, and he returned the smile. "He never trusts anyone else's knot, do you, Tsam? Especially in a cave."

"Especially inna de caves, I no trust," Tsam laughed, as he began to loosen girths and belly bands on the saddles so the horses could enjoy a breather. *"I tie de rope, den I know we come out again."* It was true. Already there had been several times when her life had depended on Tsam's knot.

"You can each take your personal stuff-bag down to the river," said Alexis, as she dismounted. "But leave your water canteens on the horses. We have food and juice, and if you want water, you can drink out of the river. It's guaranteed to be safer than anything you drink out of a tap in the U.S."

Strapping on her *machete*, she swung the heavy horse-sweat-soaked food saddlebags over her shoulder, and stood at the edge of the canyon.

"It's about a hundred and fifty feet to the bottom, and the pine needles are super slick. Hang on to the trees as you descend, or you might get there faster than the slip-and-slide at a water park. Everybody ready? Let's go." Alexis called back over her shoulder. "OK, Tsam. See you at the bottom in a few minutes."

Reaching the river, the group stood awestruck as the water roared over the horseshoe-shaped precipice some eighty feet above, and crashed into the pool before them.

"Come on gang," said Alexis. "I'll show you how to soothe those aches and pains and saddle sores. Follow me through the lower pool, and then I'll lead you to the hydro-massage. There are no changing rooms, so pick a rock, or go naked if you want. Believe me, nobody cares. And don't worry about crocs," Alexis teased. "They ate two soldiers on Tuesday, so they won't be hungry for a few more days." Everybody laughed and followed her into the river, fervently hoping she was kidding

The lower pool was only about twelve to fifteen feet deep, and with little current, it was ideal for inexperienced swimmers. Above, a narrow throat created promontories of rock extending from both sides. The restricted flow created an area of rapids with one particular fissure that acted as a natural jacuzzi. Jenny opted to stay in its bubbling comfort, but the others chose to press on towards the base of the falls itself.

Nobody knew how deep the upper pool was. Experienced divers had told Alexis they were unable to touch the bottom. The consensus of opinion was about twenty-five feet. The fierce current was challenging, even for strong swimmers.

"The only way to get into the falls is to dive off the rocks here and swim diagonally over to that rock face," Alexis shouted above the roar. "Then we'll have to inch our way up the wall. When you get to the bottom of the shoot, you'll need to push off the rocks and launch yourself back across again. Then climb out, and I'll show you how to ease into the channel at the base of the falls. But, fair warning, you'll have to brace yourself against the force. The falls will be right behind you. Everybody ready?"

The three remaining riders managed to reach the bottom of the thunderous waterfall, and they took turns lowering themselves into the channel. But Ross was the first to find out that any delay in locating the foot-brace in the torrent resulted in a quick trip down the chute and into the upper pool.

"Oh, it makes you feel so good," said Sandy, as she thrilled to the feel of the rushing water.

"I read that negative ions raise endorphin levels, creating a natural euphoria," Chuck explained. "Apparently, people who get cabin fever, or live in the desert, suffer from a lack of negative ions. It's not the effect of aerated water, but rather, of the hydrogenated air." Whatever the cause, it was a joy that created laughter and camaraderie, an experience that turned strangers into friends.

A few minutes later, Alexis spotted Tsam, so she left the guests to help him set up the food. When everything was ready, she gave the signal, and the riders didn't need to be called twice. After two and a half hours of vigorous activity, they ate hungrily. After lunch, Tsam took the guests for a second swim and another trip to the falls.

Now it was Alexis' time to relax. She spread her towel on the warm rocks and lay down for a short *siesta*. Closing her eyes, she felt the warmth on her skin. For a brief time she was conscious of the rushing river and the chirping birds overhead. But soon the sounds faded into a hazy daydream... *Effortlessly, she sailed upward as the winds wafted her high into the air. She'd been to this place before. Alexis looked down on the familiar landscape. The green river threaded its way northward through the cool shade of the forested banks. She could see the submerged mossy boulders. Then she was flying south, upstream, farther and farther. At last she came to the bend where the river curved sharply to the east. Alexis had never seen the great elbowed canyon before, but somehow she had always known that it must be there. The water became a brilliant turquoise blue, sparkling with unmatched clarity. As she wheeled in flight like a bird, boulders of pink and black granite rose from the riverbed and she saw herself stretched out on the rocks...* Abruptly, her mind was sucked back into her body, and she sat up looking at the glistening water.

"This is it," she exclaimed in wonder. "The river of my dreams. The green and the turquoise. It's all the same river. This river, the Rio On, is the primary source of the Macal. It's so obvious. All these years and I never put it together before. It has always been here. It exists. Not merely a dream, a premonition of what was to be."

Outward bound, the horses had been easy-going, even a little reluctant. But now on the return trip they picked up their pace as thoughts of corn, bran, and molasses lured them homeward. The attitudes of the guests were quite the opposite. Happy, but exhausted, they had climbed the canyon after lunch and hauled themselves, wearily, into the saddles. Cantle-bags were retied, and stirrups were adjusted to accommodate sore rear ends and the need for more clearance.

As the group got underway, conversation died completely. Each rider became lost in his or her own thoughts. They rode through the tall pines and crossed pockets of vegetation of tree fern and tiger bush, while clouds in the distance made a dappled patchwork on the forested hills. When Alexis brought the riders to a halt, she heard Chuck groan.

"God, my ass hurts. And to think that I paid good money to hurt like this. "

"Listen, Chuck. I read a book about a rich man who went to Africa to hunt for big game," said Alexis. "At some point during the safari, he and his guide found themselves without food, water, fuel, or ammunition. When the guide began to apologize, the white hunter interrupted him and told him to shut up. He said he'd paid a lot of money to be that uncomfortable!

"Anyway, I know you guys are tired, but I'd still like to suggest a side trip to a cave if you have the energy. There's no pottery in this one but it has some terrific limestone formations. It would add about forty-five minutes to the ride. Are you up for it?"

"Yu should do it. Yu would like it, fu true, " Tsam encouraged.

"We came for adventure. I vote we go for it," said Sandy.

"Don't look at me. I'm not going to wimp-out," mumbled Jenny.

The pine savannah changed once more to jungle. There, the fertile soil allowed for an abundance of mahogany, sapodilla, hog plum, and wild fig, all of it festooned with giant split-leaf philodendrons. Central American brown jays fanned their white tail feathers, calling to each other in raucous cacophony. As the horses stepped over a rotted log, hundreds of yellow butterflies took flight and lingered around the riders in a cloud of butterscotch, as hummingbirds sipped the nectar of tiny red wild hibiscus. Ten minutes later, the group arrived at the mouth of the cave.

"Okay everybody," Alexis announced. "We'll tie up the horses here. Tsam can help you dismount if *rigor mortis* is setting in."

"What is this little trail cutting across right here?" asked Chuck. "See it? About two inches wide? Is that from snakes?"

"Oh no, that's made by the *wee-wees*, leaf-cutter ants," said Alexis. "They have these little highways all through the jungle. Sometimes they go on for miles. In this case, this is the end of the trail. Here, I'll show you." She walked over to a large sandy mound of bare earth about fifteen yards from the cave. "This is their home. As you can see they have many trails that feed in from different directions. See? Here are the ants."

Mostly obscured by the little pieces of leaf, at first it was hard to see the ants themselves. The long weaving line looked like a bobbing column of shredded lettuce. Only under closer inspection could they see the insects beneath their leafy burdens. Alexis continued by saying that the ants didn't actually eat the leaves, but rather composted them to grow a particular type of fungus. The ants grew their own food.

"Is everybody ready? Tsam, does everyone have their headlamp?"

"Wait one nex' minute. I wan' cut one fresh vine fu go down inna de cave. Dis vine too old an' dry already, " he replied.

With a quick look around Tsam picked out a fresh pliable vine and slashed it with his razor-edged *machete*. In one fluid motion, he looped the new vine around the tree near the mouth of the cave and lashed it securely.

"Okay, Miss Alexis. We ready now."

Only the upper half of the cave was visible from the outside, but once inside, the drop was about six feet. Using the vine as a rope, Tsam showed them the footholds to lower themselves into the cave.

"What is that awful smell?" asked Sandy.

"There's not much air circulation," said Alexis. "The odor is caused mostly by molds and bat droppings. Pretty soon you won't even notice it."

"What kind of bats?"

"Mostly vampires," she replied, matter-of-factly.

"You're kidding again, right?" said Ross. "Like the crocodiles at the falls?"

"Not this time. But they're not really dangerous," Alexis admitted. "Sometimes they bite the horses at night, and the next day we find long streaks of dried blood on their necks, but the rest is Hollywood. It's really no big deal, more of a nuisance. We have a lot of fruit bats, too. Bats are a necessary part of the ecological balance in the jungle. They're very useful when it comes to seed dispersal, insect control, and pollination."

"So does anything really live in here?" asked Jenny, timidly.

Alexis couldn't resist the temptation to tease a little. "Why? Are you nervous? Not really being sure is part of the adventure you know."

"Hey, listen Ms. Bush-woman," Chuck said, laughing. "How about a straight answer to the question? I want to leave Belize with all the tender body parts I arrived with."

"Okay," she relented. "All joking aside, there are no animals that live in these caves. I used to suspect big cats and poisonous snakes, but I've never seen anything but bats and an occasional albino bug."

"Excep' for de time we find de peccary bones where de tiger eat it," Tsam offered.

"That's true. Once we found what was left of a jaguar's dinner. But I think it was just his picnic site rather than living quarters. Cats prefer cozy places in the underbrush where they can make a den of soft bedding, and since snakes can't produce any body heat of their own, caves are too cold and damp. Of course, there may be exceptions, but that's been our experience so far."

Gradually their eyes became accustomed to the semi-darkness and, as the group moved farther into the shadows, their headlamps began to focus on a spectacular variety of limestone formations. Alexis pointed out the differences between stalactites and stalagmites, and where they joined to form a column. Hugging the right, they skirted the edge of a short drop-off. The walls were sweaty with condensation, and the sloping floor was slick with clay.

"We're going to be going through a hole," said Alexis, forewarning them. "You don't have to crawl on your hands and knees, just stoop down low. It's about seven feet long. On the other side it opens into a huge room. But watch out. You have to clear the hole by at least three feet before you can stand up. There are stalactites directly above your head. Is everybody ready?"

"I don't know if I want to do this," said Jenny.

"Of course you do," said her husband. "You don't want to stay here alone do you?"

"No!" she cried.

"Come on, Jenny. You'll enjoy it. I promise," said Alexis, reassuringly. "Remember, Tsam and I come here once or twice a week. It's quite safe, and will be well worth it."

"Come on, honey," Ross coaxed. "You wanted an action vacation. We could be lying on the beach right now getting fat on piña coladas. Besides, they wouldn't be taking us in here if it wasn't safe. I'll protect you."

"Okay, but to hell with you – I want my Tsam!"

"No problem, Miss Jenny, I stay close by yu."

Alexis entered first and helped each guest through. Once on the other side, she pointed out a piece of stalactite that had been intentionally wedged across the top of the hole.

"You can see that this is completely unnatural. Limestone formations always grow up and down with gravity, never horizontal. The Mayas placed this here, positioning this piece crosswise to prevent the hole from closing up."

"What did the Mayas do in these caves?" asked Chuck. "There are different theories," replied Alexis. "Some people believe they were used as a refuge from the Spanish. Other experts think they were used for sacrifices."

"I thought the sacrifices were done on top of the temples."

"Sometimes, but that was a more common practice with the Aztecs. Caves were also important to collect holy water. You see, the rain came from the Overworld and fell on the Middleworld," she explained. "By the time it filtered through to the caves, the Underworld, it was considered purified. The Mayas collected it in pots and used it in religious ceremonies. That's why so much pottery is found in some caves."

"True. Dose Mayas was somet'ing else," Tsam added.

"You say 'those Maya' as if you weren't one of them," Chuck teased.

"Well, I tell yu, Mista Chuck. Dose Maya did one lot of good t'ings, buildin' temples, an' studyin' de stars. But it mek me vexed because my grandfathers were kings – and dey neva left me not'ing!"

Tsam's remark was amusing, yet he had spoken the truth; it was a question that had no resolve. How could such an advanced civilization just disappear, taking with it centuries of progress, and leaving its descendants to toil in poverty as if there had never been a glorious ancestral past?

The shafts of light from their headlamps pierced the gloomy darkness as more formations materialized. Alexis showed her guests various configurations: drapery, columns of popcorn, and a cascade of white crystalline flowstone on the far wall. They saw hump-backed flooring that Tsam called 'the turtle,' and another rounded hanging formation named 'the cow's udder.'

"I can't believe I'm doing this," Jenny remarked in a small voice, "but it's fantastic."

"Now we are entering the 'moon room,'" said Alexis. Here, ridges of limestone stood proud from the surface by perhaps four or five inches. The ripples were at least a half-inch thick and ran crookedly across the uneven surface in meandering patterns, sometimes forming large ovoid or circular areas.

"Amazing formations. Look at the size of this place," Ross exclaimed.

Scanning with their headlamps, the riders began to realize how large the cavern really was. With an arched ceiling perhaps a hundred feet high, the dimensions of the cave were so distant that the beams were unable to penetrate the outer limits.

"Just a little further," said Alexis. They were almost a quarter mile inside the cave when they reached the most spectacular columns. One looked like a giant ice cream cone piled high with extra scoops. Another looked like an abstract skull. Yet another bore an uncanny resemblance to madonna-and-child. Some formations were ivory colored; others were orange, green, or yellow.

"This is a great photo-op location. We'll stop here. Everybody give me your cameras, and pose together on these rocks." Using each of their cameras, one by one, Alexis took the photographs. Looking through the viewer, she was amused at the degree to which the tourists had changed during the course of the day. Six hours earlier, these 'greenhorns' had arrived at the ranch in their spotless Banana Republic clothing, looking like a stylized Gunga Din, or Indiana Jones. Now, sweat-stained and weary, the tourists with mud-streaked faces and stringy hair had become seasoned explorers. Years later, they would point to the photograph and boast of their courage.

"Okay, now it's time for a regular feature of the tour," said Alexis, returning the cameras. "Lights out. And no talking."

"Oh shit," Ross said. "I'm not sure if I want to see how dark it really is in here."

"Lights out," she insisted.

Hesitantly, the headlamps snapped off one by one, and the impact of the darkness hit them. All the guests had gone camping and knew what it was like to be in darkness, away from the lights of the city. But, even on a moonless night, there is always the dim light of the stars, and even in the darkest of rooms, the human eye will dilate, adjusting to let in the smallest amount of light.

Not so in the vast depths of the earth. As many times as Alexis experienced it, she could never quite get used to the feeling. The oppressive blackness was palpable, and seemed to squeeze her physically, as her eyes fought to adjust to a light that wasn't there. It was darker than the womb, darker than the vision of the blind. There was no light, a perfect void where the human senses cried out for something to perceive, and found nothing.

The journey back was quicker.

"There it is," said Chuck. "I can see daylight." He turned the corner and saw the mouth of the cave ahead. Suddenly, there was a crescendo of beating wings from the rear of the cave. A swarm of bats came straight towards them, heading for the opening, and everyone ducked involuntarily as they swooped low over their heads.

"I don't suppose we really needed to duck, did we?" said Sandy, after the fact. "They have that radar thing, right?"

"It's called echo-location, but it's better to duck. It's not a perfect system," said Alexis. "Sometimes they brush your cheeks with their wing tips. One guest got a bat tangled in her hair."

"Eeeuuuww," shrieked Jenny. "Now you tell me."

"If I had told you before, you probably wouldn't have gone in the cave."

You're right. But now I'm glad I went."

"I'm glad we all went," Sandy agreed. "What an experience. I'll certainly never forget it."

A few miles away, the hunter shaded his eyes and squinted as the last glint of afternoon sun disappeared behind the blue-black clouds. He knew that it was the lighter gray sky just behind that would bring the heavy rains. Luciano was tired. The shotgun felt heavy in his hand, and shifting the load to his shoulder didn't help much. He knew that Anna would not chide him if he returned home without meat. But, with eight children and another baby on the way, the responsibility of providing food weighed heavily on his mind. The deer had been solidly in his sights, yet the shot had gone wild. The animal had taken the hit in the hind quarters and vanished into the bush. Now, Luciano had been tracking the wounded deer for over an hour. As the light grew dimmer in the coming storm, he was starting to lose hope. Thunder could be heard from the distant ridge and, when it rained, the blood trail would be washed away. Suddenly, he noticed broken twigs and a dark blood clot. The buck was dragging the leg badly.

Just ahead, the big female jaguar crouched restlessly under a large tree fern and paused again to sniff the breeze. Her tawny golden coat, dappled with black rosettes, camouflaged her perfectly, and her stiff whiskers twitched in studied concentration. With the storm approaching, the frivolous wind kept changing directions. Earlier, she thought she'd picked up the scent of blood, but couldn't be sure; her sense of smell wasn't as keen as it used to be. She and her babies had undertaken a long journey earlier that day, and her belly growled with hunger. Now that the three hungry cubs were nestled in their new den, the cat took off, determined to make a kill.

Throughout her lifetime, the jaguar had mothered many litters. Now beyond the normal reproductive age, it was only a freak of nature that she had been impregnated one last time by a persistent young suitor. The cubs were boisterous, and she had no patience with them. They demanded large quantities of food, yet were too young to help in the hunt.

Suddenly, the deer stepped into her field of vision. Weakened by the loss of blood, it staggered forward and collapsed to the ground. The big cat froze. The wind was behind her now, but instinct told her to stay motionless. With her ears forward and every muscle tensed in anticipation, she began to inch closer, waiting for the right moment. The jaguar leapt on the dying animal, breaking its neck with the power of her jaws. Then she began to gnaw into the underbody of the deer, systematically biting through the anus and genitalia to the soft viscera. She would engorge herself with food, and later regurgitate it for the cubs.

A twig crackled as Luciano stepped through the brush and found himself face-to-face with his competitor. The great cat pulled her head out of the body cavity, her beautiful coat slick with blood and intestinal juices. She was a massive cat, a full six feet long from her head to the base of her tail. He saw the clear yellow eyes narrow into slits as she snarled at his intrusion. The small neat ears were laid flat on her head; her lips curled, exposing great terrifying teeth.

Luciano's adrenalin raced, his lungs could not draw breath. The sweat burst from his body, and in a sickening rush, he felt his bowels void. Still clutching the shotgun, Luciano began to back away slowly, raising his gun at the same time. Seeing the movement, the jaguar rose from her kill and began to stalk him. She roared and the bush reverberated with the echo. The hunter brought the gun up slowly, his finger on the trigger. Backing up, his foot caught on an exposed root.

The shot blasted upward, striking the jaguar in the forepaw as she vaulted into the air and bore him to the ground.

With one stroke of her powerful rear claws, she split Luciano's torso from clavicle to pelvis. The whiteness of his ribs showed beneath the torn muscle, and his exposed entrails quivered. The blood-slathered face of the jaguar, just inches above his own, filled the breadth of his vision. He could smell the acrid stink of carrion on her breath, and tried to scream, but no sound came out.

In his mind's eye, he saw the moments of his life: his parents, the days of his youth, his wife, and the births of his children. Yet all he could see in the physical world were the golden eyes of the great cat, glaring at him like the fires of hell. It was the last thing he saw. The jaguar snarled again and sank her teeth deeply into the man's neck, crushing the cervical vertebrae. A sudden rush of bright arterial blood arched skyward and seeped slowly into the earth.

A short distance away, the riders heard the roar followed by the blast of the shotgun.

"What was that?" said Chuck. "One of those howler monkeys?"

"Sounded like it," Alexis lied, coolly. "Listen, Chuck. Would you stay here and hold the lead position for a minute? I want to go back and talk to Tsam."

"Sure, no problem."

She reined Ash around sharply and cut to the rear.

"Tsam, I don't like the sound of that at all. What do you think? Big cat?"

"I got one bad feelin' 'bout dat noise. Dat a jaguar for sure. Somebody shoot de shotgun. Why yu don' stay with the tourists and continue to de ranch, Miss Alexis? I will go see what gwine on."

"Okay. The ranch isn't far. We were planning on cantering for the last stretch anyway. If you're not back in thirty minutes, I'll send someone after you."

"Bueno. I gone then."

"Con cuidado, amigo mio," Alexis called after him as he rode into the forest.

On the way home, she tried to appear calm, but knew something was wrong. It was a sixth sense developed by living close to the land, and now a dozen possible scenarios were playing in her mind. She told the guests that Tsam was running an errand. Then she tried to keep the conversation lighthearted, and concentrated on getting them back to the ranch as quickly as possible. They cantered on the last stretch for an exhilarating finish.

"Listen up everybody," said Alexis, arriving at the corral. "Please make sure you remove all your possessions from the horses. We don't want to inherit anything at your expense. Then you can head over to the cantina for refreshments. There's lemonade and rum. Help yourselves. I'll be with you in a minute."

Alexis dismounted quickly, handed the reins to Genaro, and ran up to the house for the shotgun, grabbing the pistol as an afterthought. Back at the little *cantina*, she put Uberto in charge of hosting the guests. He didn't speak much English, but all he really had to do was get some rum and lemonade into them. The taxi driver had spent the day waiting; it was cheaper than driving all the way to San Ignacio. He would be ready to go as soon as the guests had had a drink or two. Then, she tactfully offered her apologies, making the excuse that something had fallen out of her saddlebags on the trail. They had been a delightful group, and they expressed their gratitude for the adventure of a lifetime. Ash was raring to go, and strode out with the same energetic spirit he'd had at the beginning of the long day.

Without the burden of the extra riders, Alexis picked up Tsam's tracks quickly. She rode hard and fast, cutting through the bush, ducking the low limbs of scrub oak and rattan palm. The wind had begun to blow harder and a light rain had started to fall. She looked up and noticed turkey vultures circling ahead, and urged Ash to go faster.

Chani was tied to a tree, snorting and stomping the ground. Smelling the stench of blood and feces, Alexis swung down and tied her horse quickly. Securing the *machete* scabbard to her waist and thigh, she grabbed the shotgun, and tucked the pistol into her waistband.

Just at that moment, Tsam came stumbling out of the bush. His face was pale and his hands were bloody.

"Tsam! Are you all right? What happened? Is that your blood?"

He could hardly speak. *"A big jaguar. De blood is not mine. It is Luciano Perez. He dead, Miss Allie. De jaguar done gone. Look like maybe dey was both hunting de same animal. As I reached dere, I saw de place where de cat drag away de deer. Luciano get tear up bad. It look plenty ugly."*

Alexis followed Tsam through the bush. Although she anticipated the worst, nothing could have prepared her for the grisly scene. At her feet lay the torn body of the dead man. His head had been almost completely severed at the neck and a piece of the scalp had been torn from the skull. His torso was twisted sideways at an impossible angle. The intestines spilled out of the abdominal cavity, and he had been emasculated. Blood was everywhere.

Alexis turned away and vomited. She staggered back to the horse and drenched her bandanna with water from the canteen. Wiping her face, she rinsed out her mouth and fought to regain composure. She spied a small bloody object in the grass, picked it up, and put it in her pocket.

Tsam simply sat on a nearby rock holding his head. Tears ran down his cheeks. *"Sorry. I neva in my life cry in front of a woman before."*

"It's all right, Tsam. He was your friend."

"We must mek a longeria, fu carry de body back to Anna."

Alexis nodded. "There's a poncho behind each of the saddles. We could use one to wrap him and one to string between the poles."

A steady drizzle came down now as Tsam cut two long straight thin trees, then went back along the trail to where the rattan palms grew and chopped a length of vine. Avoiding the wicked spines, he peeled away the black outer layer and split off long strips of the pliable inner bark. Cutting several shorter sticks, he used the rattan to bind them securely to the long poles. Passing more rattan through the grommets of the heavy military poncho, he lashed it securely to the framework. Rock-steady and oblivious to the smell of death, Ash stood still as Tsam bound the rig to Alexis' saddle. The whole effort had taken less than thirty minutes.

Finally, the skies opened and the hard rain began. With heavy hearts, Tsam and Alexis lifted the small shrouded body onto the *longeria* and began their slow muddy journey to the Perez homestead.

Suddenly remembering, Alexis reached into her pocket and pulled out the bloody object. It was a jaguar claw.

THE CAVE

chapter 18

It was now the third tourist season since the inception of the business, and besides the exposure from local advertising, more and more riders came to the ranch as a result of wholesale packages sold the U.S. and Europe. With Ted's help, Alexis had appealed to two wholesale outfits that offered horseback tours on a global basis. Once the principals had visited and personally experienced the magnificent trails, Belize-By-Horseback had been immediately qualified as a world-class facility. Accordingly, Alexis set up an addendum to the brochure outlining specifics of the package tours: four days of riding with five overnights at Tarpon Run, plus three days and nights on Ambergris Caye. Although it had taken time to build up a reputation, the concept of the 'turf and surf' package was becoming very successful. Wives wanted to ride; husbands wanted to scuba dive, and these packages appealed to both. Now, rain or shine, there were guests nearly everyday – greenhorns, soft adventurers, or hard-core endurance riders – Sundays and holidays notwithstanding.

Returning from the feed mill at Spanish Lookout, Alexis helped Tsam and Genaro unload the corn, bran, and molasses, and then drove up to the house to put away the other provisions. The unopened letter from Jack lay on the counter and she eyed it with excitement. They had been in constant correspondence since her initial trip to Miami, and had become the best of friends. Jack was her confidant and mentor. Resisting the temptation to open it immediately at the Post Office, she had chosen instead to savor the potential, hoping, once again, that the letter would bear news of a forthcoming trip to Belize. So she fixed a cup of tea, sat down in an easy chair, and opened the envelope.

Alexis had barely begun to read the joyful news of Jack's impending arrival when she heard the commotion of barking dogs at the gate. A taxi had arrived from Cayo, bearing a single passenger. Her eyes flew wide open when she saw who it was, and she ran down the hill with winged feet.

"I can't believe you're really here," said Alexis, as Jack released her from a big bear hug.

"It's so great to see you. I can't tell you how curious I've been to see your ranch and riding operation after working together on the brochure. I am way overdue."

"Well, come on in and let's put your stuff upstairs in the guestroom," said Alexis. "You won't believe this, but I just got back from town, and I only opened your letter five minutes ago. What would you have done, if I hadn't been home?"

"Jumped your fence, made friends with your dogs, grazed from your garden, dug a comfortable nest in the forest, and waited for you," Jack laughed. "I never trifle with details."

A few minutes later, Alexis and Jack relaxed together outside on the veranda. The sun was setting, and the brilliant green mixed with pink-hued gold, creating a surreal quality. They leaned back on the cushioned wooden lounge chairs, drinking a glass of red wine, and enjoying each other's company. Before them stood the magnificent *llora sangre* tree with its spectacular hanging bromeliad.

"So," said Jack. "Tell me everything. The long version."

"Well, it's taken several years to get going, and the work is physically hard, but overall, the business has been doing great," Alexis told him. "Of course, I've also had some major obstacles. One of them is getting the guests here on time, which ties directly with the second problem – all the really good attractions on the trails are just a bit too far away. If the caves and waterfalls were only a mile or two closer, it really would make a difference, but they are where they are. Our tour group only has a certain amount of time to get to the falls, eat, swim, maybe stop at a cave, and get back in time to catch their taxi back to Tarpon Run. I'm always concerned that, one of these days, we'll all get caught in the bush at night with no supplies. If that does happen, hopefully it won't be pouring down rain as well."

"Can't you keep a cache of food or dry firewood out there somewhere?" Jack suggested.

"Not really. The trails branch out in many different directions. We cover so much territory that, chances are, if we got stranded on the trail, we wouldn't be anywhere near the cache. Besides, now that we've created these trails, local hunters use them, so any cache would be ransacked in no time. What we really need is to have a resort here on the ranch instead of always sub-contracting the lodging portion of our riding package. That way, if we got back late it wouldn't matter. And we'd be making a lot more money."

"Have you checked into financing a hotel operation?"

"I was hoping to toss that around with you," said Alexis. "We're losing too much money by having someone else provide the accommodations for the riding packages. I want to see if Ted would seriously consider turning this place into a full-scale resort. It's not a new thought, but the problem has always been the water supply. Rick and Suzy have the Macal River. We have one small *ojo de agua*. Americans are used to having water come from a tap. They don't think about where it's coming from when they shower, and you know how wasteful they are."

"That's true," Jack agreed. "And it's not just the showers. You'd need a full-blown restaurant too, instead of just your little cantina. You'd either have to find some investors or get financing from the bank. So what made you think about considering a resort now?"

"I was reviewing the bottom-line. This place is missing out on a big chunk of the profits by farming out the accommodations for the package tours. Ted's been very generous, but I don't know if I should push the envelope. After all, a major earthquake or a couple of hurricanes could bring tourism to a screeching halt. I suppose that, at some point or other, I need to get Ted to come down so we can talk about it."

Just then, a giant black and gold *oropendula*, largest member of the oriole family, warbled its unique call and flew across the yard into its huge woven basket-nest suspended from the limb of another large tree. Alexis excused herself briefly, went into the house and brought back the bottle of wine. She hugged him then, and refilling the glasses, they toasted.

"You know what's funny?" said Alexis, resuming her seat. "This lifestyle is what most people would wish for if they won the eight-figure lottery. Most people would give anything to live the way I do, but it's only good for a short fantasy. Once in a great while I'll invite a guest or two up here to the house, and you know what they say?"

"No. What?"

"First it's, 'Wow, what a beautiful view.' Then it's, 'Gee, it sure is quiet up here.' And then it's, 'what the hell do you do up here all day anyway?' See what I mean? They go from paradise to burn-out in sixty seconds."

Jack nodded. "So, when you're in the mood for entertainment, what do you do?"

"I remember the last time I decided to take myself out for a night on the town. I put on a dress and some nice shoes and decided to go to Belmopan and treat my self to a real restaurant. Except that it was raining like hell; the mud sucked one of my shoes right off my foot and the backs of my legs were splattered black before I ever made it to the truck. The pick-up leaked rusty water all over my dress – there's a small gap in the windshield seal – and then the truck got stuck in a big rut near the Jamaican's ranch on the Mountain Pine Ridge Road. By the time they pulled me out, all I wanted to do was go home. Even so, I still had to suffer the banging, leaking truck, and potholes all the way back."

Jack started to laugh softly. He knew the reality of life in the jungle.

"In retrospect, I guess it's funny," said Alexis. "But it wasn't funny then. So the next time I had the urge to go out, I put on my loincloth, drank a glass of red wine, and squatted bare-breasted next to the fire pit like a Neanderthal while I roasted an entire deer tenderloin." Now Alexis was laughing too. "And it was a much better evening."

"So you have this fantastic natural paradise, but that's all," said Jack. "You can't go to the movies, an art gallery, a museum, or a concert. You can't borrow books from a library, or take computer classes at a local community college. From one standpoint, this life has everything. But in other ways, you feel you have no real options for the future."

"Exactly," Alexis said with relief. He really did understand.

"What about your kids. Where do things stand?"

"I found a decent attorney named Errol Knight, and finally started proceedings seeking visitation rights for both kids. I realized I need to stand up to Max, not only for Jordan and Jessie, but for my parents, and myself. God knows I can't keep living this way. Max uses the children to punish me, and believe me, he's nothing short of an artist. I've simply got to find a legal solution so we can all go about our lives. And that's another thing – I need to look at the big picture and decide what I want to do for the next ten to twenty years. Maybe I should go back to the States. If I can't see my kids, what difference does it make which country I'm in? I need to make money, because money buys power, and there's no way I intend to be permanently tied to a madman who holds my heart on a leash."

"But enough about that for now," she changed the subject. "Will you be ready to ride tomorrow? Or will you want a day to recover from jet lag?"

"Jet lag? Never touch the stuff," Jack quipped. "I'll be ready to ride bright and early. What time do you usually get up?"

"Tsam will get here at about six. His three-wheeler is our alarm clock. Uberto and Genaro will be dressed and waiting for him to arrive. Then they'll round up whichever horses are on the list, while Tsam loads the tack on the truck and backs it out to the corral. As soon as the horses come in, all three of them will start grooming and saddling. Meanwhile, I'll be up here at the house getting the food together, packing the survival kit, preparing the lemonade, ice, and rum for afterwards. There's always a lot to do before a ride," she concluded. "So who do you want to hang out with in the morning?"

"Everyone," said Jack, smiling.

At five-thirty the following morning, Jack was already down the hill, chatting in Spanish with Uberto outside the corral in the early light before dawn. By the time Tsam arrived, the unlikely duo had already circled the far side of the herd on the two little mares, and had cut the selected horses from the herd. The local cowboys were impressed. *Señor* Madera was a man of the people. Once Tsam had the tack out at the corral, Jack stayed with the cowboys to help them saddle the tour horses. An hour later, he was back at the house in the kitchen asking if he could help Alexis. It was now eight-thirty, and the sixty-nine year old man, who had been helping everyone on the ranch for three hours, was now ready for a full day's adventure.

"BBB, Belize-By-Horseback. Come in. Tarpon Run. Over."

Alexis heard the two-way marine band radio, dried her hands on a dishtowel, and picked up the transmitter.

"Go ahead Tarpon Run. This is BBB, Belize-By-Horseback. Come back."

"Bad news, I'm afraid," said Rick. "Your riders have changed their minds. Over."

"Come back Tarpon Run? You say they've changed their minds? Are you saying they are not riding today? Over."

"That's a roger. The party has decided to go to Tikal instead."

"Bummer. Everything's ready on this end. I've got seven horses saddled and all the food packed. Did you inform them that they'll lose their deposits?"

"Roger. Affirmative. They say they don't care. They want to go to the ruins instead."

"Okay. Copy."

"Sorry, Alexis," Rick apologized. "I encouraged them as best I could. Apparently they're just too sore from diving yesterday in San Pedro."

"Okay, Rick, we copy. They're officially canceled. Thanks for the info. Anything else?"

"Negative BBB. This is Tarpon Run. Out."

Alexis sighed as she hung up the transmitter. "Now, you see what I mean?"

"I can see it's not fair. Yet it's no one's fault," Jack sympathized. "If those folks were staying here, it wouldn't matter if they changed their minds. You could just take them on the tour to Tikal instead, or just let them hang around the ranch. You'd still be making money."

"Right."

"So what do we do now?" asked Jack.

"Well, on one hand, I'm bummed out, but on the other hand, I feel really liberated. Let's go anyway. It'll be fun. We won't have to deal with guests, so we'll be able to move as fast or as slow as we want. Do you have any preferences as to where we go?"

"Oh, I'd love to go to someplace totally different," he said. "Do you have anything special on reserve?"

"You know, as a matter of fact, Tsam and Uberto were telling me about a cave they just found," said Alexis. "A new one. An untouched cave is extremely rare around here. This one is southeast of Lazzaro on the way to Baron's Creek. Tsam said it looked undisturbed. But it has a real tricky entry, pretty scary, but of course—"

"—the more difficult the entry, the better the find," said Jack, knowingly.

"Exactly!" Alexis laughed. Jack would be the perfect companion.

With Jack on Ash, and Alexis on Cisco, they rode side by side while Tsam set the pace on Trigger. The dew sparkled in the morning sunlight, and doves cooed in the treetops. It was a rare treat not having any tourists along, and Alexis was able to finally ask Jack some of the many questions on her mind.

"So would you consider yourself a professional adventurer?"

"I don't really consider myself to be anything," Jack answered, unpretentiously. "I take pictures and write articles on the places I go. I don't try to analyze beyond that. I'm too busy living it."

Alexis nodded. "Helen Keller said, 'Life is an adventure, or nothing at all.' You're lucky that family doesn't hold you back."

"Years ago I had extensive business and family ties. But at this stage of my life – yes, I can do what I want. People are the hardest concession. You can compromise your own time, or even your personal interests, because they are your own. But in our society, we're obliged to accommodate the feelings of those we love, and we violate a whole array of emotional taboos if we don't. For example, suppose two people are sight-seeing together. Isn't it silly that they have to check with each other, so they can make a united decision about when to move on down the street, or when to linger a bit longer? I can't tell you the number of times I've witnessed or experienced something extraordinary that other people passed up, just because one of them was in a hurry. That's why I travel alone most of the time. I have a feel for serendipity. Alone, I can explore what's around the corner, and do so at my leisure."

Alexis ducked under a low-hanging bush that Tsam had missed. She swung expertly with her *machete*, clearing the trail for Jack to follow.

"So you're more of a loner than a people-person?"

"Not exactly. I guess I'd describe myself as a gregarious loner," said Jack, and Alexis laughed again. The description was most fitting, for both Jack and herself.

Riding in a northeasterly direction through the bush, they broke into a clearing. Heading east along a fence line, a flock of parrots squawked raucously overhead, while small creatures scampered away into the underbrush, frightened at the riders' approach.

Jack had been to nearly every country in the world, except for a few of the most obscure islands. Latin American culture was his favorite, and he visited Central or South America at least a half dozen times a year. He'd been attacked in the Amazon when some unfriendly natives shot poison arrows at him. Luckily, the arrows missed, but when one got stuck in a tree, he went back and calmly retrieved it as a souvenir. He'd eaten strange foods like mealy worms, snake meat, and moose nose. Once in China, he'd had noodles served with pond scum.

"It was actually quite good, and I've eaten lots of insects – cockroaches, beetles, caterpillars, and grubs. Most of them aren't bad toasted on the fire. They have lots of protein."

Alexis learned quickly that Jack either had guardian angels, or a guiding star. Almost all of his travel was spent exploring the nether regions of the world, through jungles, crossing oceans, or climbing mountains. He avoided cities and traveled lightly, carrying only personal documents, cameras, film, money, and a change of clothes. Most of the time, he slept in the open air, and his journeys were mostly via horse, mule, raft, truck, canoe, sailboat, windsurfer, or on foot. Jack ate whatever nature provided. Fruit, fish, or snails; it didn't matter. And when there was nothing to eat, he went without. There was no competition between them. She applauded his heartiness, but preferred her adventure in the daytime. At night, she wanted a hot shower, with some nice clean sheets, and no bugs.

"The longer the deprivation, the more intense the pleasure," he continued. "You know that feeling at the end of the day when you're browned, hungry, overexposed, and exhausted? Then finally you find a river to bathe in, you put on a clean *dhoti*, and you're offered a simple meal. Afterwards you sit on a rock and watch the sun go down. It is the ultimate moment of being."

About an hour had passed, and the riders were now in deep jungle. There was very little light and, as it was not an established trail, Alexis and Tsam had to swing their machetes often and with precision, just to get through. All around them were magnificent tropical giants, laden with bromeliads and orchids, and festooned with creeping lianas, and strangler figs. Just ahead, they caught a glimpse of Tsam as he dismounted by some giant boulders and signaled. They tied their horses and Alexis started to remove the headlamps and ropes from the saddlebags when Tsam stopped her.

"I could do it, Miss Alexis," said Tsam. *"Just pass between dese rocks. Dey mek a circle inside. Wait fu me dere. I will bring de lights."*

Following Tsam's directive, Jack and Alexis slipped between the huge stones and found that, indeed, the rocks formed a circular enclosure, a sanctuary of sorts, well-hidden from the outside. Within the perimeter was a hole about twenty feet in diameter. Perfectly round with straight sides, it was as if a large geometric plug had been pulled out of the ground. An ancient mahogany tree perched on the edge of the hole, its gnarled roots gripping the side of the pit like writhing snakes.

"This place," said Alexis. "It's incredible."

"Sentinels of stone," Jack mused, as he stared at the boulders.

Moments later, Tsam appeared suddenly. He looped the rope around the mahogany tree, tied a bowline knot, and leaned back with all of his weight to test it. Again, Tsam was fanatical about ropes when it came to caving. It would be their lifeline.

"Ready?" asked Tsam. *"Yu want dat I go first?"*

"Sure. Go ahead Tsam. You've been here before," Alexis conceded. "Lead the way."

In turn, each of them used the rope to descend the fifteen feet to the bottom. From topside, the floor of the pit looked relatively flat, but as Alexis landed she found that it was spongy with debris. Besides the leaf mold of countless seasons, the compost undoubtedly contained several million seed-ticks and probably a yellow-jaw or two. The footing was so uneven it was impossible to tell which mounds were soft, which were jagged rock, or which might be concealing cool reptilian flesh.

As they crossed to the opposite side, Alexis noticed a small opening at the base of the far wall. The triangular shape had been created by a wide stalactite, obscuring most of the aperture. To access the cave, the three explorers would have to squeeze through this triangle which was no more than seventeen inches at the apex and twelve inches at the base.

"What's on the other side, Tsam? Is it flat? Or does it go up, or down, or what?"

"To tell yu dis truth, I never seen inside dat cave. Genaro was de one who looked inside wit' de flashlight. Betta we check it firs' before we go thru."

"I'll do it," Jack volunteered. Without hesitation, he crouched low and poked his head and shoulders through the triangular hole.

"Looks good," he said. "We'll be on top of a boulder. Then there's a short drop on the other side of maybe a few feet. I can't really see much of what's beyond. But it definitely opens up into a chamber."

"Good enough," said Alexis. Lying down, she wriggled sideways, and barely squeezed through on her hip. Sliding over the rounded boulder, she dropped feet-first onto the sandy ground. Seconds later, Tsam and Jack were there beside her, and they squatted together in the semi-darkness, waiting for their eyes to adjust.

The same excitement always gripped Alexis at the beginning of such an expedition. There was a heightening of the senses, her nose and ears overcompensating for her restricted vision. From deep inside, a solitary bat squeaked, and there was the faint echo of a dripping stalactite. She sensed the pressure within the living rock, and felt its darkness as an entity. No one spoke. The three secured their headlamps and prepared to go deeper. Alexis knew through experience that, unlike the movies, real caves didn't have smooth level floors or predictable tunnels with gentle curves and conveniently placed columns and stalactites. In this world of subterranean wonder, the size and dimensions of caves was limited only by the imagination. Some caves consisted of a network of chaotic fissures that fractured upward through the rock like spider webs, or the branches of a tree. Caves of that type often revealed vertical drops of hundreds or even thousands of feet. Some ran horizontally for miles. Other caves could barely be considered caves at all. Mere crawl spaces, they were nothing more than separations between the rocky strata where the spelunker's body might be wedged between ceiling and floor with their faces in the dust and no room to turn around. Real caves were replete with treachery in all forms – loose shale, spiky ceilings, crevasses, falling rock, oozing minerals, crags and peaks, sheer drops, jagged edges, and steep inclines coated with greasy clay. A caver, thinking his footing safe, might be, at any time, walking on a paper-thin limestone shell above a bottomless pit.

The horizontal shafts of ivory light from their headlamps cut through the gloom of the cave, illuminating millions of dust particles that swirled in the vacuum created by their moving bodies. The cave was dank, poorly ventilated, and musky with bat guano. Shining his headlight as they crept deeper, Tsam was first to notice the smudges of carbon along the bottom of the far stone wall. Then Jack found charred matter, wedged between the crevices of the rocks.

"The Mayas must have put corn-cob torches in these spots to light their way," said Alexis. "Imagine how much oxygen a fire would consume in here. It seems like it would be suffocating."

"You never know," said Jack. "It could have been much different back then. Seismic activity could have shifted things. There might have been more air holes to the surface."

Tsam was still far ahead and to the left, and now his voice was full of excitement.

"Mista. Jack, Miss Alexis! Come back dis way! See dis back here! It look like de

floor drop!"

"Just a minute," said Jack. "I'm coming." He turned to extend a hand to Alexis but found she was no longer behind him.

"I'm over here." Her voice also came from ahead, perhaps a dozen yards to the right of Tsam. "I'll be there in a minute. I just saw a big round...oh my God!"

Both Jack and Tsam scrambled over the broken rocks to her side.

"Look at this giant pot!" Alexis cried. "It's enormous, and completely intact! This is the largest unbroken Mayan pot I've ever seen."

"Big, fu true," Tsam agreed.

"The Mayas always shattered their pottery in a yearly ritual," Jack said. "Why isn't this broken? Something must have happened here."

"Dat's what I start to tell yu before," said Tsam. *Yu must come back wit' me and see over de edge."*

"In a minute, Tsam." Alexis could hardly take her eyes from the perfect clay pot. Although the temperature in the cave was relatively cool, she was sweating from the exertion and excitement. Little rivulets of perspiration had snaked through the fine coating of dust on her arms and hands. "Well, I know one thing. Nobody could have stolen this pot from the cave, even if they'd been able to find it. Look at the size of it. Bigger than the opening we crawled through to get in here."

"Good point," said Jack. "How old do you think it is? I would guess mid-classic to late classic period. How about you, Alexis? You're pretty good at rough-dating."

"Well, the lack of polychromic finish, and the fact that there's no geometric design would suggest mid-classic, but I think it is actually late classic. My suspicion is that the only reason it lacks the fancy paint-work is because it's not a ceremonial piece. This was for utilitarian use. Look there. Aren't those more fragments?"

Tsam had disappeared again. Now he called to them once more from the precipice ahead, this time more insistently. *"I really t'ink yu should come see dis."*

"Okay, we're coming," said Alexis, clambering over the rock fall. "What did you find?"

The diffused light of Tsam's headlamp focused on the stalactites of the vaulted ceiling ahead. The three explorers inched closer to the brink and stared over the edge.

"The floor is gone," Alexis gasped. "Like the bottom dropped out and disappeared."

"Except for the shelf over there," said Jack. "See that lip along the side?"

"I want to go down there," said Alexis, with finality.

"Yu wan' to go down more? We no got more ropes unless I go get de udder ones from de saddles."

"Yes, please Tsam. And the extra batteries for the headlamps too. We might be here a little while."

"I come back direc'ly." Within seconds Tsam had disappeared.

"You feel the vibes too, don't you?" said Jack.

"Intensely," Alexis replied. "Somehow, I feel sure that we are the first human beings to be in this cave in five or six hundred years. It's so different from every cave I've ever been in. You can see it by looking around. No footprints, no evidence of anything having been touched. Look at all the pot shards. Every speck of dust on the surface of the fragments is undisturbed."

"But there's more you're feeling, isn't there?"

"Yes. Something dramatic happened here," she said, almost trance-like. "I feel a sense of transience and fragility. Something extraordinary. Passion and terror."

"I feel it too. I have goose bumps all over my body," said Jack. "There's always excitement in caves, but there's something more. It feels strangely sacred. I can't explain it. But whatever it is, the answer's down there."

It took a full ten minutes before Tsam returned with the extra equipment. He secured the additional ropes on a sturdy stalagmite about two feet from the edge of the drop-off.

"Yu sure yu wan' to do dis, Miss Alexis?" asked Tsam. He would never get used to the *cojones* of this particular white woman. Belizean women were subservient in every way, spending their days in the kitchen, stirring pots, and making tortillas. Alexis ignored him.

"Since there's no footing directly below, you'll have to push hard off the wall and then drop over to the shelf on the other side," said Jack. "That's the only piece that didn't collapse. But even so, it may not be solid. You really should have a harness and proper rock climbing equipment for this."

"So I'll tie the rope around me," said Alexis. "A loop around my back and one under my butt. If it can't be done, or the lip collapses, you guys can always haul me up."

"Be careful, Alexis," Jack cautioned. "This wall below us is new flowstone. Those quartz crystals are like razors. We can't let the rope touch them."

She looped the rope around her, and let Tsam create the makeshift harness. Then she turned and inched backwards over the edge of the precipice while the men paid out the line. Careful not to look down, she focused on the white sparkling wall in front of her eyes and tried not to think of the pit below. Suddenly her foot slipped and she fell hard against the jagged wall. Sharp quartz sliced through her pant leg and cut into her thigh. She winced but did not cry out.

"Yu okay?"

"Yes, I'm almost level with the shelf. I'm going to count to three and then push hard off this wall with my feet. You'll need to let out about another four feet of rope so I can drop onto the shelf. Without the extra rope, I'll miss the angle, swing back, and smack this wall."

"OK. No problem," said Jack. "I'll judge the drop and Tsam will pay out the last few feet. Are you ready? You'll have to push hard."

"Yeah, I got it. Ready? One – two – three."

In coordinated effort, Alexis swung across the crevasse and dropped on the far shelf, absorbing the impact with her knees. For a few seconds, she waited for the rocky shelf to crumble under her weight, but nothing happened. For the moment, her footing seemed secure. Trembling with exhilaration she took a few steps, moving around the large chunks of rock and pot shards that littered the limestone shelf.

It was then that Alexis saw a sight so macabre she was sure her vision had betrayed her. There were bones. Small human bones, vertebrae. A scapula, part of a clavicle, a few ribs. As if in a dream, she bent down to examine that which could not possibly be real. Yet, it was real. The skull of a human child lay in the dust at her feet, impaled by a great spear of limestone.

Kneeling beside the fragile remains, Alexis picked up the small ancient skull and held history in her hands. Faces of the past seemed to swarm around her in silent echoes. Overwhelmed by the spell, the hairs on the back of her neck stood on end, and a cold chill passed through her body. Alexis tried to imagine what might have come to pass on that fateful day of the child's death. How had an infant gotten inside the cave? And why had the child died alone?

Tsam rode ahead on the way home and left Jack and Alexis immersed in their own thoughts. She was overwhelmed, and still lost in the afterglow.

"You're very quiet," said Jack.

"How could I not be after what we saw today? I can't think of anything else."

"Me neither. I've seen many archaeological sites in my life, but the feeling inside that cave was rare, and powerful. You could feel such presence."

"A child. Such a young child," she murmured.

"Speaking of children, tell me more about the legal proceedings." said Jack.

"Mr. Knight is working on it," said Alexis, "but we're still trying to get a court date. The idea of fighting Max still terrifies me. I'm the only one who really knows how dirty he plays. Seeking visitation is scary enough, but now things are even more difficult."

"Why? What happened?"

"Because the last time I saw Jessica, she started crying and said that she doesn't want to live with her dad; she wants to live with me full time. Meanwhile, Jordan doesn't want to live with me; he is quite happy living with his father. Can you imagine changing the lawsuit – filing for custody of my daughter, and only visitation for my son?" Alexis shook her head. "He's eleven now, very much influenced by Max, and his attitude has always been not to rock the boat."

"And you don't agree?" Jack said, gently.

"It's smarter and more realistic than you might think. My son knows his dad, and so do I. Jordan figures that shaking things up is not worth the risk. Unfortunately, not rocking the boat adds up to exactly what I did during my ten years of marriage – just taking it. I don't have the courage to fight him, and I don't have the stomach to keep taking it either."

Ash tossed his head, as if in agreement, and Jack stroked the big gray's neck to sooth him.

"That could get very difficult."

"Especially if I don't know if I want to stay in Belize forever. What will I do if I want to leave? Ted may or may not be interested in building accommodations here, and his decision will have an impact on whether I stay. That's why I'm doing everything I can to reach a legal resolution. I have to find closure so I can move forward with my life. If I could win custody of both children, I could leave and go back to the States if I wanted to, and get away from Max's influence once and for all. But if I win custody for Jessica, and only visitation for Jordan, I'll end up staying here in Belize and fighting with Max for the rest of my life. Worse yet, if I lose both visitation and custody, I'll lose both of my children forever. As it is, Max could go back to South Africa." She fought for control; her voice quavered. "I feel like I am doomed to lose my daughter in one grim scenario, and doomed to lose my son either way! What kind of a choice is it – going back to the States alone, or staying near the kids I can't have?"

"Isn't it better to keep one of your kids than to lose both?

Alexis looked into Jack's eyes and felt the tears welling up inside.

"I can't even begin to deal with that. It's Sophie's Choice. You're talking about sacrificing one child so I can have the other. How would Jordan feel if he thought that I had chosen Jessie over him – even if he doesn't want to live with me?" She tried to envision the years ahead – a future in which she could not clearly see the images of her children. Suddenly, it was a future that now seemed just as uncertain as it ever had.

The jungle trail before them opened up into a nice stretch of flat with a banana plantation on the left and a large fenced field of peanuts to the right. A toucan flew across their path, its festoon-like flight pattern unmistakable. Cisco was ready to run so Alexis urged him forward into a gallop, and Jack kicked Ash into gear as well. After flying over the terrain for a quarter mile or so, they reined in their animals, and Jack pulled up beside her.

He looked over at Alexis, smiled, and then sighed. "I have a son."

"You do?" she queried. "I thought you only had the three girls with Marina."

"I was married before, and I had a son by my first wife," said Jack. "I almost never see him. Jackie and I just don't have anything in common."

"How can that be?" she asked. "He's not an adventurer like you?"

"Adventurer?" Jack laughed. "Actually, he's kind of a redneck. He likes country western music, drinks beer, and works a blue-collar job. He cares nothing about the arts, and hates to travel. He lives right in Miami. I have seen him twice in seven or eight years. If he calls me on the phone, which is maybe once a year, we have nothing to talk about. He's never even sent me a birthday card."

"I can't relate to that. Doesn't it bother you?"

"No, not anymore," said Jack. "You see, the older you get, the more you realize that you can't always be close to someone just because you're related to them. Relationships, be they blood or otherwise, take time and care and nurturing. Sometimes the basis for a relationship just isn't there. That's how it is with my son."

"I don't want it to be like that with Jordan. I love him and he loves me."

"Then it will work out. It may be sooner than you think, or it may take a long time. Things may get tougher for you before they get easier. But, even if everything falls apart for a few years, life spans many decades. The kids will grow up, and they'll seek you out."

"You talk as if I've already lost them."

"Not at all. I'm just trying to give you an overview," he counseled. "I have learned to see things on a broad spectrum in all my years of living. Believe me. Time has a way of working these things out."

"Things never worked out with Max."

"He is not your child. Max is a batterer – a controller, with a need to convince you that you were responsible for everything. He fits the profile perfectly. The insults and threats, the physical punishing, then the please-forgive-me-it-will-never-happen-again."

"But in all fairness, he was a victim too."

"Oh, come on! You're not defending him, are you?" Jack said, surprised.

"No, I'm just saying he had a past to overcome, a tough life when he was growing up. Max's mother was a tyrant. During his school years, he lived in a youth hostel away from home. Later, he was a despised member of a minority group in somebody else's army. Then, on top of it all, the girl he loved ran away with his best friend. Max has had some tough breaks. It wasn't easy for him. I guess what I'm trying to say is, aren't we all shaped by the parameters of our upbringing?"

"We are and we aren't. Blaming one's faults on childhood is just a convenient rationalization. If a person grows up with a certain inadequacy or handicap, a limitation, a dubious background, or any weakness they're aware of – then isn't it their responsibility to work extra hard in those particular areas? To overcome them, and in doing so, encourage their growth as healthy spiritual beings on the planet? The point is that Max had a choice to remain a victim of his past, or to define his personal problems and work to overcome them. Unfortunately, he chose to remain blind."

"Does that mean my children will also be victims of their experience? Will Jordan beat his wife? Do you think Jessica will hate men?"

"No one can know the future. But Belize doesn't breed wimps. Remember, they have their mother's blood too."

Alexis smiled. "Do you think there's a God, Jack?"

"You mean the kind that watches over our every move as we go about our daily living? No, I don't think so. There was probably a Great Spirit, or God Force that got things started, and I think we humans have been, pretty much, screwing it up ever since. It's all about freewill."

At that exact moment, Alexis saw a golden ray of late afternoon sunshine strike the canary-yellow flowers of a Cortez tree in full bloom, electrifying and illuminating it, a brilliant beacon that could be seen for miles.

THE LAST RESORT

chapter 19

With the seasonal rains of June, the flowers seemed to burst forth from every green living thing, adding a bold element of vibrant color to the landscape. Unlike the typical three-month break in the States, school vacation in Belize was a short seven weeks, and Max had promised that the kids would spend the first half of the summer with their mother on the ranch. Alexis had already made arrangements with her Belizean cowboys that, as long as the kids were visiting, they would be in charge of leading most of the tours. Not to say that the children didn't enjoy the trails. Already Jordan handled his small gelding with strength and finesse, and tough little Jessica clung to her mother, straddled bravely behind her on Cisco or Ash. But when hosting tourists, Alexis was still on the job, and responsible for everyone's safety and well-being, so it was important that she spend quality off-time with her kids as well, just talking, teaching, playing, and interacting.

They were all sitting on the floor of the living room, playing cards, laughing, and listening to music when the call came in over the radio. As if delivering a summons, Max abruptly informed Alexis that the kids were booked to fly with him to southern California where they would stay until school started. Disney was his red herring. It was great news for Jordan and Jessica, and bad news for Alexis. Their visit had lasted a mere four days.

"Disneyland!" shouted Jordan. "Yay! Daddy's going to take us to Disneyland!" He jumped up and started dancing around the room.

"Are we going to see Mickey Mouse?" Jessica asked, shyly.

"Oh yes. Mickey, and Donald, and Pluto – and Goofy too," the eleven-year old replied with the authority of a well-informed older sibling. "And there will be rides and hot dogs and shows and music..."

Alexis tried to hide her feelings in front of the children, but inside, she was crushed. She couldn't deny them Disneyland, and Max knew it. Yet, he had legal custody, and she had no rights. There was nothing to do except let them go, and simply persist in getting the case heard as soon as possible. But there was something else, something more.

In the still of night, when Alexis lay in bed, alone in the house, alone with her thoughts, a dark force nagged and filled her with dread. Why was it that, just when her case got close to being on the docket, civil hearings were discontinued, and the venue changed to criminal sessions? Everyone in her inner circle had encouraged her to pursue legal recourse. Yet, since February, she'd gotten four court dates, and four times it had been postponed. At one point, she'd begun to suspect Max might have administrators or judges in his pocket, and now she was starting to believe it was true. And if so, that meant she was dealing with a crooked system, and the whole effort would be in vain. Besides, she wasn't a Belizean, she thought bitterly. What did anyone care if some obscure *gringa* was granted justice?

As a result, a two-fold certainty crept icily over her mind: one, it didn't make sense to fight unless she could win; and two, it was dangerous for Max to put her in a position where she had nothing to lose. After all, Alexis thought grimly, if the legal battle dragged on long enough, the law just wouldn't matter anymore.

The next day when she dropped off the children, Alexis tried to avoid Max's eyes. She didn't want to see him gloating or his look of triumph as she kissed the children goodbye.

"Bye Mum," said Jordan happily. "I'll send you a postcard from Disneyland."

"Me too, Ma," echoed Jessica. "I'll get Angelina to help me write one. And, you know what?" She beckoned to her mother to come close. Alexis got down on one knee and listened to her little girl whisper in her ear, "Next year I'm going to stay with you for the whole summer," she stated simply.

Six months passed and just after the Christmas holiday, Ted came to visit the ranch. Again, the cowboys handled the guiding duties, and for the next three days, he and Alexis realistically researched the idea of a resort on the property. A potential site was chosen on the north hill, and Ted brought in a surveyor and a drilling expert to evaluate the lay of the land and the water supply. After compiling the results, he put together a realistic prospectus of approximate costs and returns. Although Ted was a wealthy doctor, for an enterprise like this, he would need more.

Approaching the Belizean banks turned out to be a colossal joke, as there was no such thing as a long-term inexpensive loan. All lending programs were short-term, nothing longer than ten years, with a ridiculously high interest rate. He calculated it would cost about four hundred and fifty thousand dollars to borrow two hundred and fifty thousand. In short, the expenses would be overwhelming and the returns, an illusion.

Now, as Alexis and Ted sat together on the veranda of the hexagonal house watching the sun set, she wondered if the sun was also setting on what she now thought of as "the last resort."

"…So throughout the course of ten years, the total amount of the loan, including interest, would be almost twice the cost of the principle," Ted explained. "Plus, the interest rate stinks, and the collateral is intolerable. We'd have to put up the entire ranch and everything on it."

"What! That's insane!" she cried.

"Yep," he said, shaking his head. "Think about it. The ranch, the horses, the tack, the trails, the cantina, all the work that you've done with regard to networking, contacts, agencies, all the international riding packages with the wholesalers I helped line up – everything that makes this business function. According to the bank manager, it would take everything, just for another roll of the dice. We'd be gambling there would be no substantial fluctuations in the world market, nothing to prevent people from spending money on overseas vacations, no earthquakes, no hurricanes, and no major wars – for ten whole years."

"Yes, I understand," Alexis admitted. "It was a good thought and I appreciate your consideration. You've done so much already, and I'm grateful."

"Hey, you're the one who's made it happen. I may own the ranch, but it's been your business from the start," said Ted. "You've been honorable in every way, and I've gotten profits every month for, how long now? Two years?"

"Almost three on the profits," she said, "but we've been operational for almost four."

"Well," said Ted, sighing heavily, "I can't swing the finances for a resort, but I'll do whatever you want. There's no pressure. I am well-aware of your situation with the kids, and I know my decision will greatly impact your decision. So, here's the offer: we can keep things as they are, with you running the riding business as is, with no accommodations, or we can get someone else to run it, so you can leave Belize, if that's what you want. It's your choice."

"I don't know how to feel – happy or sad," said Alexis. "But I guess certain things have to fall out of the equation in order for me to fine-line my choices. Let me see how it goes with the court case. Depending on what happens, and how soon, it will either influence or dictate a direction."

More time passed. The dry season ended, and with it had come more court dates and postponements. After months and months of sparse and sporadic visits, summer had arrived again, and at least now Alexis would have a long unbroken visit with her children, the first such opportunity in several years.

But times had changed. Jordan and Jessica were growing up, and Alexis found they could no longer be treated collectively as "the children." They were two very different young people with minds of their own. Jordan felt that this school holiday should be like any other, shared by both parents, three and a half weeks each. On the other hand, seven-year old Jessica was determined to spend the entire summer with her mother to make up for the previous one. From the beginning of the visit, Jordan seemed quiet and sullen. Although he enjoyed the ranch and horseback riding, his heart didn't seem to be in it, and after just a few days he told his mother he was bored. He missed his buddies, his soccer games, his bike, and his new Nintendo. Not wanting her son to be unhappy, Alexis returned Jordan to Max's house after only one week on the ranch. Regardless of her own feelings, she had always put his happiness first. Conversely, little Jessica was thrilled to be spending the time with her mother. She never seemed to tire of the riding, waterfalls, and caves, especially now that she was big enough to ride solo on her own horse, instead of sitting behind Alexis. Tsam had fashioned a custom pair of shorty stirrups, so she could get enough lift off the saddle. Guests and guides alike admired her endurance. Jessica paid close attention to her mother's trail commentary, and soon she was parroting the information to the tourists, answering their questions as junior guide *extraordinaire*.

Three weeks later Max called on the radio. Half of the summer was over, and now he wanted Jessica to return home.

But Daddy, you're not being fair," Jessica argued into the transmitter, "I was with you all of last summer when we went to California. So this summer I get to stay with Mommy the whole time."

"You listen to me," Max's voice crackled angrily over the radio. "You're coming home. You're my daughter, and the law says you belong to me. You're only up there on the ranch because I was nice enough to let you. Now look what I get for it. Nothing but trouble."

"You're only going to push her away," Alexis broke in. "Have you no feelings for what Jessica wants or needs?"

"This has nothing to do with her feelings," he made the pronouncement. "This is a legal issue. Now, are you bringing her back or what?"

"Jordan wanted to go back, so I brought him back. Jessie doesn't want to go back, so I'm not going to make her," argued Alexis.

"Well, I've got news for you. If you think you're going to keep my daughter away from me, there's going to be trouble," he threatened. "Big trouble."

True to his word, Max showed up at the front gate with a local policeman the next afternoon. The German shepherds barked angrily at the would-be intruders, baring their teeth, so even Max didn't dare to cross the line. His face was scowling and vicious. Alexis knew that look. She was afraid, and grateful for the dogs' protection.

All around them, again nature had bloomed in all its wet season glory. The royal poincianas over their heads had put forth a riot of orange flowers, and the giant crepe myrtle nearby was engulfed in a lavender mist of blossoms. In this setting of verdant gardens, bright flower beds, and tropical birds overhead, it was hard to reconcile the paradox of contrasting beauty and unnecessary ugliness.

"I told you," explained Alexis, from the other side of the gate. "Jessica doesn't want to go with you."

"You're only telling me what you want. I don't believe you're speaking for her. Bring her down here," Max insisted angrily. "Let her tell me herself."

Alexis went back up the hill, and Jessica returned with her. Dragging her feet, the little girl began to cry as she saw her father pacing angrily back and forth on the other side of the gate. She trembled as she clung to her mother's hand, but made her opinion clear when she reached the gate.

"Dad, I told you I want to stay here." Turning to Alexis, she cried, "Mommy, please don't make me go. I want to stay with you."

"She's a seven-year-old girl, Max," said Alexis, kneeling down and hugging her tight. "Girls need to be with their mothers. Can't you understand that?"

"Look. I didn't come here to argue. I've come for my daughter. I have custody, and I demand you give her to me."

Jessica was first vehement, then angry. "Dad, I told you I want to be with Mommy! You don't even spend time with me when I am at your house. You just lie in the hammock and make me pour your smelly whiskeys for you! Besides, Mommy doesn't spank me with a stick."

Max's face colored at the truth. Then his temper snapped, and he went for the latch on the gate in an attempt to open it. The guard dogs charged him, roaring and snapping, and he backed off in haste.

"I wouldn't do that if I were you. They bite," Alexis assured him.

"So you're refusing then?" Max shouted. "It's official? I have a witness here you know."

"Yes," said Alexis, angrily. "I see. Witnessed by this officer. I understand. Now get the hell off this property, and go get yourself a warrant. In fact, why don't you just go back to South Africa with the rest of the human rights oppressors?"

For the very first time, Max had lost a round. There was nothing more to be said. He spun on his heel, got into the truck and left. And in spite of the aggressive confrontation, the rest of the summer passed without incident. The long-range radio at BBB received no signals from the Lost Gringo Trading Company. It was obvious that Max was biding his time, and Alexis was grateful for the radio silence, even if it was ominous.

The pace had been rigorous throughout the summer. Guiding duties had to be constantly rotated between Tsam, Alexis, Uberto, and Genaro. Yet, almost without exception, Jessica went along on every ride her mother led, proudly seated on Snickers, and reining the filly with a firm hand. In fact, she was such a good role model that many guests were embarrassed into jumping a stream, or entering a spooky cave, just because they saw a little girl do it. Indeed, after Tsam's discovery of another untouched cave, which Jessica proudly named White Hawk, she enjoyed the distinction of being the first child in modern history to explore its ancient secrets. The ties of love between mother and daughter strengthened dramatically that summer, and it served to console them both. Every night Alexis tucked Jessica into bed, read her stories, and said prayers with her. During their waning season of togetherness, she used the time to instill a sense of values in her daughter, to teach her to be strong and understand that life was not always fair. Alexis' happiness was only overshadowed by two things: a sinking feeling of having lost touch with Jordan, and the innate certainty that this quiet summer with Jessica would be the last calm before the storm.

Alexis and Jessica were both in a fine mood as they skipped up the steps to the second floor Post Office at Central Farm. It was late August and only a week was left before school started. Tsam and Genaro were on the tour for the day, so Alexis had taken her daughter to run a few errands. They bought their stamps at the window and picked up the mail. Jessica stood close to her mother, holding her hand. But just as they turned to leave, Alexis found herself face to face with Max Lord. He snarled at her with that familiar black scowl and snatched up the little girl, physically tearing her away from her mother.

"Don't, Daddy! No!" Jessica screamed. "Let me down. Stop it! Leave me alone."

"I knew I'd catch you sooner or later, you bitch," Max growled at Alexis. "I saw the truck and knew I had you cornered. No bad-ass dogs are going to protect you this time."

"I was going to bring her back in a few days anyway," Alexis insisted. "The summer's over. Don't make it end like this. She's been traumatized enough."

"Traumatized by you," he sneered, as he pulled her to the top of the staircase. "You're the one who created the problems by not respecting the law. I'm the one who has legal custody, remember?"

"As if you'd ever let me forget?"

"Daddy, no. Please!" cried Jessica, struggling to get down. "At least let me kiss Mommy goodbye."

"You've had all summer to do that. We're outta here."

Max turned and manhandled Jessica down the steps. She continued to squirm and struggle to get away, so he gripped her harder.

"You're hurting me, Daddy! Stop squeezing me. You're hurting my arm!"

Alexis ran down the stairs after them, her heart breaking at the look on Jessie's face, her arms stretched out imploringly. As they got to Max's truck, she reached towards her daughter, but Max seized her by the shirt collar, pulling it tight around her neck, and cutting off her air flow.

"Stay out of this, God damn it!" he shouted. "Or, I swear, this time I'll kill you. I'll take a shotgun, hunt you down like a fucking animal, and tack your stinking hide on the wall of my tool shed. Now back off! Jessica, get in that truck, now!"

He opened the passenger's door and shoved the little girl onto the seat, locking the door behind her. As he walked to the driver's side, Jessica made a last ditch effort to unlock it and get out before Max hauled her roughly back across the seat.

"Jordan!" Max shouted. "Come on out of there. Let's go!"

Alexis had been unaware of her son's presence, but suddenly, Jordan jumped out from behind some bushes and climbed in the back of the truck.

"How could you, Mom?" Jordan rebuked her. "How could you not bring Jessie back? You were supposed to let her spend half the summer with Dad and me, but you kept her instead. You broke the law. How could you do it? Why do you keep making trouble for us?"

Max turned the key and sawed the wheel viciously. The engine roared to life and the truck sped down the dirt road, leaving Alexis in a cloud of dust. Tears rolled furiously down her cheeks.

"I'm so sorry, Jordan," she whispered her reply. "I did what I've always done – what I had to do."

Alexis' neck was bruised and swollen. The doctor at the hospital explained that since the neck was a vital area, the injury could be considered 'assault and grievous harm.' As Alexis was no longer Max's wife, he could no longer hide behind the "rule of thumb." So she decided to file charges against him – the very first time he'd ever been held accountable for his abuse. At first she was pleased to take a stand, but once again the plan backfired. Max retaliated by refusing to let Alexis see the children, period, until the assault charges had been dropped.

Time dragged on, and aside from once or twice when she was able to catch them at lunch or in the school yard, her isolation was complete. Months went by without a visit to the ranch until finally, in late November, Jessica called her on the radio, begging her to comply with Max's demand. Alexis felt like she was dying inside. Her inner spirit told her not to give in, otherwise, when would it end? But her maternal instincts couldn't stand it anymore; she was only flesh and blood. Yet Max had to be shown the line – it was the very first time she ever had documented medical evidence. Finally she had something solid; she couldn't give in now. But how much longer could she hold out?

At last, the assault case was heard in a tiny courtroom in Belmopan, and it was an unmitigated disaster. Max denied ever touching Alexis. Jordan testified against his mother. The medical documentation at the hospital had mysteriously disappeared, and the case was thrown out. In the end, Alexis had gained nothing by making her stand against Max, other than to widen the gulf between herself and her son. It had been almost nine months since Jordan had visited the ranch. Alexis didn't blame him, nor did she love him any less. Caught in a tangle of emotions that threatened to tear him apart, Jordan only wanted peace. It was all he had ever wanted. The boy was not blind to the failings of either of his parents, and in his own way, was fiercely loyal to both. But, like all the other players, he was most driven by his own pain. Jordan merely did what he felt he had to do.

* * * *

Tree ferns were her favorite, but Alexis also adored orchids, and now she had a collection of almost two hundred varieties thriving on the second-floor veranda. Every once in a while, the cowboys would bring her an orchid or two from the jungle, something unique, still attached to its host of wood or bark. Sometimes Alexis had discovered a rare flowering beauty on her own. Now the entire upper floor was alive with tropical flora. Repotting some of the larger ones had been on her mind for quite some time and, as there were no riding guests for this day in late November, she decided to take the opportunity. As she sat on the veranda with the canvas tarp piled with plants, a bucket of acid-rich humus on the right, and another of manure on the left, she was reminded of an old Japanese proverb.

If you want to be happy for three days, kill a pig and eat it.
If you want to be happy for a week, get married.
If you want to be happy for a lifetime, grow a garden.

Working with green growing things had always been therapeutic; they helped take her outside of her analytical self. Even so, she could not quite escape the terrible choice that loomed before her, and the need for a decision weighed heavily on her mind.

This time the radio call came as a wonderful surprise.

"Come in BBB, Belize-By-Horseback. This is Tim and Maggie. Over."

"Tim Davis? Wow, what's up with you guys? How's Texas these days? Over."

"Hot and dusty, sweetie, just like the movies. Hey, Maggie and I are here in Belize City. Would you like to have some company up on the ranch?" It was not surprising that, even though they'd been out of the Belize loop for quite some time, they had already been apprised of her current situation. Usually, every *gringo* who ever returned knew the low-down on everyone within thirty minutes.

Coincidentally, Tsam was working in the corral when the vehicle arrived two hours later, so he shouted up to Alexis and opened the gate for Tim and Maggie. The Land Rover drove under the heavily-laden avocado trees, past the pineapple patch, and up the hill to the house. As she saw their smiling faces, Alexis knew it was going to be a good time with old friends.

"Maggie!" Alexis called. "It's so good to see you! Hi Tim! Gosh, it's been a long time. What's been going on?" Hugging them both, she beckoned, inviting them into the house. For the next few hours, they ate and drank and reminisced about the early days in Belize.

With the exception of the few years he and Maggie had lived in Baron's Creek, Tim had spent his entire life in Texas, working on ranches owned by huge produce companies. But Belize had made a lasting impression during their tenure in the valley, and now, inspired by new religious conviction, they'd decided to check out new opportunities and make their return.

"The only problem is we don't know where," Tim explained. "We'd like to be up in Cayo again, but not in Baron's Creek. That was just too primitive – too many snakes and bugs. Wherever we are, we're going to be doing the Lord's work."

"I'm confused. You're talking like missionaries," Alexis commented, hesitating a little. "Are you here in some type of official religious capacity?"

"We don't think of ourselves as religious, exactly. Unfortunately, thanks to certain televangelists, religion has gotten a bad rap," he laughed. "But I guess you could say we've become spiritual. We believe that the Holy Spirit speaks through us and we'd like to help. Wherever we end up, we intend on building a small church. And yes, we have some backing from our congregation in San Antonio."

"Tim and I heard that you're fighting a legal battle with Max over your kids?" said Maggie, changing the subject. Again, the population of young white Americans in Belize was small, and the grapevine, most efficient.

"Yeah," Alexis took a deep breath. It was difficult to talk about, even under the best of circumstances. "I just need a court date, but they keep screwing me around, and now there's another twist that further complicates things." She shook her head. The ramifications were almost too great to bear. "There has been a split between what the children want. So, according to their wishes, I'm now suing for visitation for Jordan and custody for Jessica."

Maggie's eyes filled with tears for her friend's sake. She and Tim now had two of their own, and only a mother could know another mother's pain.

"Does Max let them come here to the ranch?"

"They visit here and there, but it's always on Max's terms," said Alexis, "and unfortunately, his promises are contrived to be made and broken. He is very good at maintaining a facade of cooperation, just in case the authorities ever examine his actions. Then, of course, there was a long period when Jordan didn't want to come up at all. He was very angry with me. Now he visits with Jessica, but only once in a while. Things are not right between us. I don't know if Max is brain-washing him, or whether Jordan's reached his own conclusions that his mother is a bad person."

"You're not a bad person," Maggie said warmly, reaching out for her hand.

Alexis bit her lip to fight the response that came to her mind. Seeing her track record from Jordan's perspective, she could understand why he might easily feel she was bad; there had been so many misunderstandings. Sometimes she wondered if she had done the wrong thing by merely surviving. Maybe her life would have been more meaningful as a martyr. But that was ridiculous, purely self-pity.

"God wants you to be fruitful," said Tim, as if reading her thoughts. "Sometimes the grand plan takes a while to reveal itself, but you've survived. You have two children who adore you – though one of them might have temporarily forgotten. Look around you. You have done wonders with this ranch and horseback business. You have a reason for being here."

Alexis' eyes opened wide as serendipity dawned on her.

"You're right. There's a reason why I'm here, and there's a reason why you're here too. I don't know why I didn't think of it sooner. Let me tell you a little bit about a newly available opportunity regarding this ranch and horseback business..."

* * * *

When Alexis' attorney called her from Belize City in late January, informing her of another court date, she was skeptical. After nine individual postponements in the course of one year, she had no reason to believe this one would be any different. But after hearing Mr. Knight explain that the Court Registrar had been caught taking bribes and had been replaced, she was sure that, at last, the case would come to fruition. Of course, it wasn't definitive that Max was the culprit, but it was a darn good guess. Regardless, Errol assured her, she would get her day in court. The date was set for March 23rd. There would be no more postponements, and now it was time to align her strategy. She still didn't know what she'd do about Jordan, but as soon as the court case was over, a bold move would be in order. The legal battle was a gamble at best, and she was betting heavily on winning. After all, even if she won, she would still only secure a future with one of her children, not both.

The potential offer she'd presented to Tim and Maggie seemed full of promise, so immediately after their visit, Alexis put them both in touch with Ted. As it turned out, he was thrilled with the idea of having the Davis family take care of his property and run the business. Tim and Maggie were equally grateful, feeling that the Lord was guiding their destiny. Three weeks later, the deal came together with only one small hitch – Tim and Maggie didn't want to just run the ranch; they wanted to buy it, and Ted had decided he wanted to sell. On the upside, Alexis would make a large chunk of money by selling out her share of the riding business, but on the other hand, it would no longer be her option to stay. She would now have to leave Belize. The reality was tougher than the hypothetical. Similar to selling *Emoyeni* to the Swiss, Alexis knew this was an unparalleled opportunity; she might never have another chance to walk away with some money. The torrent of conflicting emotions ran rampant in her head; she could not reconcile herself to new certainties, and felt she was going to explode.

Frustrated and disheartened, Alexis walked down the hill and got her saddle, blanket, and bridle from the tack room. It was already late in the day, but as she approached the pasture and whistled for Cisco; he came running, always eager and willing. As she threw the saddle on his back and tightened the belly band, she thought of losing her horse, her beautiful trails, her orchids, and all the memories.

So many *gringos* had left Belize with their tails tucked between their legs. Pride was involved; she didn't want to feel that she had failed, that she was a loser. But wouldn't she be a winner? Nobody made money out of Belize. It was a standard joke in Belize: "To make a small fortune in Belize, you have to start with a large one." Unlike others who brought everything and left with nothing, she had come there with nothing and was leaving with a substantial sum of money. Like Las Vegas, if she stayed and played her winnings, she'd probably lose what she'd won. The only way to truly win was to walk away with the jackpot.

But how could she walk away from her children? It would kill her to leave them a second time. Alexis had already left them once when she'd fled to Mexico, and had spent five years trying to get them back. She absolutely had to win custody over Jessica.

Jordan wouldn't have the option. By aligning himself so strongly with Max, he had made his choice. Her throat closed tight with emotion as she realized she wouldn't even be able to tell him she was leaving, and now would bear guilt for that subterfuge as well.

The cold reality was that Max would probably put a contract out on her life if she took Jessica out of the country, even if she won her fair and square. Time had not lessened the menace of Max's threat; she was sure it was just as valid as ever. There did not seem to be any answer. If she didn't win, she would lose both children, and now she would be compelled to leave anyway.

Jumping on Cisco's back, she reined him with an uncharacteristically savage jerk, and launched him into the full gallop down the driveway. Instead of turning right at the bend to head towards the road, she headed left, and went west, back into the valley. Alexis didn't know where she was going and didn't care. After a mile or two, she came to a fork where Tsam and Genaro had started chopping a new trail and then abandoned it. She took the horse as far as she could before the bush closed in around her, then dismounted. Tying the horse to a tree, she continued running on foot. Alexis still didn't know where she was going or why. There was no destination, no shelter, and there would be no respite. Desperately, she ran through the virtually impenetrable jungle vegetation as sharp thorns plucked at her clothes. A deadly poisonous coral snake slithered across her path, but she jumped over it and kept going. On and on she ran, ducking through the vines and creepers until, at last, exhaustion overcame her and she collapsed against a moss-covered wall of stone. As her eyes closed, she went back in time. The visions whirled...

...the Dark One had returned. She could see his scowling evil face lurking in the shadows just beyond the gray curtains of sanity. The harpy claws of the menacing fiend lashed out, the razor tips grazing her bare skin. Terrified beyond all reality, Alexis could smell death and the stench of decomposed flesh on its hot stinking breath. Only a heartbeat away from the depths of hell, the sulfuric fumes enveloped her. She was running, running, but he was almost upon her...

Alexis awoke with a scream, staring into the face of a hideous gargoyle carved in stone. Her aimless flight had brought her to the hidden ruins of the city-state of Chan'pa'tan, and an ancient Mayan temple that had once stood high above the forest primeval, now long forgotten and ravaged in the mists of time. But as she confronted the gruesome carving, a transformation took place, and a new strength and courage began to course through her veins. It was somehow Max, but it was not Max. Reaching out tenuously, her fingers traced the lines of the evil visage with its cruel eyes and terrifying grimace. The demon is set in stone, thought Alexis, long dead, even to its own ancestors, and separated from me by centuries. It is decayed and weak; grass grows from its mouth. It cannot pursue me or harm me.

Suddenly, she stood tall and touched the jade bead around her neck with reverence, the center and color of her being.

"No," Alexis said aloud. "These dreams and fears will not defeat me. I am master of my own fate, and I will win. Not by leaving Belize, nor by staying. Not by winning my children, nor by losing them."

A ray of evening sun suddenly came piercing through the deep bush, the pillar of golden fire landing at her feet, as though lighting her way.

"I will win, because I will live on. This too, I will survive."

TRIAL BY FIRE

chapter 20_____

"All rise," the bailiff said. "This court is now in session. You may be seated."

The Courthouse in Belize City was located on Regent Street and once housed the former colonial administration under British rule. Built of wood, painted brilliant white with green trim with wrought-iron gingerbread railings and a clock tower, it was completed in nineteen twenty-six after a fire destroyed an earlier building on the same site. Outside, the sunny parking lot was crowded with flower vendors and dry goods solicitors. Inside, the undersized windows were covered with so much grime that very little light penetrated the interior, a misfortune further magnified by the electricity being out, leaving the courtroom in virtual darkness. Although Alexis had seen something of the justice system during the assault trial in Belmopan, she was appalled at the dingy and unprofessional atmosphere of the highest court in the land. Courtrooms of this era had once been used to hang people, or banish them to dungeons. The judge wore the Olde English white sheepskin wig, made more laughable by his contrasting dark skin and his nappy-head black hair poking out around its edges. Alexis sat on the chair within the heavy dark mahogany witness stand as the cross examination began.

"Mrs. Lord, please tell the court why do you feel you deserve custody of the child, Jessica?"

"As I am divorced, please address me as Alexis Dubois. Regarding your question, I am here because I was never given the opportunity to appear at my divorce proceedings when custody of the children was initially given to my ex-husband. No one ever deemed me to be unfit—"

"Slow down, slow down, Miss Dubois," said Max's attorney. "This is not the United States. You must speak slowly so that our clerk may take down the testimony."

"I was never given..." Alexis began.

"'I was never given...'" the clerk repeated.

"The opportunity..." she said.

"'The opportunity...'" said the clerk.

"To appear at my own divorce proceedings..." Alexis carried on doggedly.

"'To appear...,'" he paused. "Sorry, what was that last part?"

"To appear at my own divorce proceedings..."

"Yes. Go on."

"When custody was given to my ex-husband…"

"'Given to your ex-husband...'" repeated the clerk.

"Also, I was never..."

During the first recess, Alexis talked to her attorney, Errol Knight, on the sidewalk outside the courthouse.

"It's not only ridiculous; it's impossible. There's no court stenographer, just some half-literate clerk taking notes longhand! I can't possibly present my thoughts in a cohesive fashion. Here I am, trying to point out what happened, and this judge, who must be at least ninety years old, can't even keep track of who Angelina is."

"I will admit that he's quite elderly," said Errol, "and to be honest, this particular judge has been known to pass out on the bench."

"Great. How, in heaven's name, are we ever going to get a fair trial?" Alexis pleaded. "Did you hear him get all bent out of shape when I mentioned the divorce proceedings were skewed to begin with?"

"That's because he's the same judge who officiated over your divorce," he replied. "He doesn't want anyone to think he did the wrong thing."

"Does anyone around here understand the words 'conflict of interest?'" cried Alexis. "Max's attorney certainly understood it when he refused to represent me. How can justice be done?"

Errol put his hand on her shoulder. "I agree. It doesn't look good. At this point, I feel that our best bet would be to have the judge speak with Jessica, privately, in his chambers."

"How's he going to do that when I can't even get through my testimony? I've been on the stand for two hours, and I haven't even gotten through half the story. Not at four words a minute."

One hour later the court session reconvened.

"Milord," said Mr. Goodwin, using the proper form of address for a British court. "Due to the lack of electric lights, which is making the recording of the transcripts difficult, I would like to request a postponement of these proceedings until tomorrow."

"No!" Alexis stood up in the courtroom and shouted aloud. "You can't do that!"

The judge slammed his gavel down. Alexis realized her blunder immediately, and her color rose. Max sat next to his attorney with his arms crossed, a smug expression on his face.

"Miss Dubois, you are out of order. You will kindly deport yourself in a manner befitting this legal proceeding, or I will find you in contempt."

"I'm sorry, Your Honor. I mean 'Milord.'"

Mr. Knight spoke. "Milord, may we three confer at the bench?"

Alexis watched anxiously as the two attorneys talked to the judge. After convening for less than a minute, they returned to their seats. With one look at her lawyer's face, she knew it was over. The judge banged his gavel again.

"It has been determined that this proceeding will terminate for today, due to the lack of electricity," said the judge. "We will reconvene next week on Tuesday at nine o'clock. Due to the extensive wait already endured by both parties, consecutive follow up dates will be set for Wednesday and Thursday, and continue through Friday if necessary. This case will suffer no more postponements. A settlement will be reached next week. Court dismissed."

No sooner did the gavel slam down, and Max disappeared with the children. He was gone almost before Alexis could stand up and turn around.

"I thought I'd at least be able to talk to them a little bit," Alexis told her attorney, bitterly, as they walked out of the gloom and into the brilliant sunshine. "But that was probably unrealistic. This was a court proceeding, not a family reunion."

"At least we'll get it finished this time." Errol's dark brown eyes were kind. How could he tell her the real answer? The deck was stacked and he knew it. "I don't know what more I can do for you, but at least it appears there will be a conclusion of some kind."

"God just has to let me win this time," she implored. "My friends, Tim and Maggie, say that with enough faith, all prayers will be answered, and I have been the loser for so long..."

"Yes, I understand," he said, "and if not for your sake, then at least for the sake of your children. I firmly believe that, even if we adults deserve no consideration, the children should get what they want and need." He shook her hand. "I will be in touch."

Two days later, the unthinkable happened when Mr. Knight radioed that her case had been canceled indefinitely. The courts were reconvening early with criminal sessions. It was not even a postponement; no date had been set to continue the litigation. Not even when civil cases were due to resume in the fall. It was as if the case had never existed.

Alexis hung up the transmitter and began to wander aimlessly. Outside, the sun was shining, mocking her pain. All around her was the breathtaking beauty of the jungle, yet she was alone in the big beautiful house on the hill. No one to care. No one to comfort her. Once again, the vast sadness and awesome reality of the situation overwhelmed her. In a daze, she walked down the hill through the bountiful yard, lingering briefly under the shade of the tall palms. Climbing the pasture fence, she stood on the second rung, and leaned into the morning sunshine. Several of the horses sauntered over with their lovely horsy-smell and nuzzled her with their velvety-soft noses.

Returning to the house, she went to the mirror and stood there, grim with determination. Yes, there will be an ending, Alexis thought. After all these years, I'm going to make an ending. I'm going to take Jessica and leave, without legal custody.

There was nothing she could do about Jordan. She couldn't even offer him the choice of leaving, as it would expose her plan. A choice created in hell; it would be one child, or none. Suddenly overwhelmed with need, she jumped in the truck and drove all the way to Central Farm to use the phone. Alexis would call Jack, and beg him to fly down one last time.

Three days later, Jack rode alongside Alexis in silence, considering her question carefully. Throughout the years, the two had grown to love each other in a most unconventional way. It was not the love of a father and daughter, nor the ardor of lovers, but rather a unique devotion, a kinship of mind and spirit, a metaphysical bond of understanding. Jack had become her best friend and closest confidant. With him, she could discuss the most delicate issues, those too volatile to discuss with anyone else.

The horses reflected their mood and ambled along, neither hurried, nor lazy. Cutting through a relatively unused section of deep jungle, the two riders wound their way down into a vast ravine, crossed the small creek at the bottom, and made their way up the other side, breaking into the open pine ridge. Still pensive, Jack raised his eyes to the horizon, searching for the words that might ease her.

"I'm trying to see it from every angle. But unfortunately, by spiriting Jessica away from Belize – yes, you'll break Jordan's heart," he said somberly. "There's no avoiding it."

"But if I tell him we're leaving Belize, thereby giving him the opportunity—"

"He most certainly will expose your intentions to Max and blow the whole thing wide open. Then you'll lose Jessie too."

"Is there any way you can think of that I could, sort of, feel him out, and see if he'd be willing to leave with us?" said Alexis. Every time she tried to accept the situation, she found herself back in denial.

"I don't know that you can. Not at this point. Besides, don't you already know, in your heart, that his alliance is here with his father?" Jack asked. "Aren't you only deceiving yourself that it could be any other way?"

"That's probably because I can't resign myself to it. Besides, I'll be stealing his sister; it's ten times worse than when I left for Mexico. First, Jordan will be worried, just like his father. Then the anger will come. If it was his father's cause before, it will most certainly become his personal crusade now. I'm afraid he will hate me – that he'll never forgive me."

"What's your alternative?" he asked gently.

"The only other thing I can do is to leave Jessica too. Then I'd be abandoning both of them for the second time. I couldn't live with betraying her – just dumping her, when all she ever wanted was to be with me."

"You're doomed to feel like that anyway with Jordan," said Jack. "But then again, if he only wanted to be with you because he liked the idea of the States, he'd be going for the wrong reason."

"That's true," she replied. "He has to want me, as well as whatever I can provide for him. God knows I love him. I want him to have the best in life, even if it means not being with me. But I never wanted him to suffer, and yet now, through some obscene paradox, I am abandoning him all over again."

Jack and Alexis rode of the top of the ridge, and came to the edge of a precipice. Looking out over the vast panoramic view of a grand forested valley to the north, there was also an awe-inspiring three-hundred foot cliff of limestone to the west, its immense white face pockmarked with hundreds of caves. A solitary king vulture in magnificent plumage of white, black, and red, hovered effortlessly on the thermal updrafts. Loosening their reins, they allowed the horses to graze while they talked.

Jack tried to validate her. "You've only done what you had to do."

"I've told that to myself a thousand times," Alexis replied. "There's no comfort in it. What I want is to be vindicated, to be understood."

"Emerson said 'to be great is to be misunderstood.'"

"It's more than being misunderstood. Innocence is never important to the guilty, but it is critical to the falsely-accused. Sometimes I wish I could tie Max to a chair, tape his mouth shut, and tell the world what really happened."

"Why don't you?" Jack said, with a smile. "Tell the world, express yourself. Write it all down, the whole story. The jungle and the injustice. Survival of the fittest. Perhaps you'll get your vindication, with interest, and inspire others at the same time."

"Me?" Alexis shrugged modestly. "You're the role model. You're the adventurer. You're the one who's larger than life."

"Don't sell yourself short. I know you feel that way about me, but did you ever stop to think how many have been influenced by you? Think of the inspiration you have provided to hundreds of tourists here on your horseback rides, the sense of wonder and fantasy. I've ridden the trails, I've experienced it myself, and I've read their comments in your little guest book. What's more, I know the context of their lives and how they assimilate the experience after the fact. Those people return to their big cities, their jobs, their computers, and their otherwise fatuous little lives, but they go back with renewed faith in their own abilities. Don't you see that you have shown them the kind of reality that can be accomplished when someone dares to dream?"

"I...don't know what to say," she stammered.

"Think about the abuse issue," said Jack. "Thousands of women are abused by their husbands. Battering is a disease; it ravages American society. Don't you realize how reading your story could inspire them to do something, to take action? You could save lives. And," he said, lovingly, "you have inspired me as well."

"You?" Alexis looked at him incredulously. "In what way?"

"I have known many fascinating people in my life: writers, photographers, inventors, athletes, the famous, the wealthy, super models, movie stars – even a couple of presidents and kings. I've had many cherished friends, young and old, men and women both. I've had countless lovers, and have been involved in hundreds of relationships. But you are especially dear to me, Alexis, because you are one of the most vital people I have ever known. Like me, you refuse to be anything less than unstoppable. You act the part until you feel the part if necessary, but you still keep going, despite all odds, and for that I love you. You have the soul of a poet and the heart of a jaguar. You are one of the most precious beings in my life, and they are less in number than the fingers of one hand."

Her eyes full of tears, Alexis reined her horse closer and held out her hand to him.

"Jack? Why can't I grow myself a hard shell of cynicism like everybody else? I just never seem to wise-up."

"I don't know, but I hope you never do. Look how you have grown through the years. You're older and wiser, and have become far more beautiful. You no longer care about id and ego, cynicism, winning, losing, or proving a point. You have become more forgiving of the faults of others, more compassionate to the needs and fears of others. No doubt it stems from your own need for absolution, but that's okay. After all, isn't personal experience the very birthplace of empathy? Isn't suffering is the only true catalyst of human growth?"

"It's true," said Alexis quietly, "but now I only want peace,"

"And you will have it, in due time. Once you sought a different lifestyle. Now you've lived the adventure, tasted its joys, sorrows, and regrets. Your uphill struggle has taken many twists and turns but you have had success in your search for a meaningful life."

His face glowed with a magic that seemed surreal. Like Merlin, Jack only seemed to grow younger. To Alexis, he embodied all that was good in humankind, all the strength and excellence beyond the realm of mere mortals.

"You always say the right thing, don't you?"

"No," Jack replied, laughing. "Sometimes I just get lucky."

Alexis looked into his eyes. "Do you think I am wrong to leave and take Jessica?"

"Is a person, who is deprived of any lawful means of reclaiming their basic human rights, justified in breaking the law? Sometimes a person cannot obey a law his conscience tells him is unjust."

"I'm afraid of the consequences."

"Of course you are," said Jack, eyes shining with love. "And you should be. Acts of courage are always dangerous. It is the very nature of the beast."

* * * *

In the dark of the night, a freak dry-season rainstorm broke over the Maya Mountains. The storm howled and moaned while tridents of lightening lashed the skies. Fitfully, Alexis tossed as strange dreams plagued her subconscious mind. Suddenly, she sat straight up, wide awake, and looked out into the darkness just in time to see a bolt of lightening strike the great *llora sangre* tree. With an explosive crack, terrifying in volume, booming and thundering like cannon fire, the magnificent tree began its slow-motion fall to the earth, still illuminated by the eerie strobe lights of the storm.

The next morning, Alexis awoke to a surreal landscape, a chaotic jumble of splintered limb, branches and leaves in the yard that was once the crown of the magnificent tree. She was inconsolable. The hanging bromeliad had been the focal point of her every waking moment. Never ceasing to appreciate its beauty and grace, she had watched the plant sway in the breeze for over five years.

Alexis pulled out the painting she had made of the tree two years before. Looking like a silly cartoon, she was irritated by her lack of mastery. But how could any creation of such majesty ever be captured? Many people had tried to photograph it; none had succeeded. The tree, and its hanging monster, had been too vast in magnitude, too difficult to frame within the lens of a camera.

There was no fitting epitaph until she found the piece of prose among her papers:

Here is a tree...one of a myriad and yet alone.

Its roots go down into the earth, the earth into the marl, the marl into unimaginable depths of pressure and dark fire. And the tree thrusts upward; its branches reach up with hungry arms toward the blue sky above.

And now at last it is the monarch of all trees, its crown broad and free against the sky. The sun and rain strike down upon it, and a storm roars and passes and a rending and splitting shake the earth. Crown, branch, and bole topple. Creepers, ferns, and orchids lie at the foot of the tree among the fallen branches. And then all is still. There is no sound now, only the drip of the raindrops on the sodden mass of foliage. Nothing moves...

The great mother tree was gone. It was time to leave Belize.

So many things needed to be done, yet utmost secrecy had to be maintained, especially since riding tours would continue right until the very end when the transfer was to take place. Few people knew about the deception Alexis planned, and extreme caution was crucial. Even the local agencies couldn't be allowed to find out. Belizeans were a snoopy lot, and with so many willing spies throughout the country, the juicy information could easily find its way to Max.

Personal possessions had to be packed away into boxes, a few at a time, and taken to a warehouse in Belize City. The furniture would stay behind for Tim and Maggie, as would the appliances and machinery that made the ranch functional. The German Shepherds would also stay. They were Ted's, and a part of the ranch's legacy; they would live out their days with the new owners.

The passport for Jessica had almost been her downfall. Alexis knew that Max had passports made for both kids five years earlier. Being ready to take them to Africa on a moment's notice was always part of his threat. It also meant that if the current documents hadn't already expired, they were due to expire any day. Alexis picked up an application from the American Consulate in Belize City and then searched for pictures of Jessica, desperate to find something appropriate. The chances were slim. Passport photos must be in color with a light background, and very specific dimensions of the facial area. Even more difficult, the application demanded two identical shots. If none were suitable, it would be impossible to take her to a photographer without exposing their plans. Even Jessica couldn't be allowed to know they were leaving until the very end. Alexis caught her breath sharply as she pulled out one of her favorite pictures. Jessica wore a little pink, green, and yellow cotton shirt that made her look like a peppermint candy. Wasn't there a second one like that? Yes, there were two. The photos weren't exact duplicates. But, as they were taken only seconds apart, they looked the same. With her heart pounding, she measured the length and width of Jessie's face. They fit. The pictures would work.

Of all the details, buying the airline tickets to Miami was the most likely to result in exposure. If the right person put two-and-two together and called Max, the ruse would be over. Alexis couldn't possibly use substitute names, and tickets had to be issued two weeks in advance. She could easily be denounced.

During that time, Alexis thought she would go mad with worry. Every nerve-wracking moment brought the possibility of police showing up to take her to jail. She didn't even know where she was going to live, but figured Florida was probably the most obvious choice. Come to think of it, she should be avoiding the obvious, but there were still limitations. She would still need to hang around Florida long enough to receive her household goods. Then she would put everything in a truck and go north or west or whatever. There were so many things to consider. She didn't want to be too far away from Jordan, and she didn't want to be too close to Max. One thing she was absolutely certain of – he would come after her.

The thought of Pennsylvania came to her mind. Did she really want to return to the frozen north? A place that represented everything she spent years trying to get away from? Then, suddenly, it hit her. Her priorities were different. Family was the only thing that really meant anything to her now. What if she was only a few miles, or even a few hundred miles from her folks? How wonderful it would be to live close to them again. Alexis had robbed them of many years, years away from her, years away from their grandchildren. Now she could make it up to them.

The final turmoil that lived inside Alexis dwelled there in the form of a young teenage boy, her own first-born child, a victim in the cruelest sense of the word. She was leaving him. Every potential contingency was pre-meditated to insure success, so how could it not appear malevolent? The thought of masterminding this clearly illegal act, and at the same time grieving for the sin she had yet to commit, was a staggering paradox. How could she love Jordan so much and still leave him? Worse yet, there would be no grand goodbye, not a word or a hug beyond the usual ones exchanged after a visit. There would be no ability for Alexis to explain, and no ability for Jordan to understand. Most of all, there would be no guarantee of mother-son reconciliation.

Although she went through the thought process over and over, from beginning to end, a thousand different ways, she could not resolve the dilemma. Alexis prayed to God with fervency beyond faith. She prayed for a blind and holy intervention that would take away this bitter cup, but nothing happened. Jesus did not return in the Rapture of the Second Coming. No immense change of heart caused Jordan to approach his mother quietly on the side, saying he would prefer to live with her. Maddeningly, Max lived on, free of injury, fatal accident, or terminal disease. No magical passport for Jordan arrived from heaven on the back of a silver steed. There were no signs, no earthquakes, and no natural disasters. She was still leaving Belize with Jessica, providing her plans continued to fall into place undetected.

Alexis would never really remember the details of the deception that succeeded in isolating Jessica from Jordan on that particular weekend. It was some kind of ruse, but the end result was that Jessie would visit the ranch alone. She had often come by herself. There had been many times when Jordan hadn't wanted to go, so it wasn't an unusual arrangement.

But when the moment came to separate the children, Alexis was numb. Jordan's innocent face filled her soul, imprinting on her mind forever. The words burbled out like madness while a freight train seemed to scream in her ears. Her blood ran hot and cold. She was overwhelmed by a sense of presence, a feeling of *now*, and as sure as the approaching stroke of midnight on New Year's Eve, the feeling of *now* fading. Alexis was in the truck with the two children. She'd picked them up from school and was giving Jordan a ride to Max's house before continuing with Jessie back to the ranch.

"So, I'll just see you next week then when you both come up together?" Alexis couldn't even hear her own words as she spoke them. It was a lie.

"Sure, Mom," Jordan said, happily, kissing and hugging her. "No problem. I'll see you next week." Alexis kissed him back, and hugged him hard. Her heart was tearing in two, and her guts twisting. She looked over his shoulders and beyond, down through the dark corridors of the many years ahead. Would she ever see him again? When? How long would it be?

"I love you, Jordan."

"I love you too, Mom," he replied. "Mom? Are you all right? You feel kind of shaky."

"Just a little chill," she said, feeling the gooseflesh. "I'm okay."

"Okay, see you then," he said. "Bye Jess. See you Monday. Bye Mom."

"Bye bye."

That was it. Bye. Goodbye to Jordan. Goodbye to her son.

Alexis only had a few minutes. Within the short ride back to the ranch, she would need to prep Jessica for a huge shock. Done incorrectly, it could blow everything apart. Done right, it would still hurt, and she would still need to explain the subterfuge she'd used on her son.

"Jess?"

"Yes, Mommy?" The little girl smiled, and wiggled comfortably next to her mother.

"I have something very important to explain to you. Remember how I said maybe we'd go back to the States one day and live there? Well, we're going to go."

"Really?" Jessica didn't seem shocked, or even very surprised, mostly excited. "When?"

"Tomorrow. I need to know if you want to go with me, or if you want to stay here with your Dad?" It took a moment for the words to sink in.

Jessica turned and asked seriously, "What about Jordan?"

"What do you think he'd rather do?"

"He'd want to stay with Daddy," she replied, firmly.

"That's what I thought." Now the real question arose. The tickets had already been purchased, the passport secured, the house packed up. Everything in Alexis' world depended on Jessica's next words. "What about you?"

"Are you saying that you and me are going to leave Belize? Tomorrow?" asked Jessica.

"Yes, but only if you want to go. I'm sorry this is such a shock. There was no other way to arrange it."

"Yeah," she said pensively. "You couldn't tell Jordan, right? He would have told Dad." She paused. "I guess you couldn't really even ask him if he wanted to go either."

"You are very perceptive."

Jessica still hadn't given her an answer, and this had to be her daughter's decision.

"You're really sad, aren't you, Mommy? It's not fair, is it?"

"Yes, I'm sad, honey. I love your brother very much. And, like I told you a long time ago, life isn't always fair."

"Okay," said Jessica. "I'll go with you to the States. I've always wanted to be with you."

Alexis was too choked up to talk. She continued to drive while Jessica patted her knee, playing the role of little mother.

"Don't worry, Mommy. It'll be okay."

In the evening hours just before sunset, Alexis and Jessica said goodbye to Tsam, the cowboys, the dogs, the orchids, the trees. The hexagonal house seemed forlorn. Gutted of its humanity, it seemed to be a mere shell now, waiting to be filled with the spirits of others. Would Tim and Maggie love it as much as she had? Could anyone love it as much? Would they care for the flowering plants that had been nurtured so carefully? So many thoughts raced through Alexis' mind, she couldn't believe what was actually happening. Here she was saying goodbye to the *cantina*, the corral, and the horses. She saw Cisco munching contentedly in the pasture, and thought of the joy he'd given her.

Belize was a silly little country, rough and rude, but it had been her home for thirteen years. Her son had been raised here, and her daughter, born here. And she,

Alexis, had grown up here. No longer the starry-eyed wild child, she was a woman now, forged in the joy and pain of the refiner's fire. Now she was leaving her only son behind. Now she was leaving the lifestyle of a lifetime. It was over.

Only Jessie slept that night, her young mind free from the strife that rioted quietly in Alexis' mind. The anguish of the waking nightmare would not subside, and in those final hours she cried out over and over.

Oh my son! I can only hope you'll understand this someday. You'll be angry, you'll be hurt, and you'll surely hate me for a long time. Oh God, I pray you can accept it. Even if it's not right away, will you ever be able to forgive me? Will you ever come to realize the pressure I was under? How can I accept that it could be years and years before I see you again? Will you forgive me by then? Or will it take longer? Will it take until you have children of your own to really understand why I had to do it? Will you ever know the depth of my love, and commitment, and heartbreak?

They left the next morning under the lingering cover of darkness, and Alexis sighed as the last glimpses of western Belize disappeared from sight. The emotional upheaval was so intense that she could not stay focused. Despite her trauma, she must still make the escape. Everything depended on the next few hours. Jessica was quietly lost in her own thoughts. When asked if she was okay, the little girl nodded and squeezed her mother's hand. Alexis was moved by her daughter's supreme trust. Jessica believed in her mother; she would get them away safely. Dressed in oversized jeans, old un-tucked cotton plaid shirts, baseball caps, hiking boots, and sunglasses, the twosome looked like a man and his little boy returning from a Belizean fishing expedition. Alexis wore no makeup or jewelry, and her long blond hair was rolled up in a knot underneath her hat, as was Jessica's. Together, they just looked like a couple of 'good old boys' from Texas.

"Don't look at anyone in the eye," she warned, as they arrived at the airport. "Nobody can really be sure it's you, unless you make eye contact. Then you've acknowledged them."

"I won't," said Jessica. "But Mommy, I'm scared. If Daddy sees us, he'll stop us. He said he'd kill you if you ever stole us kids away." The threat had been long before Jessica's birth. How could she know?

"He told you that?" said Alexis, angrily.

"I heard him tell Angelina when he thought I was asleep. But once when he was really mad at you, he still told me he was going to kill my rotten mother. That scared me, Mom. I want to go with you but, if you want, I'll stay with Daddy so he won't come and kill you."

"Nobody's going to kill anybody," said Alexis. They pulled into the airport, and she explained the plan to her daughter. "I'll do the Immigration papers and check the baggage. You just sit over here in the corner on this bench and wait. Just do not look up or talk to anybody. Everything depends on it."

Although some children might have been caught up in the drama of a real-life movie getaway, it was all serious business to Jessica. She knew this was one game being played for keeps. She sat quietly, stayed in character, and didn't say a word. When Alexis came back with the papers, she did a double-take. With her head bowed and eyes downcast, Jessica was completely unrecognizable.

"Okay. You just give me your hand. We're going to walk right through this airport and get on the plane. Just pretend we don't know anybody and keep looking at the ground. Act like you're very shy."

Nerves jangled with anticipation. This was the moment when anything could happen. As they walked in slow-motion Alexis kept imagining that Max would show up any minute. Her blood pounded and her head buzzed as she waited for someone to shout in recognition. Max would somehow show up here, not because of a hot tip, but because of some weird twist of fate. He had always foiled her plans. Now, surely, some coincidence would bring him to the airport unexpectedly. Any moment the public address system would announce that the flight would be late, or canceled, or that the plane had a malfunctioning engine. Things always went wrong – this was Belize. Someone would see them, recognize them, and give them away. When the flight was called, they began to board the plane. Alexis cringed, waiting for news of a delayed departure, waiting for Max to violently shove people aside, brandishing a firearm. In that final moment, she fully anticipated the crack of a gunshot, and waited for the impact of a bullet in her heart.

Instead, the door was closed by the attendant, the engines came to life, and the taxiing process began. Alexis searched the faces, looking for Max, but he was not aboard. In the end, nothing happened.

Alexis and Jessica looked at each other, full of indescribable emotion, intense and palpable, afraid to say a word that might burst the bubble. Had they beat the odds? Was it real? Neither of them spoke; there was no gloating, no pleasure in the grief caused by slipping out the back door. Alexis felt no satisfaction in the necessity of the deed. Given a choice, she would not have done this to her worst enemy, and Max was her worst enemy. The plane rose from the ground and banked sharply. Squeezing Jessie's hand, Alexis saw one last flash of her beloved landscape. She saw the high-bush clumped like broccoli heads and the thread of the serpentine river of her dreams.

Goodbye to breadfruit and *tamalitos*. Goodbye to the scent of humus in the rainforest and wood smoke and ozone before a storm. Goodbye to double rainbows and coral reefs and crystal-clear oceans. Goodbye to her first born child. Goodbye to the past. Only the future was left.

"All passengers please fasten your seat belts," said the captain. "We are now making our final approach to Miami International Airport. For those of you visiting Miami we hope you have a pleasant stay. For residents, let us be the first to welcome you home."

Jessica wriggled with nervous excitement, but maintained a serious demeanor.

"Mommy? Would you have really left me in Belize with Daddy if I had wanted to stay?"

"Yes. It wouldn't have been easy, but I would have left you there if that had been what you wanted. Just like your brother. Bringing you here was for your sake, not mine. You have a right to live your life the way you want. The last thing I ever wanted was to prolong the warfare with your father. I did it for everyone's sake, yours, mine, and Grandma and Grandpa's."

"But you really miss Jordan, don't you?"

"Yes," said Alexis. "Inside my mind, I'm crying all the time.

"Is it okay if I miss Daddy too?" Jessica asked.

"Of course, honey. It's all right for you to miss your dad. We all know it was a terrible way to have to leave. There was no other way to do it."

"I know," the little girl empathized. "I may only be eight, but I understand better than you think. Daddy didn't really mean to be so bad. He just was, sometimes. Will I be able to call him on the phone?"

"Yes, but not right away," Alexis explained. "Then you can call him. But, for a while, we won't be able to let him know where we are."

"Because he might come to the States and hurt you, right?"

The plane cut a huge arc in the sky, tipping its wing to the ground as it prepared to make the final approach. Alexis looked into her daughter's dark green eyes. Already her little spirit had suffered more than any child should.

"When will it all end Mommy?" Jessica asked quietly.

"I don't know," Alexis replied.

"Are you going to keep me from being with Daddy ever again?"

"Heavens no, baby. I don't want you to miss out on any good influence your father may be able to offer. When things calm down, you'll be able to see him again. We just need to make sure that your rights are protected first."

* * * *

There was a supreme irony in the return of this prodigal child named Alexis. Once, she balked at the idea of being an integral link in United States society, being traceable by social security number or driver's license. Alexis had monumentally and conspicuously rejected all that the U.S. stood for: its laws, politics, pollution, seemingly limitless taxation, and political wastefulness; even junk mail was an imposition. She had once bristled at the idea of being just another sheep in the flock, but now everything was different. It didn't mean the same failings were not still to be found; the United States would always have its faults, and Alexis would learn to deal with these as a matter of necessity. But she had learned that when it came to choices, life gave you two: you could make this mistake, or make that mistake, and if she didn't have faith, she'd better manage to find some.

Now Alexis looked forward to the idea of living in a country where the roads were paved, where mail took three days, where hot water was always hot, where telephones were dependable, and where electricity was available at the flick of a switch. Businesses would be functional. Professionals would be reliable. People would open and close their shops according to the posted hours. What a revelation! Wouldn't it be nice to go to a bookstore and pick out a best seller? Or call a girlfriend and have coffee? She would take Jessie to see Disney movies at the theater. There would be good dentists, doctors, and proper hospitals. Alexis didn't know if she was ready for shopping malls, K-Mart, and Sears, but a nice little air-conditioned sports car with a sun-roof sounded pretty nice, especially one with a great sound system and big speakers. Maybe she'd even eat a Big Mac.

Springtime had broken in Georgia and the air was sweet with the scent of peaches as mother and daughter drove the rental truck north to Pennsylvania. Crossing the state line into Tennessee, Alexis was reminded of the last time she had passed this way. She noticed the curve in the road and marveled how the sides of the mountains had been carved away to allow for a feasible road gradient. In one place, the diagonal strata of exposed rock gave way to a huge outcropping of rock that protruded from the jagged mountainside. It looked as if it were a waterfall cast in stone…a tumbling cascade frozen in time…then the recollection hit her.

Alexis remembered this place, a place indeed frozen in time – for it was the very same place that had marked the beginning of her journey some twenty years before. It seemed a lifetime had passed. Yet, to this mountain, it had been the blinking of an eye, a trifling insignificance.